Financial Literacy: Planning for the Future

Insurance Strategies to Protect Your Family

Financial Literacy: Planning for the Future

Insurance Strategies to Protect Your Family

2018 Edition

GREY HOUSE PUBLISHING

FINANCIAL RATINGS SERIES

WeissRatings

& Grey House Publishing

https://greyhouse.weissratings.com

Grey House Publishing
4919 Route 22, PO Box 56
Amenia, NY 12501-0056
(800) 562-2139

Weiss Ratings
4400 Northcorp Parkway
Palm Beach Gardens, FL 33410
(561) 627-3300

WeissRatings

Independent. Unbiased. Accurate. Trusted.

Published by Grey House Publishing, Inc., located at 4919 Route 22, Amenia, NY 12501; telephone 518-789-8700. Grey House Publishing neither guarantees the accuracy of the data contained herein nor assumes any responsibility for errors, omissions or discrepancies. Grey House Publishing accepts no payment for listing; inclusion in the publication of any organization, agency, institution, publication, service or individual does not imply endorsement of the publisher.

Grey House
Publishing

2018 Edition
ISBN: 978-1-64265-020-4

Table of Contents

Welcome!

Grey House Publishing and Weiss Ratings are proud to announce the second series of guides in their popular *Financial Literacy* series, *Planning for the Future*. Each volume in this series provides readers with easy-to-understand guidance on how to manage their finances. This new eight-volume set provides helpful guidance for readers who are ready for the next step in their financial planning–starting a family, buying a home, weighing insurance options, protecting themselves from identify theft, planning for college and so much more. Designed as a complement to *Financial Literacy Basics, Financial Literacy: Planning for the Future* takes readers even further towards their financial goals.

Written in easy-to-understand language, these guides take the guesswork out of financial planning. Each guide is devoted to a specific topic relevant to making big decisions with significant financial impact. Combined, these eight guides provide readers with helpful information on how to best manage their money and plan for their future and their family's future. Readers will find helpful guidance on:

- Financial Planning for **Major Life Events: Living Together, Getting Married & Starting a Family;**

- **Buying a Home** for the First Time & Mortgage Shopping;

- **Insurance Strategies** to Protect Your Family;

- Making the Right **Healthcare Coverage** Choices;

- Protect Yourself from **Identify Theft**;

- Steps for **Career Advancement**;

- Saving for Your **Child's Education**; and

- **Retirement Planning** Strategies & the Importance of Starting Early.

Filled with valuable information alongside helpful worksheets and planners, these volumes are designed to point you in the right direction toward a solid financial future, and give you helpful guidance along the way.

Planning for the Future: Insurance Strategies to Protect Your Family

Life is full of unexpected turns. While we may not be able to ward off unhappy experiences – we can't, as they say, buy happiness – we can at least purchase some assurance that our family's finances won't be devastated by certain unexpected events. This assurance is called *insurance,* and it's an important feature of everyone's lives in the modern world.

Insurance first arose hundreds of years ago as accounting, statistics, civil government, and modern business enterprises all reached new levels of sophistication. Today, there are certain forms of insurance that are mandatory for all or most citizens.

Health insurance is required of everyone by the federal government. Car insurance is required for all drivers. Your mortgage institution, following federal mandates, may require you to purchase homeowner's insurance.

Beyond these, it can be hard to know what kinds of insurance or types of policies you should consider for yourself and your family, if you have one. A lot depends on your circumstances. Many financial planners, however, recommend life and disability insurance, especially if you are married or have children.

Insurance Needs: Life, Health, Auto, Disability

Life Insurance

The point of life insurance is to provide for those you leave behind at the time of your death. This is especially important if you've started a family and have dependents. A common recommendation is that your policy should pay out ten times your annual salary, but the amount of the benefit is up to you. It should be enough to pay for your funeral expenses, of course, but it should also give your beneficiaries a substantial cushion so that they can recover from the loss of your income.

Health Insurance

Sixty-two percent of bankruptcies in the United States begin with healthcare costs that spiral out of control. The Affordable Care Act requires everyone to carry health insurance, but the kinds of coverage vary dramatically. It is difficult to find affordable health insurance; this is especially true outside of employer-sponsored health insurance programs.

Auto Insurance

According to data from the non-profit National Safety Council, an organization that works with the federal government on auto safety issues, 40,200 people died in motor vehicle accidents in 2016. Unfortunately, that number has been rising for several years. Every state in the union requires drivers to carry at least liability insurance.

Disability Insurance

You may not think disability insurance is important. But, according to the Social Security Administration, one in four of us will become disabled for a period of at least ninety days – and thus unable to work – at some point before we reach the age of retirement. Further, most disabling accidents are *not* work-related, which means that workers' compensation programs will not assist you. Having disability insurance in addition to your

savings will make a huge difference if you face a devastating injury or illness.

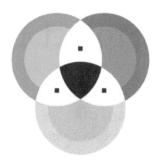

Life Insurance

Life insurance is intended to provide protection against financial losses resulting from the early death of the insured person. The amount of money to be paid is called the **benefit**, and the person to whom it is paid is called the **beneficiary**.

Who needs life insurance? Most of the time, buying life insurance only becomes important when you're starting a family. Once you have children, you will want them to be provided for in case you should die prematurely. But life insurance makes sense in other circumstances, too. If you are a newlywed, then you will want your spouse to be taken care of if you die unexpectedly. You might have a mortgage payment and a financial plan that depends on the salaries of two adult earners, and your spouse could be left in the lurch.

★ As your family situation – and your financial situation – changes over time, you should periodically re-evaluate the safety net that is in place for your family and heirs.

How Life Insurance Works

The purpose of life insurance is to provide some financial security for your family or other beneficiaries after you die – especially in the case of a sudden or early death. For this reason, the decision to purchase life insurance, as well as your selection of a beneficiary and the type and amount of insurance policy, should only be made after careful consideration of your financial plan. Do you want to leave enough to support your dependent children until they reach the age of maturity as well as pay off the mortgage so that your survivors will not be forced to move? Do you only want to leave enough to pay for one of those things? It is wise to reconsider any life insurance policy that you own as your situation changes. Things like marriage, divorce, the birth of a child, or the purchase of a business are all events that might require a re-thinking of your life insurance strategy.

Life insurance policies can be of two types, which will be discussed in this guide: **term life insurance** and **permanent life insurance**, sometimes also called **whole life**.

The two most important monetary elements in a policy are the **death benefit** and the **premium**. In addition, a permanent life insurance policy will have a **cash value**.

The **death benefit** is the amount of money that the insurance company will pay out to the beneficiaries named on the policy after you die. There is no set amount; it will depend on your circumstances and your choice, but the insurance company will use its actuarial statistics and other information – like your age, your health, and your lifestyle, among other things – to determine their risk.

The risk to the insurance company will largely determine the amount of the **premium**, or what you have to pay for the insurance. For term insurance, the premium pays just for the cost of the insurance. For permanent policies, on the other hand, your premium may also include payments toward the cash value.

From the perspective of the insured, **cash value** resembles a kind of tax-deferred savings account; a portion of your premium will be used to accumulate the cash value of the policy. It has two functions. First, the cash value can be drawn on while the insured is still alive. Second, the cash value works for the insurance company to mitigate their risk. This is because the larger the cash value that has accumulated, the lower their risk of having to pay the full death benefit.

How Much Life Insurance Should You Have?

Carrying life insurance doesn't always make sense. If you are single with no dependents, then life insurance may not belong on your agenda, especially if you have assets enough to pay for costs related to your death, like funeral expenses, etc. If you have dependents, and you also have plenty of investments that can provide for them in case of your death, then life insurance may not be necessary.

On the other hand, if you have dependents but you don't have a significant portfolio of wealth, then life insurance might be a great way to make sure that your dependents will be okay if you die. The insurance benefit could be used to pay off the mortgage, for example, and support your children until they are adults.

Before buying insurance, you should sit down and determine your insurance plan. Ask yourself: How much money will your dependents need? As you formulate your plan, consider these factors:

- **Debt payment**. You should purchase enough life insurance to pay off the debts that will be inherited by your spouse and

will affect your children's lives. This includes, above all, your mortgage, car loans and all debts that you share with your spouse. (Your own personal debt, like your student loans, are not inherited.)

- **Support for dependents**. Suppose you are the primary provider for your family, and your salary brings in $75,000 annually. You should consider buying a policy that will replace this income for a given number of years. Add some extra to account for inflation.

For example, if you want to leave enough to provide for your family's needs for ten years, then you would want a policy for $750,000 plus something more for inflation. It's common to simply add one more year's worth of your salary to handle this. In this case that would be $750,000 + $75,000 = $825,000.

Most insurance experts recommend that people purchase a life insurance policy that covers six to ten years' worth of their annual salary. But there are other ways to think about the amount you need. Suppose, for example, that you are a 45-year-old man with a wife who stays at home to care for a disabled adult child. You might want, in this case, to buy enough life insurance to replace your annual income until your age of retirement, allowing your retirement plan to take care of the rest. In this case, you would purchase a policy for twenty times your salary.

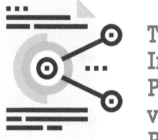

Types of Life Insurance Policies: Term versus Permanent

Term Life Insurance

The most common kind of life insurance sold in the United States is called **term life insurance**, accounting for 64% of individual life insurance policies sold. "Term" means that the policy has an end; it provides coverage for a limited period of time. The cost of term life insurance is typically much more reasonable than a permanent life insurance policy. Term life insurance will not have a cash value, unlike permanent policies.

Term life insurance is generally a good fit for people in their twenties and thirties who have children. The temporary nature of the policy makes it a flexible tool for protecting your family against financial devastation if you die unexpectedly before your children are grown.

How Does It Work?

Suppose you are 32 years old, and you purchase a term life insurance policy for $500,000. A term life insurance contract is for a limited number of years. Let's suppose that, in this case, the policy is for ten years. You might pay a monthly premium of around $50. If you die at any time during that period, whether the day after you sign or the day before the policy expires, the insurance company will pay $500,000 to the beneficiary or beneficiaries named in the policy. If you die the day after the policy expires, then your beneficiaries will receive nothing.

You will typically be able to renew your term life insurance policy before it expires. But this is often the same as signing for a new policy, in practice. It will likely mean qualifying for insurance again at your current age, and your premium will likely be higher.

Term life insurance makes sense for the majority of people seeking life insurance for one simple reason: it costs much less than permanent life insurance. Typically, in fact, it makes more sense to buy term life insurance and then keep renewing the policy – up to a point – than it does to buy permanent life insurance. Especially if you invest the difference in the cost between a term and a permanent policy for many years, you will have a tidy sum.

Your premium will be decided on the basis of some things over which you have no control, like your age and your sex. It will also be decided on the basis of factors that are in your control, at least to some extent. You will be required to have a medical exam and answer questions about your lifestyle. If you smoke, you should quit smoking as soon as possible. Typically, insurance companies will not insure you at nonsmoker rates until you've been a nonsmoker for at least twelve months. Your occupation and even your driving record will all be used to determine your risk of dying during the period in which the policy is in force.

Three Types of Term Life Insurance

- **Level Term**. This is the most common type of term life insurance. Level term means that your premium will be the same from the start to the end of the policy. Your rate will be determined by averaging the annual costs based upon your risk as you age across the

period of the policy. This means that you'll pay slightly more at the beginning but slightly less toward the end.

- **Decreasing Term**. In a decreasing term policy, the death benefit is reduced each year as the policy ages. This kind of insurance is designed with asset protection in mind. It makes sense if you want a policy that will cover the remaining payments on the mortgage for your house, for example. A decreasing term policy costs less than a regular policy, and the monthly payments are typically level for the term of the policy.

- **Yearly Renewable Term (YRT)**. This kind of policy is renewable annually but doesn't require that you undergo a medical examination or other determinations of your insurability each year; the rates are based upon actuarial tables without the additional, personal input. The policy premiums on a yearly renewable term policy can become very expensive as you get older.

Permanent Life Insurance

This kind of insurance differs from term in that it doesn't expire, and it includes a **cash value**. There are two kinds of permanent life insurance, **whole** and **adjustable**; the most common kind of adjustable insurance is **universal**. The cash value portion of the policy is a sort of savings account. Usually after a certain period of time, you will be able to borrow funds against or even withdraw the cash value.

Does it make sense to buy permanent life insurance? It depends on your circumstances. Note that permanent life insurance premiums are typically much higher. This is because, unlike term life, which is likely to expire before your die, permanent insurance will, in fact, pay out a guaranteed benefit when you die. The insurer's risk is calculated on the basis of *when* you will die, not *if* you will die before the policy expires. Further, many financial advisers warn that the cash value component of a life insurance policy may not be the most robust savings plan or investment strategy available to you, so be careful when shopping for policies.

On the other hand, if you have a lot of wealth, then a permanent life insurance policy might make more sense for a number of reasons, including managing your tax liability.

Whole Life

This is the standard form of permanent life insurance, also called **straight life**. As noted, it will include an investment portion in which you can grow equity in a savings account with tax-deferred interest dividends.

History of Whole Life

From the 1940s through the 1970s, whole life insurance was the preferred type of policy. Because it included an investment component, whole life formed a comprehensive product that individuals could purchase as part of their larger retirement and financial planning strategy. Beginning in the 1980s, however, a greater diversity of investment and insurance products became available, including more flexible products that allow consumers to invest in the stock market and achieve higher rates of return than were typically available from whole life policies.

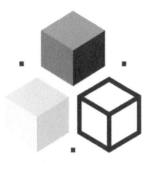

Adjustable Life Insurance

The most common kind of **adjustable life insurance** is called **universal**. This is a form of permanent insurance that is more flexible than standard whole life. It is called universal because it combines certain features of term life with permanent insurance. In a universal policy, the various components – things like the death benefit, the savings component, and the premium – can typically be altered.

The chief idea behind a universal policy is to allow interest earned in the savings component of the policy to pay the premium. Also, any payments that you make beyond the minimum payment will go to the cash value savings, and these additional funds, too, can be applied against the premiums. This means that your monthly premium for a given type of coverage will be smaller than it would be if you had an ordinary whole life policy, although it only works up to a point. (As you age, the rising cost of your insurance policy will make the dividend from your savings seem less and less significant.) Another helpful feature of a universal plan is that if the savings component isn't returning a high dividend, you can simply use it as if it were cash on hand to pay the

premium while you grow money elsewhere.

Term Life Insurance versus Permanent

The choice between term or permanent life insurance is partly a matter of your circumstances and needs and partly a matter of your mindset. If what you want is a life insurance policy that can be used by your spouse and children to pay off whatever remains on your mortgage if you die before its paid, then you really only need a term policy. In fact, a **decreasing term life insurance policy** would be an appropriate financial instrument for you.

If you conceive of life insurance as, first, a tool to provide for your heirs in the case of an early death, and *also* a source of income for your beneficiaries whenever you die, and if you feel that the tax-advantaged savings component is worthwhile, then you may opt for a whole or universal life policy.

If you buy a term life insurance policy, then one of the things you will probably have to face is the following situation. (*Probably* is used advisedly because of the risk calculation behind term policies.) Suppose you bought a term life insurance policy twenty years ago, and you made twenty years' worth of payments into it. Now its term is up. *You have nothing to show for it.* Was it worth it? Should you have bought a whole life policy instead?

Consider, however, that the term life insurance policy may have cost you around $50 per month. If you *had* purchased a whole life policy instead of term twenty years before, your monthly payment might have been more like one or two thousand dollars each month. And you might have had a smaller benefit. Having a higher payment might make sense to you if you conceive of your life insurance as, say, one more instrument for your funds, or as a way to manage a tax liability. But most people are better off not thinking of their insurance benefit as an investment like savings. You don't *want* to die prematurely, after all. And chances are that you won't.

Term insurance plans will get more expensive as you age; your whole life policy won't change. You'll pay the same monthly premium for your whole life policy when you're ninety-eight that you paid when you purchased it back in 1950. You'll have paid it for many, many years, however. Regardless who "wins" – you or the insurance company – your beneficiary will receive the payout,

and you will have been nicely insured throughout your life. As you can see, buying permanent life insurance usually makes more sense if you are wealthy. And, if you are wealthy, it can make sense to buy the policy when you are relatively young.

Some advisers recommend that you purchase a term policy unless you want to use a permanent life insurance policy to prevent or pay for estate taxes that would kick in when you die. According to the Tax Bill of 2018, estate taxes only apply to estates assessed at $10 million dollars or more, and that amount increases to $20 million if you are married. Before the 2018 Tax Bill was passed, the estate tax kicked in on estates assessed at five million dollars.

Convertible Term Life Insurance

A **convertible term policy** is a term life insurance policy that allows the insured to convert the policy to a permanent one without going through the insurability process again. If you opt for this, typically the benefit remains the same, but your monthly premium will increase when the policy switches. This would be an excellent choice in certain circumstances. Suppose you bought a 10-year convertible term policy, and in the ninth year, your health declined. You would be able to convert your policy to a permanent one and the premium would be determined on the basis of your previous medical examination and not your current health status.

Another reason you might opt for a convertible term policy is if you cannot afford a permanent policy but think you might want one in the future. You can purchase a term policy now and when you are ready – say, in 10 years – convert it.

If you are interested in convertible term policies, be careful to look at the details. There are often windows that limit when you can convert the policy. There are also typically age limits at which a conversion isn't allowed – age 65 or age 75, for example.

Average Annual Life Insurance Rates for Women

Age at purchase	Policy amount	20-year term life	30-year term life	Whole life
30	$250,000 $500,000 $1,000,000	$141 $208 $347	$206 $335 $585	$2,114 $4,142 $8,150
40	$250,000 $500,000 $1,000,000	$185 $306 $534	$314 $553 $1,026	$3,008 $5,897 $11,677
50	$250,000 $500,000 $1,000,000	$375 $669 $1,233	$689 $1,284 $2,349	$4,569 $9,003 $17,760
60	$250,000 $500,000 $1,000,000	$1,033 $1,911 $3,637	Not available.	$7,293 $14,387 $28,670

Average Annual Life Insurance Rates for Men

Age at purchase	Policy amount	20-year term life	30-year term life	Whole life
30	$250,000 $500,000 $1,000,000	$156 $242 $415	$240 $403 $720	$2,385 $4,675 $9,217
40	$250,000 $500,000 $1,000,000	$210 $348 $631	$384 $687 $1,281	$3,508 $6,910 $13,700
50	$250,000 $500,000 $1,000,000	$491 $898 $1,692	$913 $1,725 $3,301	$5,436 $10,802 $21,483
60	$250,000 $500,000 $1,000,000	$1,477 $2,793 $5,393	Not available.	$8,783 $17,487 $34,853

Source: https://www.nerdwallet.com/blog/insurance/average-life-insurance-rates/

Your Life Insurance Medical Exam

What about the life insurance medical exam? The exam is usually performed by a nurse, not a doctor, and it may be performed in your home or in a location contracted by the insurance company. Do not take the exam lightly. It is key to determining your insurability and your premiums. Don't do anything excessive or strenuous before the exam. Don't be hungover, for example, and don't exercise vigorously at the gym just before your appointment. (On the other hand, regular exercise for a few weeks or months – or years – prior to the exam would be an excellent idea.)

If the personal and health information that you gave on your application is contradicted by the medical exam, then you might be denied coverage. Alternatively, you might have to undergo more tests. If you fail the

---

Life Insurance Medical Exams

The life insurance medical exam has two parts:

- A verbal questionnaire about your personal and family health. This is typically a confirmation of the information you already provided in the paperwork of your application. The questionnaire will cover your physical health and also ask you about matters of your mental health, like depression.

- Standard readings of vital signs and sample collections. You will have your blood pressure checked, and the nurse will collect tissue samples from you, usually blood, urine, and saliva.

The entire exam will take approximately thirty minutes. The exam is intended to measure health indicators like:

- Body mass index (BMI)
- Blood pressure
- Cholesterol levels
- Liver and kidney function

You will also be tested for:

- Diabetes
- Hepatitis
- HIV
- Drug use
- Nicotine use
- Early signs of Alzheimer's

exam or if feel like something on the medical exam is incorrect, ask the insurance company to send you a copy of the results. Show them to your doctor. If you failed because of a mistake made by the insurance company, then your doctor should be able to help you remedy the situation quickly.

Disability Insurance

Think of **disability insurance** as an income replacement insurance if you should become unable to work. Disability insurance differs from **worker's compensation**. Worker's compensation is a government-mandated insurance system that varies from state to state, but in all cases it is set up to pay short-term benefits only when an employee suffers a job-related injury or illness. Disability insurance, by contrast, is meant to replace some of your lost wages if you are injured or ill for reasons that are not work-related – the majority of disabling injuries and illnesses. Disability insurance makes sense for single and married people. If you have a family or dependents who are reliant upon your income, then

purchasing disability insurance is a good investment in their well-being.

What about **Social Security Disability Insurance (SSDI)**? This is a federal insurance program that you already participate in if you have social security deducted from your pay. There are over 150 million workers currently enrolled in the program. Social Security has strict definitions for disability, usually more strict than private insurance. There are also lengthy determination periods, often taking years. Further, the benefits are not robust. There is cap on the monthly benefit – around $2,700 in 2018. This is a small percentage of a high-income earner's regular monthly salary. Moreover, the Social Security Administration uses a complex formula to determine benefits; the average benefit is around $1,100 monthly.

Private disability insurance, by contrast, offers more liberal coverage and higher benefits, as well as more flexibility. For example, SSDI requires beneficiaries to prove that they are unable to perform any of the work required in any job, whereas private policies can be written to offer so-called **own occupation coverage**. This would mean, for example, that a brain surgeon who breaks a finger and is unable to operate for several months would qualify as disabled.

Social Security Disability Insurance

The determination of **disability** for Social Security Disability Insurance (SSDI) has three parts:

1. You cannot do the work that you did before.

2. You are unable to take other work because of your disability.

3. Your disability has lasted, or is expected to last, for at least a year.

Social Security Disability Insurance isn't intended to help you during short-term periods of disability. It is only for total and long-term disability, where *total* means that you are unable to do *any* work and *long-term* means that you are disabled for more than one year.

None of this meant to downplay the role of Social Security Disability Insurance. It meets a vital need, and if you become disabled you should make use of SSDI if you qualify. Sometimes, a private insurer will deduct the amount of your SSDI payments (if you qualify for SSDI) from the benefit that they pay.

Disability insurance comes in two kinds: short-term and long-term. **Short-term disability insurance** typically pays benefits for a maximum of twenty-six weeks (six months). **Long-term disability** benefits can extend until retirement. As you might imagine, long-term disability insurance is more costly than short-term.

About 30% of people in the work force have disability insurance provided through their employer. Some states require employers to provide short-term disability insurance to their employees. Other employers freely offer it as part of the benefits package. However, the trend is to provide less and less and to ask the employee to pay for more and more. Sometimes employees will be given a sort of *a la carte* list of options for disability insurance, as they are with other benefits, like retirement accounts.

Historically, your employer would pay the full cost for disability insurance, at least for coverage up to a minimum level, and all employees were automatically enrolled. More recently, however, when employers offer disability insurance as a benefit, it's commonly offered as a **voluntary benefit**. This means the employee will pay the full cost. Even if your employer pays nothing toward the cost of the disability insurance, however, remember that participation through group plan is still usually cheaper than anything you can purchase as an individual.

Short-Term and Long-Term

Which should you have? It's important to realize that these are not mutually exclusive options but two different tools. You *can* have both. Short-term disability is more commonly provided as a workplace benefit than long-term, so you may already have it. If not, many advisers say that having an emergency savings fund that can keep you afloat for several months is a better option than buying a private short-term disability policy. Consider what you can afford. However, when it comes to long-term disability insurance, advisers will often encourage it.

Keep in mind as you consider your options that the majority of personal bankruptcies in the United States result from medical expenses that get out of hand. Anything you can do to reduce that risk is a good idea.

Short-Term Policies: How They Work

Short-term plans typically provide a benefit that is up to 80% of your gross income.

Disabilities usually include chronic conditions such as heart disease, back problems, and cancer. They also include injuries sustained while *not at work*. Pregnancy is sometimes covered, too. *Injuries received at work are not covered*.

Most policies will replace a percentage of your income for a duration between one month and six months.

Your coverage can begin as soon as one day after your injury or a diagnosis, or up to 14 days after. This is one of the features that distinguishes short-term from long-term disability insurance.

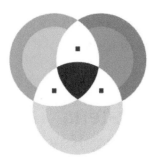

Long Term Disability Policies: How They Work

Long-term disability insurance usually kicks in after a few months have passed since you stopped working. This is called the **elimination period**, or how long you have to wait before the benefit starts paying. A longer elimination period is a key feature distinguishing long-term policies from short-term ones.

Long-term disability insurance typically replaces up to about two-thirds of your income, never more than that. This is called the **benefit amount,** usually expressed in terms of your monthly income. A figure of sixty percent is a common higher limit. Of course, lower benefit amounts will cost you less.

The **benefit period** is how long you will receive payments. Some policies have benefit periods of only two years, while others will continue payments until you reach retirement age. Typical policies last for 2, 5, or 10 years, or until retirement.

An **exclusion** is a condition under which the benefit won't be paid. For example, this could be a pre-existing condition or an injury resulting from a dangerous hobby like mountain climbing.

How much are the premiums? Typically, long-term disability insurance will cost around *one to three percent* of your annual income. This will change dramatically if you are older when you are applying for a policy or if you work in a high-risk job. If you are getting coverage through an employer-sponsored plan, your employer may pay some of the premium. If you are not covered through your employer, then you will have to take a medical exam that will help to determine your rate.

Long-term disability insurance makes the most sense for people whose careers require an investment of time and money. It also makes sense if you have family and children to support. Young professionals who are starting their careers with debt can also benefit from it.

What to Look for in a Long-Term Disability Policy

Here are some important features that many financial advisers recommend for inclusion in a premium long-term disability policy. You can opt for others.

- A 90-day elimination period.

- A monthly benefit of 60% of your total gross income. Because the benefit on a personal policy is nontaxable income, this will be close to your existing take-home pay.

- An "own occupation" policy. This defines disability as the inability to work at your regular occupation. You don't want your insurer to tell you that you can always get a lower salary job in an entirely different industry.

- A benefit period that lasts until age 67 or retirement. This type of policy costs more, but if you are permanently disabled and you have a ten-year policy, think of the situation you will be in when that policy expires.

- A non-cancelable and renewable policy. This way, your premiums will remain unchanged if you want to keep the policy.

Other Things to Consider

Who will make medical decisions on your behalf if you are unable to do so?

It can be a difficult subject to approach, but it is important to discuss end of life decisions with your family.

You can plan for future health care decisions by setting up an **Advance Directive**. This is a legal document that provides your directions or preferences concerning your future health care, also known as a **Living Will**. This document also allows you to appoint someone—a spouse, partner, trusted friend or relative—to act as a Health Care Proxy to make these decisions on your behalf if you are unable to make them on your own.

Be sure to discuss your healthcare wishes with the individual you select as a Health Care Proxy. You can also

name one or two individuals to serve as backup agents.

Guidelines to set up an Advance Directive and to assign a Health Care Proxy vary by state. You can download forms for your state from the American Bar Association here: https://www.americanbar.org/groups/law_aging/resources/health_care_decision_making/Stateforms.html

Sign and date these forms in front of a witness or witnesses. Some states also require that the form be notarized. The individual you select as a Health Care Proxy should have a copy of this document, along with your doctor.

Weiss Ratings' Recommended Life Insurance Providers

The following pages list Weiss Ratings' Recommended Life Insurance Providers (based strictly on financial safety). These insurers currently receive a Weiss Safety Rating of A+, A, A-, B+, or B, indicating their strong financial position. Companies are listed by their Safety Rating and then alphabetically within each Safety Rating grouping.

If an insurer is not on this list, it should not be automatically assumed that the firm is weak. Indeed, there are many firms that have not achieved a B- or better rating but are in relatively good condition with adequate resources to cover their risk. Not being included in this list should not be construed as a recommendation to cancel a policy.

To get Weiss Safety Rating for a company not included here, go to https://greyhouse.weissratings.com.

Insurer Name   The insurance company's legally registered name, which can sometimes differ from the name that the company uses for advertising. An insurer's name can be very similar to the name of other companies which may not be on this list, so make sure you note the exact name before contacting your agent.

Weiss Safety Rating   Our rating is measured on a scale from A to F and considers a wide range of factors. Highly rated companies are, in our opinion, less likely to experience financial difficulties than lower-rated firms. See "What Our Ratings Mean" in the Appendix for a definition of each rating category.

City & State   The city in which the company's corporate office is located and the state in which the company's corporate office is located.

Licensed In   The states in which an insurer is licensed to conduct business.

Website   The company's web address

Telephone   The telephone number to call for information on purchasing an insurance policy from the company.

The following list of Recommended Life Insurance Providers is based on ratings as of the date of publication.

A+ Rated Life Insurers

Insurer: **AMERICAN FAMILY LIFE INS CO**
Rating: A+
City & State: MADISON, WI
Licensed In: All states except NY, PR
Website: https://www.amfam.com
Telephone: (608) 249-2111

Insurer: **COUNTRY LIFE INS CO**
Rating: A+
City & State: BLOOMINGTON, IL
Licensed In: All states except CA, DC, HI, NH, NJ, NY, VT, PR
Website: https://www.countryfinancial.com
Telephone: (309) 821-3000

Insurer: **PHYSICIANS MUTUAL INS CO**
Rating: A+
City & State: Omaha, NE
Licensed In: All states except PR
Website: https://www.physiciansmutual.com
Telephone: (402) 633-1000

Insurer: **STATE FARM LIFE & ACCIDENT ASR CO**
Rating: A+
City & State: Bloomington, IL
Licensed In: CT, IL, NY, WI
Website: https://www.statefarm.com
Telephone: (309) 766-2311

Insurer: **STATE FARM LIFE INS CO**
Rating: A+
City & State: Bloomington, IL
Licensed In: All states except MA, NY, WI, PR
Website: https://www.statefarm.com
Telephone: (309) 766-2311

Insurer: **TEACHERS INS & ANNUITY ASN OF AM**
Rating: A+
City & State: NEW YORK, NY
Licensed In: All states, the District of Columbia and Puerto Rico
Website: https://www.tiaa.org
Telephone: (212) 490-9000

A Rated Life Insurers

Insurer:	**ALLIANZ LIFE INS CO OF NY**
Rating:	A
City & State:	New York, NY
Licensed In:	CT, DC, IL, MN, MO, NY, ND
Website:	https://www.allianzlife.com/new-york?legacy=/new
Telephone:	(763) 765-2913

Insurer:	**BERKLEY LIFE & HEALTH INS CO**
Rating:	A
City & State:	URBANDALE, IA
Licensed In:	All states except PR
Website:	http://www.wrberkley.com
Telephone:	(609) 584-6990

Insurer:	**FEDERATED LIFE INS CO**
Rating:	A
City & State:	OWATONNA, MN
Licensed In:	All states except AK, DC, HI, PR
Website:	https://www.federatedinsurance.com
Telephone:	(507) 455-5200

Insurer:	**FIRST RELIANCE STANDARD LIFE INS CO**
Rating:	A
City & State:	New York, NY
Licensed In:	DC, DE, NY
Website:	http://www.reliancestandard.com
Telephone:	(212) 303-8400

Insurer:	**FRANDISCO LIFE INS CO**
Rating:	A
City & State:	Toccoa, GA
Licensed In:	GA
Website:	http://www.1ffc.com
Telephone:	(706) 886-7571

Insurer:	**GUARDIAN LIFE INS CO OF AMERICA**
Rating:	A
City & State:	NEW YORK, NY
Licensed In:	All states except PR
Website:	https://www.guardianlife.com
Telephone:	(212) 598-8000

Insurer:	**LIFEWISE ASR CO**
Rating:	A
City & State:	Mountlake Terrace, WA
Licensed In:	AK, CA, ID, MD, OR, WA
Website:	http://www.lifewiseac.com
Telephone:	(425) 918-4575

Insurer:	**MIDWESTERN UNITED LIFE INS CO**
Rating:	A
City & State:	FISHERS, IN
Licensed In:	All states except NY, PR
Website:	https://www.voya.com
Telephone:	(770) 980-5100

Insurer:	**NATIONAL WESTERN LIFE INS CO**
Rating:	A
City & State:	Denver, CO
Licensed In:	All states except NY
Website:	https://www.nationalwesternlife.com
Telephone:	(512) 836-1010

Insurer:	**PARKER CENTENNIAL ASR CO**
Rating:	A
City & State:	STEVENS POINT, WI
Licensed In:	All states except NY, PR
Website:	https://www.sentry.com
Telephone:	(715) 346-6000

Insurer:	**SENTRY LIFE INS CO**
Rating:	A
City & State:	STEVENS POINT, WI
Licensed In:	All states except NY, PR
Website:	https://www.sentry.com
Telephone:	(715) 346-6000

Insurer:	**SHELTERPOINT LIFE INS CO**
Rating:	A
City & State:	GREAT NECK, NY
Licensed In:	CA, CO, CT, DC, DE, FL, IL, MD, MA, MI, MN, NJ, NY, NC, PA, RI, SC, TN
Website:	https://www.shelterpoint.com
Telephone:	(516) 829-8100

Insurer:	**SOUTHERN FARM BUREAU LIFE INS CO**
Rating:	A
City & State:	Jackson, MS
Licensed In:	AL, AR, CO, FL, GA, KY, LA, MS, NC, SC, TN, TX, VA, PR
Website:	https://www.sfbli.com
Telephone:	(601) 981-7422

Insurer: **UNITED FARM FAMILY LIFE INS CO**
Rating: A
City & State: Indianapolis, IN
Licensed In: AZ, CA, IL, IN, MD, MA, NH, NJ, NC, ND, OH, PA
Website: https://www.infarmbureau.com
Telephone: (317) 692-7200

Insurer: **UNITED FARM FAMILY LIFE INS CO**
Rating: A
City & State: Indianapolis, IN
Licensed In: AZ, CA, IL, IN, MD, MA, NH, NJ, NC, ND, OH, PA
Website: https://www.infarmbureau.com
Telephone: (317) 692-7200

A- Rated Life Insurers

Insurer: **AMALGAMATED LIFE INS CO**
Rating: A-
City & State: WHITE PLAINS, NY
Licensed In: All states except PR
Website: http://www.amalgamatedlife.com
Telephone: (914) 367-5000

Insurer: **AMERICAN FAMILY LIFE ASR CO OF NY**
Rating: A-
City & State: Albany, NY
Licensed In: CT, MA, NJ, NY, ND, VT
Website: https://www.aflac.com
Telephone: (518) 438-0764

Insurer: **AMERICAN HEALTH & LIFE INS CO**
Rating: A-
City & State: Fort Worth, TX
Licensed In: All states except NY, PR
Website:
Telephone: (800) 316-5607

Insurer: **AMERICAN REPUBLIC INS CO**
Rating: A-
City & State: Des Moines, IA
Licensed In: All states except NY, PR
Website: http://www.americanrepublic.com
Telephone: (800) 247-2190

Insurer:	**ANNUITY INVESTORS LIFE INS CO**
Rating:	A-
City & State:	Cincinnati, OH
Licensed In:	All states except NY, VT, PR
Website:	http://www.greatamericaninsurancegroup.com
Telephone:	(513) 357-3300

Insurer:	**ANTHEM LIFE INS CO**
Rating:	A-
City & State:	INDIANAPOLIS, IN
Licensed In:	All states except NY, RI, VT, PR
Website:	https://www.anthem.com
Telephone:	(614) 433-8800

Insurer:	**AUTO-OWNERS LIFE INS CO**
Rating:	A-
City & State:	LANSING, MI
Licensed In:	All states except AK, CA, CT, DC, DE, HI, LA, MD, MT, NJ, NY, OK, RI, TX, WV, WY, PR
Website:	http://www.auto-owners.com
Telephone:	(517) 323-1200

Insurer:	**CENTRAL STATES H & L CO OF OMAHA**
Rating:	A-
City & State:	Omaha, NE
Licensed In:	All states except NY, PR
Website:	http://www.cso.com
Telephone:	(402) 397-1111

Insurer:	**CIGNA LIFE INS CO OF NEW YORK**
Rating:	A-
City & State:	NEW YORK, NY
Licensed In:	AL, DC, MO, NY, PA, TN
Website:	http://www.cigna.com
Telephone:	(215) 761-1000

Insurer:	**COTTON STATES LIFE INS CO**
Rating:	A-
City & State:	ALPHARETTA, GA
Licensed In:	AL, FL, GA, KY, LA, MS, NC, SC, TN, VA
Website:	https://www.countryfinancial.com
Telephone:	(309) 821-3000

Insurer:	**COUNTRY INVESTORS LIFE ASR CO**
Rating:	A-
City & State:	BLOOMINGTON, IL
Licensed In:	All states except CA, DC, HI, NH, NJ, NY, UT, VT, PR
Website:	https://www.countryfinancial.com
Telephone:	(309) 821-3000

Insurer:	**ERIE FAMILY LIFE INS CO**
Rating:	A-
City & State:	Erie, PA
Licensed In:	DC, IL, IN, KY, MD, MN, NC, OH, PA, TN, VA, WV, WI
Website:	https://www.erieinsurance.com
Telephone:	(814) 870-2000

Insurer:	**FARM BUREAU LIFE INS CO OF MICHIGAN**
Rating:	A-
City & State:	LANSING, MI
Licensed In:	MI
Website:	https://www.farmbureauinsurance-mi.com
Telephone:	(517) 323-7000

Insurer:	**FARM BUREAU LIFE INS CO OF MISSOURI**
Rating:	A-
City & State:	Jefferson City, MO
Licensed In:	MO
Website:	https://www.mofbinsurance.com
Telephone:	(573) 893-1400

Insurer:	**FIDELITY INVESTMENTS LIFE INS CO**
Rating:	A-
City & State:	Salt Lake City, UT
Licensed In:	All states except NY, PR
Website:	https://www.fidelity.com
Telephone:	(401) 292-4616

Insurer:	**GARDEN STATE LIFE INS CO**
Rating:	A-
City & State:	GALVESTON, TX
Licensed In:	All states except PR
Website:	https://www.americannational.com
Telephone:	(409) 763-4661

Insurer:	**LIFE INS CO OF BOSTON & NEW YORK**
Rating:	A-
City & State:	Athol Springs, NY
Licensed In:	NY
Website:	http://www.lifeofboston.com
Telephone:	(800) 645-2317

Insurer:	**MASSACHUSETTS MUTUAL LIFE INS CO**
Rating:	A-
City & State:	SPRINGFIELD, MA
Licensed In:	All states, the District of Columbia and Puerto Rico
Website:	https://www.massmutual.com
Telephone:	(413) 788-8411

Insurer:	**MEDICO CORP LIFE INS CO**
Rating:	A-
City & State:	Omaha, IA
Licensed In:	All states except CA, CT, MA, NH, NJ, NY, PR
Website:	http://www.gomedico.com
Telephone:	(800) 822-9993

Insurer:	**MUTUAL OF AMERICA LIFE INS CO**
Rating:	A-
City & State:	New York, NY
Licensed In:	All states except PR
Website:	http://www.mutualofamerica.com
Telephone:	(212) 224-1600

Insurer:	**NEW YORK LIFE INS CO**
Rating:	A-
City & State:	NEW YORK, NY
Licensed In:	All states, the District of Columbia and Puerto Rico
Website:	http://www.newyorklife.com
Telephone:	(212) 576-7000

Insurer:	**NIPPON LIFE INS CO OF AMERICA**
Rating:	A-
City & State:	West Des Moines, IA
Licensed In:	All states except ME, NH, WY, PR
Website:	http://www.nipponlifebenefits.com
Telephone:	(212) 682-3000

Insurer:	**NORTHWESTERN MUTUAL LIFE INS CO**
Rating:	A-
City & State:	MILWAUKEE, WI
Licensed In:	All states except PR
Website:	https://www.northwesternmutual.com
Telephone:	(414) 271-1444

Insurer:	**PACIFIC GUARDIAN LIFE INS CO LTD**
Rating:	A-
City & State:	Honolulu, HI
Licensed In:	AK, AZ, CA, CO, HI, ID, IA, LA, MO, MT, NE, NV, NM, OK, OR, SD, TX, UT, WA, WY
Website:	http://www.pacificguardian.com
Telephone:	(808) 955-2236

Insurer:	**PACIFIC LIFE INS CO**
Rating:	A-
City & State:	OMAHA, NE
Licensed In:	All states except NY, PR
Website:	http://www.pacificlife.com
Telephone:	(949) 219-3011

Insurer: **PHYSICIANS LIFE INS CO**
Rating: A-
City & State: Omaha, NE
Licensed In: All states except NY, PR
Website: https://www.physiciansmutual.com
Telephone: (402) 633-1000

Insurer: **STANDARD LIFE & ACCIDENT INS CO**
Rating: A-
City & State: GALVESTON, TX
Licensed In: All states except ME, NH, NJ, NY, PR
Website: https://slaico.americannational.com
Telephone: (409) 763-4661

Insurer: **STANDARD LIFE INS CO OF NY**
Rating: A-
City & State: WHITE PLAINS, NY
Licensed In: NY
Website: https://www.standard.com
Telephone: (914) 989-4400

Insurer: **SYMETRA NATIONAL LIFE INS CO**
Rating: A-
City & State: WEST DES MOINES, IA
Licensed In: All states except AK, HI, ME, MA, NH, NJ, NY, RI, VT, WY, PR
Website: https://www.symetra.com
Telephone: (425) 256-8000

Insurer: **TRANS OCEANIC LIFE INS CO**
Rating: A-
City & State: SAN JUAN, PR
Licensed In: FL, PR
Website: http://tolicpr.com
Telephone: (787) 620-2680x2319

B+ Rated Life Insurers

Insurer:	**ADVANCE INS CO OF KANSAS**
Rating:	B+
City & State:	Topeka, KS
Licensed In:	KS
Website:	http://www.advanceinsurance.com
Telephone:	(785) 273-9804

Insurer:	**AETNA HEALTH & LIFE INS CO**
Rating:	B+
City & State:	HARTFORD, CT
Licensed In:	All states except PR
Website:	https://www.aetna.com
Telephone:	(860) 273-0123

Insurer:	**AMERICAN FAMILY LIFE ASR CO OF COLUM**
Rating:	B+
City & State:	Omaha, NE
Licensed In:	All states except NY
Website:	https://www.aflac.com
Telephone:	(706) 323-3431

Insurer:	**AMERICAN FIDELITY ASR CO**
Rating:	B+
City & State:	Oklahoma City, OK
Licensed In:	All states except NY
Website:	https://americanfidelity.com
Telephone:	(405) 523-2000

Insurer:	**AMERICAN UNITED LIFE INS CO**
Rating:	B+
City & State:	INDIANAPOLIS, IN
Licensed In:	All states except PR
Website:	https://www.oneamerica.com
Telephone:	(317) 285-1877

Insurer:	**AMICA LIFE INS CO**
Rating:	B+
City & State:	LINCOLN, RI
Licensed In:	All states except PR
Website:	https://www.amica.com
Telephone:	(800) 652-6422

Insurer: **ASSURITY LIFE INS CO**
Rating: B+
City & State: LINCOLN, NE
Licensed In: All states except NY, PR
Website: http://www.assurity.com
Telephone: (402) 476-6500

Insurer: **AXA EQUITABLE LIFE INS CO**
Rating: B+
City & State: New York, NY
Licensed In: All states, the District of Columbia and Puerto Rico
Website: https://us.axa.com
Telephone: (212) 554-1234

Insurer: **BEST LIFE & HEALTH INS CO**
Rating: B+
City & State: Austin, TX
Licensed In: All states except AK, AR, CT, DE, ME, MA, MN, NH, NJ,
                NY, RI, VT, WV, WI, PR
Website: http://www.bestlife.com
Telephone: (949) 253-4080

Insurer: **BLUEBONNET LIFE INS CO**
Rating: B+
City & State: Flowood, MS
Licensed In: AL, AR, LA, MS, TN
Website:
Telephone: (601) 664-4218

Insurer: **BOSTON MUTUAL LIFE INS CO**
Rating: B+
City & State: Canton, MA
Licensed In: All states, the District of Columbia and Puerto Rico
Website: https://www.bostonmutual.com
Telephone: (781) 828-7000

Insurer: **COMPANION LIFE INS CO**
Rating: B+
City & State: Columbia, SC
Licensed In: All states except CA, HI, NJ, NY, PR
Website: http://www.companionlife.com
Telephone: (803) 735-1251

Insurer: **DEARBORN NATIONAL LIFE INS CO**
Rating: B+
City & State: Chicago, IL
Licensed In: All states except NY
Website: http://www.dearbornnational.com
Telephone: (800) 348-4512

Insurer:	**DEARBORN NATIONAL LIFE INS CO OF NY**
Rating:	B+
City & State:	Pittsford, NY
Licensed In:	NY
Website:	http://www.dearbornnational.com
Telephone:	(800) 348-4512

Insurer:	**DELAWARE AMERICAN LIFE INS CO**
Rating:	B+
City & State:	Wilmington, DE
Licensed In:	All states except PR
Website:	https://www.metlife.com
Telephone:	(302) 594-2000

Insurer:	**EMPIRE FIDELITY INVESTMENTS L I C**
Rating:	B+
City & State:	New York, NY
Licensed In:	NY
Website:	https://www.fidelity.com
Telephone:	(401) 292-4616

Insurer:	**FAMILY HERITAGE LIFE INS CO OF AMER**
Rating:	B+
City & State:	Cleveland, OH
Licensed In:	All states except NY
Website:	http://www.familyheritagelife.com
Telephone:	(440) 922-5200

Insurer:	**FARM BUREAU LIFE INS CO**
Rating:	B+
City & State:	West Des Moines, IA
Licensed In:	AZ, CO, ID, IA, KS, MN, MT, NE, NV, NM, ND, OK, OR, SD, UT, WA, WI, WY
Website:	https://www.fbfs.com
Telephone:	(515) 225-5400

Insurer:	**FIRST SYMETRA NATL LIFE INS CO OF NY**
Rating:	B+
City & State:	NEW YORK, NY
Licensed In:	NY
Website:	https://www.symetra.com
Telephone:	(425) 256-8000

Insurer:	**GERBER LIFE INS CO**
Rating:	B+
City & State:	White Plains, NY
Licensed In:	All states, the District of Columbia and Puerto Rico
Website:	http://www.gerberlife.com
Telephone:	(914) 272-4000

Insurer:	**GLOBE LIFE INSURANCE CO OF NY**
Rating:	B+
City & State:	LIVERPOOL, NY
Licensed In:	NY
Website:	https://www.globelifeofnewyork.com
Telephone:	(315) 451-2544

Insurer:	**GOVERNMENT PERSONNEL MUTUAL L I C**
Rating:	B+
City & State:	San Antonio, TX
Licensed In:	All states except NJ, NY, PR
Website:	https://www.gpmlife.com
Telephone:	(210) 357-2222

Insurer:	**JACKSON NATIONAL LIFE INS CO**
Rating:	B+
City & State:	LANSING, MI
Licensed In:	All states except NY, PR
Website:	https://www.jackson.com
Telephone:	(517) 381-5500

Insurer:	**LOCOMOTIVE ENGRS&COND MUT PROT ASSN**
Rating:	B+
City & State:	Southfield, MI
Licensed In:	MI, NE, NM, TX
Website:	https://www.lecmpa.org
Telephone:	(800) 514-0010

Insurer:	**MIDLAND NATIONAL LIFE INS CO**
Rating:	B+
City & State:	West Des Moines, IA
Licensed In:	All states except NY
Website:	https://www.midlandnational.com
Telephone:	(515) 273-0874

Insurer:	**MINNESOTA LIFE INS CO**
Rating:	B+
City & State:	ST. PAUL, MN
Licensed In:	All states except NY
Website:	https://www.securian.com
Telephone:	(651) 665-3500

Insurer:	**MML BAY STATE LIFE INS CO**
Rating:	B+
City & State:	ENFIELD, CT
Licensed In:	All states except NY, PR
Website:	https://www.massmutual.com
Telephone:	(413) 788-8411

Insurer: **MUTUAL OF OMAHA INS CO**
Rating: B+
City & State: OMAHA, NE
Licensed In: All states, the District of Columbia and Puerto Rico
Website: http://www.mutualofomaha.com
Telephone: (402) 342-7600

Insurer: **NATIONAL BENEFIT LIFE INS CO**
Rating: B+
City & State: Long Island City, NY
Licensed In: All states except PR
Website: http://www.nationalbenefitlife.com
Telephone: (718) 361-3636

Insurer: **NATIONAL FARMERS UNION LIFE INS CO**
Rating: B+
City & State: Dallas, TX
Licensed In: All states except AL, CT, DE, FL, GA, HI, LA, ME, MD, MA, NH, NJ, NY, NC, RI, SC, TN, VT, WV, PR
Website: http://www.americo.com
Telephone: (816) 391-2000

Insurer: **NATIONAL INCOME LIFE INS CO**
Rating: B+
City & State: LIVERPOOL, NY
Licensed In: NY
Website: http://www.nilife.com
Telephone: (315) 451-8180

Insurer: **NEW YORK LIFE INS & ANNUITY CORP**
Rating: B+
City & State: NEWARK, DE
Licensed In: All states except PR
Website: http://www.newyorklife.com
Telephone: (212) 576-7000

Insurer: **OHIO NATIONAL LIFE ASR CORP**
Rating: B+
City & State: Cincinnati, OH
Licensed In: All states except NY
Website: https://www.ohionational.com
Telephone: (513) 794-6100

Insurer: **PACIFIC LIFE & ANNUITY CO**
Rating: B+
City & State: PHOENIX, AZ
Licensed In: All states except PR
Website: http://www.pacificlife.com
Telephone: (949) 219-3011

Insurer:	**PAN AMERICAN ASR CO**
Rating:	B+
City & State:	NEW ORLEANS, LA
Licensed In:	All states except AK, IA, ME, MA, NH, NY, RI, SD, VT, WY
Website:	https://www.palig.com
Telephone:	(504) 566-1300

Insurer:	**PRINCIPAL LIFE INS CO**
Rating:	B+
City & State:	DES MOINES, IA
Licensed In:	All states, the District of Columbia and Puerto Rico
Website:	https://www.principal.com
Telephone:	(515) 247-5111

Insurer:	**SB MUTL LIFE INS CO OF MA**
Rating:	B+
City & State:	Woburn, MA
Licensed In:	All states except NY, PR
Website:	https://www.sbli.com
Telephone:	(781) 938-3500

Insurer:	**SHELTER LIFE INS CO**
Rating:	B+
City & State:	COLUMBIA, MO
Licensed In:	AR, CO, IL, IN, IA, KS, KY, LA, MS, MO, NE, NV, OH, OK, TN
Website:	https://www.shelterinsurance.com
Telephone:	(573) 445-8441

Insurer:	**SOUTHERN PIONEER LIFE INS CO**
Rating:	B+
City & State:	LITTLE ROCK, AR
Licensed In:	AL, AR, GA, IN, KS, KY, LA, MS, MO, NM, OK, SC, TN, TX
Website:	https://www.securian.com
Telephone:	(651) 665-3500

Insurer:	**STANDARD INS CO**
Rating:	B+
City & State:	PORTLAND, OR
Licensed In:	All states except NY
Website:	https://www.standard.com
Telephone:	(971) 321-7000

Insurer:	**SYMETRA LIFE INS CO**
Rating:	B+
City & State:	WEST DES MOINES, IA
Licensed In:	All states except NY
Website:	https://www.symetra.com
Telephone:	(425) 256-8000

Insurer:	**TENNESSEE FARMERS LIFE INS CO**
Rating:	B+
City & State:	Columbia, TN
Licensed In:	TN
Website:	https://www.fbitn.com
Telephone:	(931) 388-7872

Insurer:	**TRANS WORLD ASR CO**
Rating:	B+
City & State:	San Mateo, CA
Licensed In:	All states except NH, NY, VT, PR
Website:	http://www.twasite.com
Telephone:	(650) 348-2300

Insurer:	**TRUSTMARK INS CO**
Rating:	B+
City & State:	LAKE FOREST, IL
Licensed In:	All states, the District of Columbia and Puerto Rico
Website:	http://www.trustmarkcompanies.com
Telephone:	(847) 615-1500

Insurer:	**TRUSTMARK LIFE INS CO**
Rating:	B+
City & State:	LAKE FOREST, IL
Licensed In:	All states except PR
Website:	http://www.trustmarkcompanies.com
Telephone:	(847) 615-1500

Insurer:	**VOYA RETIREMENT INS & ANNUITY CO**
Rating:	B+
City & State:	WINDSOR, CT
Licensed In:	All states, the District of Columbia and Puerto Rico
Website:	https://www.voya.com
Telephone:	(860) 580-4646

B Rated Life Insurers

Insurer: **4 EVER LIFE INS CO**
Rating: B
City & State: Oakbrook Terrace, IL
Licensed In: All states, the District of Columbia and Puerto Rico
Website: http://www.4everlife.com
Telephone: (630) 472-7700

Insurer: **AAA LIFE INS CO**
Rating: B
City & State: Livonia, MI
Licensed In: All states except NY, PR
Website: https://www.aaalife.com
Telephone: (734) 779-2600

Insurer: **AAA LIFE INS CO OF NY**
Rating: B
City & State: Harrison, NY
Licensed In: NY
Website: https://www.aaalife.com
Telephone: (734) 779-2600

Insurer: **AETNA LIFE INS CO**
Rating: B
City & State: HARTFORD, CT
Licensed In: All states, the District of Columbia and Puerto Rico
Website: https://www.aetna.com
Telephone: (860) 273-0123

Insurer: **ALLIANZ LIFE INS CO OF NORTH AMERICA**
Rating: B
City & State: Minneapolis, MN
Licensed In: All states except NY
Website: https://www.allianzlife.com
Telephone: (763) 765-6500

Insurer: **ALLSTATE LIFE INS CO**
Rating: B
City & State: NORTHBROOK, IL
Licensed In: All states, the District of Columbia and Puerto Rico
Website: http://www.allstate.com
Telephone: (847) 402-5000

Insurer: **AMERICAN FARM LIFE INS CO**
Rating: B
City & State: Fort Worth, TX
Licensed In: NM, OK, TX
Website: http://www.americanfarmlife.com
Telephone: (817) 451-9550

Insurer: **AMERICAN FEDERATED LIFE INS CO**
Rating: B
City & State: Flowood, MS
Licensed In: AL, IL, LA, MS, MO
Website:
Telephone: (601) 992-6886

Insurer: **AMERICAN FIDELITY LIFE INS CO**
Rating: B
City & State: Pensacola, FL
Licensed In: All states except NY, VT, PR
Website: http://www.amfisite.com
Telephone: (850) 456-7401

Insurer: **AMERICAN GENERAL LIFE INS CO**
Rating: B
City & State: Houston, TX
Licensed In: All states except NY
Website: http://www.aig.com
Telephone: (713) 522-1111

Insurer: **AMERICAN HERITAGE LIFE INS CO**
Rating: B
City & State: JACKSONVILLE, FL
Licensed In: All states except NY
Website: http://www.allstate.com
Telephone: (904) 992-1776

Insurer: **AMERICAN MATURITY LIFE INS CO**
Rating: B
City & State: Hartford, CT
Licensed In: All states except PR
Website: http://www.thehartford.com
Telephone: (860) 547-5000

Insurer: **AMERICAN MODERN LIFE INS CO**
Rating: B
City & State: CLEVELAND, OH
Licensed In: All states except NH, NJ, PR
Website: https://www.securian.com
Telephone: (651) 665-3500

Insurer:	**AMERICAN NATIONAL INS CO**
Rating:	B
City & State:	GALVESTON, TX
Licensed In:	All states except NY
Website:	http://www.anico.com
Telephone:	(409) 763-4661

Insurer:	**AMERICAN NATL LIFE INS CO OF NY**
Rating:	B
City & State:	GLENMONT, NY
Licensed In:	NY
Website:	http://www.anicony.com
Telephone:	(409) 763-4661

Insurer:	**AMERICAN PUBLIC LIFE INS CO**
Rating:	B
City & State:	Oklahoma City, OK
Licensed In:	All states except NY, PR
Website:	https://www.ampublic.com
Telephone:	(601) 936-6600

Insurer:	**AMERICAN REPUBLIC CORP INS CO**
Rating:	B
City & State:	Omaha, NE
Licensed In:	All states except AK, CA, CT, FL, HI, ID, ME, MA, MI, NH, NJ, NY, RI, VT, WA, PR
Website:	http://www.americanrepublic.com
Telephone:	(866) 705-9100

Insurer:	**AMERITAS LIFE INS CORP**
Rating:	B
City & State:	Lincoln, NE
Licensed In:	All states except NY, PR
Website:	https://www.ameritas.com
Telephone:	(402) 467-1122

Insurer:	**ANTHEM LIFE & DISABILITY INS CO**
Rating:	B
City & State:	NEW YORK, NY
Licensed In:	NY
Website:	https://www.empireblue.com
Telephone:	(212) 476-1000

Insurer:	**AURORA NATIONAL LIFE ASR CO**
Rating:	B
City & State:	LOS ANGELES, CA
Licensed In:	All states except CT, ME, NH, NY, PR
Website:	http://www.auroralife.com
Telephone:	(800) 265-2652

Insurer:	**AXA CORPORATE SOLUTIONS LIFE REINS**
Rating:	B
City & State:	Wilmington, DE
Licensed In:	All states except FL, PR
Website:	
Telephone:	(201) 743-7217

Insurer:	**AXA EQUITABLE LIFE & ANNUITY CO**
Rating:	B
City & State:	Highlands Ranch, CO
Licensed In:	All states except NY, PR
Website:	https://us.axa.com
Telephone:	(704) 341-7000

Insurer:	**BALTIMORE LIFE INS CO**
Rating:	B
City & State:	Owings Mills, MD
Licensed In:	All states except NY, PR
Website:	https://www.baltlife.com
Telephone:	(410) 581-6600

Insurer:	**BANKERS FIDELITY LIFE INS CO**
Rating:	B
City & State:	Atlanta, GA
Licensed In:	All states except CA, CT, NY, VT, PR
Website:	http://www.bankersfidelitylife.com
Telephone:	(800) 241-1439

Insurer:	**BENEFICIAL LIFE INS CO**
Rating:	B
City & State:	Salt Lake City, UT
Licensed In:	All states except NY, PR
Website:	http://www.beneficialfinancialgroup.com
Telephone:	(801) 933-1100

Insurer:	**BERKSHIRE LIFE INS CO OF AMERICA**
Rating:	B
City & State:	PITTSFIELD, MA
Licensed In:	All states except PR
Website:	https://www.guardianlife.com
Telephone:	(413) 499-4321

Insurer:	**BLUE CROSS BLUE SHIELD OF KANSAS INC**
Rating:	B
City & State:	Topeka, KS
Licensed In:	KS
Website:	http://www.bcbsks.com
Telephone:	(785) 291-7000

Insurer:	**BLUE SHIELD OF CALIFORNIA L&H INS CO**
Rating:	B
City & State:	San Francisco, CA
Licensed In:	CA
Website:	https://www.blueshieldca.com
Telephone:	(888) 800-2742

Insurer:	**BRIGHTHOUSE LIFE INSURANCE CO**
Rating:	B
City & State:	Wilmington, DE
Licensed In:	All states except NY
Website:	https://www.brighthousefinancial.com
Telephone:	(212) 578-9500

Insurer:	**BROOKE LIFE INS CO**
Rating:	B
City & State:	LANSING, MI
Licensed In:	MI
Website:	
Telephone:	(517) 381-5500

Insurer:	**CARIBBEAN AMERICAN LIFE ASR CO**
Rating:	B
City & State:	SAN JUAN, PR
Licensed In:	PR
Website:	http://www.assurantsolutions.com/puertorico
Telephone:	(787) 250-6470

Insurer:	**CHESAPEAKE LIFE INS CO**
Rating:	B
City & State:	OKLAHOMA CITY, OK
Licensed In:	All states except NJ, NY, VT, PR
Website:	http://www.healthmarketsinc.com
Telephone:	(817) 255-3100

Insurer:	**CHRISTIAN FIDELITY LIFE INS CO**
Rating:	B
City & State:	Dallas, TX
Licensed In:	All states except AK, CA, CT, DC, DE, HI, IA, ME, MD, MA, MI, MN, NH, NJ, NY, NC, PA, RI, VT, WI, PR
Website:	http://www.oxfordlife.com
Telephone:	(602) 263-6666

Insurer:	**CHURCH LIFE INS CORP**
Rating:	B
City & State:	New York, NY
Licensed In:	All states except PR
Website:	https://www.cpg.org/global/about-us/about-cpg/ch
Telephone:	(212) 592-1800

Insurer:	**CIGNA HEALTH & LIFE INS CO**
Rating:	B
City & State:	BLOOMFIELD, CT
Licensed In:	All states, the District of Columbia and Puerto Rico
Website:	http://www.cigna.com
Telephone:	(860) 226-6000

Insurer:	**CIGNA WORLDWIDE INS CO**
Rating:	B
City & State:	WILMINGTON, DE
Licensed In:	DE
Website:	http://www.cigna.com
Telephone:	(302) 797-3207

Insurer:	**CINCINNATI LIFE INS CO**
Rating:	B
City & State:	FAIRFIELD, OH
Licensed In:	All states except NY, PR
Website:	http://www.cinfin.com
Telephone:	(513) 870-2000

Insurer:	**CM LIFE INS CO**
Rating:	B
City & State:	ENFIELD, CT
Licensed In:	All states except NY
Website:	https://www.massmutual.com
Telephone:	(413) 788-8411

Insurer:	**COLUMBIAN MUTUAL LIFE INS CO**
Rating:	B
City & State:	Binghamton, NY
Licensed In:	All states except PR
Website:	http://www.cfglife.com
Telephone:	(607) 724-2472

Insurer:	**CONSUMERS LIFE INS CO**
Rating:	B
City & State:	Cleveland, OH
Licensed In:	All states except AL, AK, CA, CT, FL, HI, ID, ME, MA, NH, NY, NC, RI, TN, VT, WA, PR
Website:	https://www.consumerslife.com
Telephone:	(216) 687-7000

Insurer:	**CONTINENTAL AMERICAN INS CO**
Rating:	B
City & State:	Omaha, NE
Licensed In:	All states except NY, PR
Website:	http://www.caicworksite.com
Telephone:	(888) 730-2244

Insurer: **DESERET MUTUAL INS CO**
Rating: B
City & State: SALT LAKE CITY, UT
Licensed In: HI, ID, UT
Website: https://www.dmba.com
Telephone: (801) 578-5628

Insurer: **EAGLE LIFE INS CO**
Rating: B
City & State: WEST DES MOINES, IA
Licensed In: All states except ID, NY, PR
Website: http://www.eagle-lifeco.com
Telephone: (515) 221-0002

Insurer: **EMC NATIONAL LIFE CO**
Rating: B
City & State: DES MOINES, IA
Licensed In: All states except NJ, NY, PR
Website: https://www.emcnationallife.com
Telephone: (515) 237-2000

Insurer: **FARM FAMILY LIFE INS CO**
Rating: B
City & State: GLENMONT, NY
Licensed In: CT, DE, ME, MD, MA, NH, NJ, NY, PA, RI, VT, VA, WV
Website: http://www.farmfamily.com
Telephone: (518) 431-5000

Insurer: **FIDELITY SECURITY LIFE INS CO**
Rating: B
City & State: Kansas City, MO
Licensed In: All states except PR
Website: http://www.fslins.com
Telephone: (816) 756-1060

Insurer: **FIDELITY SECURITY LIFE INS CO OF NY**
Rating: B
City & State: Brewster, NY
Licensed In: MS, NY
Website: http://www.fslins.com
Telephone: (800) 821-7303

Insurer: **FIRST ASR LIFE OF AMERICA**
Rating: B
City & State: BATON ROUGE, LA
Licensed In: AL, LA, MS, TN
Website:
Telephone: (225) 769-9923

Insurer:	**FIRST PENN-PACIFIC LIFE INS CO**
Rating:	B
City & State:	Fort Wayne, IN
Licensed In:	All states except NY, PR
Website:	https://www.lfg.com
Telephone:	(260) 455-2000

Insurer:	**FIRST SECURITY BENEFIT LIFE & ANN**
Rating:	B
City & State:	New York, NY
Licensed In:	KS, NY
Website:	https://www.fsbl.com
Telephone:	(800) 355-4570

Insurer:	**FORETHOUGHT LIFE INS CO**
Rating:	B
City & State:	INDIANAPOLIS, IN
Licensed In:	All states except NY
Website:	https://www.globalatlantic.com
Telephone:	(317) 223-2700

Insurer:	**GENERAL AMERICAN LIFE INS CO**
Rating:	B
City & State:	St. Louis, MO
Licensed In:	All states except NY
Website:	https://www.metlife.com
Telephone:	(314) 843-8700

Insurer:	**GENERAL RE LIFE CORP**
Rating:	B
City & State:	Stamford, CT
Licensed In:	All states except PR
Website:	http://www.genre.com
Telephone:	(203) 352-3000

Insurer:	**GOLDEN RULE INS CO**
Rating:	B
City & State:	INDIANAPOLIS, IN
Licensed In:	All states except NY, PR
Website:	https://www.uhone.com
Telephone:	(317) 290-8100

Insurer:	**GPM HEALTH & LIFE INS CO**
Rating:	B
City & State:	Spokane, WA
Licensed In:	AZ, CA, CO, GA, HI, ID, IL, IN, KS, KY, MD, MI, MS, MO, MT, NV, NM, NC, OH, OR, PA, SC, TX, UT, VA, WA, WY
Website:	http://www.nclife.com
Telephone:	(509) 838-4235

Insurer:	**GREAT SOUTHERN LIFE INS CO**
Rating:	B
City & State:	Dallas, TX
Licensed In:	All states except NH, NY, RI, VT, PR
Website:	http://www.greatsouthern.com
Telephone:	(816) 391-2000

Insurer:	**GREAT WESTERN INS CO**
Rating:	B
City & State:	Ogden, UT
Licensed In:	All states except AK, CT, HI, NY, PR
Website:	http://www.gwic.com
Telephone:	(801) 689-1401

Insurer:	**GREATER GEORGIA LIFE INS CO**
Rating:	B
City & State:	ATLANTA, GA
Licensed In:	AL, GA, MS, NC, SC, TN, VA
Website:	https://www.bcbsga.com
Telephone:	(404) 842-8000

Insurer:	**GREAT-WEST LIFE & ANNUITY INS OF NY**
Rating:	B
City & State:	New York, NY
Licensed In:	NY
Website:	http://www.greatwest.com/NY
Telephone:	(303) 737-3000

Insurer:	**GREENFIELDS LIFE INS CO**
Rating:	B
City & State:	West Des Moines, IA
Licensed In:	CO, IA
Website:	http://www.greenfieldslife.com
Telephone:	(515) 225-5400

Insurer:	**GUARANTEE TRUST LIFE INS CO**
Rating:	B
City & State:	Glenview, IL
Licensed In:	All states except NY
Website:	http://www.gtlic.com
Telephone:	(847) 699-0600

Insurer:	**GUARDIAN INS & ANNUITY CO INC**
Rating:	B
City & State:	WILMINGTON, DE
Licensed In:	All states except PR
Website:	https://www.guardianlife.com
Telephone:	(212) 598-8000

Insurer: **HANNOVER LIFE REASSUR CO OF AMERICA**
Rating: B
City & State: Orlando, FL
Licensed In: All states, the District of Columbia and Puerto Rico
Website: https://www.hannover-re.com
Telephone: (407) 649-8411

Insurer: **HARLEYSVILLE LIFE INS CO**
Rating: B
City & State: HARLEYSVILLE, PA
Licensed In: All states except AK, CA, CO, HI, ID, KS, LA, ME, MS, MO, MT, NV, NY, OK, OR, VT, WA, WY, PR
Website: https://www.nationwide.com/harleysville-insuranc
Telephone: (215) 256-5000

Insurer: **HCC LIFE INS CO**
Rating: B
City & State: Indianapolis, IN
Licensed In: All states except PR
Website: http://www.tmhcc.com
Telephone: (770) 973-9851

Insurer: **HM LIFE INS CO OF NEW YORK**
Rating: B
City & State: New York, NY
Licensed In: DC, NY, RI
Website: https://www.hmig.com
Telephone: (800) 328-5433

Insurer: **HOMESTEADERS LIFE CO**
Rating: B
City & State: West Des Moines, IA
Licensed In: All states except NY, PR
Website: http://www.homesteaderslife.com
Telephone: (515) 440-7777

Insurer: **HORACE MANN LIFE INS CO**
Rating: B
City & State: SPRINGFIELD, IL
Licensed In: All states except NJ, NY, PR
Website: http://www.horacemann.com
Telephone: (217) 789-2500

Insurer: **ILLINOIS MUTUAL LIFE INS CO**
Rating: B
City & State: Peoria, IL
Licensed In: All states except AK, DC, HI, NY, PR
Website: http://www.illinoismutual.com
Telephone: (309) 674-8255

Insurer: **INTRAMERICA LIFE INS CO**
Rating: B
City & State: HAUPPAUGE, NY
Licensed In: AZ, AR, CT, FL, HI, IL, IN, KY, LA, MD, MA, MI, MO, NE, NV, NJ, NM, NY, NC, OR, PA, TX, UT, VT, WY
Website: http://www.allstate.com
Telephone: (631) 357-8923

Insurer: **INVESTORS LIFE INS CO NORTH AMERICA**
Rating: B
City & State: Dallas, TX
Licensed In: All states except NY, PR
Website: http://www.americo.com
Telephone: (816) 391-2000

Insurer: **JACKSON NATIONAL LIFE INS CO OF NY**
Rating: B
City & State: PURCHASE, NY
Licensed In: DE, MI, NY
Website: https://www.jackson.com
Telephone: (517) 381-5500

Insurer: **JAMESTOWN LIFE INS CO**
Rating: B
City & State: LYNCHBURG, VA
Licensed In: VA
Website: https://www.genworth.com
Telephone: (434) 845-0911

Insurer: **JOHN HANCOCK LIFE & HEALTH INS CO**
Rating: B
City & State: Boston, MA
Licensed In: All states, the District of Columbia and Puerto Rico
Website: http://www.johnhancock.com
Telephone: (617) 572-6000

Insurer: **JOHN HANCOCK LIFE INS CO (USA)**
Rating: B
City & State: Lansing, MI
Licensed In: All states except NY
Website: http://www.johnhancock.com
Telephone: (617) 572-6000

Insurer: **JOHN HANCOCK LIFE INS CO OF NY**
Rating: B
City & State: Valhalla, NY
Licensed In: MI, NY
Website: http://www.johnhancocknewyork.com
Telephone: (914) 773-0708

Insurer:	**KANSAS CITY LIFE INS CO**
Rating:	B
City & State:	Kansas City, MO
Licensed In:	All states except NY, VT, PR
Website:	https://www.kclife.com
Telephone:	(816) 753-7000

Insurer:	**LAFAYETTE LIFE INS CO**
Rating:	B
City & State:	CINCINNATI, OH
Licensed In:	All states except NY, PR
Website:	https://www.llic.com
Telephone:	(513) 362-4900

Insurer:	**LIBERTY LIFE ASR CO OF BOSTON**
Rating:	B
City & State:	Boston, MA
Licensed In:	All states except PR
Website:	https://lifemadeeasy.libertymutual.com
Telephone:	(617) 357-9500

Insurer:	**LIBERTY NATIONAL LIFE INS CO**
Rating:	B
City & State:	OMAHA, NE
Licensed In:	All states except NY, PR
Website:	https://www.libertynational.com
Telephone:	(972) 569-4000

Insurer:	**LIFE INS CO OF ALABAMA**
Rating:	B
City & State:	Gadsden, AL
Licensed In:	AL, AR, FL, GA, KY, LA, MS, NC, OK, SC, TN
Website:	http://www.licoa.com
Telephone:	(256) 543-2022

Insurer:	**LIFE INS CO OF NORTH AMERICA**
Rating:	B
City & State:	PHILADELPHIA, PA
Licensed In:	All states, the District of Columbia and Puerto Rico
Website:	http://www.cigna.com
Telephone:	(215) 761-1000

Insurer:	**LIFE INS CO OF THE SOUTHWEST**
Rating:	B
City & State:	Addison, TX
Licensed In:	All states except NY, PR
Website:	https://www.nationallife.com
Telephone:	(214) 638-7100

Insurer:	**LINCOLN LIFE & ANNUITY CO OF NY**
Rating:	B
City & State:	Syracuse, NY
Licensed In:	All states except PR
Website:	https://www.lfg.com
Telephone:	(260) 455-2000

Insurer:	**LINCOLN NATIONAL LIFE INS CO**
Rating:	B
City & State:	Fort Wayne, IN
Licensed In:	All states except NY
Website:	https://www.lfg.com
Telephone:	(260) 455-2000

Insurer:	**LONGEVITY INS CO**
Rating:	B
City & State:	Addison, TX
Licensed In:	All states except HI, ME, MA, NH, NY, ND, RI, VT, WY, PR
Website:	
Telephone:	(215) 956-8000

Insurer:	**M LIFE INS CO**
Rating:	B
City & State:	Centennial, CO
Licensed In:	AZ, CO, DE, MI, NE, NJ
Website:	http://www.mfin.com
Telephone:	(503) 232-6960

Insurer:	**MANHATTAN LIFE INS CO**
Rating:	B
City & State:	Great Neck, NY
Licensed In:	All states, the District of Columbia and Puerto Rico
Website:	http://www.manhattanlife.com
Telephone:	(713) 529-0045

Insurer:	**MEDAMERICA INS CO OF FL**
Rating:	B
City & State:	Orlando, FL
Licensed In:	FL
Website:	https://www.medamericatc.com
Telephone:	(585) 238-4464

Insurer:	**MEDICO INS CO**
Rating:	B
City & State:	Omaha, IA
Licensed In:	All states except CT, NJ, NY, PR
Website:	http://www.gomedico.com
Telephone:	(800) 228-6080

Insurer: **MEDICO LIFE & HEALTH INS CO**
Rating: B
City & State: Des Moines, IA
Licensed In: AZ, CO, ID, IN, IA, KS, KY, MI, MN, MT, NE, NC, ND, OH, OK, OR, PA, SD, UT, WI, WY
Website: http://www.gomedico.com
Telephone: (800) 247-2190

Insurer: **MERIT LIFE INS CO**
Rating: B
City & State: EVANSVILLE, IN
Licensed In: All states except AK, MA, NY, VT, PR
Website: https://www.onemainsolutions.com
Telephone: (800) 325-2147

Insurer: **MONITOR LIFE INS CO OF NEW YORK**
Rating: B
City & State: Utica, NY
Licensed In: AZ, AR, CO, CT, DC, FL, IL, IN, IA, KS, LA, MD, MA, MS, MO, MT, NV, NY, OH, OK, PA, TN, TX, UT, VA, WV
Website: http://www.monitorlife.com
Telephone: (601) 956-2028

Insurer: **MONY LIFE INS CO OF AMERICA**
Rating: B
City & State: Phoenix, AZ
Licensed In: All states except NY
Website: https://www.axa.com/en
Telephone: (212) 554-1234

Insurer: **MOTORISTS LIFE INS CO**
Rating: B
City & State: COLUMBUS, OH
Licensed In: AR, FL, GA, IL, IN, IA, KY, MA, MI, MN, MO, NE, NH, OH, PA, RI, SC, TN, VA, WV, WI
Website: https://www.motoristsinsurancegroup.com/who-we-a
Telephone: (614) 225-8211

Insurer: **MUTUAL SAVINGS LIFE INS CO**
Rating: B
City & State: ST. LOUIS, MO
Licensed In: AL, FL, GA, IN, LA, MS, TN
Website: http://www.kemperhsc.com/mutualsavings.htm
Telephone: (314) 819-4300

Insurer:	**MUTUAL TRUST LIFE INS CO**
Rating:	B
City & State:	Oak Brook, IL
Licensed In:	All states except NY, PR
Website:	https://www.mutualtrust.com
Telephone:	(630) 990-1000

Insurer:	**NATIONAL FARM LIFE INS CO**
Rating:	B
City & State:	Fort Worth, TX
Licensed In:	TX
Website:	http://www.nflic.com
Telephone:	(817) 451-9550

Insurer:	**NATIONAL FOUNDATION LIFE INS CO**
Rating:	B
City & State:	Fort Worth, TX
Licensed In:	All states except CT, FL, HI, IL, MD, MA, MI, MN, NH, NJ, NY, RI, VT, WV, WI, PR
Website:	http://www.nfl-ins.com
Telephone:	(817) 878-3300

Insurer:	**NATIONAL LIFE INS CO**
Rating:	B
City & State:	Montpelier, VT
Licensed In:	All states except PR
Website:	https://www.nationallife.com
Telephone:	(802) 229-3333

Insurer:	**NATIONAL SECURITY INS CO**
Rating:	B
City & State:	Elba, AL
Licensed In:	AL, FL, GA, MS, SC, TN, TX
Website:	http://www.nationalsecuritygroup.com
Telephone:	(334) 897-2273

Insurer:	**NATIONAL SECURITY LIFE & ANNUITY CO**
Rating:	B
City & State:	New York, NY
Licensed In:	AZ, AR, DC, IL, IN, IA, KS, LA, NE, NH, NJ, NY, OH, OK, OR, PA, SC, SD, TX, UT
Website:	https://www.nslac.com
Telephone:	(877) 446-6060

Insurer:	**NATIONAL TEACHERS ASSOCIATES L I C**
Rating:	B
City & State:	Addison, TX
Licensed In:	All states except NY, PR
Website:	https://ntalife.com
Telephone:	(972) 532-2100

Insurer:	**NEW ENGLAND LIFE INS CO**
Rating:	B
City & State:	Boston, MA
Licensed In:	All states except PR
Website:	https://www.brighthousefinancial.com
Telephone:	(617) 578-2000

Insurer:	**NIAGARA LIFE & HEALTH INS CO**
Rating:	B
City & State:	Amherst, NY
Licensed In:	CT, NY
Website:	
Telephone:	(803) 735-1251

Insurer:	**NORTH AMERICAN CO FOR LIFE & H INS**
Rating:	B
City & State:	West Des Moines, IA
Licensed In:	All states except NY
Website:	https://www.northamericancompany.com
Telephone:	(515) 226-7100

Insurer:	**NORTH AMERICAN INS CO**
Rating:	B
City & State:	Madison, WI
Licensed In:	AL, CO, DC, IL, IN, KS, LA, MD, MI, MN, MO, NM, ND, OH, OK, OR, PA, SC, TX, WI
Website:	http://www.oxfordlife.com
Telephone:	(877) 667-9368

Insurer:	**NORTHWESTERN LONG TERM CARE INS CO**
Rating:	B
City & State:	MILWAUKEE, WI
Licensed In:	All states except PR
Website:	https://www.northwesternmutual.com
Telephone:	(414) 661-2510

Insurer:	**NTA LIFE INS CO OF NEW YORK**
Rating:	B
City & State:	Addison, TX
Licensed In:	NY
Website:	https://www.ntalife.com
Telephone:	(972) 532-2100

Insurer:	**NYLIFE INS CO OF ARIZONA**
Rating:	B
City & State:	SCOTTSDALE, AZ
Licensed In:	All states except ME, NY, PR
Website:	http://www.newyorklife.com
Telephone:	(212) 576-7000

Insurer:	**OHIO MOTORISTS LIFE INSURANCE CO**
Rating:	B
City & State:	INDEPENDENCE, OH
Licensed In:	OH
Website:	
Telephone:	(216) 606-6045

Insurer:	**OHIO NATIONAL LIFE INS CO**
Rating:	B
City & State:	Cincinnati, OH
Licensed In:	All states except NY
Website:	https://www.ohionational.com
Telephone:	(513) 794-6100

Insurer:	**OLD UNITED LIFE INS CO**
Rating:	B
City & State:	Phoenix, AZ
Licensed In:	All states except ME, NH, NY, PR
Website:	http://www.oldunited.com
Telephone:	(913) 895-0200

Insurer:	**OPTUM INS OF OH INC**
Rating:	B
City & State:	Columbus, OH
Licensed In:	All states except ME, NY, PR
Website:	https://www.optumrx.com
Telephone:	(800) 282-3232

Insurer:	**OXFORD LIFE INS CO**
Rating:	B
City & State:	Phoenix, AZ
Licensed In:	All states except NY, VT, PR
Website:	http://www.oxfordlife.com
Telephone:	(602) 263-6666

Insurer:	**PACIFIC CENTURY LIFE INS CORP**
Rating:	B
City & State:	Phoenix, AZ
Licensed In:	AZ, HI
Website:	
Telephone:	(602) 200-6900

Insurer:	**PAN AMERICAN LIFE INS CO OF PR**
Rating:	B
City & State:	GUAYNABO, PR
Licensed In:	PR
Website:	https://www.palig.com
Telephone:	(787) 620-1414

Insurer:	**PAN-AMERICAN LIFE INS CO**
Rating:	B
City & State:	NEW ORLEANS, LA
Licensed In:	All states except ME, NY, VT
Website:	https://www.palig.com
Telephone:	(504) 566-1300

Insurer:	**PARK AVENUE LIFE INS CO**
Rating:	B
City & State:	WILMINGTON, DE
Licensed In:	All states except HI, NY, PR
Website:	https://www.guardianlife.com
Telephone:	(800) 538-6203

Insurer:	**PATRIOT LIFE INS CO**
Rating:	B
City & State:	Frankenmuth, MI
Licensed In:	ME, MI, OH, VT
Website:	http://www.patriotlife.com
Telephone:	(989) 652-6121

Insurer:	**PEKIN LIFE INS CO**
Rating:	B
City & State:	PEKIN, IL
Licensed In:	AL, AZ, AR, GA, IL, IN, IA, KS, KY, LA, MI, MN, MS, MO, NE, OH, PA, TN, TX, VA, WI
Website:	http://www.pekininsurance.com
Telephone:	(309) 346-1161

Insurer:	**PENN MUTUAL LIFE INS CO**
Rating:	B
City & State:	Philadelphia, PA
Licensed In:	All states except PR
Website:	http://www2.pennmutual.com/content/public/indivi
Telephone:	(215) 956-8000

Insurer:	**PHILADELPHIA AMERICAN LIFE INS CO**
Rating:	B
City & State:	Houston, TX
Licensed In:	All states except NY, RI, PR
Website:	http://www.neweralife.com
Telephone:	(281) 368-7200

Insurer: **PIONEER MUTUAL LIFE INS CO**
Rating: B
City & State: FARGO, ND
Licensed In: All states except AK, NY, PR
Website: https://www.oneamerica.com
Telephone: (800) 437-4692

Insurer: **PRENEED REINS CO OF AMERICA**
Rating: B
City & State: Phoenix, AZ
Licensed In: AZ
Website: https://www.nglic.com
Telephone: (608) 257-5611

Insurer: **PRIMERICA LIFE INS CO**
Rating: B
City & State: Boston, MA
Licensed In: All states except NY
Website: http://www.primerica.com
Telephone: (770) 381-1000

Insurer: **PRINCIPAL NATIONAL LIFE INS CO**
Rating: B
City & State: DES MOINES, IA
Licensed In: All states except NY, PR
Website: https://www.principal.com
Telephone: (515) 247-5111

Insurer: **PROTECTIVE LIFE & ANNUITY INS CO**
Rating: B
City & State: BIRMINGHAM, AL
Licensed In: All states except MN, PR
Website: http://www.protective.com
Telephone: (205) 268-1000

Insurer: **PROTECTIVE LIFE INS CO**
Rating: B
City & State: BRENTWOOD, TN
Licensed In: All states except NY
Website: http://www.protective.com
Telephone: (205) 268-1000

Insurer: **PROVIDENT AMER LIFE & HEALTH INS CO**
Rating: B
City & State: Cleveland, OH
Licensed In: All states except AL, CT, ME, MI, MN, NH, NJ, NM, NY, RI, TN, VA, WA, PR
Website: http://www.cigna.com/medicare/supplemental/?camp
Telephone: (512) 451-2224

Insurer:	**PRUDENTIAL INS CO OF AMERICA**
Rating:	B
City & State:	NEWARK, NJ
Licensed In:	All states, the District of Columbia and Puerto Rico
Website:	https://www.prudential.com
Telephone:	(877) 301-1212

Insurer:	**RELIANCE STANDARD LIFE INS CO**
Rating:	B
City & State:	Schaumburg, IL
Licensed In:	All states, the District of Columbia and Puerto Rico
Website:	http://www.reliancestandard.com
Telephone:	(267) 256-3500

Insurer:	**RELIASTAR LIFE INS CO OF NEW YORK**
Rating:	B
City & State:	WOODBURY, NY
Licensed In:	All states except PR
Website:	https://www.voya.com
Telephone:	(770) 980-5100

Insurer:	**RX LIFE INSURANCE CO**
Rating:	B
City & State:	ALGONA, IA
Licensed In:	All states except AK, FL, HI, ME, MA, NH, NJ, NY, VT, PR
Website:	
Telephone:	(515) 295-2461

Insurer:	**S USA LIFE INS CO INC**
Rating:	B
City & State:	PHOENIX, AZ
Licensed In:	All states except CT, NH, NY, PR
Website:	http://www.prosperitylife.com
Telephone:	(212) 356-0300

Insurer:	**SBLI USA MUT LIFE INS CO INC**
Rating:	B
City & State:	NEW YORK, NY
Licensed In:	IL, IA, MI, MS, NH, NJ, NY, NC, OH, PA, SD, VT, PR
Website:	http://www.prosperitylife.com
Telephone:	(212) 356-0300

Insurer:	**SECURIAN LIFE INS CO**
Rating:	B
City & State:	ST. PAUL, MN
Licensed In:	All states, the District of Columbia and Puerto Rico
Website:	https://www.securian.com
Telephone:	(651) 665-3500

Insurer: **SECURITY BENEFIT LIFE INS CO**
Rating: B
City & State: Topeka, KS
Licensed In: All states except NY, PR
Website: https://www.securitybenefit.com
Telephone: (785) 438-3000

Insurer: **SENTRY LIFE INS CO OF NEW YORK**
Rating: B
City & State: SYRACUSE, NY
Licensed In: MN, NY, ND
Website: https://www.sentry.com
Telephone: (315) 453-6301

Insurer: **SETTLERS LIFE INS CO**
Rating: B
City & State: Madison, WI
Licensed In: All states except NY, PR
Website: https://www.settlerslife.com
Telephone: (608) 257-5611

Insurer: **SHELTERPOINT INS CO**
Rating: B
City & State: WEST PALM BEACH, FL
Licensed In: All states except CA, MI, NY, PR
Website: https://www.shelterpoint.com
Telephone: (516) 829-8100

Insurer: **SOUTHERN NATL LIFE INS CO INC**
Rating: B
City & State: Baton Rouge, LA
Licensed In: LA
Website: http://www.bcbsla.com
Telephone: (225) 295-3307

Insurer: **STANDARD SECURITY LIFE INS CO OF NY**
Rating: B
City & State: New York, NY
Licensed In: All states, the District of Columbia and Puerto Rico
Website: https://www.sslicny.com
Telephone: (212) 355-4141

Insurer: **STARMOUNT LIFE INS CO**
Rating: B
City & State: Baton Rouge, LA
Licensed In: All states except NY, PR
Website: http://www.starmountlife.com
Telephone: (225) 926-2888

Insurer:	**STATE LIFE INS CO**
Rating:	B
City & State:	INDIANAPOLIS, IN
Licensed In:	All states except NY, PR
Website:	https://www.oneamerica.com
Telephone:	(317) 285-2300

Insurer:	**STATE LIFE INS FUND**
Rating:	B
City & State:	Madison, WI
Licensed In:	WI
Website:	
Telephone:	(608) 266-0107

Insurer:	**SUNSET LIFE INS CO OF AMERICA**
Rating:	B
City & State:	Kansas City, MO
Licensed In:	All states except AL, NH, NJ, NY, TN, VT, WI, PR
Website:	https://www.sunsetlife.com
Telephone:	(816) 753-7000

Insurer:	**SWBC LIFE INS CO**
Rating:	B
City & State:	San Antonio, TX
Licensed In:	GA, LA, MI, OK, TN, TX, UT, VA
Website:	https://www.swbc.com
Telephone:	(210) 321-7361

Insurer:	**TEXAS LIFE INS CO**
Rating:	B
City & State:	WACO, TX
Licensed In:	All states except NY, PR
Website:	http://www.texaslife.com
Telephone:	(254) 752-6521

Insurer:	**THRIVENT LIFE INS CO**
Rating:	B
City & State:	Minneapolis, MN
Licensed In:	All states except GA, ME, MA, NH, NY, NC, RI, VT, WY, PR
Website:	https://www.thrivent.com
Telephone:	(800) 847-4836

Insurer:	**TIAA-CREF LIFE INS CO**
Rating:	B
City & State:	NEW YORK, NY
Licensed In:	All states except PR
Website:	https://www.tiaa.org
Telephone:	(212) 490-9000

Insurer:	**TPM LIFE INS CO**
Rating:	B
City & State:	Lancaster, PA
Licensed In:	DC, DE, IN, KY, MD, MS, NJ, OH, PA, VA, WV
Website:	http://www.tpmins.com
Telephone:	(601) 956-2028

Insurer:	**TRANSAMERICA FINANCIAL LIFE INS CO**
Rating:	B
City & State:	Harrison, NY
Licensed In:	All states except PR
Website:	https://www.transamerica.com
Telephone:	(914) 627-3630

Insurer:	**TRANSAMERICA LIFE INS CO**
Rating:	B
City & State:	Cedar Rapids, IA
Licensed In:	All states except NY
Website:	https://www.transamerica.com
Telephone:	(319) 355-8511

Insurer:	**TRUSTMARK LIFE INS CO OF NEW YORK**
Rating:	B
City & State:	ALBANY, NY
Licensed In:	NY
Website:	http://www.trustmarkcompanies.com
Telephone:	(847) 615-1500

Insurer:	**UNIFIED LIFE INS CO**
Rating:	B
City & State:	Austin, TX
Licensed In:	All states except NY, PR
Website:	http://www.unifiedlife.com
Telephone:	(877) 492-4678

Insurer:	**UNIMERICA INS CO**
Rating:	B
City & State:	MILWAUKEE, WI
Licensed In:	All states except NY, PR
Website:	http://www.unitedhealthgroup.com
Telephone:	(763) 732-8837

Insurer:	**UNIMERICA LIFE INS CO OF NY**
Rating:	B
City & State:	NEW YORK, NY
Licensed In:	DC, NY
Website:	http://www.unitedhealthgroup.com
Telephone:	(877) 832-7734

Insurer: **UNION LABOR LIFE INS CO**
Rating: B
City & State: SILVER SPRING, MD
Licensed In: All states except PR
Website: http://www.ullico.com
Telephone: (202) 682-0900

Insurer: **UNION NATIONAL LIFE INS CO**
Rating: B
City & State: BATON ROUGE, LA
Licensed In: AL, AR, FL, GA, LA, MS, OK, TN, TX
Website: http://www.kemperhsc.com/unionnational.htm
Telephone: (314) 819-4300

Insurer: **UNION SECURITY INS CO**
Rating: B
City & State: TOPEKA, KS
Licensed In: All states except NY, PR
Website:
Telephone: (651) 361-4000

Insurer: **UNION SECURITY INS CO**
Rating: B
City & State: TOPEKA, KS
Licensed In: All states except NY, PR
Website:
Telephone: (651) 361-4000

Insurer: **UNITED HERITAGE LIFE INS CO**
Rating: B
City & State: MERIDIAN, ID
Licensed In: All states except NY, PR
Website: http://www.unitedheritage.com
Telephone: (208) 493-6100

Insurer: **UNITED HERITAGE LIFE INS CO**
Rating: B
City & State: MERIDIAN, ID
Licensed In: All states except NY, PR
Website: http://www.unitedheritage.com
Telephone: (208) 493-6100

Insurer: **UNITED HOME LIFE INS CO**
Rating: B
City & State: Indianapolis, IN
Licensed In: All states except AK, MA, NH, NY, PR
Website: http://www.unitedhomelife.com
Telephone: (317) 692-7979

Insurer:	**UNITED HOME LIFE INS CO**
Rating:	B
City & State:	Indianapolis, IN
Licensed In:	All states except AK, MA, NH, NY, PR
Website:	http://www.unitedhomelife.com
Telephone:	(317) 692-7979

Insurer:	**UNITED LIFE INS CO**
Rating:	B
City & State:	CEDAR RAPIDS, IA
Licensed In:	All states except AK, CT, DC, GA, HI, ME, MA, NH, NY, OR, RI, SC, VT, WA, PR
Website:	https://www.ufginsurance.com
Telephone:	(319) 399-5700

Insurer:	**UNITED LIFE INS CO**
Rating:	B
City & State:	CEDAR RAPIDS, IA
Licensed In:	All states except AK, CT, DC, GA, HI, ME, MA, NH, NY, OR, RI, SC, VT, WA, PR
Website:	https://www.ufginsurance.com
Telephone:	(319) 399-5700

Insurer:	**UNITED NATIONAL LIFE INS CO OF AM**
Rating:	B
City & State:	Glenview, IL
Licensed In:	AZ, AR, CO, ID, IL, IN, KS, KY, MN, MO, NE, NV, NM, NC, ND, OK, SD, TN, TX, UT, WV, WY
Website:	http://unlinsurance.com
Telephone:	(847) 803-5252

Insurer:	**UNITED NATIONAL LIFE INS CO OF AM**
Rating:	B
City & State:	Glenview, IL
Licensed In:	AZ, AR, CO, ID, IL, IN, KS, KY, MN, MO, NE, NV, NM, NC, ND, OK, SD, TN, TX, UT, WV, WY
Website:	http://unlinsurance.com
Telephone:	(847) 803-5252

Insurer:	**UNITED OF OMAHA LIFE INS CO**
Rating:	B
City & State:	OMAHA, NE
Licensed In:	All states except NY
Website:	http://www.mutualofomaha.com
Telephone:	(402) 342-7600

Insurer: **UNITED OF OMAHA LIFE INS CO**
Rating: B
City & State: OMAHA, NE
Licensed In: All states except NY
Website: http://www.mutualofomaha.com
Telephone: (402) 342-7600

Insurer: **UNITED STATES LIFE INS CO IN NYC**
Rating: B
City & State: New York, NY
Licensed In: All states except PR
Website: http://www.aig.com
Telephone: (713) 522-1111

Insurer: **UNITED STATES LIFE INS CO IN NYC**
Rating: B
City & State: New York, NY
Licensed In: All states except PR
Website: http://www.aig.com
Telephone: (713) 522-1111

Insurer: **WESTERN & SOUTHERN LIFE INS CO**
Rating: B
City & State: CINCINNATI, OH
Licensed In: All states except AK, CT, ME, MA, NH, NY, VT, PR
Website: https://www.westernsouthernlife.com
Telephone: (513) 629-1800

Insurer: **WESTERN-SOUTHERN LIFE ASR CO**
Rating: B
City & State: CINCINNATI, OH
Licensed In: All states except AK, ME, NH, NY, RI, PR
Website: https://www.westernsouthernlife.com
Telephone: (513) 629-1800

Weiss Ratings' Weakest Life Insurance Providers

The following pages list Weiss Ratings' Weakest Life Insurance Providers (based strictly on financial safety). These insurers currently receive a Weiss Safety Rating of E+, E or E-, indicating their very weak financial position.

These companies currently demonstrate what we consider to be significant weaknesses and have also failed some of the basic tests that we use to identify fiscal stability. Therefore, even in a favorable economic environment, it is our opinion that policyholders could incur significant risks.

Companies are listed by their Safety Rating and then alphabetically within each Safety Rating grouping.

To get Weiss Safety Rating for a company not included here, go to https://greyhouse.weissratings.com.

Insurer Name
The insurance company's legally registered name, which can sometimes differ from the name that the company uses for advertising. An insurer's name can be very similar to the name of other companies which may not be on this list, so make sure you note the exact name before contacting your agent.

Weiss Safety Rating
Our rating is measured on a scale from A to F and considers a wide range of factors. Highly rated companies are, in our opinion, less likely to experience financial difficulties than lower-rated firms. See "What Our Ratings Mean" in the Appendix for a definition of each rating category.

City & State
The city in which the company's corporate office is located and the state in which the company's corporate office is located.

Licensed In
The states in which an insurer is licensed to conduct business.

Website
The company's web address

Telephone
The telephone number to call for information on purchasing an insurance policy from the company.

The following list of Weakest Life Insurance Providers is based on ratings as of the date of publication.

E+ Rated Life Insurers

Insurer:	**ALABAMA LIFE REINS CO INC**
Rating:	E+
City & State:	TUSCALOOSA, AL
Licensed In:	AL
Website:	
Telephone:	(205) 247-3417

Insurer:	**AMERICAN LIFE & SECURITY CORP**
Rating:	E+
City & State:	Lincoln, NE
Licensed In:	AZ, CO, HI, ID, IL, IN, MI, MO, NE, NM, OK, SD, TX, UT
Website:	http://www.americanlifeandsecurity.com
Telephone:	(402) 489-8266

Insurer:	**CAPITAL RESERVE LIFE INS CO**
Rating:	E+
City & State:	Jefferson City, MO
Licensed In:	KS, MO
Website:	
Telephone:	(402) 489-8266

Insurer:	**DELTA LIFE INS CO**
Rating:	E+
City & State:	ATLANTA, GA
Licensed In:	GA, MS, SC
Website:	http://www.delta-life.com
Telephone:	(404) 231-2111

Insurer:	**FINANCIAL AMERICAN LIFE INS CO**
Rating:	E+
City & State:	Overland Park, KS
Licensed In:	All states except CA, IA, LA, ME, NH, NJ, NY, OH, OR, VT, VA, WA, WV, PR
Website:	http://www.famli.com
Telephone:	(904) 407-1097

Insurer: **KILPATRICK LIFE INS CO**
Rating: E+
City & State: Shreveport, LA
Licensed In: AR, LA, MS, OK, TX
Website: http://www.klic.com
Telephone: (318) 222-0555

Insurer: **LILY LIFE INS CO**
Rating: E+
City & State: Beaumont, TX
Licensed In: TX
Website:
Telephone: (866) 884-6542

Insurer: **NETCARE LIFE & HEALTH INS CO**
Rating: E+
City & State: Hagatna, GU
Licensed In: No States
Website: http://www.netcarelifeandhealth.com
Telephone: (671) 472-3610

Insurer: **PHOENIX LIFE & ANNUITY CO**
Rating: E+
City & State: Hartford, CT
Licensed In: All states except CA, GA, ME, MA, MN, NY, PR
Website: https://phoenix.nsre.com
Telephone: (860) 403-5000

Insurer: **RELIABLE LIFE INS CO**
Rating: E+
City & State: Monroe, LA
Licensed In: LA
Website:
Telephone: (318) 387-1000

Insurer: **RELIABLE LIFE INS CO**
Rating: E+
City & State: Monroe, LA
Licensed In: LA
Website:
Telephone: (318) 387-1000

Insurer:	**UNITED SECURITY ASR CO OF PA**
Rating:	E+
City & State:	SOUDERTON, PA
Licensed In:	All states except AL, CT, HI, ME, NH, NJ, NY, RI, VT, WY, PR
Website:	http://www.usa-cal.com
Telephone:	(215) 723-3044

E Rated Life Insurers

Insurer:	**AMERICAN HOME LIFE INS CO**
Rating:	E
City & State:	North Little Rock, AR
Licensed In:	AR
Website:	
Telephone:	(501) 758-1778

Insurer:	**CROWN GLOBAL INS CO OF AMERICA**
Rating:	E
City & State:	Wilmington, DE
Licensed In:	DE
Website:	http://www.crownglobalinsurance.com
Telephone:	(302) 357-9349

Insurer:	**DIRECTORS LIFE ASR CO**
Rating:	E
City & State:	OKLAHOMA CITY, OK
Licensed In:	AR, KS, OK, TX
Website:	http://www.directorslife.tv
Telephone:	(405) 842-1234

Insurer:	**INVESTORS PREFERRED LIFE INS CO**
Rating:	E
City & State:	RAPID CITY, SD
Licensed In:	SD
Website:	http://www.iplinsurance.com
Telephone:	(303) 782-0004

Insurer: **JACKSON GRIFFIN INS CO**
Rating: E
City & State: Harrisburg, AR
Licensed In: No States
Website:
Telephone: (870) 523-5822

Insurer: **LOMBARD INTL LIFE ASR CO**
Rating: E
City & State: Philadelphia, PA
Licensed In: All states except NH, NY, PR
Website: http://www.lombardinternational.com
Telephone: (484) 530-4800

Insurer: **PHOENIX LIFE INS CO**
Rating: E
City & State: East Greenbush, NY
Licensed In: All states, the District of Columbia and Puerto Rico
Website: https://phoenix.nsre.com
Telephone: (860) 403-5000

Insurer: **SMITH BURIAL & LIFE INS CO**
Rating: E
City & State: STAMPS, AR
Licensed In: AR
Website:
Telephone: (870) 533-2070

E- Rated Life Insurers

Insurer: **AMERICAN INDEPENDENT NETWORK INS CO**
Rating: E-
City & State: New York, NY
Licensed In: NY
Website: http://www.penntreaty.com/ainic/home.aspx
Telephone: (610) 965-2222

Insurer: **NORTH CAROLINA MUTUAL LIFE INS CO**
Rating: E-
City & State: Durham, NC
Licensed In: AL, AZ, CA, DC, GA, ID, IL, IN, KY, LA, MD, MS, MO,
                NV, NJ, NC, OH, OK, PA, SC, TN, TX, VA
Website: http://www.ncmutuallife.com
Telephone: (919) 682-9201

Insurer: **RHODES LIFE INS CO OF LA INC**
Rating: E-
City & State: Baton Rouge, LA
Licensed In: LA
Website:
Telephone: (225) 383-1678

Insurer: **SENIOR HEALTH INS CO OF PENNSYLVANIA**
Rating: E-
City & State: Harrisburg, PA
Licensed In: All states except CT, NY, RI, VT, PR
Website: http://www.shipltc.com
Telephone: (317) 566-7500

Appendices

Helpful Resources

Contact any of the following organizations for further information about purchasing health insurance.

- **Your state department of insurance** - See next page for a specific contacts

- **National Association of Insurance Commissioners** - www.naic.org

- **Insurance Information Institute** - www.iii.org

- **Independent Insurance Agents & Brokers of America**
  www.independentagent.com/default.aspx

- **Weiss Ratings, LLC** provides financial strength ratings for health insurance plans nationwide: www.weissratings.com

- **United States Department of Labor**
  Telephone: 1-866-4-USA-DOL www.dol.gov

State Insurance Commissioners' Departmental Contact Information

State	Official's Title	Website Address	Telephone
Alabama	Commissioner	www.aldoi.org	(334) 269-3550
Alaska	Director	https://www.commerce.alaska.gov/web/ins/	(800) 467-8725
Arizona	Director	https://insurance.az.gov/	(602) 364-2499
Arkansas	Commissioner	www.insurance.arkansas.gov	(800) 852-5494
California	Commissioner	www.insurance.ca.gov	(800) 927-4357
Colorado	Commissioner	https://www.colorado.gov/pacific/dora/node/90616	(800) 866-7675
Connecticut	Commissioner	http://www.ct.gov/cid/site/default.asp	(800) 203-3447
Delaware	Commissioner	http://delawareinsurance.gov/	(800) 282-8611
Dist. of Columbia	Commissioner	http://disb.dc.gov/	(202) 727-8000
Florida	Commissioner	www.floir.com/	(850) 413-3140
Georgia	Commissioner	www.oci.ga.gov/	(800) 656-2298
Hawaii	Commissioner	http://cca.hawaii.gov/ins/	(808) 586-2790
Idaho	Director	www.doi.idaho.gov	(800) 721-3272
Illinois	Director	www.insurance.illinois.gov/	(866) 445-5364
Indiana	Commissioner	www.in.gov/idoi/	(800) 622-4461
Iowa	Commissioner	https://iid.iowa.gov/	(877) 955-1212
Kansas	Commissioner	www.ksinsurance.org	(800) 432-2484
Kentucky	Commissioner	http://insurance.ky.gov/	(800) 595-6053
Louisiana	Commissioner	www.ldi.la.gov/	(800) 259-5300
Maine	Superintendent	www.maine.gov/pfr/insurance/	(800) 300-5000
Maryland	Commissioner	http://insurance.maryland.gov/Pages/default.aspx	(800) 492-6116
Massachusetts	Commissioner	www.mass.gov/ocabr/government/oca-agencies/doi-lp/	(877) 563-4467
Michigan	Director	http://www.michigan.gov/difs	(877) 999-6442
Minnesota	Commissioner	http://mn.gov/commerce/	(651) 539-1500
Mississippi	Commissioner	http://www.mid.ms.gov/	(601) 359-3569
Missouri	Director	www.insurance.mo.gov	(800) 726-7390
Montana	Commissioner	http://csimt.gov/	(800) 332-6148
Nebraska	Director	www.doi.nebraska.gov/	(402) 471-2201
Nevada	Commissioner	www.doi.nv.gov/	(888) 872-3234
New Hampshire	Commissioner	www.nh.gov/insurance/	(800) 852-3416
New Jersey	Commissioner	www.state.nj.us/dobi/	(800) 446-7467
New Mexico	Superintendent	www.osi.state.nm.us/	(855) 427-5674
New York	Superintendent	www.dfs.ny.gov/	(800) 342-3736
North Carolina	Commissioner	www.ncdoi.com	(855) 408-1212
North Dakota	Commissioner	www.nd.gov/ndins/	(800) 247-0560
Ohio	Lieutenant Governor	www.insurance.ohio.gov	(800) 686-1526
Oklahoma	Commissioner	www.ok.gov/oid/	(800) 522-0071
Oregon Insurance	Commissioner	http://dfr.oregon.gov/Pages/index.aspx	(888) 877-4894
Pennsylvania	Commissioner	www.insurance.pa.gov/	(877) 881-6388
Puerto Rico	Commissioner	www.ocs.gobierno.pr	(787) 304-8686
Rhode Island	Superintendent	www.dbr.state.ri.us/divisions/insurance/	(401) 462-9500
South Carolina	Director	www.doi.sc.gov	(803) 737-6160
South Dakota	Director	http://dlr.sd.gov/insurance/default.aspx	(605) 773-3563
Tennessee	Commissioner	http://tn.gov/commerce/	(615) 741-2241
Texas	Commissioner	www.tdi.texas.gov/	(800) 578-4677
Utah	Commissioner	www.insurance.utah.gov	(800) 439-3805
Vermont	Commissioner	www.dfr.vermont.gov/	(802) 828-3301
Virgin Islands	Lieutenant Governor	http://ltg.gov.vi/division-of-banking-and-insurance.html	(340) 774-7166
Virginia	Commissioner	www.scc.virginia.gov/boi/	(804) 371-9741
Washington	Commissioner	www.insurance.wa.gov	(800) 562-6900
West Virginia	Commissioner	www.wvinsurance.gov	(888) 879-9842
Wisconsin	Commissioner	oci.wi.gov	(800) 236-8517
Wyoming	Commissioner	http://doi.wyo.gov/	(800) 438-5768

Glossary

Adjustable Life Insurance: A kind of policy that offers flexibility in modifying the benefit, premium, or savings component.

Beneficiary: In life insurance, the person selected by the insured to receive the death benefit.

Benefit: Money paid out by the insurance company.

Cash Value: In permanent life insurance, cash value refers to a component of the plan that works like a tax-deferred savings account. Otherwise, the cash value is the amount of money that the life insurance policy owner would receive as a refund if the policy owner decided to cancel the policy. In this second sense, also called "cash surrender value."

Convertible Term Life Insurance: A term life insurance policy that is written to allow conversion into a permanent life insurance policy in the future.

Death Benefit: The amount of money that the insured person's beneficiaries will receive from the insurer when the person dies.

Decreasing Term Life Insurance: A type of term life insurance in which the death benefit decreases at a pre-determined rate across the duration of the policy.

Elimination Period: In disability insurance policies, this is the period before the policy starts paying the benefit.

Exclusion: A condition in an insurance policy under which the benefit will not be paid.

Level Term Life Insurance: A type of term life insurance in which the premium remains the same for the duration of the policy.

Long-Term Disability Insurance: Disability insurance that pays benefits for longer periods than short-term disability insurance, up to retirement.

Own Occupation Coverage: A kind of disability insurance that covers the insured whenever they are unable to perform the work required for their occupation.

Permanent Life Insurance: Life insurance in force for the insured person's entire life and that pays a benefit whenever that person dies. Sometimes called "whole life."

Premium Payment: The amount paid for an insurance policy, usually a monthly payment.

Short-Term Disability Insurance: Disability insurance that pays benefits for, typically, no more than six months.

Social Security Disability Insurance: (SSDI) A federal disability insurance program for U.S. workers managed by the Social Security Administration and funded through a payroll tax.

Straight Life: Another term for Whole Life.

Term Life Insurance: Life insurance payable only if the death of the insured occurs within a specified time called the "term" of the policy, such as 5 or 10 years.

Universal Life Insurance: An adjustable life insurance in which premiums and coverage are adjustable, and money or especially interest earned in the savings component is used to pay premiums.

Whole Life Insurance:

Life insurance in force for the insured person's entire life and that pays a benefit whenever that person dies. Also called "permanent life insurance."

Workers' Compensation:

A state-run system of short-term insurance that provides for the continued payment of salaries to employees when they have been injured or made ill in the course of employment.

Voluntary Benefit:

Employment benefits that are offered by the employer although the employer doesn't contribute to the cost.

Yearly Renewable Term:

(YRT) A type of term life insurance that is renewed each year.

Further Reading

"Disability Insurance Learn Center." Policy Genius. www.policygenius.com/long-term-disability-insurance/learn/

Monaco, Kristen. "Disability Insurance Plans: Trends in Employee Access and Employer Costs." Beyond the Numbers, Feb. 2015. Bureau of Labor Statistics. United States Department of Labor. www.bls.gov/opub/btn/volume-4/disability-insurance-plans.htm.

Reavis, Marshall Wilson III. Insurance: Concepts and Coverage. FriesenPress, 2012.

Steuer, Tony. Insurance Made Easy: A Comprehensive Roadmap to the Coverage You Need. Life Insurance Sage Press, 2017.

Weiss Ratings: What Our Ratings Mean

A   **Excellent.**   The company offers excellent financial security. It has maintained a conservative stance in its investment strategies, business operations and underwriting commitments. While the financial position of any company is subject to change, we believe that this company has the resources necessary to deal with severe economic conditions.

B   **Good.**   The company offers good financial security and has the resources to deal with a variety of adverse economic conditions. It comfortably exceeds the minimum levels for all of our rating criteria, and is likely to remain healthy for the near future. However, in the event of a severe recession or major financial crisis, we feel that this assessment should be reviewed to make sure that the firm is still maintaining adequate financial strength.

C   **Fair.**   The company offers fair financial security and is currently stable. But during an economic downturn or other financial pressures, we feel it may encounter difficulties in maintaining its financial stability.

D   **Weak.**   The company currently demonstrates what, in our opinion, we consider to be significant weaknesses which could negatively impact policyholders. In an unfavorable economic environment, these weaknesses could be magnified.

E   **Very Weak.**   The company currently demonstrates what we consider to be significant weaknesses and has also failed some of the basic tests that we use to identify fiscal stability. Therefore, even in a favorable economic environment, it is our opinion that policyholders could incur significant risks.

F   **Failed.**   The company is deemed failed if it is either 1) under supervision of an insurance regulatory authority; 2) in the process of rehabilitation; 3) in the process of liquidation; or 4) voluntarily dissolve after disciplinary or other regulatory action by an insurance regulatory authority.

+   The plus sign is an indication that the company is in the upper third of the letter grade.
-   The minus sign is an indication that the company is in the lower third of the letter grade.
U   Unrated. The company is unrated for one or more of the following reasons: (1) total assets are less than $1 million; (2) premium income for the current year was less than $100,000; or (3) the company functions almost exclusively as a holding company rather than as an underwriter; or, (4) in our opinion, we do not have enough information to reliably issue a rating.

Terms and Conditions

This document is prepared strictly for the confidential use of our customer(s). It has been provided to you at your specific request. It is not directed to, or intended for distribution to or use by, any person or entity who is a citizen or resident of or located in any locality, state, country or other jurisdiction where such distribution, publication, availability or use would be contrary to law or regulation or which would subject Weiss Ratings, LLC or its affiliates to any registration or licensing requirement within such jurisdiction.

No part of the analysts' compensation was, is, or will be, directly or indirectly, related to the specific recommendations or views expressed in this research report.

This document is not intended for the direct or indirect solicitation of business. Weiss Ratings, LLC, and its affiliates disclaim any and all liability to any person or entity for any loss or damage caused, in whole or in part, by any error (negligent or otherwise) or other circumstances involved in, resulting from or relating to the procurement, compilation, analysis, interpretation, editing, transcribing, publishing and/or dissemination or transmittal of any information contained herein.

Weiss Ratings, LLC has not taken any steps to ensure that the securities or investment vehicle referred to in this report are suitable for any particular investor. The investment or services contained or referred to in this report may not be suitable for you and it is recommended that you consult an independent investment advisor if you are in doubt about such investments or investment services. Nothing in this report constitutes investment, legal, accounting or tax advice or a representation that any investment or strategy is suitable or appropriate to your individual circumstances or otherwise constitutes a personal recommendation to you.

The ratings and other opinions contained in this document must be construed solely as statements of opinion from Weiss Ratings, LLC, and not statements of fact. Each rating or opinion must be weighed solely as a factor in your choice of an institution and should not be construed as a recommendation to buy, sell or otherwise act with respect to the particular product or company involved.

Past performance should not be taken as an indication or guarantee of future performance, and no representation or warranty, expressed or implied, is made regarding future performance. Information, opinions and estimates contained in this report reflect a judgment at its original date of publication and are subject to change without notice. Weiss Ratings, LLC offers a notification service for rating changes on companies you specify. For more information visit WeissRatings.com or call 1-877-934-7778. The price, value and income from any of the securities or financial instruments mentioned in this report can fall as well as rise.

This document and the information contained herein is copyrighted by Weiss Ratings, LLC. Any copying, displaying, selling, distributing or otherwise delivering of this information or any part of this document to any other person or entity is prohibited without the express written consent of Weiss Ratings, LLC, with the exception of a reviewer or editor who may quote brief passages in connection with a review or a news story.

Weiss Ratings' Mission Statement
Weiss Ratings' mission is to empower consumers, professionals, and institutions with high quality advisory information for selecting or monitoring a financial services company or financial investment. In doing so, Weiss Ratings will adhere to the highest ethical standards by maintaining our independent, unbiased outlook and approach to advising our customers.

https://greyhouse.weissratings.com

Financial Ratings Series, published by Weiss Ratings and Grey House Publishing offers libraries, schools, universities and the business community a wide range of investing, banking, insurance and financial literacy tools. Visit www.greyhouse.com or https://greyhouse.weissratings.com for more information about the titles and online tools below.

- Weiss Ratings Consumer Guides
- Weiss Ratings Financial Literacy Basics
- Weiss Ratings Financial Literacy: Planning for the Future
- Weiss Ratings Guide to Banks
- Weiss Ratings Guide to Credit Unions
- Weiss Ratings Guide to Health Insurers
- Weiss Ratings Guide to Life & Annuity Insurers
- Weiss Ratings Guide to Property & Casualty Insurers
- Weiss Ratings Investment Research Guide to Bond & Money Market Mutual Funds
- Weiss Ratings Investment Research Guide to Exchange-Traded Funds
- Weiss Ratings Investment Research Guide to Stock Mutual Funds
- Weiss Ratings Investment Research Guide to Stocks
- Weiss Ratings Medicare Supplement Insurance Buyers Guide
- Financial Ratings Series Online – **https://greyhouse.weissratings.com**

Lavery Library

St. John Fisher College
Rochester, New York

CHAMFORT

Chamfort. Photo: Roger-Viollet.

CLAUDE ARNAUD

Chamfort

A BIOGRAPHY

Translated by Deke Dusinberre

With a Foreword by Joseph Epstein

THE UNIVERSITY OF CHICAGO PRESS

Chicago & London

CLAUDE ARNAUD is a novelist and scriptwriter. He has also published a play, *Les Salons*, set in the eighteenth century.

DEKE DUSINBERRE is an adjunct professor at the University of Paris.

The University of Chicago Press, Chicago 60637
The University of Chicago Press, Ltd., London
© 1992 by The University of Chicago
Foreword © 1991 Joseph Epstein
All rights reserved. Published 1992
Printed in the United States of America
01 00 99 98 97 96 95 94 93 92   5 4 3 2 1
ISBN (Cloth) 0-226-02697-3

Originally published as *Chamfort: Biographie, suivie de soixante-dix maximes, anecdotes, mots et dialogues inédits, ou jamais réédités.* © Editions Robert Laffont, S.A., Paris, 1988.

The following aphorisms and anecdotes in Appendixes 3 and 4 are from "Maxims and Meditations" nos. 36, 60, 150, 194, 434, 447, 545; and from "Characters and Anecdotes" nos. 721, 888, 920, and 1223, published in *Products of the Perfected Civilization* (North Point Press). Reprinted by permission of Georges Borchardt Inc. for the author. Copyright © 1968, 1969 by W. S. Merwin.

Library of Congress Cataloging-in-Publicaton Data

Arnaud, Claude.
    [Chamfort: A Biography. English]
    Chamfort / translated by Deke Dusinberre : with a foreword by Joseph Epstein.
        p.   cm.
    Translation of: Chamfort.
    Includes bibliographical references and index.
    1. Chamfort, Sébastien Roch Nicolas, 1740?-1794—Biography.
    2. France—History—Revolution, 1789–1799—Literature and the revolution.   3. Authors, French—18th century—Biography.
    I. Title.
    PQ1963.C4A8913   1992
    848'.509—dc20
    [B]   91-31913
                                                                       CIP

⊗ The paper used in this publication meets the minimum requirements of the American National Standard for Information Sciences—Permanence of Paper for Printed Library Materials, ANSI Z39.48-1984.

CONTENTS

FOREWORD

CHAMFORT: AN INTRODUCTION

Admirers of the form known as the aphorism have always been few and aphorists of the first-class, naturally enough, many fewer. The aphorism is an acquired taste; it provides something substantial, tangy, yet more than a touch sour, rather like the best Greek olives. Aphorisms are generalizations of universal, or as nearly universal as possible, significance, written out of one's experience, or more likely disenchantment with one's experience. If proverbs tend to tell us that we shouldn't expect people to be better than they are, aphorisms are more likely to tell us just how bad they can be. "We all have strength enough," writes La Rochefoucauld, nicely striking the characteristic note of the aphorist, "to endure the troubles of others."

Those among us who take pleasure in aphorisms do not, then, come to them for cheering up. They can of course be immensely amusing, which the best among them generally are, and this, to be sure, can provide its own sort of cheer. But the bone truth is that aphorisms, while they need not be bitter, are usually better for being so. The closest synonym to an aphorism is a maxim, and sometimes the two words are used interchangeably, though the notion of advice that clings to the word *maxim* does not cling to the aphorism, which has tended to seem freer to observe the pretentious, ridiculous, paradoxical, and sometimes though not very often surprisingly majestic quality of human conduct.

The aphorist is by nature, if not necessarily by birth, aristocratic. He is a man who does not bother either to argue or to explain; he asserts, and, if he has got it right, his assertion is sufficient unto the day. Implicit in the brevity of the aphorist's assertions is an impatience with logical proof. He also operates at a high level of generality. "Great thoughts are always general," wrote Dr. Johnson, "and consist in positions not limited by exceptions, and in descriptions not descending to minuteness." When the aphorist stylishly remarks upon the conduct of human behavior—and without style, that preservative of literature, the aphorist has no hope of his works living beyond the time it takes to write them—he assumes that readers as worldly as he will recognize instantly that what he says is true. If not, too bad, and, come to think of it, not too surprising, either. One doesn't, after all, expect the butterfly being pinned to the velvet cloth to appreciate the elegance of the lepidopterist's efforts.

Universal though the truth of the aphorism attempts to be, it is very far from impersonal. On the contrary, the true aphorist leaves the stamp of himself, through his style, on each of his aphorisms. Scarcely could it be otherwise, for the literary act that is the aphorism is one in which the author sets out to tell you precisely what he thinks. Usually what he thinks is opposed to the received wisdom on most subjects. In asserting his own truths, the aphorist separates himself from the platitudes and received wisdom on every subject that he touches. Nietzsche, who was himself partial to the form of the aphorism, once noted that every idea has its autobiography. So, one might add, does every aphorism. "The artist doesn't see things as they are, but as he is," an anonymous aphorism runs, and it applies nicely to that artist in the briefest of all prose forms, the aphorist. His power, like that of all artists, is to convince us that the way he sees things is the way they truly are.

Not long ago, as the editor of an intellectual quarterly, I received a batch of aphorisms from a man of whom I had never heard, but whom I took to be in his forties. He had sent these aphorisms to me for publication. They were not at all bad, his aphorisms, and I found myself writing to tell him that I would indeed publish them if only his name were Winston Churchill or Charles de Gaulle, but I could not do so as long as his name was what it was—it was, such is the heavy irony life dispenses, Smith—nor, I quickly added, would I be able to publish them if they were written by someone named Joseph Epstein.

My logic here—if logic be the right word—is that aphorisms have become so old-fashioned a form that, in order to have one's aphorisms published, one really ought to be well known to begin with. It was no longer possible, I felt, simply to have thought long and written with high style and concision about general subjects, and expect to find someone willing to publish one's lucubrations. To publish fewer than a fairly large body of someone's aphorisms, or at least those of someone who is not otherwise known to the world, seemed to me a bit beside the point. The point here is that the composition of powerful aphorisms implies a life behind them of the most varied and interesting experiences. If one wants to publish aphorisms today, it is best as a precondition, my advice is, to become very famous before doing so.

The honor roll of the great aphorists requires only a very small scroll. The fingers of both hands can almost include all those who can make some claim to have a place in world literature. Let me count their names: La Rochefoucauld, La Bruyère, Vauvenargues, Pascal, Joubert, Rivarol; switching from French to Teutonic culture now, let us add G. C. Lichtenberg, Schopenhauer, Nietzsche, Karl Kraus; and a lone Rumanian, a contemporary named E. M. Cioran. William Hazlitt wrote aphorisms, jolly dark ones too—"The youth is better than the old age of friendship" and "I believe in the theoretical benevolence and the practical malignity of men"—but not enough of them are superior. Emerson is often included among the ranks of the great aphorists, but, to my taste, he is too vatic, not to say uplifting, though I am prepared to say boring. But then Emerson did not, strictly speaking, write aphorisms but instead in an aphoristic style, which allows anthologists to pluck discrete aphorisms from the often heavy pudding of his prose.

My list of aphorists shows the form to have been taken up overwhelmingly by Frenchmen. A certain amount of sense inheres in this fact of literary history. If vengeance, as the Italians say, is a dish best served cold, for the French disgust is best served cool and with disdain, and cool disdain is perhaps the key ingredient for the aphorist. When Germans express disgust—as in Schopenhauer or Nietzsche —it tends, like so many things German, to be rather overdone. Apparently neither the English nor Americans have felt disgust with sufficient intensity to produce a strong line of aphorists, which is a testament either to their respective societies or to the naivete of their writers.

I have delayed including the name Chamfort (1740–1794) among the great aphorists until now because his place among them is not an altogether understandable one. "A passionate man," an aphorism of Stendhal's has it, "is never witty." Yet Chamfort, one of the great aphorists of his own or any other age, gives the lie to this particular aphorism. Few men have been wittier, and perhaps none more passionate, if one measure of passion be sustained agitated feelings. ("You cannot believe," Chamfort wrote, "how much wit it takes to avoid ever being ridiculous.") Even for an aphorist, Chamfort could be very dark. In his excellent biography of Chamfort, Claude Arnaud quotes the Abbé Morellet on his frequent conversations with this extraordinary man:

There were two features to his conversation. It always touched on people and never on things, and it was constantly misanthropic and excessively denigrating. The turns of phrase with which he demonstrated his hatred for humanity in general as well as his specific aversions were captivating in their originality . . . but I left Auteuil hundreds of times with a heavy soul—after mornings of listening to him recount anecdote after anecdote for two hours, inventing epigram after epigram with indefatigable ease—as though I were leaving the scene of an execution.

Yet Chamfort has always had his admirers, and they have made up a most impressive literary cast. Tell me who admires you, Sainte-Beuve somewhere says, and I shall tell you who you are. Schopenhauer much admired Chamfort and Nietzsche did so even more. Stendhal read him with appreciation. Everything Chamfort wrote, said Cocteau, that connoisseur of tomorrow, "seems as if it were written yesterday." Camus thought him *un écrivain classique* and thought it possible to speak of him without paradox as a novel-ist. Closer to our own day the poet W. S. Merwin has translated a generous selection of Chamfort's aphorisms, characters, and anec-dotes under the title *Products of the Perfected Civilization* (North Point Press, 1984). E. M. Cioran has spoken of the impulses of gratitude that he feels toward Chamfort—and Job.

Yet Chamfort remains considerably less than a household name. Even among people who know and care about literature, he is not always known; or if his name is known, what he stands for is a bit blurred. Part of the problem is that Chamfort was both a political figure—though a minor and for the most part behind-the-scenes one—and a writer, and that much of what he wrote in the earlier phases of his career—plays, pamphlets, criticism, poetry—today is quite negligible. Adding to the complication is that his career is parted by that most tumultuous of events of the eighteenth century, or perhaps of modern history itself, the French Revolution, and so one must consider, in effect, not one but three Chamforts: the career-ist of the Ancien Régime, the flamingly enthusiastic revolutionist, and the dispossessed and disenchanted figure on whom the Revolu-tion turned.

What anyone with the least biographical interest wants to know about an aphorist he admires is whether he had more wit than character—or, to put the case more positively, whether his character was commensurate with his wit. This question, I suspect, must often have occurred to Chamfort himself. This exquisite writer— with all the strengths and weaknesses that the adjective implies— was a misfit: in some ways a misfit by fortune, in some ways by na- ture, and in more important ways a self-made misfit. Chamfort was a man who made and unmade himself, not once but several times in the course of his life.

The first and crucially significant fact about Chamfort was that he wasn't born Chamfort—a name he took up later in life—but was born out of wedlock, to an aristocratic mother and an obscure cleric, in 1740, in Clermont-Ferrand, whence also derived Pascal. The child was, in effect, farmed out to the family of a grocer and his wife, who lost a child of their own born on the same day as he. He was raised by this family under the name Sébastien Roch Nicolas. The boy learned who his true mother was when he was seven or eight. This knowledge established him for life in his ambiguous, highly charged relation with the aristocracy of the Ancien Régime, and with an early notion of what people will do to maintain appearances. It left the young boy with a sense of himself as a vic- tim, but a victim always with a high opinion of himself. He grew up, consequently, with great ambition and an ample grudge. Medi- ating between the two—between his aspirations and his anger— became the story not alone of his career but of his life.

Careers open to the talents was scarcely the motto of the Ancien Régime, but talent of a certain kind, combined with ambition, could, with luck, find its way. Chamfort, clearly, did. He was a brilliant stu- dent, and won various medals in competitions open to students across France. He was adept at languages, ancient and modern, and the clerical principal of the school in Paris at which he was educated thought he might make an excellent priest. Chamfort (still young Nicolas), according to his biographer, M. Arnaud, quickly disabused the principal of that notion. "I'll never be a priest," he informed him. "I'm too fond of sleep, philosophy, women, honor and real fame; and not fond enough of quarrels, hypocrisy, honors, and money." M. Arnaud also tells us that Chamfort even then considered himself a genius; and later in life he would write that "geniuses belong to no family, no century, no nation—they have neither ancestors nor de- scendants."

Few things so improve the appearance as a good opinion of oneself. But in this realm Chamfort stood in little need of improve- ment. As a young man, he was devastatingly handsome and very well turned out. A woman with whom he slept reported: "You think he's only Adonis, yet he's Hercules"—a remark every young man would like on his calling card. Like many a delicious remark in that day, it got around, accruing to the young Chamfort's reputation for charm and—how to put it?—dexterity. In an age of artifice, he created himself with careful attention to detail: changed his name while leaving the truth about his birth a mystery; dropped two years off his age to create the impression that he was even more precocious than he was; acquired the knack of gaining the patronage of the most important personages of the time; "and mastered the art," as M. Arnaud puts it, of "knowing exactly when to go too far."

In short, the young Chamfort was turning into a man of precisely the kind the mature Chamfort would despise. Do we have a case here, in Chamfort's ability easily to insinuate himself into the most select segments of society, of the well-known Groucho Complex, which holds that there can be no point of joining any club whose standards are so low that they are willing to accept oneself as a member? Only in part, I think, for to get Chamfort right one has to add the elements of a heightened critical sensibility that led into something akin to self-hatred at the sign of his willingness to abase himself before his putative superiors.

Chamfort quickly enough grasped, then mastered, the artificiality of Parisian life. As Sainte-Beuve says of the young Joseph Joubert, a near contemporary of Chamfort, [H]e lived there [in Paris] as one lived then: "he chatted." So did Chamfort—brilliantly. He also produced a rather callow play, *La jeune indienne,* that received the approval of Voltaire. D'Alembert extended him his patronage. He corresponded with Rousseau, the one writer among the great French prose writers of the age—and the age was clearly one for prose, not poetry—whose work he seems unstintingly to have admired. He understood that literary talent meant an entree into the highest society, yet he also sensed, as M. Arnaud puts it, that "high society appears to respect those who appear to hold it in contempt." Contempt Chamfort did not have to feign, especially for aristocrats, whose pretenses to superiority he despised.

Along with literary talent, the art of seduction had its utility in the Paris of Chamfort's days. Laclos, author of *Les liaisons dangereuses,* was born only a year later than Chamfort. It is perhaps well to recall that Chamfort wrote the aphorism around which Laclos might be said to have constructed his novel: "Love, such as it exists in high society, is merely the exchange of whims and the contact of skins." He himself knew no shortage of women who were ready to transact precisely this exchange, among them the actress Mlle. Guimard, who was famous for the perfection of her bosom and who did her makeup each day before the portrait that Fragonard had painted of her.

Chamfort often used his amatory powers to revenge himself on aristocrats for what he felt were social slights. His own beauty, as M. Arnaud nicely puts it, "was one injustice that Chamfort bore lightly." But then, at the age of twenty-five, he was struck by one of fate's mysterious darts, and in a single shot his own good looks and his health were gone. A still unknown disease hit him—some allege it was venereal—affecting his nerves, his complexion, his chest, his bladder, his eyes, leaving him unable to read, or to walk, and turning him over to the horror of eighteenth-century medical treatment. His elegant appearance, his youthful air, were destroyed. He took to his rooms. His onward and upward progress ceased. His already advanced misanthropy had found its autobiographical raison d'être.

Those who have written about Chamfort differ on the question of the origin of his dark views: some say they are owed to the socially demeaning facts of his birth, some to this devastating illness, some to a superior lucidity let loose in a rotten age. About the darkness of these views there can be no controversy. After the unexplained attack of his illness, he steeled himself. Removed from the sex wars—in which, as he would later write, "the heart must break or turn to bronze"—he devoted himself more earnestly to literature. But try as he might, he was unable to kill entirely the aspirations that seemed inseparable from his character. Chamfort remained a man who desired everything and detested himself for his own desires. His was a case, perhaps not all that uncommon, of eating your cake and hating it, too.

To be sure, there are tableaux of Chamfort that soften the view of him as the always angry young man, in a state of perpetual perturbation, the persistent good hater. In the pages of M. Arnaud's biography, we discover Chamfort stroking Mme. Helvetius's angora cats, who were fed on a strict diet of chicken breasts; meeting Benjamin Franklin, who himself had an idea or two on the art of seduction; actually in love for a brief time with Marthe Buffon, a woman older than he who died only six months after their relationship had got underway in earnest and of whom a contemporary said that Chamfort had loved her "as ardently as a mistress, as tenderly as a mother." A not uncommon sight in the rarified circles in which he traveled was that of Chamfort holding forth, talking brilliantly, captivating everyone. One witness to his talk, who for a long stretch saw him daily, said that he never repeated himself, another that he made people laugh and think simultaneously.

These scenes of the gentle life are counterposed against the almost endless internecine literary squabbles for which the time was famous, a time of impressive ingratitude, relentless jealousy, and devastating put-downs. (Of Jean-Francois de La Harpe, a rival and exceedingly rivalrous man of letters, Chamfort said that he frequently "hid his vices behind his faults"—a very crisp little two-cushion shot.) Chamfort took a good thumping from critics for his second play, *Mustapha et Zéangir*. Owing to this thorough shellacking, Chamfort acquired paranoia, the disease of the intellectuals, of serious dimensions. Given the general disputatiousness, not to say backstabbing, of intellectual life in the Ancien Régime, and the non-metaphorical backstabbing in the Revolution that followed hard upon it, his paranoia would serve Chamfort well. So would it serve his aphorisms, which he began writing around this time—roughly 1777, when he was thirty-seven—for it was in these aphorisms that he first dropped the dry and artificial style of neoclassicism in which all his public writing had been composed and wrote as he spoke, lucidly, beautifully, devastatingly.

"Genius," noted Ortega y Gasset, "is the ability to invent one's own occupation." By this standard, Chamfort qualifies as a genius, even though it is a bit difficult to say what, precisely, his occupation quite was. Continually—one is almost ready to say continuously—attracted and repelled by the rewards of society, he fairly regularly ducked in and out of it, but in 1780, when he was forty, he resolved no longer to write for the public. (The following year, 1781, he was finally elected to the Académie française, to which he had been seeking membership for many years.) But now he planned to rusticate himself. He was a man who could live well enough on his despair, bemoaning the fate of the literary man in his time, contemptuous of the class whose approval he also sought—that, along with the various government pensions he had accrued, made life, however dark, endurable.

M. Arnaud remarks that Chamfort was "born at the wrong time." He tells us that both he and Laclos perhaps shared "the intuition that their half century would be remembered less for its literature than for its mores and fashions, ideas and conversation." Chamfort himself noted, in one of his aphorisms: "Reading through the memoirs and literary monuments of the century of Louis XIV, one finds even in the bad company of the age something that is missing in the good of our own." The period tossed up odd talents such as Retif de la Bretonne and Chamfort himself; today the only writer of the period who is still considered of central importance is Rousseau. Yet Chamfort's life was not so much divided as cleaved by that event of singular significance, the French Revolution—an event that simultaneously shortened his life and lent him part of the significance he has today. Without the intercession of the French Revolution, Chamfort would have been remembered if at all as an elegant fop with an impressive control of language, another literary man on the make, a Julien Sorel who missed the guillotine.

There are times in intellectual history when politics sweep the boards. During such times politics absorb, become, and are everything. All talent turns to politics, and art, literature, music, family life, and everything else is secondary, if not altogether beside the point; or so at least they seem to those who live during such times. The years leading up, through, and immediately after the French Revolution were such a time. Chamfort, despite his claims to wish to live outside society, was quite as swept up as any intellectual of his day in the events of the French Revolution. He might, in his aphorisms, mock society as "nothing but the contentions of a thousand clashing petty interests, an eternal conflict of all the vanities that cross each other, strike against each other, are wounded and humiliated by each other," but when the action of the Revolution began Chamfort was there, a player very close to its center. Nietzsche, in *The Gay Science*, remarks: "That a man who understood men and the crowd as well as Chamfort, nevertheless joined the crowd and did not stand aside in philosophical renunciation and resistance, I can explain it to myself only in this way: He had one instinct that was even stronger than his wisdom and had never been satisfied— hatred of all nobility by blood."

As late as 1784, Chamfort accepted the post of principal secretary to Mme. Elizabeth, the sister of Louis XVI, which didn't stop him from writing, in collaboration with Mirabeau, *Considerations on the Society or Order of Cincinnati*, a Rousseauistic pamphlet making a strong case against nobility. ("He is," said Mirabeau of Chamfort, "the flint I need for my musket.") He had earlier joined a number of younger political intellectuals, known as the Bellechasse group, of whom Talleyrand would go on to become the most famous member.

Chamfort wrote one of the first arguments for republican government during the Ancien Régime. Later, along with Mirabeau and
Talleyrand, he joined the Club of Thirty, which prepared the ground
for the first democratically run election ever held in France. As
M. Arnaud says, "Chamfort was born too early—or too late—to
produce a major literary work, but he had arrived just at the right
time to change the world."

Chamfort's deep antipathy to the nobility is not difficult to
trace. It had its beginnings in his own disgraced birth, and came to
its maturity with Chamfort himself, who needed the approval of
the nobility for any advancement he wished to make. This antipathy to the nobility plays throughout Chamfort's aphorisms. He
took what Montaigne said of nobility, "Since we can't attain it, let's
get even by maligning it," and remarked that it would be better rewritten as "I loathe nobility which made me flee that which I loved,
or would have loved." Behind much of the rancor in the aphorisms
lie the sad twists that Chamfort felt he had to undergo in his own
personality before those who were above him in rank but, as he
well knew, in nothing else. A man without money or a title, he aver-
red, was more estranged than "a Frenchman in Peking or Macao or a
Lapp in Senegal." "To acquire fortune and distinction in spite of the
disadvantage of having no ancestors, and to do it in the midst of that
crowd who received everything at birth, is like winning, or stale-
mating a game of chess after giving one's adversary a rook or castle. . . . One can manage without the castle but not without the
queen."

The French Revolution was thought to give everyone back the
queen through beheading the real queen and her husband, Louis
XVI. Chamfort exulted in the Revolution, at least for a time. His resentment, his Rousseau-like idealism, his quite genuine feeling for
the underdog, all got a good workout in the first years of the Revolution. "Society is made up of two great classes," Chamfort wrote, in
one of his most famous aphorisms, "those who have more dinners
than appetite and those who have more appetite than dinners."
Now at last he didn't have to hide the side on which his own true
feeling lay. M. Arnaud reports that "he was a happy revolutionary . . . . [hewing] a middle path between intrigue and uprightness, pragmatism and utopia." Where once he claimed a noble
ancestry, now he vaunted his lowly upbringing. He stripped away
all the luxuries from his personal life. He justified the early days of
the Terror. Heads on pikes, the creaking inexorable wheels of the

tumbril, the persistent snap of the "national razor" didn't cause him to flinch. "These days you have to be cruel out of humaneness," he said. He was himself asked to be director of the Bibliothèque Nationale. He demurred but eventually agreed to accept a codirectorship.

As Chamfort's generation was replaced by the generation of Danton and Robespierre, with Marat overlapping both, the second Terror began in horrendous earnest. Chamfort's own position became precarious under this reign of lawyers turned revolutionists. He was twice arrested, first accused of advocating criminal behavior by a spy who wanted his job at the Bibliothèque Nationale and who claimed to hear him approve of the assassination of Marat by Charlotte Corday, the granddaughter of Corneille; and the second time for putatively refusing to dissociate himself from Charlotte Corday and thus, in the mad logic of the Revolution, proving his accuser correct.

Upon this second arrest, Chamfort was sent to the prison known as Madelonnettes, where, M. Arnaud reports, meat went untouched because it was rumored to have come from the bodies of victims of the guillotine. What wasn't rumor was the filth and stench of this, the beastliest jail in Paris. Chamfort was made to spend two nights in Madelonnettes, among rats real and metaphorical. His brief sojourn in this prison was a jolt to more than his, Chamfort's, metabolism; he, who felt he had sacrificed so much for the Revolution, now could not but know that he was likely soon to be sacrificed to it himself. Come what may, he vowed never to return to Madelonnettes.

Revolutions, like many varieties of slug, ingest their own kind, and so eventually did the French Revolutions swallow Chamfort, one of its most ardent early provocateurs, ideologues, and ardent supporters. When told that the theater in Paris was being poorly attended, he remarked that "tragedy no longer has the same effect once it roams the streets." And so when it was announced to Chamfort, who after his stay at the Madelonnettes was under house arrest, that he would have to return to prison, he quietly finished his simple dinner of soup and coffee, retired to his bedroom, and proceeded hideously to butcher himself.

M. Arnaud provides the graphic details of Chamfort's attempted suicide. I shall here offer the Parental Guidance version and say that with a mis-aimed pistol shot he first blew out his right eye; he then attempted to cut his throat; and finally he slashed himself about the arms and legs. In all he inflicted twenty-two wounds upon himself without completing the job. He would later claim that Seneca, a richer man, had servants to help him and so was able to make a tidier job of his own suicide. Chamfort would live five or so months longer, but inept treatment of his wounds—in closing them up, the attending physician neglected to leave drainage slits— brought about his death on April 13, 1794. "When a man lies dying, he does not die from his disease alone," wrote Peguy. "He dies from his whole life."

No one would have known about Chamfort's aphorisms but for their having been discovered and saved by his faithful friend, Ginguené, who eventually brought them to the public under Chamfort's own ironically intended title of *Products of the Perfected Civilization*. The irony, heavy-handedly bitter, is that Chamfort found civilization, both under the monarchy and under the Revolution, as far as possible from perfected. "Prejudice, vanity, scheming," wrote Chamfort, "these are what govern the world," and he goes on to report that "he whose only principles of conduct are reason, truth, and sensibility has nothing in common with society," concluding that "it is within himself that he must seek out and find virtually all his happiness." Here we have the *donnée* for nearly all aphorists. Ah, if only man had the simple good sense to be content in solitude. Pascal said it first: "All the misfortunes of men derive from one single thing, which is their inability to sit quietly in a room." La Bruyère chimed in with: "In France, it takes much firmness of spirit and a great breadth of understanding to do without offices and positions, and be willing to stay at home and do nothing." Chamfort, too, maintains that "the world hardens most men's hearts," and giving oneself up to several days of society leaves one troubled and sad, and the only advantage of having been out in the world is "the pleasure it lends to retirement." Elsewhere he says that the ability to say "no" and "the ability to live to oneself are the only two ways of preserving one's liberty and one's character." The problem, for Chamfort and for the others, was managing to stay home, out of the tumult, in repose, quietly, thinking.

"The most wasted of days is the one lacking laughter," wrote Chamfort. Yet, one's sense is, he was more likely to have been the cause of laughter in others, with his lacerating wit, than in himself, who was often the object of his witty lacerations. Traditionally, aphorists come on coolly elegant in their disdain, but Chamfort, as Sainte-Beuve remarked, "scorched the paper" on which he wrote. He is almost always the angry aphorist. He claims no wisdom, unlike La Rochefoucauld or La Bruyère or Vauvenargues. They used scalpels, he a broadax; they took lessons from life, he remained furious about it; they aimed for the most heightened objectivity, he could never slip his passion; they wrote as if from outside looking in, he wrote as if fully caught in life's whirlpool. "Living," he wrote, "is an ailment which is relieved every sixteen hours by sleep. Death is the cure."

The history of literature could be written around the subject of writers finding their true forms. Sometimes the forms are there waiting, and sometimes they have almost to be invented. Although he came to it late in his life, the aphorism was perfect for Chamfort, though he himself never had the time to make perfect his own aphorisms. W. G. Moore, in *La Rochefoucauld: His Mind and Art*, has recounted the social context in which La Rochefoucauld, who is the father of the form, created his own aphorisms. They began in a game, played among the circle of Mme. de Sable, where social observations were set out and then honed to their greatest possible pungency and brevity, in the attempt to turn them into epigrams. La Rochefoucauld's manuscripts show how he would often begin with a full paragraph and then, slowly, thoughtfully, clip and prune and boil a thought down to its quintessence. Final approval in many instances awaited the word of Mme. de Sable. In this purifying process, where economy was so highly valued, abstraction naturally emerged prominent. Who knows out of how much in the way of discussion, writing, and editing La Rochefoucauld's "The head is always fooled by the heart" was born?

None of this is meant to imply that La Rochefoucauld's elegant, economical aphorisms were made by method alone. They were made, above all, by experience. La Rochefoucauld lived in what the Chinese, in their famous curse, called "interesting times"—that is, a time in which men had plenty of latitude to show their more disgraceful sides—during those civil wars in France during the minority of Louis XIV known as the Fronde; and he lived long enough to have been disappointed by life, which used perhaps to take a bit longer then than it does now. Like La Rochefoucauld, Chamfort, too, lived in interesting times wherein men's motives were revealed at their worst; he also lived long enough to be disappointed in love and by ambition. Add to this the rancor that, as a bastard, was part of his birthright, and you have the classical profile of the natural aphorist.

George Poulet has written that Chamfort is only of interest from the time that he began to write his aphorisms. "Before that there had undoubtedly been other versions of Chamfort: an ambitious hack, a dandy, a passionate lover." All of these, of course, were grist for the mill, which ground exceedingly fine, of the aphorist. "Love," wrote Chamfort, "doesn't allow its secret to be revealed. A man who knows it is incapable of divulging it, and he forgets it the moment his passion ceases, for the secret is nothing other than love itself." As M. Poulet rightly notes, the man Chamfort constantly executes in his aphorisms "is indeed Chamfort himself." The bitter lessons learned by that unhappy young man went into the stiletto-like sentences of the mature writer. "A philosopher," he wrote, "must start by experiencing the happiness of the dead."

A good part of what impresses the modern reader with Chamfort is not only his essential loneliness but his own lucid sense of how precisely alone in the world he was. "Preserve, if you can, the interests that attach you to society, but cultivate the feelings that separate you from it," he writes. Yet the feelings that separated Chamfort from society, from his fellow man, from nearly everyone seemed to come naturally enough to him. He is one of those loners in literature, in the line of Baudelaire, Dostoyevsky, Schopenhauer, Nietzsche, Camus. The reason all were essentially alone is that each was intent on discovering an ethic that would comport with the prominent fact of evil in man and in nature, all were contemptuous of intellectual mediocrity and philosophical sham, all permitted no easy optimism or belief in the rehabilitation of man through progress in history. "What is a philosopher?" asked Chamfort. "A man who pits nature against the law, reason against custom, conscience against opinion, and his own judgment against injustice."

Chamfort was a moralist who distrusted even his fellow moralists. The argument has been made that even the relatively rough form of some of Chamfort's aphorisms is based on the almost systematic hatred of systematic thinking in Chamfort. Professor Eve Katz has written that Chamfort's aphorisms "do not, like La Rochefoucauld's, for example, rest on the assumption that one can enclose an entire philosophy in one or two sentences. They do not lay claim to certainty. They do not presuppose that there are limits to ideas and that one can give them definitive expression." She quotes, in support of her argument, another of Chamfort's aphorisms:

> In order to view things correctly, one must give words the opposite sense to the one the world gives them. Misanthrope, for instance, means philanthrope; bad Frenchman means good

citizen, which implies certain monstrous abuses; philosopher means "a simple man, who knows that two and two makes four, etc."

Perhaps the best way—which is also to say, the best reason—to read Chamfort today is for his honesty. For honesty, if it cuts deeply enough, is itself a variant of truth, and discrete touches of penetrating honesty may have to do until a more elaborate or systematic version of truth is available to those of us of an even gently skeptical nature. It is this Chamfort, the Chamfort who wrote,

> It is commonly believed that the art of pleasing is a great means of achieving wealth; knowing how to be bored is an art which succeeds still better. The talent for acquiring wealth, like the one for succeeding with women, can be reduced practically to that.

who gives pleasure of a lighter kind. It is the Chamfort of the quick and deadly definition—"Love: agreeable folly. Ambition: serious imbecility," or "Celebrity: the advantage of being known by those who do not know you"—whom one finds so companionable, however oddly the word "companionable" may seem to fit this all but friendless writer. Yet it was Chamfort who remarked that "in certain friendships one enjoys the happiness of the passions and the approbation of reason as well," which constitutes a quite respectable blurb for the intellectual profit his own writing brings.

In his aphorisms, Chamfort is a writer dedicated to acting with honesty, living with limitations, and striving always for truth. "Give and take pleasure, without doing harm to yourself or anyone else— that, I think, sums up morality," he wrote. His own was a life far from filled with pleasure, and in the end he did the ultimate harm to himself, yet today, roughly two hundred years after he wrote it, Chamfort's encapsulated prescription for morality rings true, and the ring of truth is the only serious criterion for judging an aphorism. Coming from the man who wrote that "pleasure may be based on illusion, but happiness rests on truth," this is in itself a small but impressive and, yes, finally happy tribute to Chamfort the aphorist, the artist of truth.

Joseph Epstein

Chicago
July 1991

PREFACE

Even though man explains as much as he can through knowledge, even though he appears as objective as possible, all he ever obtains is his own biography.

Nietzsche

Chamfort remains an author apart. Though he was quoted, often plagiarized, and regularly republished, the secrecy and ambiguity with which he cloaked his life still clings to him. Chamfort is appreciated as a particularly lucid observer—someone who had seen it all, who could laugh at his own despair, who wrote down his insights each evening on little scraps of paper found after his death. These scraps became bedside reading for a long line of critical minds, from Stendhal to Cioran and from Schopenhauer to Nietzsche (who described Chamfort as the "wittiest of all moralists"). "Reactionaries" consider him a revolutionary, while "progressives" think of him as a misanthrope. Yet he continues to be a favorite writer for those interested in the negative underside of feelings and history.

Up till now, Chamfort's life has remained an enigma. Most hypotheses concerning the birth of this illegitimate son of an aristocratic lady and a canon were erroneous. Little or nothing was known of his links to Mirabeau, Talleyrand, Rivarol, Chateaubriand, and Robespierre, nor of his affairs with Mlle. Guimard, Marthe Buffon, and Julie Talma. The extent to which he was a protégé of the Ancien Régime was unappreciated, as was his enthusiasm for the new order. There were only short brilliant essays devoted to Chamfort; two woefully incomplete biographies (one in the nineteenth century, another in 1944) wound up crushing him by trying to justify him. The eighteenth century knew Chamfort but not his aphorisms, whereas today we know only of his aphorisms. Like Sade prior to being rediscovered, Chamfort has remained a notorious stranger.

I had to rummage in archive basements and library attics in order to reassemble the remnants of his life, to revive this revolutionary who was hounded by fate from the day of his birth to the ultimate theft of the major part of his manuscripts. I discovered a man even more ironic and unhappy than his maxims suggest, a man as complex as Rousseau, the most mysterious of his contemporaries. Chamfort was given to constant metamorphosis and personal revolutions, yet he steadfastly maintained his independence. From a moral standpoint, his case defies judgment; from the standpoint of psychology, his case is complex and fascinating. Unpublished documents probably still exist here and there, scrawls of ink on yellowed paper which could be brought back to life on whiter sheets. Shadowy areas remain—but perhaps that is all for the best. Sometimes I think I know as much about Chamfort as he himself did when, at the end of his life, he reviewed his past.

Malraux had a well-known contempt for biography, which he called "a wretched little heap of secrets." Talleyrand used to say, "No man is considered great by his valet." Yet every "great man" harbors a little man in himself, just as, inversely, all of humanity resides in each of the bit players who entered Chamfort's life. Such are the secrets I wanted to uncover—which is only fair, since Chamfort himself X-rayed his contemporaries with striking acuteness and, therefore, deserves the same treatment. Indeed, his case especially lends itself to such an approach.

For Chamfort has escaped the academic dictum that "the life explains the work" as well as its no less academic refutation that "the work has nothing to do with the life." Chamfort's life was sometimes fanciful, sometimes tragic. And his "book," which he showed to no one, is above all a collection of comments, of things seen, of indirect confessions. It is the distillation of existence, an elixir of courage and spleen, a vital organ. The man cannot be divorced from his work; together they form a seamless mass of raw material. Chamfort's personal fate was the fertilizer, the complement, practically the companion volume to his writings—a biographer's dream.

Chamfort underwent two incarnations. At twenty, he considered himself a great writer, a sort of genius destined to renew the values of his age. He tried comedy, eulogy, and tragedy (a genre as moribund as the French novel is today). Yet he died, during the Terror, as a middling, almost forgotten writer. Nothing remains of this literary mortal, except his long death throes as glimpsed through the aphorisms and thoughts attributed to his second, postliterary incarnation. His very failure, however, provided Chamfort with that special perspective and lucidity the victorious lack. Nothing seemed natural to him; everything raised questions leading to still other questions. Chamfort adopted this perspective aggressively rather than complacently, which is something of a paradox for a man warmly received by the aristocracy. But he intended to be an *antiwriter* who reserved his verbal brilliance for conversation, just as later he would become a sworn enemy of the nobility and the Académie française (which it had taken him twenty years to enter).

Illegitimacy has one advantage—it complicates the human issue in the same way that homosexuality, Jewishness, or any other minority status does. It produces a twin, often simultaneous, attitude toward society, split between the desire to prevail over or to destroy society, to transcend or annihilate it. On this score, Chamfort was an exemplary case of illegitimacy. Possessing two identities (his mother's aristocracy and his adoptive family's humble status), he assumed the non de plume of Chamfort at the age of twenty. Nevertheless, he would always remain as schizophrenic as this bogus name, with its whispery beginning and chiseled conclusion. He was born in Clermont-Ferrand as Sébastien Nicolas, but once in Paris called himself Monsieur de Chamfort, then Chamfort, and finally Citizen, until he was ultimately arrested as "the former Chamfort." He was a protégé of the prince de Condé, the comte de Vaudreuil, and Louis XVI himself, yet was also precursor, along with Mirabeau, of revolutionary ideology; closely linked to the Polignacs, whose excesses hastened the fall of the monarchy, he was nevertheless a conspicuous partisan of republican austerity; more aristocratic in tone than all the nobility together, he could jeer at the salons with plebeian fury; a star actor in an extremely theatrical society, he was also a harsh critic of one of the most refined and, therefore, most unjust civilizations. Such was Chamfort, a double agent loyal only to himself, with a boundless energy which prevented him from choosing between these two versions of his "self." Chamfort was pulled to the left and to the right, venerated by Mirabeau as a sort of superman and praised by Nietzsche for his elitism, misanthropy, and pessimism (yet also discernible between the lines of *The Genealogy of Morals* as a model for the man of rancor); but his two facets ultimately remained inseparable.

For the core of his personality was very hard and very dark. He had enjoyed a golden age as a handsome, graceful, effervescent, and successful libertine. But an illness disfigured him at twenty-five, also leaving him sexually traumatized. Then he was betrayed by a patron and a friend (who never relented in his efforts to destroy Chamfort) forced him to adopt a mask to repress his intense sensitivity. Then came the crushing failure of his tragic drama *Mustapha*, followed by his decision to never publish again. Chamfort's most moving period began the day he left Paris for a woman—who subsequently died in his arms. So Chamfort hardened himself again, "bronzed" his heart a little more and, hoping to break with his past, unsuccessfully attempted to lead a second life (as Rimbaud and T. E. Lawrence would later do).

There is always a key passage in the text certain writers weave. In Chamfort's case, this springs from his constant need to define himself, fully aware of the relativity of that definition. He knew himself to be the product of civilization, yet he aspired to change civilization by changing himself. Which explains his precocious desire to start society (and the human race) afresh, and his enthusiasm for the French Revolution. His *self* fell along with the Bastille; he became reconciled with the world. He decided to abandon the "old man" still lingering in him, forget his past and origins, become one with the masses. He was going to resolve his own problems and those of the monarchy at the same time, simultaneously appeasing his own bitterness and national famine.

Everything was glorious until 1791. He distributed his epigrams and his money to the people and served as a speechwriter to the orators. He plotted in the Assembly with Mirabeau and Talleyrand and laid great plans in the clubs alongside Sieyès and Condorcet. Then came the bloody repression of the Champs-de-Mars demonstration, with Chamfort joining the far left in its forced retreat. He destroyed all external signs of his aristocratic connections and became a sort of republican saint. But the war (which he had been against) and the Gironde (to which he gave lukewarm support) pulled him back from the brink of total self-sacrifice, ultimately placing him among the "privileged" class of 1793. Denounced for having hailed the assassination of Marat, imprisoned, released, and denounced again, he shot and stabbed himself to avoid returning to prison. He thereby punished himself for the failure of the Revolution, all the while remaining steadfast to it. Life is a legacy which cannot be turned down, but it had been illegitimately imposed on Chamfort, and he had always reserved the right to disown it. This led to the most violent and horrible suicide attempt during the Terror—a suicide from which Chamfort, to his despair, was temporarily resurrected.

As lively as he was sickly, preaching cheerfulness yet reduced to sarcasm, Chamfort sought human and social truths everywhere. He exposed role-playing and unmasked feelings, reaching the innermost self where things become indeterminate once again. Chamfort's oddness—like that of Balzac's Louis Lambert and Valéry's Monsieur Teste—derives from his superior intelligence which had seen all, intuited all, and understood all, yet was itself incapable of movement or achievement. Such intelligence prefers ideas to things, plays at being both patient and doctor. "We have no doubt today that sickness is instructive, much more instructive than health," Nietzsche would claim—from personal experience—in *The Genealogy of Morals*. To a certain extent, therefore, Chamfort never really wanted to recover.

A distinction can be made between free spirits and the spirit of freedom. Strangely, Chamfort embodies both of these. He was fiercely attached to his own independence, and wanted the Revolution to free mankind from social "charlatanism" by replacing false hierarchies (birth and money) with valid ones (intelligence and talent). These complex aspirations involved a measure of resentment and self-destructiveness, a desire for progress and a yearning for the past. Although Chamfort represented sophistication itself, deep down he belonged to an ancient era predating humanity's commitment to work, trade, and technology. He was a sort of highly civilized savage, who wanted to *be* rather than *do*. Which explains why Chamfort was read by a long and fertile line of major thinkers, and why he remains today—at a time of sheeplike individualism—a particularly bracing symbol of resistance.

Chamfort revealed the seamy and negative side of a century that considered itself happy, playful, sociable, healthily promiscuous, and resolutely opposed to neurosis and pathos—which, to a certain extent, it was. As early as 1728, Vaucanson planned to build an artificial human and by 1780 had predicted travel to the moon. During the Regency, the abbé de Sainte-Pierre anticipated a sort of League of Nations, and released balloons in the Tuileries gardens to symbolize the key values of lightness and progress. It was thus the eighteenth century that coined religious, sexual, and political freedom; for the most part, the twentieth century merely rediscovered such values, with less freshness and in reaction to the heritage of the nineteenth century. In Chamfort's day, licentiousness precluded pornography (an upshot of puritanism), and his contemporaries' optimism could take wing, whereas today we are only too aware of the wars, revolutions, dictatorships, and famines which, in certain respects, have made the twentieth century a monumental museum of horrors.

It is nevertheless tempting to draw comparisons. Cocteau claimed that a journalist could become famous by publishing Chamfort's thoughts as his own, then revealing the hoax. "Everything seems as though it were written yesterday," commented Cocteau. The 1750s, like the 1950s, favored theory, essays, and social sciences, whereas the years 1770–1780 represented a return to classical literary genres. But history only repeats itself in snatches, or in cycles. The intellectual revolution of the Englightenment preceded the 1789 Revolution by thirty years (while the post–World War II period wedded intellectual movements to political movements), allowing for a dramatic shift to a *staged society* in the interval. Though nothing is truly comparable, certain phrases sound strangely familiar. Revolution is not a bowl of cherries, said Chamfort, long before Chairman Mao argued—and proved—that it is not a banquet either. Chamfort's sacrificial phase in 1792 inevitably evokes the voluntary proletarization of late nineteenth-century Russian populists, not to mention certain French and Chinese Maoists.

It was never my intention, overtly at least, to write a book concerning the present day—such a task requires another volume. Yet in describing the original "staged society," I have stressed certain details which seem to recur in history, whose influence can only really be felt over the long term. Perhaps the eighteenth century inaugurated an era marked by a certain type of society and revolution, an era the twentieth century is seeing out. Or perhaps the alternation between revolution and restoration will continue for a long time, as the instability of democracies suggests. In either case, Chamfort will have been a particularly acute observer of a specific moral sensibility which France has historically incarnated to the point of caricature.

How do revolutions start? What are the social, historical, and even "metabolic" factors behind the events of 1789? Does history have its own inherent rhythms, like living cells which are apparently renewed every seven years? It is these vagaries of history, in fact, that intrigued me as much as the secrets behind Chamfort's life or the genesis of his "book." Few centuries appear to be as carefully plotted out as the eighteenth century. It began with the immoralist excesses of the Regency, Watteau's balls and Marivaux's trysts, continued with Montesquieu's liberalism, the *Encyclopédie*'s positivism, Holbach's atheism, and Rousseau's *Social Contract*, ending with those well-known revolutionary events. Yet there was also much reverting to the past, much nostalgia for the reign of Louis XIV and for the ancient Greeks and Romans. History heavily marks the European consciousness, and Chamfort inevitably shared these revertings and revisions.

The aura that France has managed to retain to this day, from Latin America to Mittel Europa, is largely due to two accomplishments: the aristocratic style of the 1760s (which even today remains the unconscious model to which the bourgeoisie aspires), and the ideals of 1789 (the freshness and spontaneity of which sharply distinguish them from, for instance, the "professionalism" of the Bolshevik Revolution). In spite of his pessimism, Chamfort helped forge both these models by coining phrases of fascinating conciseness. His true talent lay in being able to express the essential in only two sentences, in prophesying revolution with Ancien Régime style.

Alienated from God, from the elements, from the land, and from his ancestors, Chamfort grew up among books, eventually growing old as the head of the Bibliothèque Nationale. Words were his only landscape, his only nature. Thanks to words, he managed to start afresh each time following periods of aphasia and inner exile. His conversation was like a high-wire act which spanned the abyss of his neurosis, and this social climber's brilliant verbal acrobatics would seem to be of special interest in today's thoroughly image-oriented society.

Along with Pericles' Athens and the Italian Renaissance, the eighteenth century represents one of the high points of European civilization. It nevertheless worried about the weak quality of its literature, as if the nobility already suspected its own decline. Such anxiety haunted Chamfort to the point where he unfairly assessed his times. For the eighteenth century eased his bitterness, lightening his almost Dostoevsky-like personality. Without the extremely social and contented ambience of aristocratic civilization, Chamfort would probably have shared the solitary and tragic fate of those nineteenth-century lay saints canonized by the twentieth century in the name of art—Nietzsche, Rimbaud, Van Gogh, etc. This volume is no hagiography, therefore; it merely presents two sides of a single portrait—positive and negative—and is to be read as both social document and authentic novel.

Despite recent bicentenary celebrations, the French Revolution does not currently enjoy a good reputation. Stress is usually placed on its economic impact and on the massacres in the Vendée region. Much is made of the rancor that shaped it (rancor exemplified, once again, by Chamfort). But the Revolution also sought happiness, plenty, and freedom for all. It hoped to spread the benefits of the Enlightenment, to democratize the promise of bliss held out by France. Chamfort, as will be seen, believed above all in a cataclysmic flood that would regenerate mankind, making the earth fertile once more. He kept his most noble gestures secret but spared no one his criticism; he was admired by a core of friends but attacked by most of his contemporaries. It is this oddness I wanted to convey, avoiding the simplistic moral rehabilitation that so often hampers biographies.

For although fictional characters are sometimes encouraged to be odious (see Dostoevsky), real people are supposed to be "nice." Chamfort, however, was not always kind. There is nevertheless something moving about this man who was never able to escape his own ego for long and whose fate was so typically Western, masculine, even barren. As lucid as Chamfort tried to be, he inevitably fell into every trap set by his own neurosis. It may even be somewhat cruel to hound Chamfort this way, constantly setting his strict principles against his lifelong opportunism, comparing word to deed. I trust I have not taken the process too far.

The Revolution obviously should not be judged on Chamfort's case alone, anymore than on its two years of Terror. Much of Europe still enjoys the fruit of the accomplishments of 1789, and even the Revolution's staunchest opponents now wave its flag. It is interesting to note that although no street is named after Robespierre, Napoleon—who is responsible for a million deaths from Toulon to Moscow—lies peacefully in the *Invalides* mausoleum (next to the ashes of Napoleon II, brought back to Paris by Hitler). And while the humanitarian crown with which the Third Republic tried to cap the Revolution is now contested (often legitimately), the Revolution is attacked for reasons too closely linked to present-day concerns. The 1789 Revolution was designed to resolve the Ancien Régime's financial crisis, and from that standpoint it was a resounding failure. But the event was also political and symbolic, for it entailed a shift in worldview, in *Weltanschauung*, and thus remains incomprehensible to those who attempt to economize on history. Revolution is the business of the masses, just as war had been the business of the elite up until 1792. Both undertakings should be assessed in terms of the cost in lives, though such calculation is rarely made for the industrial revolution, usually measured only by how long it lasted. Unlike the generals in 1914–1918, those who assumed leadership in 1789 paid for their mistakes by exile or guillotine; Chamfort paid through prison and suicide. His fate should be disturbing to those who experienced or witnessed the events of May 1968 with total impunity. But it is also an end worthy of a man accused by Chateaubriand of having been behind the "plot" which led to 1789, and who was one of France's very first republicans.

Understanding Chamfort requires an appreciation of the social issues as well as of the literary impasse in which he languished (along with almost everyone at the time) until he discovered a last-minute escape via his maxims. The bourgeoisie had been trying to translate its economic influence into political power ever since Etienne Marcel's uprising in the fourteenth century. By the mid-eighteenth century, the bourgeoisie was separated from the aristocracy only by a symbolic barrier. Chamfort embodied this proximity through his "birth," his style, his ideas, his position, his skin-deep aristocracy, and his gut-level plebeianism. Such proximity generated constant social conflict (at first extremely formal, later armed) which high society initially absorbed, spilling it all back out in 1789. Chamfort thus incarnated not only the French language but also the contradictions of a nation alternately seduced by elitism and equality, those twin engines of history. His disease-plagued body was the site, the most *telling* emblem, of this social upheaval.

Chamfort was an extravagant symptom of history in the making, as if the pus oozing from his sores announced the volcanic eruption of 1789. This was during a century in which geniuses appeared to be happy, in which madmen were few and far between (not even de Sade nor Marat was mad), in which few cases spark psychological investigation, in which the calculating moderation for which France is so often reproached actually bore fine fruit. Hence Chamfort— unhappy in love, literature, and revolution, yet livelier and more profound than most of his contemporaries—was simultaneously the antithesis and the symbol of his epoch. It is with reluctance that I am now bidding farewell to that special period he embodies, when Ancien Régime was inseparable from the new order.

AUTHOR'S ACKNOWLEDGMENTS

I would like to thank all those who helped me with and during my research, most especially: Simone Balayé, Jean-Claude Bonnet, Gabriel de Broglie, Odile Cail, Mme. Louis Camu, Jean-Paul Caracalla, Guy Chaussinand-Nogaret, Professor Jean Ehrard (University of Clermont-Ferrand), Dr. Jacques Girard of Clermont-Ferrand, Jean Grassion of Mirefleurs (Auvergne), Marcel Le Clère, Bernard Minoret, George D. Painter, Georges Poisson, Maurice Regard, Professor John Renwick (University of Leeds), Pierre Riberette, Edouard Richard of Riom, and Professor Christopher Todd (University of Edinborough).

I would also like to thank Monsieur Cousseau and Mme. Sérulaz (Louvre Museum), Jean-Michel Pianelli (Marmottan Library), and Mme. Roland-Michel for having helped me in my search for portraits of Chamfort.

Finally, I am grateful to Philippe Arnaud, Manuel Carcassonne, Jacques Fieschi, Frédéric El-Guedj, Georges Liébert, Olivier de Magny, Bernard Minoret, and Charles Najman for the care with which they read my manuscript, and to Nancy Doyle for having helped me translate into French the maxims found in the Mirabeau papers.

TRANSLATOR'S ACKNOWLEDGMENTS

Raymond Salette and Jean-Paul Socard displayed patience and insight in helping me resolve a number of complicated passages. I am also grateful to Christine Schultz-Touge for her useful comments concerning the English manuscript.

CHAMFORT

1. A NEGATIVE FAIRY TALE

It's a story of the negation of everything, eventually including the negation of self, a race toward the absolute which ends in the fury of nothingness.

Albert Camus
Preface to Chamfort's *Maximes et pensées . . .*

Children were unfashionable in the aristocratic world of 1740, for their cries reminded that overcivilized society of its animal origins. Infants were, therefore, remanded to country-bred wet nurses—prompting Talleyrand's claim that he spent only one night in his parents' home. The eighteenth century, though ethically close to our own, seems totally alien in a social sense. Children of "high birth" were protected throughout life by the halo of their noble particle, bolstered by marriages that governed the lives of nobles to an almost incestuous extent. Chamfort was nearly of noble birth, but the "nearly" changed everything. His mother, Jacqueline de Vinzelles, belonged to a noble family from Clermont-Ferrand. Married to Jean-François Dauphin de Leyval, a public prosecutor, and mother of two girls aged sixteen and twelve, she became pregnant at age forty-four by a modest canon at Clermont Cathedral named Pierre Nicolas. With one stroke, she betrayed husband, class, and God.

As chance would have it, a young infant born to a grocer named François Nicolas—a relative of the canon—died at the moment of the future Chamfort's birth. Jacqueline Dauphin de Leyval, in the role of wicked mother, suggested a swap. The grocer agreed, and on June 22, 1740, the newborn child was baptized in Saint-Genès Church, Clermont.[1] He was given the same first, middle, and last names as the dead child (who was baptized on April 5), as well as the same godfather (a master locksmith). His godmother was the wife of a baker and his new mother a domestic servant who also happened to be aged forty-four. Thus this little unwanted Dauphin, declared to be of unknown parentage, became known to all as Sébastien Roch Nicolas, son of grocer Nicolas and his wife Thérèse. The awkward fairy tale had begun.

The winter of 1740 was a brutal one. Frost nipped harvests,

3

famine spread, and riots shook Clermont-Ferrand. Bishop Massillon of Clermont reported that people literally snatched the bread from their children's mouths in order to pay their taxes. Thérèse Nicolas nevertheless managed to avoid the worst. Short-haired (like those Auvergne women who in Caesar's day sold their hair to the Romans), Thérèse was totally devoted to her "son," as though she somehow felt guilty about the changeling. Probably aided by Jacqueline Dauphin de Leyval, she arranged for a scholar from the University of Navarre to be his tutor.[2] Still studying at an age when some children were already helping their parents, the young Sébastien Roch Nicolas, the future Chamfort, was a privileged child in an underprivileged environment. He was brought up to respect effort and frugality in a family as morally upright as a Greuze painting, fully immersed in that austere and unyielding atmosphere which had previously influenced the Jansenism of Blaise Pascal (another native of Clermont-Ferrand). Thérèse Nicolas was not just a wet nurse; she was a righteous mother. She protected the young Sébastien from both poverty and the spectacle of the aristocracy, keeping him in a social bubble where money and material possessions mattered little—because they were characterized by neither lack nor excess. His first seven years were probably the happiest in a life thereafter marked by a quest to reestablish this initial equilibrium between poverty and splendor.

Then Thérèse Nicolas punctured his world. She told Sébastien, aged seven or eight, that he was the son of Jacqueline de Vinzelles (Jacqueline Dauphin de Leyval), Dame de Montrodeix (a village situated at the foot of the Puy-de-Dome). The boy also learned that his maternal ancestors fled an Italy gripped by war between Guelphs and Ghibellines to settle on the heights of the Massif Central in France; that he was descended from the Chevaliers de Vinzelles (buried in their own chapel in Clermont Cathedral from the thirteenth century onward), as well as from fifteen generations of Seigneurs from Vinzelles, Fonfreyde, Orme, Veilles, Baussat, Nadaillat, Rochegonde, and other localities overlooking the Limagne plain. This heady discovery shattered his sense of identity. Having fallen from an ancestral chateau to a grocery store rendered bare by shortages, Chamfort experienced the most brutal social fall imaginable under the Ancien Régime. He should have been Sébastien de Vinzelles—or rather de Leyval, had his mother's husband accepted paternity—yet he now found himself the son of a shopkeeper. He began to consider himself as someone apart, different from everybody he knew, coming from somewhere else, belonging to no one: a *natural* child in the fullest sense of the term. It was as though he forever eradicated the social circumstances surrounding his birth. Yet anger at having been rejected by his real mother, at having been deprived of rank and legitimacy for the sake of appearances, sparked a profound wariness. This grew into a misanthropic tendency, a bitterness he would try to suppress all his life, sublimating it through irony and brilliant wit. Along with intelligence, charm, and sensitivity, this misanthropy would become one of the dominant traits of his personality.

His situation was all the more painful since Thérèse Nicolas worked as a servant for the Chazerats, relatives of his real mother. Thérèse fully participated in the Chazerat family life—was even godmother to one of the children—and, therefore, decided to send the young Sébastien away to spare him humiliating encounters. She also wanted to give this precocious child, so obviously little-suited to the family grocery business, every chance of success. Hence his half-sisters Marguerite de Laire and Françoise de Leyval, his relatives the Chazerats, and all the others on the Auvergne peerage list soon had a good excuse for not greeting him—he had been sent to school in Paris.

Genealogy of Rancor

Chamfort's birth, so determining in every respect, merits emphasis. Through a mixture of pride and shame, he maintained almost total secrecy concerning his origins, never able to forget them nor to consider them objectively. Commentators would offer numerous hypotheses. Some considered him to be the illegitimate nephew of Madame du Deffand, the famous letter writer, while others thought him the legitimate son of the grocer Nicolas; Chamfort was eventually overwhelmed with parents. The sole reliable testimony is that of Baron d'Espinchal, who was himself from a noble Auvergnat family. The baron was closely linked for over twenty-five years both to Augustin Dauphin de Leyval, the husband of Chamfort's half-sister, and to the prince de Condé, who became one of Chamfort's protectors. In the second, unpublished part of his memoirs, Espinchal asserts that "Chamfort is my fellow countryman, having been born in Clermont-Ferrand. He is the issue of the illegitimate love between the Dame de Montrodeix and Master Nicolas, Canon of that city." Espinchal can be believed, for he was the best informed—and more especially the most accurate—man of his day. He kept thousands of files on his contemporaries, noting genealogy and biography. According to Mme. Vigée-Lebrun, he knew everybody "from the duchess to the hussy." He once located a provincial woman's lost husband at the theater, for the man was the only person in the house unknown to Espinchal.

By revealing the secret apparently known to several noble Auvergnat families, Espinchal makes it possible to reconstruct Chamfort's maze of relatives. His real mother, the Dame de Montrodeix, descended from the Cisternes, that Italian family who fled to Auvergne around 1300. The chivalric origins of their noble title made them one of the most prestigious families in the area. In addition to the chapel in Clermont Cathedral, the family possessed another in the church at Issoire. Both father and brother of Chamfort's mother were presidents of the Clermont Court of Aids (customs and excise administration). Discreet, provincial, with no particular ties to Paris and going up to Versailles only to be presented to the king, the family was related to all the major judiciary dynasties in Auvergne. It thus constituted one of the foremost families among the *noblesse de robe* (those holding hereditary legal posts), the class that was the first to suffer from the French Revolution. Four Cisternes were officers in the army with which the prince de Condé vainly attempted to overthrow the government stemming from the events of 1789.

Chamfort's adoptive mother's maiden name was Creuzet (or Croizet). She was the daughter of Claude Creuzet, a cloth shearer who died in 1741. In January 1727 she married the grocer Nicolas in Clermont-Ferrand.[3] Some chroniclers claim that she accompanied Chamfort to Paris for his schooling, but nothing is certain. Chamfort would appear to have had no more contact with his real mother or his real father, the canon Nicolas, although he kept in touch with a "relative" through the writer Thomas, another Auvergnat.[4] Things are not quite clear here, either, but his leaving Clermont undeniably constituted a healthy break wit his childhood milieu, which extended to every level of Auvergne's social hierarchy.

Armed with a half-scholarship obtained by his tutor, the ten year-old Sébastien Nicolas left Clermont in the summer of 1750.[5] He was taken to the Collège des Grassins on Sainte-Geneviève hill, where he spent his first night in Paris. He would not get to see much of the city, however; the school, one of the best in France, was very strict. Leaving via the rue Mouffetard exit required an *exeat*, and disciplinarians were stationed in a hut near the courtyard toilets to whip unruly students. The boy's horizon was limited to classroom, courtyard, and dormitory. Taking refuge in the boarding-school syndromes of arrogance and solitude, Nicolas did not study very hard. But he blossomed in his fourth year, and in rhetoric he competed in all five subjects comprising the interschool Competitive Exam, the *ne plus ultra* of academic competitions. First in all subjects except Latin composition, he yielded to pressure from the school and put his four titles on the line again by entering a second time the following year. He won all across the board and saw his name etched in gold on the five honor rolls in the refectory.

Having become the top student in France, he looked down on his lesser rivals with an irony already betraying a sharp sense of superiority. Nicolas, handsome and high spirited, became infatuated with himself. One of his earliest friends, Nicholas Joseph Sélis, described him as "impetuous and cunning, studious and mischievous, achieving the impossible by winning every contest, learning Greek, Latin, Italian, and English all at once, reading everything, already forming judgments on things . . . and people."[6] He became the disciple of the Greek teacher, Lebeau the elder. Although strong in Greek composition, the boy displayed an unruly streak, and one day the humorless Hellenist lost his temper and dismissed him from class. Nicolas thereupon dismissed his teachers. His school days were over.

> . . . *Ces prisons où le hasard rassemble,*
> *Des esprits inegaux qu'on fait ramper ensemble.*[7]

> . . . Those prisons where chance alone tethers
> Unequal minds forced to grovel together.

France's best student intended to prove that he no longer needed an institution reserved for children of the poor in order to continue to be the best.

The Artifice of Flight

He decided to take his savings and leave for America, dragging along an accomplice named Letourneur. But once at the port of Cherbourg, the two schoolboys hesitated. "Before setting off to see the world, suppose we see to ourselves?" suggested Nicolas.[8] With this remark—worthy of Pascal—he summed up both his genius and his limitations.

Having returned to Paris with Letourneur, the future Chamfort
went back to Grassins and his top ranking. His prestige with his fellow students increased tenfold thanks to his projected departure for
America, so unusual for the times; at age fourteen, Chamfort already had a following. He let fly his first epigram against *Candide*,
parodying Voltaire's parody of Leibniz's "Everything for the best in
the best of all worlds."[9] He wrote a few poems and corrected those
of fellow-student Jean Fontaine-Malherbe (this presumed descendant of the poet François de Malherbe was a strange case, described
by Sélis as a "real Cyrano de Bergerac"). Having completed his studies, Nicolas wore, like Diderot before him and like most poor children educated by the church, the black breeches and little collar of a
priest. An interview with the principal set things straight. "I'll never
be a priest," Nicolas informed him. "I'm too fond of sleep, philosophy, women, honor and real fame; and not fond enough of quarrels,
hypocrisy, honors and money."[10] He would almost keep to his
word.

He thus abandoned school, priestly garb, security. His class-
mates scattered—Fontaine-Malherbe would translate Shakespeare
under the aegis of Letourneur, who introduced the poetry of Ossian
into France (where it became a bible for Bonaparte and the early Romantics). Nicolas's mental geography, however, was inspired by his
intensive study of the classics. As though escaping to some Greek
island, he would always flee via Homer's tales and Plutarch's *Lives*.
Like those heroes who sacrificed everything for glory, he would
struggle against anonymity all his life. He didn't want to merely exist, he wanted to exist superlatively, meriting both legend and biography at his death. Everyday acts and phrases were garnished with
riddles, for the day when a biographer would come along to explain
them. He was set on this path by the brothers Lebeau, those fine
teachers he scorned (and who—cruel paradox—would die obscure). Through their teachings and books, such as *Histoire du Bas-
empire* [*History of the Eastern Roman empire*] and *Essai sur Lucien* [*Essay
on Lucian*] they provided Nicolas with his cardinal points. Heroism
was up, cynicism down, with tragedy on the right and satire on the
left. Armed with this compass, Nicolas cut a path through Greek
values and Roman rottenness. Nourished on fragments and textbooks (like Nietzsche at Pforta), endowed with an intuitive intelligence, he would dream of being both great and morally upright, a
fabulous character yet real, passionate but always in control of him-

self. The integrity instilled in early childhood found infinite outlet in the idealized culture preached at Grassins.

There were those who suspected that a "certain liking for the Republic" was acquired through hearing about "the Senate, liberty, the justifiable death of Caesar, and Cato's dagger."[11] But the contradictions of the education provided by the grand Catholic schools would only bear fruit later. For the moment, Nicolas abandoned the ancient world where his five victories in the Competitive Exam had served as a toga of manhood. He would retain only the two key values of intellect and inspired genius, never understanding why these alone did not rule the world, why kingly scepters, worldly wealth, and noble titles were not beholden to them.

Chamfort perhaps considered himself a genius. The idea, at any rate, must have crossed his mind. Based on his reading, he somewhat academically imagined himself a Daedalus soaring over his contemporaries, above a world too small for him. "There are few men of great character who don't hold some fabulous image in mind or heart," he would say. Which was precisely his case. It required only a small step, which he seems to have taken, to consider himself one of those geniuses that heaven mercifully sends, practically fully formed, to "renew mankind and restore sanity." This would be the source of a profound and lasting misconception, expressed in what seems to be a plea on his own behalf: "Geniuses belong to no family, no century, no nation—they have neither ancestors nor descendants."[12]

2. EARLY STRUGGLE AGAINST ANONYMITY

Setting down each moment of one's being, for all eternity—is there a kinder fate, a more touching pleasure?

Chamfort

Paris was an unpleasant surprise. After suffering the trials of school, Nicolas expected a somewhat pleasant life. Like all great readers, he had drawn a certain notion of omnipotence from his excessive familiarity with words and his solitary encounters with ideas. With a puritanism typical of intellect, he imagined himself making his way abstractly through a world devoid of money. But the capital city paid no attention to this gifted, defrocked cleric. Several weeks after having left Grassins, the "best student in France" was wandering the streets.

Talent would not become associated with poverty until the Romantic era. In 1760, indigence was still commonplace. The poor gathered at dawn at the place de Grève to await work, or lined up at the kitchens of private residences to buy leftovers. Poverty lived so close to luxury that Louis Sébastien Mercier placed Parisians lower than peasants on his scale of happiness. The poor were without rights, without security, constantly threatened with becoming nonbeings. And this abyss threatened Nicolas for a long time. Thucydides had taught him the ruses of war, not of survival. Reduced to "the most wretched"[1] state, almost longing for his old status as cleric, he agreed to ghostwrite for a preacher—the start of his long career as literary mercenary.

Finally, in 1761, an attorney confided the education of his son to Nicolas. But the tutor was fired when caught in the company of his employer's wife. A pretty, twenty-five-year-old widow then engaged him to raise her child with discernment. "I want you to teach Latin, rhetoric, and ethics to me, too," she instructed him, seduced by his handsome face and blue eyes. After exhausting every subject, Nicolas "educated" first one, then two servant girls. "You've not been faithful to our agreement," the young widow stated. "Every time you make my son study, he loses weight!" "And I, too, Madame, every time you and I . . . study!"[2]

Appointed preceptor to the nephew of Count Van Eyck, Nicolas went to Liège, Spa, and Cologne, where the count's brother was prince-elector. He gave lessons to the heir to this small German court and composed couplets that the count would read during celebrations. But as a "literary valet" he was poorly paid. Outraged by these rich people "stretched out limply on their sofas . . . counting the instants"[3] to pass the time, Nicolas departed. "I know of nothing which I would have been less suited to be than a German," he said.[4] Thus ended his first, and almost only, trip abroad. It gave birth to his conviction that he belonged to a culture fundamentally French, with a touch of Greek.

His stay in Cologne, however, was not entirely wasted. It was there he wrote a poem for a friend—dated June 19, 1761—in which he flung down the gauntlet, announcing that he was ready to grapple with Paris. Doubt and questioning were over. Relegating nice Nicolas to the status of a middle name, he signed a third birth certificate by becoming, at twenty-one, Sébastien Roch Nicolas de Chamfort. The former "valet" took to literature with a name that fluttered like a banner and that, according to the duchesse d'Abrantès, he used as though it had been borne by "a hundred forebears."[5]

After completing a comedy in verse titled *La jeune indienne [Indian Girl]*, Chamfort met Jean François de La Harpe, his first significant acquaintance. Although La Harpe was only six months older than Chamfort, he had a six-year head start in life, having been received by Diderot at sixteen, congratulated by Voltaire at twenty, and his work performed by the Comédie-Française at twenty-two. Barely five feet tall, La Harpe was nicknamed "Bébé" (like the dwarf to King Stanislas of Poland), and was considered a full-fledged "Philosopher" by Voltaire and d'Alembert. Right from the start he dominated Chamfort. Brillant, charmingly nasty, and endowed with a prodigious sense of tactics, La Harpe was by nature and constitution a writer—which Chamfort was not. La Harpe always carried around three volumes of his writings, penned favorable reviews of his own plays, wanted those of his rivals censored, and was a never-satisfied sponger who was always invited back. He was convinced he was the writer that Europe awaited, the lady-killer all women desired. Chamfort was visibly seduced by La Harpe's total determination to succeed, as well as by the colossal audacity of someone consigned to minority status (not that of race or sex but of physical stature).

Meeting a prodigy endowed with contacts and privileges made

Chamfort realize that he was not the best, and he shaved two years off his age to make up for lost time. Nevertheless, after months of solitude and wandering, he was at last accepted by Paris itself, a city not so much hostile as indifferent. La Harpe sent *La jeune indienne* to Voltaire and presented it to the Comédie-Française, two gestures that sparked Chamfort's gratitude (a sentiment with which he was spontaneously generous) as well as his grandiose ideas on friendship ("one soul in two bodies," as the ancients put it). La Harpe, also illegitimate, was the brother Chamfort never had, a Pylades who would help him take vengeance. This crucial relationship led to Chamfort's confession that a long conversation with a friend provided him with the same "sweet languors" as love; he henceforth held that friendship was superior to love, due to its ability to reconcile the delights of passion with those of reason.

But as far as La Harpe was concerned, Chamfort was merely an acolyte, his creation, his "thing." La Harpe later wrote, "He showed me three books: an epistle on fame which he thought excellent, and which I advised him to throw into the fire; another on education, which I suggested he revise, and finally *La jeune indienne* on which he had no opinion, yet which delighted me. . . . He was nothing, had nothing, and I could see he was ready to accept the most petty task."[6] Which is why Bébé limited himself to introducing Chamfort to Dorat and Ximénes. These two patrons housed La Harpe and were also salon writers who went broke on their own vanity publications—Dorat was even accused of trying to redeem himself "plate by plate," thanks to the sumptuous engravings with which he spiced his work. Though surrounded by young poets and addressing verses to well-known women (most of whom he did not know), Claude Joseph Dorat was no Voltaire. He would even be dismissed by La Harpe, after their falling out, as a "scribbler of fans, zephyrs and roses."[7] Yet on encountering Dorat, Chamfort lost some of his puritanism. He began to speak less of books and more of authors, as Paris expected. He learned the fashionable art of the day, conversation, in a town already torn between a desire for profoundness and the fear of it. He discovered which gestures to avoid, which vulgarities to banish; he learned to act as though on stage. Thus he entered the civilization of masks, that product of an aristocracy that now imitated actors (whereas it had formerly served as a model for these same actors). Chamfort, in a sign typical of a society caught between greatness and decadence, seemed to undergo a split. Soon he no longer knew where his own truth lay—within the simple room in which he slept or on the stage upon which he acted. It was as though he had been divided once again into a Nicolas and a Vinzelles.

Fame at Twenty

Regarding his literary personality, however, he had no doubts—he was Chamfort, a literary creation. On his return from Germany he had met the editor of *Le Journal Encyclopédique*, one of the best papers in Europe, in which d'Alembert spread the philosophical good news. When Chamfort was appointed Paris correspondent (a post he would fill for two years), he asked to be published under his initials only.[8] His agenda called for a spotless biography, fame or nothing. He entered the contests organized by provincial academies, obligatory steps toward the Académie française, that focal point and goal of every literary career. "You consider me a poor devil," he said to Sélis. "But do you know what will become of me? I'll win a prize from the Académie, my comedy will be a hit, and I'll find myself launched into the world, received by influential people whom I despise; they'll make my fortune with no meddling from me, and I shall live as a philosopher."[9] An astonishingly precocious and lucid outline of his life—the last proposition excepted. At that very moment, Voltaire, after having read one act of *La jeune indienne*, was writing to Bébé La Harpe, "Here's a young man who will write as they did a hundred years ago."[10] Chamfort, elevated to the level of Racine, would have his play performed less than two months later.

Preceded by readings in various social circles, *La jeune indienne* premiered on April 30, 1764, at the Comédie-Française. Following tradition, Chamfort sat at the Café Procope (located opposite the theater on what is now rue de l'Ancienne Comédie), waiting to go see his players backstage after the performance. The audience applauded most especially Mlle. Doligny, an eighteen-year-old prancing naked under her tiger skin in the title role. Becoming overexcited—perhaps at the idea of seeing the actress in the buff—the crowd began to call boisterously for the playwright, and the situation began to degenerate into a farce. The administrator of the theater, Argental (who was also Voltaire's Parisian representative), accommodatingly pushed Chamfort toward the stage. It was the academician Charles Pinot Duclos who saved him from ridicule at the last minute. Despite such dubious bravos, and although Dorat had already handled the same theme in *Lettre de Zeila*, critics confirmed the qualities of this glittery trifle set in Charlestown, Virginia, as well as the talent of its author, kindly described as a "lad." Compliments abounded, and Catherine II in Saint-Petersburg received a commentary from Melchior Grimm, an influential critic linked to Denis Diderot. *La jeune indienne* benefited from French culture's crushing influence over Europe, and was performed in Berlin, Leipzig, and all across Germany (Goethe considered taking up the subject himself). It was also produced in Holland, Spain, and Russia, was translated into Danish, and even pantomimed. Chamfort was intoxicated by such early fame ("fair and sweet as dawn" in Vauvenargues's phrase), and his modesty suffered. "If you sow thorns in front of you, my friend, you'll encounter them when you pass by," said a friend as lucid as Chamfort about the future.[11]

La jeune indienne in no way heralds a "revolutionary" writer. Most plays of this period were set in Babylon, in Turkey, or among the Incas, for biblical and Greco-Roman subjects had been dealt with in the previous century, whereas "national" themes were poorly received when they glorified the monarchy and censored when they took issue with it. Faithful to this rule, which allowed for indirect criticism, Chamfort even watered down a subject already explored by Dorat. Three characters, however, explained its success: Betti, the Indian girl who sprang from nature like Venus from the waters; Mowbray, the affable, informal Quaker complete with hat, who was a prerepublican figure; and Belton, saved by the Indian girl from an island shipwreck yet betrothed to a rich heiress in America, who protested against the social laws of a country still ruled by the English monarchy (though Belton already exhibits a strange complicity with what he detests). These characters would come to haunt Chamfort, the latter prefiguring the man of rancor that Chamfort would become. He has Belton complain at the idea of marrying the poor, young Indian as a sign of gratitude:

> *Rebutés, condamnés à l'affront d'etre plaints,*
> *Tout aigrira nos maux, jusqu'à notre tendresse,*
> *Nous hairons l'amour, nous craindrons la vieillesse;*
> *En d'autres malheureux reproduits, chaque jour*
> *Nos mains repousseront le fruit de notre amour.*

> Spurned and reduced to the plight of the pitied,
> All will embitter our sorrow, wound our affection
> Till we come to detest love, fear dereliction;

Having begot other poor wretches, our hands will rebuff
Day in, day out, the very fruit of our love.

Even enthusiastic critics noted the strangeness of little Betti, that Caribbean native whose vocabulary included "ardor" and "nuptials." She praised "nature as if she weren't part of it," observed Sainte-Beuve.[12] But Indians and Quakers were fashionable, for the period considered "noble savages" and rustic America to be alternatives to its own sophistication. They evoked the golden age with which history began, and with which it would end. Thoroughly won over by that "very pretty little creature," Voltaire dismissed any lingering doubts. Of course the patriarch had always sought to turn potential rivals into heirs, yet in telling Chamfort that he "would go far,"[13] Voltaire partly made it possible. Once he became a de facto member of the Philosophers' clan, Chamfort could count on the marketing genius of the "church" founded by Voltaire.

The "Revolution" of 1750

To understand how Chamfort differed from his contemporaries, it is necessary to dwell on the "revolution" of the Enlightenment presided over by Voltaire, which hastened Chamfort's departure from Grassins. D'Alembert wrote in 1759, "Everything, from the principles of secular science to the basis of the Revelation, from metaphysics to questions of taste . . . has been discussed, analyzed, debated."[14] Philosophers sought the origin of life, for the interpretations of Genesis that set the date of Adam's birth on October 29, 4004 B.C., had become outmoded, thanks partly to geological excavations and the discovery of fossils of extinct species. The existence of an "intelligent" principle, active in plants as well as animals, relegated the Great Timekeeper—or Supreme Being—to the role of supervisor or enlightened monarch. Nature was seen as positive, balanced (a conviction even the terrible Lisbon earthquake of 1755 could not shake), composed of atoms, constituents, fluids. Belief rested in a tolerant deism, or in a natural religion—the good, the true, and the right having descended slowly from heaven to earth. Adam was no longer father to all men, for the various races were considered to be the expression of the world's infinite variety—this would be the most original contribution of a century that benefited from the theories of Galileo and Newton. Freed from superstition, the enlightened citizen became a born organizer amidst the catalog of techniques and ideas embodied in the *Encyclopédie*. With France becoming richer, it was felt that all around there lay some new resource—or pleasure—to be unlocked. Advances in astronomy transformed the map of the heavens, while the voyages of Bougainville and Cook transformed that of the earth. Man was the master of the universe—a universe whose dimensions did not yet extend to the infinite. Adam Smith laid the foundations of economic free enterprise; Montesquieu asserted that "governments are made for those governed"—and not the opposite.[15] While the social order was not yet under attack, some people began to fear the advent of a revolution abolishing "all mystery."[16]

By the time Chamfort came along, this revolution had already taken place. The *Encyclopédie* sat imposingly in libraries. For a while it had survived thanks to Diderot's courage alone (and had indirectly led to the imprisonment of several of its contributors), but the tome was now protected by Louis XV's favorite, Mme. de Pompadour, and was becoming part of the establishment. Chamfort could thus enjoy the ideological luxury of refusing to choose between physiocrats and advocates of planned economy, between free traders and materialists, between Voltaire and Rousseau (whose camps were dividing up the intellectual and financial spoils of the Enlightenment's victory). Literary down to his soul, and having neither scientific curiosity nor a taste for economics, Chamfort contented himself with studying individuals, morality, and society—the human comedy.

The intellectual "revolution" of the years 1740–1760 nevertheless marked Chamfort. Here he might compare humanity to "a crowd of intelligent atoms," there he would speak of "astonishing masses of light" which preceded the birth of the world.[17] And the eulogies he composed for academic contests would tirelessly praise the struggle for liberation from "odious tyrants" and priestly obscurantism. This struggle, however, was to remain progressive and cautious, like that of Descartes, who was "the apostle of reason, without wanting to be its martyr, [who] loved mankind . . . yet [who] feared it even more."[18] For human beings were governed by instincts as much as by conscience, by passion and vices as much as reason. Nothing should be done to spark their evil nature, while everything should be done to nurture their intelligence. Chamfort, though influenced by the ideas of his day, did not believe they had really changed human nature.

He rejected the various ideologies with which enlightened Paris teemed as well as "the disastrous revolutions" in which the people, weary of oppression, "become barbarians again, thinking they are freeing themselves." Chamfort felt that it was *genius* that would ultimately prevent kings from ruling "alone over nations" and forbid them from "debasing" their subjects. Invisible, subtle, slipping into minds everywhere and governing—like God—without doing harm, genius was destined to become, in Chamfort's eyes, both liberator and master of the world—all the while remaining in the background. Thus Montesquieu, by spending twenty years writing his *L'esprit des lois* [*The Spirit of the Laws*], did more than Voltaire to promote the idea of the need for a separation of powers and to discredit despotism. "And, after having been barbaric and ignorant, superstitious and fanatical, philosophical and frivolous, perhaps we'll wind up by becoming men and citizens," concluded Chamfort,[19] a position that did not expose him to arrest in the 1760s, yet which already set him off from the encyclopedists.

Initiation into the Clan

Thanks to Voltaire's imprimatur, however, Chamfort was viewed as one of the rising stars of the Philosophers' clan and thus of French literature. Backed by Charles Joseph Panckoucke, the most adroit publisher of the day, who also published most anti-Voltaire works, the clan in effect acted as authoritative sponsor in a country profoundly and fundamentally literary. It benefited from the discreet support of the duc de Choiseul (Louis XV's prime minister) as well as the backing of two salons—that of the wealthy bourgeoise Mme. Geoffrin, who forbad the discussion of politics, and that of Mme. du Deffand, patronness to Jean Le Rond d'Alembert in spite of her penchant for higher society. (Her patronage continued up until the day in 1765 when d'Alembert went off with the blind old lady's niece, Julie de Lespinasse, to open a rival salon reserved for the "intelligentsia.") The clan was also present in the Académie française, even though the majority of academicians were still reactionary "Bonnets." This was also the case in provincial academies, which served as relay stations for spreading literary ideas and fashions. These bastions of literary mania, crucial to any writer in search of renown, were already Chamfort's main objective—yet another reason for not refusing advances made by the Philosophers.

Honor to whom honor is due: at seventy years of age, Voltaire was the uncontested ruler of French—and therefore European— literature. A staunch partisan of civilization, tolerance, and progress, this "universal man" was considered the Racine and Corneille of his day, thanks to the tragedies he wrote in the years 1730–1740, such as *Zaire, Mahomet,* and *Mérope.* He also instigated an intellectual revolution which owed much to his *Lettres philosophiques* praising the liberal English system. Voltaire remained the most combative and most political of the Philosophers, both as historian (his *Siècle de Louis XIV* chronicled a century whose classical literary rules he continued to follow) and ferocious, hilarious pamphleteer. He was also the patron saint of Ferney, a village in the Ain region where every villager worked in his watch factory. While La Harpe, like Chamfort, rested on the laurels of the *Encyclopédie,* Voltaire battled on, in 1764, to rehabilitate Calas (a Calvinist accused of having murdered his son to prevent him from converting), just as he would do in 1771 for Sirven (another victim of the final convulsions of extreme right-wing Catholicism). To his dying day, the indefatigable Voltaire, seduced by the flashes of irony in *La jeune indienne,* also publicly backed Chamfort, in whom he glimpsed a little of his own wit.

While Voltaire remained unchallenged pope, his exile fifteen years earlier had left d'Alembert as the effective head of his "church." D'Alembert, another illegitimate child, was a brilliant thinker and mathematician, impotent in bed yet with a convincing act in public. He monitored the purity of philosophical doctrine. Voltaire instructed him to get as many disciples into the Académie as possible; excluding the roughly twenty dukes, marshals, and bishops elected out of pure deference (never having written a line), the Académie was composed of the "political" avant-garde and the most dynamic elements in literature (one could be elected at age thirty, sometimes even twenty-five). D'Alembert was short of stature and lively in nature. But his mischievousness masked an unyielding, brittle, and bitter character. He was said to be "a slave to freedom." Yet Julie de Lespinasse's hapless lover was, nevertheless, one of the first Philosophers to extend an invitation to Chamfort, twenty years his junior. Everyone pressed Chamfort to enter this "family" which corresponded with several European monarchs, including the enlightened despot par excellence, Frederick II of Prussia.

For Voltaire wanted to spread enlightenment *from above,* winning over first of all kings, princes, the elite. Believing that the higher a candle is placed, the more light it sheds, the Philosophers favored strong central governments and "progressive" monarchs in order to save time and energy. This created a strange contradiction between an unchanged social hierarchy and an elite partially won over to encyclopedic ideas. The resulting paradox, which existed right up to the Revolution, was that the urban nobility considered religion to be the heritage of medieval obscurantism, while the rural masses remained attached to a God who made the rain fall, the sun shine, and harvests ripen.

This elitist approach helps to explain the attitude of Jean-François Marmontel who, coming after Pope Voltaire and Grand Inquisitor d'Alembert, was the canon among Philosophers. Born in the Auvergne in modest circumstances, a contented and good-natured writer, librettist for Grétry and author of the famous *Contes moraux* [*Moral Tales*], Marmontel was disingenuous, a good maneuverer, ponderous even in his refinement, yet able to handle irony. He incarnated everything that Chamfort unconsciously hated: the comfortable life, the cautious peasant who quarreled with nobody (because he was a nobody himself, one of his biographers would claim). He had no complex about his Auvergne accent nor about living in the shadow of the nobility. Marmontel was a long way from the major thinkers of the enlightenment—Diderot, Holbach, Helvétius, Condillac. But in 1764, the clan had less need of ideologues than of caretakers able to manage its conquests; Chamfort considered Marmontel little more than a tool.

The "church" also included several fellow travelers located here and there, such as Abbé Delille, Saurin, and Condorcet; there were also active sympathizers closely connected to the Comédie-Française, such as Argental, Voltaire's Paris correspondent; courtiers and even archbishops were favorable to its ideas; and there were young recruits of whom the most brilliant, after La Harpe, was Jean-Baptiste Suard. Son of a professor from Besançon, Suard was a sharp journalist, Anglophile as well as Germanizing, with refined tastes yet lacking the means to have his own coffee brought up from Marseille. He took the precaution of marrying the prettiest and most conventional of publisher Panckoucke's sisters. Six years older than Chamfort, Suard would receive Chamfort at his salon (despite his wife's latent hostility), one of the first in which writers met among themselves, without the least aristocratic patronage.

The Man in Armenian Clothing

Chamfort was too temperamental and too contradictory to adopt the Philosophers' analytical attitude. Regretting that its rational approach rendered his generation blasé, Chamfort wrote, "In society's current state, mankind seems to me more corrupted by reason than by passion." In addition, Chamfort was too fundamentally individualist to become a wholehearted member of the clan; he would always prefer Voltaire to the other saints, and Voltaire's influence was more determining than that of the jealous La Harpe in investing Chamfort as a "Philosopher." Nothing, moreover could have prevented Chamfort from reaching out to the clan's favorite victim, that man known to don an Armenian caftan; the Genevan who made mountains, music, and children fashionable; author of the already legendary 1761–1762 publication of *La nouvelle Héloise, Emile,* and *Le contrat social:* Jean-Jacques Rousseau. In fact, Rousseau was the only writer with whom Chamfort really identified. His penchant for solitude and his fascinated hatred for civilization engendered a sensibility that marked the young Chamfort, a sensibility that would become known as preromantic. Breaking with the Philosophers, remaining optimistic in an era where the people no longer feared God and did not yet fear mankind, Rousseau enjoyed an astonishing cult following. The cup-and-ball games he toyed with were snatched up like relics, and he was always called by his first name, Jean-Jacques. Part of the younger generation even imitated his paranoia. He thereby attained the status of the other two idols of the day: Voltaire, and the naturalist Georges Buffon (who sang of the inexhaustible variety of birds).

Rousseau, however, had not really renounced the good life. For it was during a delightful "cream tea" on the heights of Motiers, in Switzerland, that he received *La jeune indienne* accompanied by the following note: "Monsieur, although you wish to be forgotten, you surely do not wish to be forgotten by those who are in debt to you. It is precisely on this account that I am enclosing a little play which was performed here. Your writings have for long been a source of study and delight. They present a picture of natural man. The character of Betti probably owes much to them . . . I remain, Sir, with the respect due your talents—which in you are always virtuous—your very humble and obedient servant. De Chamfort."[20]

Rousseau's reply was equally enthusiastic. "I am flattered by the honor you do me in sending your play. Although acclaimed by the public, it should be equally well-received by connoisseurs and people sensitive to the true charms of nature. The surest effect of my maxims, which is to draw down upon me the hate of wicked people and the affection of good people and which is marked as much by my misfortune as by my success, suggests that the approval with which you honor my writing is exactly what is to be expected of yours. . . . I salute you, Sir, with all my heart."[21] The draft version of this letter contains the line: "You're just beginning, whereas I'm finishing."

Chamfort had good reason to be satisfied. He had reconciled the two rival exiles on the Franco-Swiss border in his own name. Heir to both Rousseau and Voltaire, the illegitimate son of paranoia and irony, of passion and reason, of solitude and civilization, he had everything needed to succeed in a profession long considered a calling or a pastime, but which now finally benefited from royal attention and Panckoucke's brilliant undertakings. (After having bought up Paris printers one by one, Panckoucke managed to make several writers truly affluent.)

But Chamfort still needed a patron on the spot, someone able to back his long march toward the Académie française while respecting his independence. That patron was to be Duclos, the writer who saved Chamfort from making a fool of himself at the premiere of *La jeune indienne*. Duclos was also secretary of the Académie which, without him, would have split irrevocably into the two camps: the progressive "Hats" versus the reactionary "Bonnets." Practically unknown today (his finest literature having been oral), Duclos was famous at the time for his *Considérations sur les moeurs de ce siècle* [*Considerations on this century's customs*]. He was initially irritated by Chamfort's peremptory tone. But insolence loves company, and Duclos even discovered a strange similarity in their styles. A moralist and eroticist who punctuated his comments with obscenities like "bougre!" and "foutre!" and who wielded frankness like a sword which struck fear, Duclos was a convinced free-thinker who was nevertheless exasperated by the hegemonic designs of the Philosophers' clan. He taught Chamfort the rules he had followed in becoming the king's historian, the mayor of Dinan, and one of the richest writers of his day. These could be summed up in a single sentence: never become captive to any one party, remain amiable to the extreme, command respect from everyone—including an audience that "applauds" like the one at *La jeune indienne*—and steer a course midway between literature and society. This was an invaluable lesson for Chamfort, just then mapping out his life, making his veritable début in high society at the homes of Mme. de Mirepoix and Mme. de Rochefort (whom Duclos still managed to shock from time to time.[22] Here—two of the numerous strategic salons for gaining power, money, or a seat in the Académie—the author of *La jeune indienne* ultimately met more courtiers and ambassadors than Philosophers. And he discovered an especially dazzling version of the society from which his real mother had banished him.

Staged Society

Louis XIV had disciplined his nobles through Court regimen and more or less constant warfare. The regent freed them from these obligations as well as from Mme. de Maintenon's religious intolerance. Louis XV once again granted nobles their full military role, but with the lack of conviction of a king who was himself just a caretaker managing the monarchy's conquests (and who reportedly said, "Après moi, le déluge"). Losing its taste for battle following the futile Seven Years' War from 1757 to 1763 (during which it watched the Philosophers "go to work for the King of Prussia"), the nobility retreated to its drawing rooms. Henceforth expecting to conquer the world with its style, it advocated the sound of words rather than that of boots, the art of living rather than dying. Conversation would continue in the salons for up to seven hours at a stretch, in a crystalline language understood as far away as Moscow and liable to make even small minds appear brilliant. In a country at peace, everyone learned to dance, to compose riddles, to improvise stock roles. Following Louis XIV's enlightened "dictatorship," France boasted the most powerful culture, government, and population in Europe. It was, moreover, during the eighteenth century that France was the most influential and the least "nationalistic." Ignoring the loss of Canada and India, the nobility further refined its manners. A cultivated man came just behind the noble soul in the scale of values. For the first time, an elite sought not to intimidate but to please and to rhyme—and this only forty years after the Chevalier de Rohan had Voltaire flogged. A literary profession was no longer considered degrading. Duclos, who worked tirelessly for this climb to favor, even said, "They fear us the way thieves fear streetlamps."[23]

But Chamfort was still a long way from instilling fear. "His manners showed that he wasn't born into high society," said Aubin, a writer whom Chamfort met on leaving school. How could he compete with a class that had been playing this increasingly subtle game since childhood? The decline of absolutism and religion complicated the social order, a process begun under the Regency (a laboratory that spawned the eighteenth century in the same way everything in the twentieth century stems from the 1910s). Under Louis XIV, a courtier fell ill on having "displeased"; under the regent, he pleased by sharing his prince's nights of debauchery; while under Louis XV, the aristocracy simply wanted to please itself. Disguises, along with their mental equivalent, paradox, replaced uniforms and ethics. Chamfort saw duchesses wanting to pass for debauched ladies at all costs, crooks wanting to display "proud and honest" conduct, cardinals laugh at religion, and Voltaire mourn its decline ("because then who will we have to make fun of?" he asked).[24] There were writers who yearned for the Bastille to escape their creditors, and the head of the royal library, Malesherbes, spoke of emptying it—all of which which led to a growing sense of unreality. Vaucanson's automatons could be seen at work, and his mechanical ducks digested food "just like living ducks." Whereas human beings, with all their polite gestures, began to look like "wind-up toys," according to Mme. du Deffand. Pseudonyms and clothing were invented to dress up these robots. Doubles made the rounds of Paris—to the extent that the real Jean-Jacques was taken for an imposter. One writer might insult himself, using a pseudonym, in order to be able to defend himself, while another would use an already well-known name to get himself talked about. Paris teemed with phony nobles and pro-Voltaire abbés, all querying one another about the transvestite Chevalier d'Eon's true sex. "Everything is turning into fiction," observed the atheist philosopher Paul Henri Holbach.[25] Immortalized by Pierre Marivaux, this round dance accelerated to dizzying speed.

There's an explanation for such unreality. Nobility no longer rested on a principle but on a style. Previously responsible for protecting "social" as well as national borders, nobility was now distinguished only by taste and manners—things that can be imitated. Its very identity was, therefore, threatened. The problem, however, was too serious to be faced squarely. So the round dance took up again, speed warding off doubt and masks warding off emptiness. Everyone wanted to be something else, as long as it was an act. While awaiting this improbable universal stage, new disguises were adopted, new names assumed. "Special" languages originating from fictional countries were spoken in small, "secret" clubs founded in the wake of the duchesse du Maine's *Order of the Honey Bee*. The Faubourg St. Germain quarter worshipped whimsy—an interlude between Cartesian reason and the Goddess Reason erected by the Revolution—and hoped above all to be surprised. It would have been unseemly to evoke the Piranesian depths in which some, like Chamfort, floundered. Identity crises, especially theirs, were a taboo subject in this, the first "staged society"—testifying to the amazing pervasiveness of theatrical attitudes and to an almost childish obsession with amusement.

3. THE MASK

Covered in dirty garments, torn breeches, and tatters today. . . .
Powdered, shod, curled, well dressed tomorrow.

Diderot
Rameau's Nephew

Had he been a proper bourgeois, Chamfort would have seemed ordinary. As a bastard, however, he appealed to people's imaginations, and romantic stories about his background abounded. "A love child!" sighed women married by arrangement and therefore indifferent to their own offspring. Through sentimentality and snobbery, they slipped Chamfort into the deck of aristocratic families like a joker, nourishing their endless genealogical discussions.

Such curiosity carried little substance, however. Illegitimate children were still denied inheritance, remaining outcasts in their own homes. D'Alembert was abandoned on the steps of the church by his mother, Mme. de Tencin who was host of one of the most important Paris salons; Julie de Lespinasse was a servant in her own father's house prior to being yoked to her aunt, Mme. du Deffand. Chamfort preferred silence to truth (or falsehood), a silence that served as his mask. Even his best friends knew little about him. Ginguené thought he was born poor; Roederer thought he was the son of a treasurer at the Sainte-Chapelle.[1] No one was fooled by Chamfort's noble name, but no one took offense either—as they did when La Harpe claimed descent from an old family. The nobility tolerated dubious pretenders on condition that they respect this remaining class bias. Chamfort did it so well that he really seemed to come from nowhere, like a meteor passing through the aristocratic heavens.

For this is precisely where remaining class prejudices lay. Worried about its legitimacy, the nobility clung to its rank. A distinction should be made here. The word "aristocracy," in general use only since 1750, was a vague term describing the real state of things—that is, hereditary domination by a minority. Nobility, on the other hand, referred to diverse categories, given a semblance of unity only in their unanimous hostility to the Revolution. Some titles dated to the time of the crusades (as did that of the Cisternes), some were acquired in the king's service (like that of the Dauphins), others were purchased along with land, and still others were usurped. Of all these groups, it was the small core of historic nobility which most strongly resisted the intrusion of writers, actors, and illegitimate children into its extremely hierarchized world, and which refused to become a class marked by its cultural prestige alone, the French expression of good fortune. Yet in 1763 this small core continued to symbolically dominate Paris (not to mention the provinces, where Jacqueline Cisternes de Vinzelles demonstrated the price she put on maintaining the old social order by abandoning Chamfort). History, however, often makes exceptions to the rule. Thus it recorded the suppers for painters given by Mme. Geoffrin (described by Mme. du Deffand as "that greasy omelette"). It valorized the elite which, influenced by the encyclopedists' ideas, effectively slid into irreligion. It reduced the reigns of Louis XV and Louis XVI to forerunners of revolution.

There were nevertheless salons where the names of Montmorency, Rohan, and La Trémoille remained unsurpassed in merit, where a marquis de Castries could be shocked at how often people mentioned Rousseau and Diderot (those people "living in garrets")![2] Or where a d'Ormesson could wonder out loud what people "like Corneille, Boileau, and La Fontaine" were good for—without coming up with an answer.[3] "In my youth," said Chamfort, "I once went to see M. Marmontel and M. d'Alembert on the same day. In the morning I went to M. Marmontel, who was then staying at Mme. Geoffrin's place; I knocked on the wrong door, and asked for M. Marmontel; the porter replied, 'M. de *Montmartel* [a well-known financier] no longer lives on these premises,' and gave me Montmartel's address. In the afternoon, I went to M. d'Alembert's place on rue Saint-Dominique. I asked for the exact address from a porter, who said, 'M. *Staremberg*, ambassador from Venice? Third door.'"[4] Thus a hard core refused to acknowledge the existence of upstarts and clung to the idea that it had nothing in common with anyone except God, "that Gentleman on high."[5]

Chamfort was wounded by such gibes (which also prompted Stendhal to observe that remarks like the one by M. de Castries merely helped to create a Robespierre).[6] He felt they revealed the very essence of the nobility, its *undisguised* truth. The social "racism" glorified by Saint-Simon only ten years years earlier was far from dead. In 1785, Madame Royale, Louis XVI's daughter, was amazed to discover that her maid had five fingers like herself. Polite manners, in Chamfort's view, simply masked a class determined to preserve the purity of its blood, whether that be at Clermont-Ferrand or at Paris. Concern for his life-style led M. de Mugiron to deliver a pastry cook to the gallows in place of the accused thief, his favorite chef. The French nobility, possessing the wealth of the most highly centralized country in Europe, had a single agenda: change everything so that nothing would change. Chamfort was "subject to the whims [of others]," said Aubin. Illegitimate and a writer, thus granted uncertain rank, Chamfort was inclined to see personal power struggles everywhere. Quite correctly, sometimes, to judge by Dr. Fournier (himself bourgeois, but then the bourgeois always overdid it), who greeted Mme. du Deffand on entering her salon with this deferential formula: "Madame, allow me the honor of offering my most humble respect." He then addressed Judge Hénault with a kindly, "Monsieur, my honored greetings," prior to turning to the illegitimate d'Alembert with a dry, "Hello."

From Rancor to Pleasure

Chamfort could have kept aloof from the game, remaining under the protection of the Philosophers' clan. In which case he would have enjoyed the salons of Julie de Lespinasse, Mme. Geoffrin, and Mme. Suard, as well as the friendship of his equals—d'Alembert, La Harpe—even if they overshadowed him literarily. But Chamfort refused to accept automatic inferiority to the aristocrats, whose "self-assured stupidity" and self-proclaimed superiority he always detested. Through a mixture of pride and taste for the challenge, Chamfort knocked at the most firmly shut doors. He was "gauche" in the beginning, according to Aubin, but the "actor" seized the unique opportunity to perfect himself, further forging the mask Nietzsche judged indispensable to all superior men, taming what he hated in order to suffer from it no longer. The paradoxes of the nobility seduced Chamfort, and he used them in winning it over, covertly regaining his social rank. "He imitated and surpassed that curtly flattering tone, that art of caressing people in high places with a sort of harshness which earned Duclos . . . the epithet of falsely honest."[7] Chamfort's style was born. The fruit of an effort accompanied by yet other efforts, it became the chamfered edge of his social revenge.

The marquis de Créquy once said to him: "But it seems to me,

Monsieur de Chamfort, that today a man of intellect is the equal of everyone, that a name counts for nothing."

"That's easy enough for you to say, Monsieur le marquis," retorted Chamfort, "but suppose that instead of M. de Créquy your name were simply M. Criquet [Cricket].[8]

Pure Chamfort, or the art of knowing exactly when to go too far.

Thus he began to dine with the devil. Fear gave way to pleasure; hatred was replaced by curiosity toward the class that received him. Aubin pointed out, "He threw himself in its arms . . . the way libertines usually seek women of whom they speak ill."[9] After the humiliation he experienced on leaving school, Chamfort was flattered at being received, and he quickly discovered this truth: high society respects those who appear to hold it in contempt. Similarly, noted Chamfort, "Genoa, rich and powerful, offered its sovereignty to several kings, who refused it. But they went to war over Corsica, which produced only chestnuts, yet remained proud and independent." The effect of surprise, however, soon wore off. France's former best pupil considered intelligence to be the only valid criterion, and therefore the values displayed in the Faubourg Saint-German appeared exotic to him. He analyzed the reflexes of the porter who dismissed him as well as those of the marquis who received him. He defined the laws society people obeyed without realizing it (the way "May beetles remain ignorant of natural history").[10] Chamfort's hierarchy was thus reestablished: intelligent where the nobility was not, he could dominate it, in turn, at the cost of a poorly disguised arrogance.

Others eventually might have become integrated, because Chamfort was at that age when one forgets oneself at the same time one makes oneself. He then would have become a larger-than-life "aristocrat." But Nicolas, that grocer's son whose place and whose birth certificate Chamfort took, was watching. (Nicolas's birth certificate would be found among Chamfort's papers on his death.) Nicolas would oblige Chamfort to keep that "lively and innate awareness of social differences" displayed by Stendhal's Julien Sorel (a disciple of Chamfort in many ways)[11] that success usually dispels. Capable of angering a duke, Chamfort would nevertheless fear the duke's contempt, that last privilege of a class Chamfort wanted to dominate without joining. By easing its rules of exclusion and opening the door a crack, the aristocracy won a measure of gratitude. Yet in a country still extremely hierarchical, it also whetted appetites hard to satisfy, awakening a social obsessiveness of which Chamfort is a typical example. He would relentlessly circle the idea of high so-

ciety, imagining urbane scenarios in which he would dispense pleasure along with punishment (somewhat the way de Sade, another
victim of willful confinement, would do in sexual terms). The aristocracy mapped out Chamfort's social geography, just as Greece had
provided his mental landscape.

Literature would act as counterpoint to this obsession. For the
first time, writing became a moral act, good in itself. Chamfort began writing edifying epistles, under the aegis of Antoine Léonard
Thomas, a sort of secular Bossuet with a wide following despite his
bombastic style (which Voltaire found utterly "Thomsensical"). Totally forgotten today, Thomas was a professor turned writer who
also hailed from Clermont-Ferrand. In 1764, however, the thirty-
two-year-old Thomas was champion of the academic eulogy, thanks
to apologia on behalf of Descartes, Friedrich II, Marshal de Saxe, and
other philosophical and military lights of Europe. At one time reserved for saints alone, the eulogy retained a hagiographical facet
even as it became secular. Great men, especially great writers, had to
be irreproachable (just as, these days, they're supposed to be monstrous). Thomas thus became the second moral reference point,
after Rousseau, in the post-*Encyclopédie* period, all the while remaining within the "clan." (A virgin, Thomas penned an *Essay on Women*
felt to be rather cold—"to be expected," went the criticism, "he
never fully entered into his subject.") He would influence Chamfort's written style just as Duclos—in a radically different way—
influenced Chamfort's spoken style.

For at that time Chamfort considered literature to be an indirect
response to the amorality of his times. Through literature he could
praise the loftiness of writers over the lowliness of courtiers, the brilliance of enlightenment over the shadows of obscurantism, the
uniqueness of genius over the anonymity of his contemporaries. He
would target "prestigious genres"—Tragedy and, to a lesser extent,
Eulogy—in the same way he targeted prestigious social circles.
He disdained more "common" exercises such as the novel, fact-
ual accounts, and "autobiography" (in particular those singular
versions—some predating Rousseau's *Confessions*—by people such
as Rétif de La Bretonne, the comte de Lauraguais, and Chabanon,
this latter a precursor of Proustian introspection, according to a recent critic).

But here again Chamfort was divided. Wavering, indecisive, his
literary personality would be subject to every influence before coming into its own. Salon literature and comedy (which had worked well

with *La jeune indienne*) continued to tempt him all the more strongly since they offered more concrete returns. But when the highly popular comic playwright Charles Collé lucidly noted that Chamfort would have to frequent the common people for a long time before acquiring real theatrical insight ("but I doubt he'll ever acquire it," added Collé), Chamfort abandoned comedy to compete for the Académie française poetry prize, based on a subject inspired by Rousseau's *Emile: A Father Writes to His Son on the Birth of a Grandson*.[12]

Mocking the mores of Catholic teachers but recognizing the usefulness of the church, biting but never drawing blood, Chamfort won the prize for his *Epistle* in August 1764, awarded by a jury on which two of his patrons—Duclos and d'Alembert—were members. Grimm praised "the young, poor, yet proud poet" whom the Jesuit press itself congratulated, whereas a latter-day Jansenist unsuccessfully demanded that "the puny sprout from the encyclopedic colossus" be censored.[13] Chamfort then sent the text to his old Greek teacher, begging pardon for Nicolas. "I always liked Nicolas," replied Lebeau the elder, "I admire Chamfort." Legend has it that master and pupil tearfully embraced one another.

Falling Out with Rousseau

Chamfort sent his *Epître d'un père* to the author of *Emile*, assuring Rousseau: "Everywhere I encounter only people who respect you, honor you, revere you. . . . Even those who persecuted you assert, in apparent good faith, that it was with regret that they were obliged to do their duty."[14] This was an unforgivable mistake. For Rousseau valued his enemies, just as Voltaire valued his friends. He wanted it to be said of him that, like Jesus, he came to be among men, but men did not understand him. "The consequences of this affair have plunged me into an abyss of misfortune from which I shall not emerge in my lifetime, but I don't begrudge these gentlemen," Rousseau wrote back. "I know . . . that my existence and my fate don't interest them in the least. I happened to be in their path like a stone that one encounters and heedlessly shoves out of the way with a foot."[15] This was touching modesty perhaps, but at Chamfort's expense. Although Chamfort's epistle follows *Emile* in advising parents to raise their own children in order to spare them human wickedness, Rousseau accused Chamfort of "undermining the foundations of morality" through "overly philosophical" concepts. He challenged Chamfort to prove, by a second epistle, that men have inherent vices—and also virtues. Chamfort could put up with Rousseau's accusations of following "fashionable metaphysics" and with being treated as a poor student by the man he had written to "as a father." But he took badly Rousseau's reproach for having mimicked "a grandfather at [your] age."

This unflattering comparison to the actors whom Rousseau wanted to drive out of Geneva prompted Chamfort's cutting allusion in his reply: "I confess that I had to dress myself up a little, but I truly felt what I put in the character's mouth. The teacher in *Emile* would be no less interesting even if he had not educated his charming pupil."[16] This was going too far for Rousseau, whose children regularly headed for charitable institutions.

The imitation of Jean-Jacques came to an end (though not of his social teachings). Some people wear themselves out by imitating a model. But Chamfort would come to increasingly resemble his true self—not literarily but personally. Hardly a lover of nature (except in books), often impassioned but rarely lyrical, wanting simply to introduce a little "wildness" into his makeup as social actor, Chamfort would never be a "preromantic." He was so mistrustful of human nature that he penned for Rousseau this still highly hypothetical declaration: "Considering that virtue is always dangerous, or at least useless, and vice always fortunate in the popular sense of the term, what is a lofty soul to do? . . . Take refuge in a sensible and unshakeable pride, a sort of misanthropy which lets him love mankind in general yet holds individuals at bay, save those to whom he is attached by natural duty."

The encounter would nevertheless mark Chamfort. Man is a sovereign moral unit, claimed Jean-Jacques; Chamfort would forevermore see himself as a republic unto himself, an independent state for which he was both diplomat and soldier, constantly protecting the frontiers of his identity in order to avoid splitting into a Nicolas and a Vinzelles.

4. HERCULEAN ADONIS

What does a young man find, on entering high society? People who want to be his patron. . . . If he has little wit, little breeding, few principles, and if he doesn't notice . . . that they want to control him, if he becomes the tool of the people with a hold over him, then he is considered charming.

Chamfort

Chamfort entered his most rakish phase. Handsome, tall for his day at five feet eight inches, with blue eyes and flared nostrils,[1] he used his physical grace and studied attire to begin a career at age twenty-four as a seducer. Mme. de Craon, following ardent "instruction," said to her friends: "You think he's only an Adonis, yet he's Hercules."[2] The compliment caught on, even quicker than *La jeune indienne*. Chamfort became known as the writer with "exquisite sensitivity" and uncommon energy. Women effectively if unofficially reigned over society, like Mme. de Pompadour over Louis XV. They could make or break ministers and academicians, with pillow talk or in the convenient intimacy of carriages called *vis-à-vis*, "where—face to face—eyes meet, breaths mingle, legs entwine" according to the Goncourts. Women brought writers and patrons together in their salons, where conversations in their presence acquired a mellowness long since lost (even scholars abandoned specialized terms in favor of that French Rivarol praised as universal). Women not only had a decisive impact on Chamfort's career, they made their mark everywhere, whether as socialites, the demi-monde, or the favorites of a king with a particularly large sexual appetite. Men reportedly became their puppets. Here again the eighteenth century innovated, freeing the second sex from its silent role and granting it the status of mandatory go-between—as though diplomacy, politics, and literature could no longer be conducted independent of desire.

Such influence may have been largely a question of appearances, but in those days appearance counted. Male faces were adorned with beauty marks, and Quentin de La Tour embellished his pastels with rouge. The ceilings of the "pleasure houses" designed by Ledoux (which financiers had built for their "dancers") were enlivened by nymphs and goddesses painted by Nattier, de Troy, and Boucher (and, in an obsessively undressed state, by Schall). Bronze, wood, and clocks all imitated feminine curves, lead-ing to rococo intoxication with garlands of breasts, rumps, and feet designed to delight and titillate.

Women reigned—not love. For love supposed sublimation and sacrifice, two vestiges of a Christianity on the decline. Love pro-voked anxiety or elation, and French culture demanded self-control. Sex, on the other hand, was delightfully suited to an era unfamiliar with the idea of sin, in which everything glorified sensual pleasure, from poetry to painting, from the shape of divans to the plunge of neckline, from garden arbors to temples dedicated to Venus. "We attract, we take; we tire, we forsake," commented the prince de Ligne.[3] Faithfulness was considered lowly, love between spouses misplaced. Couples no longer slept together; they slept around to-gether. The bed became the last battlefield in a nation at peace—and also the first on which a bastard could shine. Launched by Mme. de Craon, the Herculean Adonis slid himself between the sheets of a caste with which he remained in constant rivalry. Yet he finally reaped the rewards of his departure from Grassins. Now envied—supreme luxury—the inglorious abbé had become a glorious liber-tine.

Beauty was one injustice Chamfort bore lightly. Loved effort-lessly, he forgot the "irreproachable" conduct of which he boasted to Rousseau—women were the first "moral units" to lose their sov-ereignty. Some of them complained, but no one objects to success for long. "Love, such as it exists in high society, is merely an exchange of whims and the contact of skins," became Chamfort's most famous epigram.[4] It summed up his times and his social debut. Stendhal would later reproach him for being content with this "cold and pretty miniature."[5] But, like his conversation, it lent Chamfort the illusion of being an aristocrat, along with that blasé attitude for which he had reproached his own generation not long before.

Everything seemed to click. La jeune indienne was performed be-fore Louis XV, and the papers published his correspondence with Rousseau. D'Alembert, Duclos, and Thomas were his patrons. He announced that he was undertaking two tragedies, Polyxena and Ino.[6] He was at that age where he thought he could re-do books he admired and write the way he talked. "I would go to see him every morning," wrote Aubin. "We would read Ariosto and Voltaire's La pucelle [The maiden] together, comparing the original with the imita-

tion, around a small stove which dried out our books. . . . Then I let
him return to the social whirlwind, which he would dissect the next
day, for me who fled it just as he sought it."[7]

In terms of appearances, nothing had changed. Living in a small
house on rue Notre-Dame-des-Victoires,[8] he remained a poor
young man. He made the acquaintance of another Auvergnat, Abbé
Delille, who already passed for a major poet, but his real friends
were literary beginners, with the exception of La Harpe. These included Aubin—remembered only for his publication of Chamfort's
most famous sayings—and Sélis, a young teacher of rhetoric in
Amiens who was amassing "material for a vast reputation." Sélis,
however, would amount to little more than an early biographer of
the Herculean Adonis, after having translated the stoic Persius ("but
the translation still needs to be translated," commented La Harpe).

The Perfect Family

Yet the virtuous Thomas had introduced Chamfort to an influential
courtier, the comte d'Angiviller, who took a liking to the young man.
Chamfort soon confided to Rousseau, "Knowing him perfectly, as I
do, he is virtue on earth, the most incorruptible virtue"; Chamfort
referred to the comte d'Angiviller as being among those influential
people who revered *Emile*.[9] Astonished to find an honest man at
court, a pure soul within that temple of intrigue, Chamfort dropped
whatever reservations remained when this Gentleman to the Royal
Children granted him a small income of 600 livres "despite
[Angiviller's] very modest fortune." Chamfort displayed no arrogance in describing this encounter, perhaps because it seemed
natural to him. Angiviller, responsible for educating the three
brothers who would one day succeed Louis XV (Louis XVI, Louis
XVIII, and Charles X), domesticated the writer who was sought after
by influential people "because he seemed to flee them."[10] This courtier thus became Chamfort's first benefactor; he was already a
browbeating patron to Auvergne writers Marmontel and Thomas. It
was through Angiviller that Chamfort became friends with Ducis,
that misanthrope who spat on the ground every morning from the
garret in which the count had housed him, before getting down to
an adaptation of Shakespeare.

The comte d'Angiviller was a complex character. Politically, he
was as hesitant—or prudent—as Chamfort, being associated with
the sanctimonious Dauphin as well as d'Alembert (who called him

the "angel Gabriel"). Angiviller occupied the intersection at court, where Rousseau's followers met the Physiocrats (such as Quesnay and Mirabeau the elder, who preached free grain trade and limited state intervention). This high-ranking royal servant used his image as an "outspoken old Roman" to mask an ambitiousness and adaptability that impressed a courtier like Bombelles, and that should have earned him the post of Master of Revels (equivalent to today's Minister of Culture). Chamfort, however, thoroughly surprised to discover an aristocrat with whom he could discuss Rousseau and through whom he could morally justify his snobbery, saw Angiviller only as a sublimated father.

While Angiviller tempered Chamfort socially, it was Mme. de Marchais, the count's mistress, who finally drew him into the elite of the Ancien Régime. She invited him along on picnics around the Gobert ponds in Versailles as well as to her suppers on rue de l'Oratoire, which were among the finest in the capital. Even shorter than La Harpe, Mme. de Marchais nevertheless completely dominated the authoritarian Angiviller, who usually remained mute in her presence. Perhaps because she was much richer, more generous and eccentric than he, but also because she could discuss metaphysics as well as flowers in a light tone her lover lacked (underscored by her doll-like feet, long ashen hair, and gypsy-style dresses—a fairy straight out of some tale). Mme. de Marchais was good and generous by nature but had become "catty by imitation" after having long been snubbed by a Versailles that found "something inferior" about her; she was capable of turning her back on the author she was feting to whisper about his book, "It's dull, so dull it makes you sick." This woman, whom Chamfort would list as one of society's four best actresses (but whom others found mincing), successfully used her salon to pull off a marriage between the style of a class and the ideas of a generation, between talent and noble birth, between Philosophy and Court. "Society people left more enlightened, literary people left more amiable," said d'Alembert, describing an arrangement that suited Chamfort after a debut hampered by his social paranoia. The Herculean Adonis discovered a milieu nostalgic for the complete Renaissance man, after a fashion; inspired by Laborde, Mme. de Marchais's brother, it was able to shift its interest from a ballet score to a projected transoceanic canal at Lake Nicaragua, from a collection of maxims to the construction of a clavichord according to Pythagorean principles. All this dazzled the illegitimate offspring of a rather narrow provincial aristocracy; in-

vited to Mme. de Marchais's Versailles residence, Chamfort probably saw the "immortal" comte de Saint-Germain play the air that the
count supposedly heard on Alexander's entry into Babylon.

The Golden Age

It was already flattering to be in the good graces of a woman related
to Mme. de Pompadour (via her mother's first marriage); but it
would be even better to be her protégé. Mme. de Marchais, despairing of ever entering the Académie herself despite d'Alembert's
promises to open it to women, shifted her ambition onto Chamfort.
With a Rousseau-inspired "father" who was educating the king's
grandchildren and an Académie-oriented godmother, the illegitimate son found the perfect family. In his euphoria, Chamfort confided the secret of his real birth to Angiviller. Laborde, meanwhile,
engaged him as librettist, thus completing Chamfort's adoption.

Jean-Benjamin de Laborde (not to be confused with the banker
Alexandre de Laborde) was born into a dynasty of *fermiers généraux*
(tax collectors) and was a confidant of Louis XV, yet dreamed of
being recognized as a full-fledged musician. He explained his fever-
ish ambition in his own way: "The love of peace of mind keeps men
in perpetual agitation." Unsurprisingly, this collaboration between
Rameau's former student and Chamfort didn't get off to a good
start. The protagonists of *Amours de gonesse* [*Loves of a little brat*],
for example, sang: "You there?"—"Who's there?"—"Oh, you rascal!"—"Who's a rascal?"; the show was hooted at the Théâtre des
Italiens in May 1765.[11] The pair nevertheless got back together for
the celebrations at Fontainebleau marking the fiftieth anniversary of
Louis XV's accession to the throne. The results were once again disappointing. The king didn't like *Palmyra*, and *Zénis et Almasie* fell flat
on November 2, in spite of Chamfort's highly personal libretto. "It's
about a father who, to test his son's virtue . . . treats him as a wretch
until, after a thousand cruel torments, he reveals himself to be the
boy's dear father," reported Grimm.[12] But the failure of this oedipal
ballet was offset by the success of *Diane et Endymion*, in which fourteen Cupids forge their arrows before falling asleep on their anvils,
and where the apparition of a starry Lunar Palace sent the court into
raptures.

Although Grimm had described him as a simpleton, Chamfort
was content. The theaters were swarming with his nymphs, the
great Jélyotte and the famous Sophie Arnould were singing his

lines. Flippant and inventive, he was certain that writing for the theater was his true calling. Mlle. Guimard, who played in *Zénis et Almasie*, became his mistress. Diaphanous—the Goncourts would later say that she invented the "psychic dance"—yet sensual and even lewd, she forgot her salaried liaison with Laborde once in Chamfort's arms. Mlle. Guimard was short and slender, well turned out, but only barely pretty, yet she represented the consecration of the Herculean Adonis's dazzling career. "Her features were so fine that at the age of forty-five, she appeared to be no more than fifteen on stage," noted Mme. Vigée-Lebrun in her memoirs. True enough, since Mlle. Guimard made herself up each morning in front of the portrait the divine Fragonard had painted of her around 1769. Although she and Chamfort had the same patron and almost the same profession—seduction—their love in the heavens of Versailles was fleeting; the dancer, described in a contemporary police report as having the finest breasts in the world, never alotted her lovers more than two weeks.

Chamfort, in extolling his golden age, wrote:

Temps heureux où régnaient Louis et Pompadour!
Temps heureux où chacun ne s'occupait en France
Que de vers, de romans, de musique, de danse . . .
Le seul soin qu'on connût était celui de plaire;
On dormait deux la nuit, on riait tout le jour.[13]

Happy times when Louis reigned with Pompadour!
Happy times when everyone in France
Indulged in poems, novels, music, dance . . .
The only care we had, was how to please;
We slept in twos by night, by day laughed all the more.

5. SHATTERED ILLUSIONS

Nature never urged me, "Be not poor," much less, "Be rich." Instead, she shouts: "Be independent."

Chamfort

Fortune will come my way only if it meets those conditions that my character dictates.

Chamfort

Chamfort, poor and worthy, was liked. But success—and probably Laborde's jealousy—changed everything. D'Angiviller was "the most virtuous man in the kingdom," according to Chamfort, and virtue is demanding. A difference arose, which the courtier described, after the Revolution, as follows: "That Chamfort, the illegitimate son of a cook who had spent all her savings to educate her children, left his wretched, aged mother housed in a sixth [floor apartment] with sixty livres of income, while he lived dressed in lace and velvet, with ladies from the opera and comic theater. I issued a sharp and stiff—though not severe—reprimand: *inde irae* [hence the wrath]."[1] That, at least, is what Angiviller said after reading the passage in Chamfort's *Maximes* where he was belittled, though not by name.[2] Despite the circumstances, Angiviller's account appears to accurately explain why their relationship cooled after 1765. "When I was young," Chamfort admitted, "driven by passions and drawn to them in society . . . I was lectured on the love of seclusion and work, and was overwhelmed with pedantic sermons."

Chamfort did not deserve Angiviller's tirade. All his friends described Chamfort as very devoted to his mother, taking care of her needs before his own with "truly filial piety," according to Pierre-Louis Ginguené. Seeing her, added Sélis, meant a return "to obscurity, for her sake only." Chamfort's reaction to Angiviller thus stemmed from the confidence he had placed in the count. Furious at having dropped his social mask in front of Angiviller only to be reminded of his background, Chamfort henceforth kept his distance. Laborde was left to his dreams of recognition—"a strange obsession
38 for a very wealthy man who wasn't a professional musician, and

whom God created to be useless," commented Grimm.[3] The aristocratic mirage dissolved, and Chamfort rediscovered old values:

> *La nature toujours rend la naissance égale.*
> *Ce n'est qu'en s'illustrant qu'on met un intervalle*
> *Entre tous les mortels et soi.*[4]

Birth is, by nature, equally based.
It is only by excelling that distance is placed
between all mortals and oneself.

He would never again sacrifice his ambition to that of an amateur, nor reveal secrets to a courtier more demanding of others than
of himself. Nor would he ever again subscribe to inequality—except
perhaps in those areas in which he excelled. This marks the true
start of his antiaristocratic paranoia, which seemed almost "out of
date" in a Paris increasingly won over by the marriage of talent and
noble particle, where writing almost conferred a sort of noble title.

It should be stressed that Chamfort was not acting out of egalitarianism but out of anger at seeing his ideal hierarchy betrayed.
"When Montaigne said, referring to nobility, 'Since we can't attain
it, let's get even by maligning it,' his comment was amusing, often
true, but scandalous, for it provided ammunition to the fools whom
fortune has favored. Inequality of station is often loathed out of pettiness; but a truly wise and honest man can loathe it as the barrier
separating souls made to come together. . . . Instead of repeating
Montaigne's remark, this latter might say, 'I loathe nobility which
made me flee that which I loved or would have loved.' "[5] Such frustration would profoundly mark the writer torn between awareness
of his talent and the fact of his poverty.

Fairy godmother Mme. de Marchais remained aloof from the
break between the men, and Chamfort continued to be her protégé;
he regularly suggested charity cases needing attention, and she, in
return, provided invitations to sessions of the Académie. Nor was
Laborde himself repudiated right away. In 1766, Chamfort wrote a
letter of recommendation to Voltaire on behalf of Laborde and his
sister, prior to their stay at Ferney. Yet such esteem would not live
on. "I feel for M. de La B. the emotion felt by a gentleman passing
before the grave of a friend," he observed in his *Maximes*.

As to Angiviller, Chamfort would get even in his own way—by
doing exactly the opposite of what was advised. The Herculean
Adonis multiplied his affairs in a frenzy of pleasure, using women

once again to settle scores with the nobility. Intoxicated by success, he boasted so much that he drove his friend Aubin away. But the young cock would soon sing a different tune. He was stricken in the eyes, ears, chest, and bladder, was unable to read or even walk, and had to call in the doctors. All noted an "excess of humor" but were unable to identify a disease thought at the time to be venereal (probably incorrectly).[6] "His nerves were affected," wrote Ginguené, ". . . his complexion [lost] its color." Everything attractive about him suddenly had a repulsive side—including his personality. His life, which he had seen as infinitely expanding, was reduced to several square feet. Baths, naps, and dermatological treatments replaced the "contact of skins." He had been the "hunter," but now he found that his prey had turned. He had wagered on his physique, now he had to hide it. Deprived of his single social advantage, he now modeled his life along the games of chess he played at the Café de la Régence—for the time being, every pawn would count.

The Misanthrope Reborn

The eighteenth century displayed a certain heroism through its very frivolity. "In those days, we knew how to laugh and how to die," wrote Aurore de Saxe, George Sand's grandmother. "If you had gout, you walked anyway, without grimacing. . . . We thought it preferable to die at a ball or at the comic theater rather than in bed surrounded by candles and nasty men in black."[7] But Chamfort wanted no more of that life, of that aristocratic stoicism. His adoption having failed, he retreated to his room where he received only two or three friends. Wounded socially by Angiviller, the Herculean Adonis was then physically wounded by the dancer or "tart" who disfigured him; seeing his strength slip away and his elegance turn harsh, he decided to protect himself against society. Already nostalgic for lost omnipotence, he chose a new, revealing emblem— a tortoise, head poking out of its shell and struck by an arrow, bearing the motto, "Happy had it been completely hidden."[8] His "heroic" destiny began where Achilles' had ended—with a wound which, having failed to kill him, would deepen with every crisis, hurling him into a sea of melancholy and blackness. At twenty-five, Chamfort was already crippled.

The origin of his misanthropy has been endlessly discussed.[9] Some attribute it to his literary failure, long after his illness struck. Others consider it a reaction to his own weakness—his sensitivity, his idealism—that Chamfort masked by his hardness, fooling even himself. Gabor has suggested that Chamfort did not want to be a hammer but merely wanted to avoid being the aristocracy's anvil. It would appear nevertheless that his misanthropy, like his fear of himself and his hatred of rank, was a basic feature of his personality. Rousseau, that other misanthrope, had already detected this in Chamfort's *Epître d'un père*. Chamfort had always mistrusted men, for high society bred self-hatred, he believed, just as it had pushed his mother to abandon him. This latter event was etched in a dark corner of his mind which the Enlightenment would never illuminate. His real mother's act of rejection—brought to the surface again by Angiviller who provoked a second exclusion from the nobility (at least from Chamfort's paranoid point of view)—was the original sin which justified the radical, Pascal-like pessimism he henceforth espoused.

For as early as 1765, every individual was considered suspect, every relationship dangerous. "Never give anyone any rights over you," he wrote to a friend (perhaps the young philosopher Suard, unless it was intended for himself).[10] "The uprightness of your character may subsequently oblige you to stop seeing them, and you will appear ungrateful. Politely keep everyone at a great distance. Prostrate yourself in declining offers. I believe in friendship, I believe in love—the concept is essential to my happiness; but I believe even more that wisdom dictates that I renounce hope of finding a mistress and a friend able to fulfill my soul. I know that what I say makes you shudder; but . . . my reasons for distrusting mankind are such that I think I can be excused."[11]

Just as, at age twenty, he could have remained outside the salons—though they were indispensable to any literary recognition—Chamfort could have ignored the question of his birth. For at that time there was a writer who served as exact counterpart and who would be—for a while—his friend: Abbé Delille. Delille was also illegitimate, also from Auvergne, and ugly and one-eyed as well. Baron de Frénilly described him as "slender, tiny, and light as a quill," yet Delille was born happy and would remain so all his life, to the point of quirkiness. He did not appear to suffer from being a "beggar" in front of nobles. But herein lay an injustice as great as illegitimacy: Chamfort had a limited talent for happiness. Angiviller and illness were all that were needed to reawaken the rancor lurking in him, the misanthrope later accused of having created man in his own image.

Farewell to Women

His complex over his illegitimacy became more apparent; the stain of his birth became more visible. Twice rejected, he prepared to reject everyone. Barbey d'Aurevilly would describe him as a "born malcontent." But Chamfort's various aversions are linked to the various meanings of the word "abandon." One minute of abandon was all Eve needed to beget mankind's misfortune, was all Jacqueline de Vinzelles needed to engender Chamfort's own, was all he himself needed to fall ill. Up to that point, women had been desired "unrestrainedly," but now they were merely the perfunctory expression of his sexuality. Chamfort dressed poorly, let himself go. Wounded, he wanted to wound in turn. "The moment when youthful illusions and passions are shattered often provokes sorrow," he observed; "but sometimes we come to hate the glamour which deceived us"—a comment that applies equally to Angiviller. "It was Armida herself who burned and destroyed the palace where she was bewitched." His misogyny became pronounced, a millstone that still weighs heavy today, as Camus has pointed out. But on Chamfort's behalf it should be said that women then were not like women now. The latter claim autonomy, the former wanted to impose their dependence. They were brought up to seduce, were frivolous almost out of duty, and enjoyed an adoration typically tempered by a contempt discernible even within their own ranks. "Women never get to the bottom of anything," said Mme. Necker,[12] annoyed by the capriciousness of her own sex. The vanity, coquettishness, and plotting are all familiar. No longer familiar, however, is the extent to which women enjoyed using cunning to conquer, the conquest being just a temporary tool in a larger rivalry with other women. This is how Laclos, in *Les liaisons dangereuses*, has Valmont express contemporary attitudes: "The most adroit man can do no more than keep pace with the most sincere woman."[13]

Such distrust was accompanied by an almost total hostility to the idea of marriage for a writer. The salons wanted them single, and writers worried that they might be disturbed by a wife. Diderot would even say to Chamfort "that a sensible man of letters could be the lover of a woman who has produced a book, but should be the husband only of one who knows how to produce a shirt."[14] Chamfort certainly sharpened the dig by rejecting both possibilities. He ferreted out the absurdities of marriage, the noxious influence of "females," the incompatibility of the sexes. But he also underlined society's wrongs and the privileges of males. "Women start a war in which men enjoy the great advantage of having all the hussies on their side."[15] Yet Chamfort found himself unequal to the conflict once some tart had wounded him, and the intensity of his misogyny soon matched that of his misanthropy. Women became the symbol of everything false, of ubiquitous role playing, of the civilization of the mask. "The heart must either break or turn to bronze."[16] Not his wittiest or best-known aphorism—but his truest. It expresses his terror of total defeat and his determination to live despite his affliction. He went from "actor in spite of himself" (his definition of a high-society creature)[17] to "man of bronze." "Guard yourself against all intense and profound feeling," he urged his friend. ". . . Don't fear losing, thereby, the sensitivity necessary to a man of letters—the dose you've already received is too large, nothing can exhaust it. Reading excellent books will sustain it better." Here began Chamfort's total commitment to literature, in the name of healthy skepticism, industry, frugality. These antiaristocratic values were designed to efface the Angiviller episode (even though they were precisely the ones advocated by the count) and to return Chamfort to his earlier economic modesty—to his *truth*. This austerity program superseded the life-style outlined prior to *La jeune indienne*, replacing the period of "We attract, we take" with "I want to neither give nor take."[18] Chamfort henceforth would harden around his individualism, accumulating defenses and masks—the very weapons used by the aristocracy and by women. Still hoping to become an Achilles *with no heel*, he rejected all forms of subjugation and dependence. He even left a mistress he loved, claimed Roederer, as soon as she mentioned marriage. He intended to be his own master—a master who nevertheless became as oppressive as a dictator, who replaced the "republic" with tyranny, who hardened Chamfort to the point of self-destruction.

But this agenda was so hard, so desperate for a century so enlightened, that Chamfort kept it secret. Almost shocked by it himself, he immediately admitted to his friend, "If someone were naturally what I counsel you to be, I would flee him wholeheartedly." And so Chamfort let himself be seduced by the only case he had not foreseen—that of a young, pretty woman who wished him well, who was as straightforward as civilization was complicated. Mme. Saurin was "frank, lively, natural, intellectual and good," according to Frénilly, and lavished "all the attention of friendship" on Chamfort during his withdrawal. Advising him to "reason little" but "feel much," she succeeded in dragging him to her husband's home. M. Saurin, a Philosopher in his sixties who owed his fame to the tragedy *Spartacus*, proposed a toast to the Supreme Being every day in gratitude for having been given such a perfect wife. There Chamfort discovered simple, almost provincial surroundings where the clan's young hopefuls met—a world that could have been his, had he so wished. Slowly, the cripple became reaccustomed to the human race.

He remained firm on one key point, however: never again would he be dependent on the aristocracy. Abbé Delaroche, a modest writer associated with the Saurins, unsuccessfully proposed that Chamfort replace him as companion to the two sons of an English lord touring Italy. The sum involved was substantial, but the educational trip was to last two years; Chamfort, already feeling better, had other ambitions for himself. Delaroche's offer yielded only "a tender, mutual friendship never refuted by either party for so much as an instant," noted Ginguené.

Bébé's Initial Tantrums

But Chamfort's "tyrannical" agenda also owed much to a change in attitude on the part of La Harpe, for their romance had not survived Chamfort's growing notoriety. Late in 1765, Bébé had taken several weeks to transmit an invitation to visit Ferney, obliging Chamfort to apologize humbly to Voltaire who, victim of one of those chronic attacks designed to test his popularity, wound up canceling all visits. The incident forgotten, Chamfort dropped by in the spring of 1766 to read La Harpe the speech he had written for the Académie.[19] As soon as Chamfort had finished, Bébé stood up to read his own speech, despite their agreement to not enter the same contests. "Save your strength for the theater," Chamfort suggested, but Bébé only snickered.[20]

Defeat was total. Beaten by La Harpe, beaten even by Fontaine-Malherbe (whose poems he had corrected in school), Chamfort finished a good fourth. Thomas vainly reminded him that Voltaire had also encountered setbacks. "Show me my conqueror, and I shall rush to embrace him," went Chamfort's speech—but he did not have the strength to do so. Voltaire intervened at that point and invited them both to write a play at Ferney. "You have a brother in him," wrote Voltaire to Bébé, ". . . highly worthy of your friendship."[21] Chamfort dropped the theme of Ino and Falkland for a more

topical subject—the rivalry between Sultan Suleiman's two sons—
and prepared to write a tragedy—Roxelane—under the eye of his
revered contemporary. But La Harpe managed to exclude Chamfort
from the trip and left for Ferney accompanied only by his wife.

Bébé shared the patriarch's meals and promenades for several
months, performing Voltaire's plays in the little private theater and
occasionally correcting them. Voltaire would merely say, "The little
fellow's right, it's better that way." For the charms of Bébé's wife (a
launderer's daughter whom he had married at nineteen) helped La
Harpe become the favored disciple of Voltaire, who had never set
eyes on Chamfort. Denied equality, barely tolerated as a protégé,
Chamfort once again found justification—even more clearly than
with Angiviller—for his misanthropy.

Chamfort was never particularly modest. "Vain, steeped in his
little airs" according to Grimm, Chamfort had a high idea of himself
early on. La Harpe's attitude nevertheless obliged him to step up the
bluster, to assert himself as an author in his own right, to become his
own patron. Paris, it should be remembered, was teeming with literati. The resulting fisticuffs were followed breathlessly by every court
in Europe via literary correspondence. All blows were permitted,
from betrayal to spectacular shifts of allegiance, to denunciations to
the police (for whom the young Suard was said to work as a spy).
Everyone raised his voice to be heard. As described by Diderot in
Rameau's Nephew, every invitation was to be accepted but gratitude
never expressed (for fear of appearing to be a mere *client*). Everyone
became his own barker. Writers at the end of the Ancien Régime
were primarily endowed with the gifts of megalomania, arrogance,
and self-indulgence. Up until 1780, Chamfort fit this mold. Though
it should be pointed out that he was more intelligent than average—
if no more talented—and had a "friendship" with La Harpe in
which any form of modesty was not only unadvisable but poten-
tially fatal.

6. LITTLE BALLOON

Concord between brothers is so rare that fables mention only two amicable brothers, and assume that they never see each other.

Chamfort

Chamfort resolved to apply his new policy to Bébé—yet once again without total conviction. "You have three sorts of friend in polite society, M—— used to say. Friends who are fond of you; friends who are unconcerned about you; and friends who detest you."[1] La Harpe apparently belonged to this latter category. Determined not to continue playing second fiddle to a second fiddle, Chamfort recommenced his tragedy, *Roxelane*.

To his great amazement, however, the piece did not progress. "I fear there are greater resemblances than I had first thought," he wrote to the virtuous Thomas.[2] "I fear similarities with the two brothers in *Rodogune*, those in *Héraclius*, those in *Adélaïde du Guesclin*, the father of *Andromaque* . . . and scenes from *Oreste et Pylade*." Crushed by this heavy legacy, he tottered. But Thomas caught him, and Chamfort retired to Meudon. There Roxelane became Suleiman—a change that changed nothing. "I was very enamored of my new approach," he explained to Thomas, "but then doubts arose."[3] Torn between conflicting ideas, Chamfort set Suleiman aside in order to measure himself directly against La Harpe. Armed with a map of France, he assessed his chances. Toulouse organized the *Jeux floraux* ([Floral games], in which the revolutionary poet Fabre would one day win the nickname "Eglantine"). There were also contests in Rouen, Marseille, Dijon. Recalling the Competitive Exam, he began to train for five of these academic Olympics; victory would normally open the doors to the Académie française.

The first confrontation took place in Toulouse, where he received a Gold Amaranth.[4] He won again in Marseille—but only barely.[5] The struggle continued in Rouen and Paris, where Bébé was crowned victor.[6] But in August 1767, it was Chamfort who successfully proved the extent to which the genius of great writers influences the spirit of their century in *Combien le génie des grands écrivains influe l'esprit de leur siècle*. Concerned to maintain harmony within his empire, Voltaire swore that La Harpe "cherished" his adversary.[7] No one was convinced.

An incident then complicated the issue: Bébé left Ferney with several of Voltaire's manuscripts in order to peddle them to a bookseller. Initially incredulous, the "good father" finally excommunicated his top "angel," who was already reeling from several flops at the theater. Chamfort, a good sport, withdrew from the Paris contest in order to prepare an epistle on Anglomania and the Juvenilia[8] (which would never see the light of day), thus leaving the August 1768 prize to La Harpe. Unable to win a friend, Chamfort at least hoped to lose an enemy.

Yet the victor was Abbé Sabatin de Langeac, a child of fifteen whose mother was sleeping with the minister who oversaw the Académie. Marmontel, a Philosopher who had written Sabatin's speech and rigged the voting out of personal motives, announced the results.[9] Shouts broke out, and a regiment from Les Invalides was called out to reinforce the porters guarding the entrance to the room in the Louvre where the Académie was then housed. Chamfort led the crowd into an adjoining room. Marmontel read the winner's speech in his Auvergnat accent—and was immediately parodied by one of the demonstrators. "That's truly appalling!" shouted Marmontel through the wall. To general glee, the same comment was instantly applied to his own speech. Marmontel was then approached by "a young poet . . . fairly talented, with the handsomest appearance in the world, the finest self-importance." Chamfort. "But he was just a little balloon, which releases a violent wind when pricked,"[10] continued Diderot in his description to his mistress, Sophie Volland. The little balloon began thus: " 'The piece which you have chosen, Monsieur, must be excellent.' Marmontel: 'And why is that?' Chamfort: 'Because it would seem to be better than the one by La Harpe.' Marmontel: 'It could be better than one you refer to and yet not be worth much.' Chamfort: 'But I've seen the latter.' Marmontel: 'And you found it good?' Chamfort: 'Very good.' Marmontel: 'Then you're not very well versed in the matter.' Chamfort: 'But if La Harpe's is bad, and if it is nevertheless better than the one by young Sabatin, doesn't that make the latter appalling?' Marmontel: 'And why didn't you raise this question when your own entry won the prize?' etc. Thus Marmontel whipped that little balloon Chamfort."

Thinking he had regained a friend by defending La Harpe before their "Philosophical" elder, Chamfort proposed a deal. "Let's divide up the world, like the triumvirate," he said, leaving La Harpe first choice. Bébé, feeling thwarted, said, "I'll take the Académie Française and the La Rochelle Prize."[11] A break was once again inevitable. Galvanized by another win in Toulouse,[12] Chamfort decided to attack the Académie. The virtuous Thomas had just been elected one of the Forty Immortals, thereby giving the Philosophers and their fellow travelers a narrow majority. The Sorbonne theologians no longer wielded veto power. Candidates streamed forth to eulogize Molière. Everything seemed to indicate that this "ham actor," whom the Forty had rejected during his lifetime due to his lowly profession, would be gloriously rehabilitated. Everything, that is, except the reactionary minority led by Abbé d'Olivet, determined to counter the offensive led by Duclos and d'Alembert. Chamfort's contribution compared the "gothic prejudice" endured by Molière to "spurious modern wit," revealing a prudence that, tempered by the occasional outburst, won him the poetry prize in 1769. Bébé, who thought he would demolish Chamfort (and whose reprisals were feared when bested), was shaken. "He's like an oven which heats up, but never cooks," commented Voltaire.[13] Chamfort's text was read at the home of the duc de Choiseul, then prime minister, in the presence of Mme. de Deffand. On August 25, the victorious Chamfort attended mass at Saint-Germain l'Auxerrois, the church of the kings of France, before being received at the Académie by the very porters who had barred his way a year earlier.

It was d'Alembert who read Chamfort's eulogy, after having seated the spectators with maniacal care and obvious pleasure (d'Alembert would become known as the Académie's "dictator"). Duclos, the first to have recognized Chamfort's talent, showered praise on his protégé, and during the applause the Forty pointed out to Chamfort a vacant place in their ranks—"pleasantly predicting the honor which will probably be his one day," wrote the press.[14] Mme. de Marchais's ambitions were about to be realized. Chamfort, at age twenty-nine, was a budding academician.

First Reverses

Infringing some more on an austerity program largely theoretical, Chamfort let himself be led by the virtuous Thomas to the home of the Neckers. Originally poor Swiss, the couple was then at their peak. Necker had his bank, and his wife had a salon where she held her own against the most brilliant Philosophers, including La Harpe, thanks to handy retorts she would prepare the morning of the salon. But this minister's daughter had set ideas. "It is called a frog's thigh, not leg!" she confided to Chamfort. "It is called a billfold, not a wallet." Chamfort smiled, thinking her in jest. But Mme. Necker was not laughing. ""Interred!" she continued. "It's impossible to get used to such expressions! Remember, M. de Chamfort, that it is only permissible to use such a term for *dogs*, and never for *humans!*" "Well then, madam, I will henceforth say *inturded* when referring to a dog."[15] Cold-shouldered by Necker in the "rudest" of ways, Chamfort moved away from the pedantic wife. But he did not succeed in seducing the very conventional Mme. du Deffand. Hostile to modern ideas ever since her falling out with d'Alembert and Julie de Lespinasse, she begged Voltaire to compose *his* eulogy to Molière. "I have just done what you want," the old man replied sarcastically. "I heard a eulogy to Molière which will last as long as the French language—it is called *Tartuffe*."[16] And to clearly mark his disagreement with the blind old lady (who accused him of maintaining a pompous "following"), Voltaire reassured Chamfort that he found him "one of the kindest of Frenchmen."[17] Such backing, however, only aggravated a war inflamed by Bébé's new pretensions; for La Harpe had just invented for himself an old noble family from Vaud (when he was in fact the son of a water carrier and a seamstress). Chamfort jeered:

> *Depuis un temps La Harpe a des aïeux:*
> *Surcroît d'orgueil. . . .*
> *Eh! mon ami, baisse les yeux sur moi:*
> *Ma race est neuve, il est vrai; mais qu'y faire?*
> *Dieu ne m'a point accordé, comme à toi,*
> *Près de trente ans pour bien choisir mon père.*[18]

> La Harpe has lately found forebears:
> Hence further pride. . . .
> Well, my friend! Look down on me:
> My stock is young, 'tis true; but then again
> God hasn't granted me, like thee,
> Thirty years to choose my kin.

The feud between the two illegitimate sons was henceforth public. As the best student in France at age sixteen, Chamfort was persuaded that he was the best writer of his generation. The doubt sown by La Harpe was only temporary. Chamfort wanted to regain the title, force La Harpe to yield, to give up the crown. This was the unstated issue behind their long quarrel which was cruel, often foul, occasionally comic, and which had finally reached the point of no return.

The tension became unbearable. Chamfort broke with the Philosopher's clan, convinced that the backing of Voltaire, Duclos and Thomas would offset any negative effects. Once again as strong, gay and self-confident as he had been before his illness, Chamfort prepared a second comedy in the style of Molière. He totally abandoned his "tyrannical" policy and resumed his career: "I'm committed to all sorts of engagements, *Le marchand de Smyrne* which will perhaps be performed this winter, another trifle which will be given at court in early November, and my tragedy which must be ready by next spring."[19] The tone became lighter still toward Thomas, who wanted to see Chamfort finish his tragedy first. "Doesn't fame come to pretty trifles almost as often as to serious works?" asked Chamfort. "A genius for gaiety is indeed worthy, and how sweet to attain immortality while laughing." Hence he dismissed reproaches from his "virtuous" fellow Auvergnat, who still occasionally commissioned sermons from Chamfort for a Clermont-Ferrand clientele. The literary mercenary was at that point overly busy. He had been commissioned to do the first two volumes of a collection of witticisms, containing "sublime replies by the Ancients" and "rebukes by valets," traces of which would be found in his own anecdotes. He was still collaborating on the *Grand vocabulaire français* published by Panckoucke and was to have written the introduction, but the project was discredited by a partisan of spelling reform who advocated spelling *affreusement* as *afrezemen*, etc.[20] The actors at the Comédie-Française, however, were already predicting "tremendous success" for his *Marchand de Smyrne* [*Merchant of Smyrna*], a comic follow-up to *La jeune indienne*.

It was a joke of a success—thanks to François René Molé and Pierre Louis Dubus Préville, two actors so popular that the public would send them cases of wine at the slightest sign of a cold (or would even carry some saint in procession to produce a cure). The audience applauded this oriental concoction where Muslims had only one wife and Frenchmen two obsessions—liberty and justice. "Oh! It's unbelievable," declaimed Mlle. Hus every night as the curtain came down. And this little one act certainly was unbelievable. But the German baron's accent and the Marseille slave's Turkish slippers made everyone laugh, and Chamfort thought his return to the theater a success.

Critics, however, were less naive. "M. de Chamfort's ideas on dramatic art have no substance, because they have no roots," Grimm observed. "You can yank them from his head in fistfuls."[21] The scalping ceremony had begun. Turgot, annoyed by the *Marchand's* jingoism, attacked Chamfort's "anteroom patriotism." Collé spoke of "less than witty witticisms," and La Harpe surfaced to accuse Chamfort of having stolen the subject from Plautus. Neither the performances given by Casanova and his troupe in Florence nor the opera based on *Le marchand* (composed by the music teacher to the princess of Orange) could belie the obvious: Chamfort's success owed everything to his actors and to his extensive reading.

A Convert to Neoclassicism

Stung by the clan, dropped by the critics, Chamfort fell to earth. He thought he had denounced, Molière-fashion, the idleness of nobles, the despotism of Turks, and inequality everywhere—and he found himself accused of pettiness. For, like *La jeune indienne, Le marchand de Smyrne* presents a man paying off a moral debt—down to the last penny (a subject that obsessed Chamfort). The ever-perfidious Grimm wrote, "I would wager that [Chamfort] is . . . made of that mixture of stuff which produces a child who matures . . . to become an old fogey."[22] Hurt at seeing a conformist future predicted for him, Chamfort lost his self-confidence. He now regretted having made fun of the Lebeau brothers and of Thomas's earnestness. Yes, those good teachers were right to warn him about superficiality. Written in several months, *Le marchand* provided only a few hours of distraction. "These days," he wrote, "one painter paints your portrait in seven minutes, another teaches you to paint in three days, and yet a third teaches you English in forty lessons."[23] In terms that seem strangely contemporary today, Chamfort forever abandoned the pompadour style and called for an art that suffers and surpasses itself, for a culture worthy of its own afflictions. In his *Eloge de Molière*, he had already denounced the silly jumble of social stations, of youth's lack of "any morality" or "sensitivity" as well as its "concern to be like everyone else."[24] At age thirty-one, he refined his philosophy. "Let us look to the heroes and geniuses of the seventeenth century as examples," he said. "Let us struggle against the decline of character and the civilization of the moment. Let us make our century a major one, so as to not wind up minor writers." The policy decreed in 1765 was fully back in effect.

Such "reactionary" outbursts might have shocked if the rest of his generation had not also become aware of its own limitations. The pendulum—the Parisian amplitude of which was never more than ten years—was swinging from the fanciful back to the serious. Weary of being modern, the century turned back to those high periods of classicism, the reigns of Pericles, Augustus, and the Sun King. Mystification and arabesques gave way to forthrightness and straight lines. In a common paradox, writers rehabilitated the seventeenth-century values they had helped to discredit (which only the rearguard faction of the Académie had upheld—along with Voltaire and Mme. du Deffand). But the new version was stricter than the original. Diderot wanted painting to follow the Spartan model, not the Athenian. Waves of men in togas elbowed aside the nymphs typical of Boucher (shortly to be described as a pornographic painter). The prince de Ligne observed, "We now prefer Cato types to alley cats." Women went into decline, as anticipated by Chamfort. Furnishings became more masculine, rococo gave way to excavations at Pompeii and Herculaneum. The German art historian Johann Joachim Winckelmann advocated imitating the "ideal beauty" of the Greeks, for this was what the soul had glimpsed during its initial sojourn with the gods, according to Neoplatonists, and what it constantly yearned for during its earthly existence. Identification replaced distraction, tragedy assumed its cathartic role again. The Louis XV style went into its death throes before an astounded Europe; but if a nation's wealth can also be measured by the values it consumes, then France was one of the richest and probably the most subject to fashion.

It was thus an entire generation that, along with Chamfort, abandoned the present. Writers—aware of their own feebleness, weary of sitting at the feet of Voltaire, Buffon, and Rousseau—dreamed of joining the Greco-Roman pantheon. "I am tormented by the desire for fame," wrote Sélis, one of Chamfort's earliest biographers. "The sad truth soon dissipates the delightful illusions sparked by the success of others."[25] One newspaper encouraged this "posterity craze" by predicting, at each death, the verdict of the centuries. Cailhava d'Estandoux had one of Molière's teeth set on a ring as a gage of immortality. The era of automatons and doppelgangers drew to a close; the day of the unique individual was dawning. The Philosophers' decline gave birth to dozens of "geniuses," like so many insects emerging at nightfall: Parny, Carbon de Flins des Oliviers, Fenouillot de Falbaire, and others were ridiculed by Rivarol in his little dictionaries (the only pantheon they would ever enter).

Following his failure to become an aristocrat and his unsuccessful return to the theater, Chamfort rediscovered the old values of his school days. He turned against the 1750s (which had suppressed art and psychology in the name of progress and science), against the marriage of talent and nobility (which was guilty of smothering sensitivity with polite manners, of replacing morality with staged society). He once again sought true fame, a glorious biography, the ancient world as revealed by the Lebeau brothers. But his strictness once again contrasted with the general revival. "He no more spared the dead than the living," wrote Mme. Suard. "One day, at supper, we were talking about Plutarch's *Lives,* and he pointed out little blemishes he had noted in those of Aristides and Camillus [classical models of moral integrity]." Jean-Baptiste Suard added, "I suppose you're planning to leave us your idea of a model of perfection?"[26]

The annoyance expressed by this Philosopher and former friend is understandable; not long before, Chamfort had been a lot less stern. The witticisms and "meringues" he whipped up had delighted high society. The duc de Duras, on behalf of a court hoping to wean Chamfort from the Philosophers' clan, had commissioned verses in honor of Christian VII, then visiting Paris. Thus in 1768 Mlle. Larivée, dressed as a fortune-teller, sang before the Danish monarch:

> *Le seul aspect d'un jeune Roi*
> *M'a de l'avenir dévoilé le mystère;*
> *Son sort est d'être heureux, d'être aimable et de plaire . . .*[27]

The mere sight of a young King's face
Removes all doubt about his future;
He shall be happy, pleasing, kind in equal measure . . .

Spartan Gruel

Chamfort was now sentenced to austerity, to republican perfection—and to hostility from the Philosophers' clan. Though Voltaire backed Chamfort from his exile in Ferney, d'Alembert, Marmontel, and Suard in Paris took La Harpe's side. Initially unconcerned,

Chamfort slowly realized the extent of the challenge (which became tougher in 1772 with the death of Duclos). How, in effect, could he earn a decent living independent of the aristocracy, of the salons, and of a philosophical "church" whose temporal power remained intact? How could he avoid being reduced to spartan gruel? A Corneille-style dilemma for a man who did not have the means to support his pride (and who, back in Athens, would not even have held the rank of citizen). Enter Claude Carloman de Rulhière, son and grandson of military officers, who had followed the baron de Breteuil to Saint Petersburg, as recounted in his remarkable *Histoires et anecdotes sur la révolution de Russie* [*Stories and anecdotes on the revolution in Russia*]. Rulhière was close to Chamfort—they were accused of preparing conversations together on the eve of certain dinners, down to their own rejoinders—and he introduced him to the baron. Breteuil, who had high-level backing for his plan to integrate writers into the regime, suggested that Chamfort accompany him on his new assignment. The literary mercenary, who always claimed to be capable of following some other profession, seized the diplomat's offer in order to serve his country—the only justification worthy of his neoclassicism. Was he headed for Vienna, perhaps, or London? While awaiting the decision, Chamfort joined Breteuil at his chateau. But the encounter with this gentleman, who was already the patron to Bernadin de Saint-Pierre (author of *Paul et Virginie*), was disappointing. "He mistakes his position for his person," commented Chamfort, forced to suffer this "grotesque personage" (met at every turn in Chamfort's *Maximes*, covered with royal trinkets).[28]

Everything was ready, however, when late in 1770 Mme. du Barry obtained the dismissal of the duc de Choiseul as prime minister; Breteuil also fell in disgrace, and Chamfort put away his court dress, retreating to Mlle. Guimard's home on the rue de Richelieu. Once again he fell victim to the illness which always followed a setback.[29] Guimard had become the best-kept courtesan of the reign (after Mlle. Deschamps), organizing highly "lascivious" shows at her suburban Pantin residence, all the while discretely coming to the aid of the poor. The dancer cut short her "interviews" (each one of which earned her as much as Rousseau made for *Emile*), in order to care for her former lover.[30] Bouvard was called in, a doctor known for making his patients talk about the hidden causes of their illness—he was supposed to have healed a bankrupt financier by placing a phony letter of credit on the mantelpiece. But Chamfort hung on to his secrets. Who, then could cure him? La Harpe diagnosed a "dark, jealous nature, quick to take offence, having a great deal of desire for fame yet limited means."[31] La Harpe, however, was reputed to be more dangerous than any disease. Chamfort was unable to read or write—the "humor" had attacked his eyes as well as his chest—and obsessed by the scar marking Bouvard's face ("a blow he gave himself while clumsily handling death's scythe," according to Diderot).[32] Chamfort aged ten years in a matter of weeks.

7. IRONCLAD IN REPELLING EVIL, A WAX MOLD IN ACCEPTING GOOD...

Happiness, M—— used to say, is no simple thing. It is very difficult to find in ourselves, and impossible to find elsewhere.

Chamfort

While Chamfort recuperated as best he could in Paris (being too poor for the spa prescribed by Bouvard), that "trollop" du Barry imposed her former lover Aiguillon on Versailles, creating a cabinet that also harked back to Louis XIV. Maupeou, Terray, and Aiguillon acted as a triumvirate, advocating austerity to combat treasury deficit. It was a return to economic interventionism and to late-night ministerial meetings—as well as to rumors of ministers enriching themselves. "The relationship between ancient moral standards and our own is identical to that between Aristides, the Athenian comptroller, and Abbé Terray," wrote Chamfort.[1] Threatened by a new tax, the privileged order joined Chamfort in denouncing Terray's phony neoclassicism through songs and epigrams, traditional safety valves under the monarchy. "Sire, these are not the people for the job," said the duc de Noailles, referring to doctors called to extract an ecu worth six livres from a guard who had swallowed it. "Who is, then?" asked the king. "Abbé Terray, Sire." Louis XV himself, according to Horace Walpole, was out of fashion.

But by removing all hope of stipend or position, these cutbacks at the end of Louis XV's reign forced Chamfort to accept money from Michel-Paul-Guy de Chabanon, a Creole friend.

Chabanon, a dilettante, joined La Harpe at Ferney bearing a letter of introduction signed Chamfort, and in many ways he resembled the "musician" Laborde (to whom he was linked). Rich and undisciplined like Laborde, and as confiding with women as Chamfort was mistrustful, Chabanon would make his strongest impression through the charm of his estate at La Verberie. There, where Chamfort often went, guests were required every morning to don the costumes for the roles they would play that evening, in order to break them in—to the amazement of the local peasants. Like Chamfort, Chabanon would be published only at his death. He left a strange autobiography, titled *Tableaux de quelques circonstances de ma vie* [*Scenes of several situations in my life*], which Stendhal described as the adventures of a couple making love, alone but simultaneously, despite the ceiling separating their bedrooms.

Thanks to this unusual dilettante, Chamfort was finally able to leave for the spa at Contrexéville and follow treatment reputed to be exorbitantly expensive. From there he was invited to the chateau of the marquis de Lezay-Marnesia, at Moutonne in the Jura Mountains, where the marquis regularly put up overworked Parisian writers. Chamfort liked the region, with its cheeses and local workshops. The gentry was liberal, and the peasants themselves seemed content. True, the countryside was not "infinitely" entertaining. He found it relaxing, however, after entire years spent in Paris. Signs of age began to disappear. He even confessed, "I'm regressing to the opposite state."[2] Chamfort then announced his arrival to Voltaire. He was impatient to see Geneva and the Swiss cantons where they still voted by raised hand, to see whether Rousseau had exaggerated the virtues of Switzerland. Chamfort later wrote, during the Revolution:

> *Je fus toujours un peu républicain,*
> *C'est un travers dans une monarchie . . .*
> *Je saluais les monts de l'Helvétie,*
> *Cherchant des yeux, dans le simple Appenzell,*
> *l'Egalité, cette fille du ciel,*
> *Faite pour l'homme et par l'homme haïe . . .*[3]

> I always was somewhat republican,
> A drawback in a kingdom . . .
> I greeted those Helvitic hills,
> Eyes seeking out, 'midst Appenzell,
> Equality, whom heaven made
> To free mankind, yet whom men hate . . .

In 1773, however, he was less categorical. How can we know whether or not freedom makes beings better, he mused to the marquise de Créquy, one of Rousseau's patronesses. "A few cases are observed, from which generalizations are made. . . . And then other observations are recorded, canceling those generalizations and . . . you die before you come to a decision."

The local academy in Marseille made the decision for him by announcing the subject of its competition. Chamfort canceled his trip to Switzerland—leaving Voltaire "grieving" at the idea of dying without having met him—and hurried home to compete against La Harpe over a eulogy to Jean de La Fontaine. War had broken out again, with its inevitable low blows. But La Harpe (to whom Necker had disclosed the subject in advance) innovated by applying pressure on the jury. Since entries were submitted anonymously, "He even wrote a letter signed by himself recommending his entry as though it were that of a friend," revealed Chamfort. "It's amusing that a man considers his recommendation better than his piece."[4] But their quarrel no longer excited the crowd; Paris had its eyes riveted on Versailles, where Louis XV was on his deathbed, exhausted by smallpox and an overly long reign. The Philosophers, paradoxically, demanded communion—by reviving his fear of hell, they hoped to induce him to send Mme. du Barry away. But his favorite departed on her own, leaving the sovereign to die at peace with his God. Louis XVI, who succeeded his grandfather in May 1774, then dismissed the triumvirate. It was a victory of Philosophy over authoritarianism, of the eighteenth century over the pseudo-seventeenth. Turgot and Malesherbes were named ministers; Suard, Morellet, and Condorcet counselors; and the Philosophers' clan celebrated the advent of a great reign. They didn't yet know that Louis XVI, then only twenty, felt as comfortable in his new role as a "man who fell from a belltower."

On the Wonderful Effect of Spas

But Chamfort was not present for this marriage of Throne and Enlightenment. He had left to convalesce at Barèges, a spa in the Pyrenees located a few miles from the Spanish border, whose sulfurous waters were renowned for treating skin diseases. It was regularly cut off by the bad weather which plagued the Bastan valley, and so the patients gave a rousing welcome to the *conversationist*. He became the favorite dinner guest of the duchesse de Gramont, Choiseul's sister. This intellectual termagant, consumed by ambition, first tried to "rape" the king despite her masculine voice and brusque manners, then slept with this brother. The Choiseul clan, all-powerful just four years earlier, adopted Chamfort. The comtesse de Choiseul-Beaupré addressed him "with all the affection of a sister," and the Comtesse de Tessé and the duc d'Ayen urged him to come to Luchon. Already delighted by the exiling of Mme. du Barry, the group exulted on learning Marseille's verdict on the eulogies to La Fontaine—a unanimous vote in favor of Chamfort. The supreme consecration was the duchesse de Gramont's suggestion that Chamfort make an autumn visit to her brother's Chanteloup estate in Touraine. "For the past three months, I've been living under the wand of the Good Fairy," wrote Chamfort. "My thoughts are light and gentle, all the stirrings of my heart are pleasant, these are truly lovely days."[5] Instead of the Helvitic utopia, Chamfort discovered the irresistible once offered by Barèges—the equality of the few.

The clan having left, he continued his mud baths and took stock of things. "I was ironclad in repelling evil, I am a wax mold in accepting good," he wrote. "Various philosophies are right; it's just a question of placing them in context. . . . I find my current way of being fine; I'd return to the other if necessary." This was the end of a dry spell begun in the name of neoclassicism, but increasingly imposed from the outside. In early October 1774, Chamfort finally left for Chanteloup, the "Ferney" of the duc de Choiseul, minister in exil (whom half of Versailles had come to see after his fall from grace in 1771, despite the king's objections). Chamfort was welcomed by duke, sister, and wife (who a year earlier had triumphed in the role of little Betti, the noble savage in La jeune indienne, on the chateau's little stage). Knowing only how "to be a society figure,"[6] Chamfort delighted the duke, who worked at a loom and read fairy tales during his enforced idleness. This former "coach-driver of Europe"—the brilliant architect of the rapprochement between France and Austria, and of the marriage between Louis XVI and Marie-Antoinette—invited Chamfort to stay on. Thus Chamfort became writer for a kingdom which got up late, dined at any hour, supped in uniform (ornamental braid for the men, indigo-blue gowns for the women), and at nightfall boarded a frigate anchored on the Loire. There, the duchesse de Choiseul danced by lantern light, sometimes until dawn, with her husband, her guests, and Abbé Barthélemy, that delightfulfactotum who consoled her—platonically—for her husband's infidelities. Chamfort had now discovered a middle road between Philosophers and court, between "republic" and monarchy—a corner of the earth free from persecution by La Harpe, who had been a protégé of the Choiseuls up till then.

Bébé Is Purged

By the time Chamfort returned, Paris knew all. The women of the
Choiseul clan had recounted the spa treatment—"four women
friends each of whom loved him four times over," wrote Julie de
Lespinasse.[7] A little mockery was aimed at the "motley troupe"
formed by an unsuccessful imitator of Catherine II (Mme. de
Gramont), a patronness to Rousseau (Mme. Tessé), a former lady-
in-waiting to Mme. de Pompadour (Mme. d'Amblimont), and "the
little saint" so dear to Mme. du Deffand (Mme. de Choiseul-
Beaupré). But Chamfort was "a truly content young man, trying his
best to be modest," stressed Julie. Launched by the Choiseul crew,
his *Eloge de La Fontaine* now met with success. Impressed by this passionate portrait, and recalling her "slavery" under Mme. du
Deffand, Julie herself secretly wrote to Guibert, her lover: "My
friend, I recommend page 44," where La Fontaine is congratulated
for the kind spirit and trust with which he accepted patrons. Dorat,
who had been Chamfort's patron, published at his own expense a
small volume showing La Fontaine smiling in heaven while thumb-
ing through the eulogy.[8] This was too much for La Harpe, who had
begun a new reading tour, the high point of which was his exclama-
tion: "Oh! Time's justice will be done!"[9] Upset at her protégé's defeat, Mme. Necker attacked the Marseille jury: "Such barbarians . . . ! Never has one written better; never reasoned better." The
public nevertheless seized the chance to put La Harpe—now called
La Harpy—in his place. Voltaire himself recommended Chamfort's
eulogy to La Harpe. "The most perfect ever seen in any academy
in the world." He continued, "It is like Phidias winning out over
Praxiteles."[10] Phidias incarnated the purest Greek classicism. Apart
from Bébé's rout, this homage was Chamfort's finest reward.

Long treated as a child, Chamfort could relax at last. Despite
hostility from the Philosophers, he was now considered a tangible
"poet"—a key criterion for neoclassicists as well as preromantics.
Mme. du Deffand herself beckoned him to her salon. La Fontaine's
good image probably had a lot to do with this. But the success of
tales inspired by the ancient Greeks, which he now read in social
gatherings, showed Chamfort that he was on the right track. The
past now provided protection from his fear of passing pleasure. The
cricket La Harpe had fiddled—while Chamfort stored up for winter.
Bébé offered a different moral: "He didn't rejoice with modesty

. . . thus he was said to be like one of those not very wealthy people who are proud of the little they have."[11]

The Age of Doubt

Chamfort was too lucid—too destructive even—to fool himself for long. His eulogy remained a poem *about* someone. What had he himself done, by the age of thirty-four? He had knocked off a few comedies and written on the art of writing. He called for an end to analysis—and he analyzed constantly. Would Sparta lead to Byzantium, and the Ancients lead to plagiary? "For some time now, everything new in literature (as in many other genres) is so excessive!" he repeated.[12] Yet he went so far in imitating his forebears that he thought he could see the statues dear to neoclassicists looking down in mockery as he rewrote—less well—the books of the past. At which point an assessment was in order. Perhaps it was not the right time to write, in the same way that certain painters live far from the landscapes suited to them. To be a great writer, he declared, "you have to find everything ready," just as Alexander inherited the outline of an empire from his father.[13] Perhaps, once again, he was of *poor birth*. Aware of the sterility threatening the post-Philosophy generation, Chamfort already contemplated silence.

Friends intruded on these reflections. Stick with the past, the posterity-minded told him. Everything done since the Renaissance has come from there. La Fontaine drew inspiration from Aesop; and anyway, who hasn't copied? Fame rests on chance, the more lucid argued. Try your luck, and the rest will follow. Just look at the nonentities who currently reign! Disturbed, Chamfort retired to Sèvres, where the widow of the Philosopher Helvétius (whom he met through the Saurins) had furnished an apartment for him. There he took up his tragedy again. And swore to stick to it. A hundred times interrupted by illness (or perhaps it was his inability to finish it that made him ill), Roxelane become Suleiman become finally *Mustapha et Zéangir* would be the test of his career. If it wasn't a success, he would abandon a game in which he wanted to be either the winner or the exception. He began to write under the eye of a home nurse. He reread all of Racine, wrote a *Dictionnaire dramatique* [*Dictionary of drama*],[14] and checked up on the rules of the art. For tragedy was demanding; it dictated use of the three unities, twelve-foot lines, and the six hundred words used by Racine (whereas Shakespeare had fifteen thousand). *Phèdre* was described as "conversations under a chandelier"—a chandelier that could not be moved. Though dead at Versailles, Louis XIV still reigned more firmly than ever over the theater—and Chamfort humbly bowed.

He went out to assess his progress with Lekain, Voltaire's pet actor, who advised Chamfort to darken the character of Roxelane.[15] Work was going well, and he regained confidence. "There you see my entire fortune," he said to Aubin, holding up his manuscript.[16] Short of funds, he agreed to write the preface to Abbé de Saint-Non's *Voyage pittoresque de Naples et de Sicile* [*A picturesque voyage to Naples and Sicily*]. The abbé had visited Italy first with painter Hubert Robert and then with Fragonard, and the book made a splash when it appeared in 1781.

But Chamfort still had to soften up the Philosophers' clan, that final obstacle to success. He took up again with Suard, around whom the clan's lieutenants gathered. Suard hoped to unite French style with English and German ideas by entertaining Chamfort (though he had criticized Chamfort's recent productions) along with Diderot, Hume, Kant, Condillac, Goethe, and Wieland. At Suard's residence on rue Louis-le-Grand, however, Chamfort once again found the clubby atmosphere he hated. Abbé Delille, the contented bastard, was reading a new eulogy from his *Jardins* [*The Gardens*] to an audience stimulated by the coffee Suard now had shipped up from Marseille. "I unwittingly glimpsed the face of M. de Chamfort at that moment," wrote Mme. Suard (who venerated La Harpe), "but I promptly turned my gaze elsewhere. Envy and its rage were written on his face."[17] Chamfort would thus focus his campaign on Louis XVI just as the American insurgents were beginning their campaign for independence from the English crown.

It was not a bad idea to concentrate on Louis XVI. The king liked tragedy as much as Marie-Antoinette liked comedy (he even knew entire monologues from Racine). He was not only cultivated, sensitive, and of an honest intelligence, but his life also seemed marked by bad omens. The courier who was to announce his birth to the court fell from his horse and died before uttering a word; several hundred spectators were smothered to death during his wedding celebrations at the place Louis XV (today place de la Concorde); six years later, in 1776, this king who amused himself by studying geography and making locks had found the path, but not yet the key, to making the queen pregnant—the throne was still without an heir.[18] Finally, Louis XVI was loath to reign, appearing by turns abrupt and overly familiar with his ministers and courtiers. His brothers, Provence and Artois, seemed to harbor certain regrets. This pained the king, who loved his younger brothers. It was only a small step from there to the rivalry reigning between Mustapha and Zéangir, sons of Sultan Suleiman. A step Chamfort took by having Roxelane exclaim:[19]

> *Encor si tu vivais dans ces climats heureux,*
> *Qui, grâce à d'autres moeurs, à des lois moins sévères,*
> *Peuvent offrir des rois que chérissent leurs frères.*

> If you could only live in happy climes
> Which, thanks to other customs, gentler laws,
> Produce kings cherished by their brothers.

The king let it be known that the theme of *Mustapha* was not displeasing to him. The queen, however, had sworn never to back another play, following the dismal *Dramomane* (in which the characters died one by one, poisoned by paté). Chamfort nevertheless obtained the signal honor of reading *Mustapha* to the royal couple, which then included it in the program of annual festivities at Fontainebleau. A stir was being created around the promising poet who had won the favor of a twenty-two-year-old king liable to reign well into the following century.

The Royal Road

The plot had gone smoothly up to that point. But in August, Lekain (who didn't like his role) dropped out with the excuse of a trip to Ferney. And then on September 1, 1776, Marie-Antoinette fell ill (due, it was said, to the air in France). Departure was postponed until she was better. The courtly procession finally left Versailles for the chateau at Fontainebleau on October 9. Trunks groaned with the clothing to be worn for horse racing, a recent import from England. Chamfort rode with Mme. de Marchais in the comte d'Angiviller's carriage—sealing a reconciliation around the king, whose education the count had supervised. They were followed by Necker, red and enormous, newly named counselor for finance. The first plays presented at Fontainebleau were judged "indecent," and the king, who loved his wife, showed interest only when the hounds from his pack arrived on stage during *Ninette à la cour* [*Ninette at court*]. Finally, on November 1, 1776, *Mustapha et Zéangir* was performed. Molé outdid himself in the role of Zéangir, and Brizard made everyone forget Lekain. Aroused from their torpor, the courtiers cried genius. Louis XVI wept at the allusion to his brothers; the queen, moved, sent for the author. As the princes of the blood looked on, Chamfort joined the pretty queen of twenty-one, to whom many courtiers had never spoken. "What flattering things did the queen say?" he was asked on exiting. "Things I will never be able to forget, nor repeat," replied Chamfort in perfect courtly fashion.[20]

The papers would reveal such secrets, however. "To the pleasure that the performance of your play has given me," Marie-Antoinette reportedly said, "I would like to add another, by telling you that the king, in order to encourage your talent and reward your success, is granting you a stipend of one thousand two hundred livres." Another account had the queen say, "I am announcing this with pleasure, but would also request a favor." "A favor, Madam!" "Yes, that of having your play performed for me again at Versailles, before presenting it in Paris."[21] That very evening, the prince de Condé, cousin to the king, appointed Chamfort "Secrétaire des Commandements" (chief secretary) of his household. Chamfort refused, but Angiviller pressed, and Chamfort finally accepted. On ceremoniously retiring to bed, Louis XVI once again indicated his satisfaction. The Académie was now only a question of months, the Comédie-Française of days. Soon afterward, Provence, the king's brother, named Chamfort a member of his Society, alongside Condorcet. "The courtiers glorified him, it was certainly a blessing," wrote Collé.[22] La Harpe himself admitted that it had been a long time since a writer had enjoyed such infatuation at Versailles.

Chamfort was triumphant. The sacrifices imposed by his "tyrannical" program had worked. The illness, the doubts, and the emotional desert of the past ten years had no lingering effect. He was now, at age thirty-six, the leading tragic playwright, the Racine of the "fourth" classicism, La Harpe's *senior*. "The author's self-esteem took off like a shot," noted Collé, "it was a real pleasure [to witness]." Installed at the Palais-Bourbon (Condé's Paris residence), the "little balloon" continued to swell until he could no longer see the string attaching him to Versailles. Paris, however, did not like to follow the court's lead. In early November, Voltaire was alerted to the existence of a play by François Belin with the same title, *Mustapha et Zéangir*, published in 1704. Several days later, Bébé addressed Chamfort in the street.

"In truth, good friend, I am delighted by your happy circumstance. . . ." "I appreciate the sincerity of the compliment," replied Chamfort, "and thank you for it."

"You would be mistaken to doubt it. But it's a long way from the Palais-Bourbon to the Louvre [where the Académie française was housed]."[23] Word of Belin's play spread through Paris, and plagiary was mentioned. The Académie, to which La Harpe had been admitted in June, judged it prudent to postpone Chamfort's election. And the actors at the Comédie-Française in turn delayed the Paris presentation of *Mustapha*.

Chantilly Torment

Chamfort shrugged it off. "Calumny is like a wasp," he claimed.[24] He concentrated on improving the fifth act, the only one criticized, when he was called to Chantilly to handle the prince de Condé's correspondence. An absurb, almost criminal chore given Chamfort's situation—but inescapable. Indifferent to the fairy-tale castle in Chantilly, Chamfort got down to work, devoting his spare time to *Mustapha*. Of the twenty-five thousand people employed at Chantilly, none felt more strongly than he the folly of having to earn a living. The prince was content and was already giving thought to the education of his grandson, the duc d'Enghien. Racine had been a protégé of the prince's forebear, "the great Condé," and the prince now housed the author of *Mustapha* on an estate envied throughout Europe. Red-headed, one-eyed and a skirt chaser, the devout Condé cared little for the Philosophers, who had courted him without success. But he had not yet become the military commander hostile to revolution, as was the case after 1789. He was still liberal, sensitive to the fate of the poor, and prayed for the health of Voltaire (who always managed to seduce influential people). The prince de Condé was also patron to several writers and scientists, including J.-L. Proust and Pilâtre de Rozier. But Chamfort, that worldly Alceste, was far superior to them, and the prince of the blood became attached to the fine mind without noticing the strongmindedness.

Chamfort was "in the lion's paw," wrote Guinguené. "He had to get out before the claws shut tight."[25] When *Mustapha* was finally programmed at the Comédie-Française, Chamfort asked to be released. Condé refused, all the while rescinding the obligation to reside at Chantilly. "The prince took every care to prove to Chamfort . . . that no one was ever truly free anywhere, that even he himself was not; that it would thus be unfortunate if one didn't forget, like him, the rank into which birth had condemned him, in short that since Chamfort loved him . . . there was no reason which could render this separation necessary."[26] A perfect expression of that attitude which, well prior to the Revolution, verbally bound the classes together.

"This letter . . . is worthy of your fine soul, your great name and your goodness; this last tribute spoils nothing, for what is there above goodness!" replied Chamfort. "The truth is that I am dyspeptically determined, driven by the freedom that I have never abandoned up till now and whose value I was unaware of, driven by literature, which I thought I could reconcile with my rank, but which my way of being, of feeling and of working do not allow me to reconcile with my new position. . . . I see only too well that it would be impossible to profit from the freedom you deign to grant me. It appears that you are currently forgetting the empire that your fortune conducts without your knowledge. It is such, this empire, that it speaks when you are silent, it orders when you command nothing, would even act, so to speak, against your own will. . . . It required no mean effort of reasoning to dispel the charm of that moment when I wanted to spend my life at your feet, had it been possible, making every sacrifice imaginable for Your Serene Highness. But I know the human heart too well."[27]

Giving in to such insistence, Condé let Chamfort go, yet continued to accord him title and official apartment. "Be content, my dear Chamfort; think, write, and be of good health; I will always greatly share in your intellectual success and in the happiness of your soul."[28] Now, Condé happened to be one of the richest men in the kingdom, and the public could not understand the separation. There were rumors of bungling, of betrayal, of outright dismissal, and the clan did not hesitate to fan the flames. Chamfort objected, but maintained his decision to leave Chantilly (where La Bruyère had passed part of his life and found several of the models for his *Caractères*). He would even declare, precociously: "A choice has to be made? I'll not waver—I want to be of the people." The only patron that Chamfort could henceforth bear was also the only one who demanded nothing in return—Louis XVI.

8. A CABAL AGAINST *MUSTAPHA*

*He affected great scorn for dogs, because he found them servile and
fawning, and a great deal of esteem for cats, because he found they had a
freer yet no less attaching personality.*

Roederer

With opinion against him, and hounded by a clan jealous of his success, Chamfort recalled his promise to the queen and attempted to coordinate the election that the Académie would hold late in 1777 with the second performance of *Mustapha* at Fontainebleau, which he expected to be triumphant. A double victory would clinch his career, so he increased peremptory declarations and pressure on the Forty with undisguised impatience. But the Comédie-Française managed to humiliate him. The Paris premiere of *Mustapha* looked to be a delicate affair following the play's second presentation before the court, and the actors were still refusing to set a date. Chamfort was thus obliged to ask Marie-Antoinette to order them to begin rehearsals. At that point—exhausted by his own behavior (straight out of La Harpe) and exasperated by that of others—Chamfort received a letter from Beaumarchais, another victim of the all-powerful actors. "The love of justice and literature has finally moved me to demand a strict and exact accounting from the actors of what is owed me for *Le barbier de Séville*. . . . Consequently, Sir, if you would do me the honor of dining with me next Thursday, I hope to convince you."[1]

Chamfort replied at once to Beaumarchais (this former music teacher to Louis XV's daughters had become in turn swindler, spy, polemicist, weapons dealer, and successful author, thanks to his comedy, *The Barber of Seville*). "I hope, Sir, that the States General of dramatic art which you are hosting will not share the fate of other States General, that of reviewing all our misfortunes without relieving a single one. . . . As to myself, I will at least have succeeded in making better acquaintance with [you]."[2] Chamfort thereby engaged in his first public struggle for freedom, though this is somewhat masked by his skepticism and irony. "You are appreciated

at Versailles not because of your wit, but in spite of it," Marie-
Antoinette told him[3]—which would prove to be the case.

The injustice denounced by Beaumarchais was flagrant. Tragedy
could be performed only at the Comédie-Française (other troupes
were entitled to only three speaking players), and the actors called
the shots. Roles they didn't like were rewritten; any resistance
meant an end to rehearsals. Authors who demanded precise accounting saw their plays performed in slow-motion, or decimated
by "illness." If receipts fell below expenses for two performances,
the actors became owners of the work; after one fiasco, an author
even had to pay for diamonds added to the Spartans' shields without his knowledge. Although actors still had to be buried at night,
contempt was now mutual, and the company—defended by the
maréchal de Richelieu, who at age eighty-one continued to draw his
mistresses from it—enjoyed privileges intolerable in the century of
enlightenment. Ten years prior to the convening of the real states
general, Cato declared war on these alley cats. The very existence of
French theater was at stake, Chamfort told Beaumarchais.

At three o'clock on July 3, 1777, Chamfort presented himself at
the residence once belonging to the ambassadors of Holland. A por-
tal bearing the carved head of Medusa opened on to the premises
of the Roderigue and Hortalez Company—the front used by
Beaumarchais to sell weapons to the American revolutionaries. The
writers were to meet on the second floor, in a salon sumptuously
decorated by Van Boucle. There were numerous absentees. La Harpe
refused to sit down with his former patron, Dorat, "a madman always ready to fight for his verses. You well know, Sir, that this
means fighting over nothing," wrote La Harpe to Beaumarchais on
the subject of that "scribbler of fans."[4] Cowards ran for cover, the
more far-sighted sat on the fence—or both. But at least the twenty-
one writers present were resolute. They dined, drank, and elected
Beaumarchais their commissioner for life. They decided on a
writers' strike until accurate accounts were rendered. Three members of the Académie joined Beaumarchais in drafting a declaration
of independence based on the American model. Revolt was declared
against "the colossal machinery of the Comédie-Française."[5]

From Independence to Court

When Chamfort went back on August 17, the commissioners had
drawn up a proposal to open a second theater. The Dramatic Arts

Bureau (which has since become the Society of Dramatic Authors and Composers) congratulated itself, sure that it would go down in history, while at the Comédie-Française the actresses were amazed to discover that they were unable to do without playwrights. But dissent had already broken out within the Bureau. Accusing the commissioners of favoring their own plays, a member suggested supping on neutral turf. Beaumarchais felt targeted (justly so, apparently) and engineered a dramatic turn of events.

Thus it was on January 18, 1778, that Chamfort, along with the entire assembly, had to beg Beaumarchais to withdraw his resignation. In the ensuing enthusiasm, an advance of fifty livres was voted for one of Racine's destitute granddaughters. But the payment proposals awakened the writers' genius for quibbling. They fought over armchairs and even candles. Though later renewing his confidence in Beaumarchais, Chamfort drifted away from a Bureau too prone to cacophony. He thus acknowledged this first check in the writers' rise to power. Writers, underpaid and self-important, acted as oracle in this theatrical society, and now they wanted the leading role. "What does [a writer] need to re-establish order?" asked Louis-Sébastien Mercier. "He needs only power." Today, however, it is easier to appreciate the weight of that *only.*

Chamfort, at any rate, was too preoccupied with *Mustapha* to indulge in the Bureau's quarrels. Programmed for November, the second performance at Fontainebleau had gone off well, though the queen preferred not to attend, given the rumors of plagiarism. Last-minute additions alluding to recent visits to the provinces of the comtes de Provence and d'Artois were well-received, and Marie-Antoinette congratulated her protégé (the only one to make a literary mark of any sort). "I felt just like Métromane[6] until the final moments," she admitted the next day.[7] *Mustapha* had become *her* play to a certain extent, as witness the Turkish touches in her boudoir at Fontainebleau and the complements she addressed to Chamfort via Rulhière.

Marie-Antoinette, however, was the only one to be reassured by this success. For everything depended on opinion-setting Paris. The premiere took place on December 15, 1777, on the stage in the Tuileries Palace. The king was represented by his two brothers, the prince de Condé by his daughter-in-law. The first two acts were well-received; but the actors began to ham things up (Roederer claimed to have seen them throw themselves on their stomachs and crawl on their knees). Whether out of revenge or not, the troupe went downhill. Brizard lost his memory, Larive was "emotive at random."[8] Applause, which had been substantial, degenerated into boos, forcing one of the actors performing the epilogue to exit. "Playwright, playwright!" shouted the audience. The commotion increased until grenadiers entered the theater, to general indignation. Whistles and jeering broke out. The nightmare of *La jeune indienne* all over again, this time without Duclos to call a halt to things.

Ten minutes went by. Exasperated, the comte de Provence left. "The author can't be found," Augé managed to declare. "Should have said so earlier," the audience replied, forcing the actors to abandon the epilogue once again.[9] A third attempt having failed, Augé announced that two boys from the theater had left for the playwright's home. The audience finally allowed *La métamorphose amoureuse* [*Amorous metamorphosis*] to be performed, when blows suddenly broke out in the gallery. The conflict threatened to spread before the comte d'Artois and the duchesse de Bourbon, who had stayed out of curiosity, but the crowd ultimately dispersed.

Agony

The next day, *that* was all Paris could talk about. "Chamfort's at odds with tragedy," said a spectator. "It would seem he's taking the affair tragically,"[10] joked singer Sophie Arnould, whose witticisms were legendary. The incident was, in fact, worthy of his paranoia—thirteen years of work destroyed by an abominable cabal, a jealous clan, and pitiless critics. The journalist Bachaumont spoke of a terribly boring play, Abbé Delille of a work "worlds away from tragedy," Collé of a play "devoid of both strength and balls. The author of *La jeune indienne* grew up, or rather wanted to grow up: He donned the body of a great tragedy," continued Collé, " . . . yet that sheeplike imitator M. de Chamfort has only cleverness to offer."[11] Belin's *Mustapha* was reprinted, in guise of homage.

Chamfort's career was at stake, so he was not about to admit defeat. Encouraged by courtiers and writers, he took up arms. The cabal having aroused curiosity—a play that made the king cry and Paris yawn just *had* to be seen—the theater was full for the third performance, which Chamfort watched from a loge with Angiviller and Mme. de Marchais. A counteroffensive was launched, and *Mustapha* was compared to Racine's *Bajazet*. The death of the two protagonists provoked streams of tears, and the adverse camp was accused of cynicism. "It's hard to know what to admire more in this writer, his genius or his soul,"[12] repeated the faithful. Despite such "salon hubbub" (as dismissed by the misanthrope Ducis, purportedly Chamfort's friend), receipts fell off.

Chamfort thereupon announced a new change in the fifth act (the murder of Mustapha by Zéangir's henchmen had been judged improper). Amazingly, the public came back. On January 3, 1778, Marmontel, his wife, and her uncle—Abbé Morellet—took their seats in the orchestra in front of a packed house. The young woman wept, and the audience applauded wildly. "Aren't you ashamed to be moved by the work of a man who isn't one of us!" cried Morellet.[13] The Philosopher's clan regained the initiative and tried to contain Voltaire, whose attachment to Chamfort was well-known. But the old man decided to read *Mustapha* to his Society. "Pure Racine, by Jove!" he exclaimed during the fourth act—the comment adding grist to Chamfort's mill.[14] On January 17, attendance climbed back almost to the level of the opening nights. The actors, however, felt they'd had enough. "His piece is as good as dead," declared La Harpe.[15] And, in fact, the play was never revived.

The agony was not over, however. Banking on readers, Chamfort had *Mustapha* printed. He included a dedication to Marie-Antoinette, which Ginguené would suppress from his edition of the *Complete Works*. "Happy if I could, Madame . . . find grace before Your Majesty through the merit of my works, rather than through my choice of themes! For, Madame, the triumph of fraternal affection . . . [has always had] much claim over your soul," etc.[16] The printed version encouraged comparison with Belin's *Mustapha*, and people spoke of the systematic pillaging of Belin's subject, characters, and scenes. "You have to read the piece to believe it!" exclaimed Bachaumont.[17] Someone finally dared tell Voltaire the truth. (He had asked if *Mustapha* were truly *black* on stage. "No," came the answer, *"puce"*—a shade of gray made fashionable by Marie-Antoinette.)[18] Only the *Journal Encyclopédique*, for which Chamfort had written, still defended a play "which will probably do this century great honor."[19] Yet even this "probably" was cruel.

The incident is worth dwelling on, due to its crucial consequences. Technically, the accusation of theft is valid:

Vous l'admiriez vous-même, et je vous vis cent fois
Transporté de plaisir célébrer ses exploits, wrote Belin.[20]

Vous l'aimâtes, seigneur, je vous ai vu cent fois
Entendre avec transport et compter ses exploits, echoed Chamfort.

You admired him yourself, hundreds of times did I perceive
You transported with pleasure by what he'd achieved . . .

You loved him, sire, for hundred of times I perceived
You listen in transport to all he'd achieved . . .

The truth is that such "borrowings" were common. Restricted to the vocabulary of "wrath" and "trespass," neoclassic tragedians rummaged through the repertory like a warehouse. Chamfort was, therefore, the scapegoat for an entire generation which realized that, unlike painting (free to reinvent a no-longer-extant Greek art), the chances of reviving classical tragedy were nil. History would confirm the judgment of critics who, by knocking Chamfort, paid homage to the inimitable genius of Aeschylus and Racine. Chamfort deserved to be panned. His characters were mere ideas subsequently decked out as sultan or quaker. "He reserved his kindness for his tragedies," noted Sainte-Beuve. Too submissive to break the rules, yet not gifted enough to do them justice, Chamfort was, after Voltaire, the prime tragic playwright of the void that existed between Marivaux and Beaumarchais. He was an average eighteenth-century writer, the victim of an overly cultivated generation.

Death Throes

La Harpe, however, persisted in the deed. Once the reviews were published, he dissected the corpse of *Mustapha* over twenty-three interminable pages.[21] Fiercely objective, refusing to attack a plan "twelve years in the meditating," La Harpe suggested that his former protégé adopt silence. Chamfort had fought back every inch of the way up till then—accusing the clan of drawing up a blacklist, the public of being "absurd, cruel and unsubtle," society of having rendered the theater effete by theatricalizing life. Now he realized that he had been born at the wrong time, and he bid farewell to posterity. Finalizing La Harpe's deed (in a troubling coincidence), the latter-day Racine committed literary suicide. "Renown is chastisement for merit and punishment for talent," wrote Chamfort. "Whatever my own talent may be, it seems to act only as informer, refusing to leave me in peace. In destroying it, I experience the elation of vanquishing an enemy."[22] The mediocre writer, direct heir to the best student in France, discovered the truth: "What poets, orators, even several philosophers said about the love of fame, was told to us at school to encourage us to win prizes."[23] The eternal candidate for a place among the forty immortal writers of the Académie française now bowed out with this laconic observation: "Before being immortal, I want to know if I'll live."

While the murder of *Mustapha* was cruel, it was punishment for undeniable shortcomings. Enslaved to unrealistic models, Chamfort's oeuvre remained marked by academicism up until his fortieth year. Always correct, argumentative, and abrupt, interesting when it indirectly concerns his life, it illustrates the slow and difficult transition from classicism to romanticism. Chamfort underwent the trials of a generation who sought to reconcile Voltaire and Rousseau, enlightenment and sentiment, yet produced only "dry, mechanical and maudlin" language, according to Georges Liébert. Chateaubriand accused them of merely "arranging words." The author of *Mustapha* wanted to rehabilitate virtue and tragedy in an amoral and frivolous century, wanted to counter desire with the good and the true so dear to Plato (whose Republic excluded poets). Chamfort committed the error made by most writers who emerged at that particular watershed, when the French language made everyone a verbal virtuoso: to escape social glibness, he dived headfirst into difficulty. Chamfort, in fact, was born at the wrong time.

His very nature led Chamfort to believe his destiny lay with drama. He was more unusual, more complex, and more violent than most of his contemporaries. Yet literature was only a critical expedient, an inappropriate tool, for Chamfort; his ideas went far beyond his writing, most of which doesn't even bear mentioning. Like Diderot (whose masterpieces were posthumous), like Mme. du Deffand (who didn't believe her letters had any value), Chamfort did not yet dare write the way he spoke. He preferred to do battle with the present by imitating the past. *Mustapha* marks the collapse of this "reactionary" tendency, this flight to the past which would consign the entire neoclassical generation to oblivion, leaving only the brilliant criticism by that unfeeling Sainte-Beuve of the day, La Harpe (whom Olivier de Magny described as that "picturesque shrew of literature"). By dismantling Chamfort's ambitiousness, the *Mustapha* crisis provided a respite from which "wisdom" would emerge. Chamfort now had only himself to conquer, could become a unique moralist after having been a mediocre writer; an autobiographer after having been a scribbler of quakers, Caribbean natives, and Turks; an egotist after having been a "master" of drawing-room exoticism. Though his personality was set by age twenty, Chamfort needed two more decades to free himself from the contradictory influences of Rousseau, Voltaire, Thomas, Molière, La Fontaine, and Racine.

Fame or nothing, he used to say. So it was to be nothing. Failure, like illness before it, sparked phenomenal rejection. Crushed by *Mustapha*, Chamfort resembled the snail described by Louis-Sébastien Mercier "which, in its spiral shell, goes around saying, 'This is the Universe.' "[24] Now sobered, he criticized the world with a fury approaching nihilism. The "public" replaced "woman" as the emblem of the phony civilization; men fell into disgrace, statues and ruins regained their priority status. Disliking the very idea of movement, he took refuge in immobility and incognito by retreating to a "house out in the fields" of Auteuil, once occupied by Boileau.[25] It was modest enough—Voltaire likened it to a shady, nasty little tavern—but it sufficed for the upright, neoclassic life that he intended to lead in *deed*. Paris, which had humiliated him, was henceforth only "a stinking and loveless" place.[26] Chamfort, who had always been free of that chauvinism peculiar to capital cities, left a town that had simultaneously placed him above his station and left him marginal. Victim of the terror that reigned in the name of Racine, he swore he would never publish again. He would *be* instead of succeed. Chamfort joined the ranks of the blessed—he became a reader.

9. AUTEUIL-PASSY

When one has been thoroughly racked, thoroughly exhausted by one's own sensitivity, one realizes that one has to live from day to day, forget a lot, and in short mop up life as it spills forth . . .

Chamfort

Auteuil would do him good. No insults to fear, no queen to thank in this village nestled between the Seine and the Bois de Boulogne, far from the maelstrom orchestrated by La Harpe. Determined to be good to himself and indifferent to everything else—"a polished ball over which events slide,"[1]—the overambitious writer reined himself in. His new agenda called for a life of "peace and quiet, away from the light." "That's a sickroom," it was pointed out.[2] Nothing, however, could affect a man now determined to be neither genius nor victim. In a sign of the times, Chamfort abandoned his career just when his oldest backers died: Lebeau the elder and Voltaire, followed shortly by Rousseau.

Women were the big winners from this newfound peace. Tarts had been taboo since the "venereal" incident of 1765, but Chamfort became friendly with his fifty-eight-year-old neighbor, "Minette" Helvétius. Widow of the materialist philosopher Helvétius (whose key work, *De l'esprit* [*Essays on the Mind and Its Several Faculties*] created a scandal in 1758), this uneducated yet drole woman became his godmother in exile. Her childish sayings and her mischievous (but never nasty) little ways distracted Chamfort after fifteen years of literary effort. Stroking the angora cats that Mme. Helvétius fed on chicken breasts, he let himself be cared for by this extremely rich heiress to one of the most important families in Lorraine (she had previously furnished his little retreat in Meudon). Walks in the woods at Boulogne replaced the headlong race for posterity. Thinking of nothing, no longer writing anything, Chamfort awaited that Oriental wisdom which would finally enable him to forget his self.

But instead of the Orient, he discovered a piece of America. Benjamin Franklin, half-bard, half-prophet, was the ambassador the insurgents had sent to France. Everyday the inventor of the lightning rod would "get some air" in nearby Passy and then visit

Minette, whom he was thinking of marrying. Franklin was surrounded by a group of "walking wounded" who gathered in Auteuil to celebrate La Fayette's second campaign (for whom "insurrection [was] the most sacred of duties") and the exploits of those "good republicans" for whom the queen herself had a tender spot. Thus Turgot would discuss his 1776 dismissal, which ended the marriage between Throne and Enlightenment as well as dashing Condorcet's hopes of seeing writers destroy "all the artificial evils of the human race." Dismayed by Necker (who succeeded Turgot as finance minister and who swore to respect the existing system), Chamfort adopted Abbé Galiani's pessimism: "This is the era of the total collapse of Europe and the transmigration to America."[3] Such conversations continued in the Nine Sisters Masonic Lodge (meaning the nine muses, in masonic parlance), into which Chamfort was inducted in 1778. Here there was no Egyptian prayer or hooded grand priest; the lodge on rue du Pot-de-Fer demanded only proof of "a given talent," and it already practiced the "clubbiness" with which it later became identified. The sculptor Houdon, painters Greuze and Vernet, and the writer Louis-Sébastien Mercier were obliged, like Chamfort, to help amateurs publish their works, while lawyers and doctors had to defend and heal brothers for free. This lodge, dedicated to the memory of Helvétius, named Franklin a "venerable member" in 1779. It promoted virtue and concord in an atmosphere diametrically opposed to the extremely hierarchical and almost pyramidal ambience of the monarchy's grand orders. Although a good part of the court (including the king's brothers) were already affiliated with one masonic lodge or another, and although Franklin himself humored Louis XVI (who was arming Franklin's compatriots in hopes of weakening France's ancestral rival, England), this atmosphere was later judged prophetic, not without reason. The revolutionary Pastoret would even claim that lodges were the only places where "primal equality" persisted. At the very least, they extended the concept "sociability" to include people of talent.

But masonic brother Chamfort was a man on the way down in a generation on the rise. Unlike revolutionaries Brissot, Condorcet, and Bailly (whose ambitions inspired Abbé Barruel's wild hypotheses on the masonic origins of the French Revolution), Chamfort did not stick with the lodge. Not even America—the country he had set out to reach at age sixteen—inspired him any longer. The only things that counted were his determination to disappear and his lone unmasking. When Panckoucke offered him the job of theater critic for *Le Mercure*, one of the leading Paris papers, Chamfort declined. "The public expects spite," he wrote. "The theater column must be eagerly awaited, must arouse curiosity, fear, hope . . . [hence] the critic is maligned [and] his outlook becomes embittered."[4] Convinced that the only way to win the game was to quit it, Chamfort refused to emerge from his lair—apart from imaginary voyages. Having retired to a spot halfway between Paris and Versailles, he pursued his flight from *Mustapha* by indulging in explorers' accounts of India, Africa, and Oceania, paradises no one ever willingly left, he claimed ("Whereas a great many Europeans . . . after having lived among savages and finding themselves back among their compatriots, have returned to the woods").[5]

Irony as Cure

Once recovered, however, his wit returned. "There were two features to his conversation," wrote Abbé Morellet. "It always touched on people and never on things, and it was constantly misanthropic and excessively denigrating. The turns of phrase with which he demonstrated his hatred for humanity in general as well as his specific aversions were captivating in their originality . . . but I left Auteuil hundreds of times with a heavy soul—after mornings of listening to him recount anecdote after anecdote for two hours, inventing epigram after epigram with indefatigable ease—as though I were leaving the scene of an execution."[6] Himself implicated in the murder of *Mustapha*, the abbé nevertheless deferred to Minette, for whom Chamfort orally recreated books, sublimating his rancor into irony.

The incisive Abbé Morellet (whose niece married Marmontel) was so hostile to religion and despotism that Voltaire gave him the punning nickname "*Mords-les*" ["Bite 'em"]. In spite of his unbending, provocative and Swift-like sharpness, he yearned for comfort to the extent of emptying the bedrooms of chateaus in which he stayed, the better to appoint his own. This drapier's son illustrates, in fact, the astonishing success of certain Philosophers. Housed by Mme. Helvétius in a little chalet in her Auteuil garden, and enjoying a stipend from the church (after having spent several weeks in prison for a stinging pamphlet which reportedly hastened the death of the pious princesse de Robecq), Morellet was the only Philosopher (along with La Harpe) who really stood up to Chamfort. He would nevertheless ask Chamfort to back his candidacy to the Aca-

démie, only to write later in his *Mémoires* that "Chamfort was as un-
worthy as he was incapable of friendship." This is how writers
behaved under the Ancien Régime, before ideology offered an unexpected new outlet for the rivalry and sterility of the most obscure
among them. The literary milieu fought and made up shamelessly,
certain only of mutual hatred, ingratitude, jealousy.

Other "cripples" lived a stone's throw from the "hospital" run
by Mme. Helvétius (nicknamed Our Lady of Auteuil thanks to her
generosity and her proximity to a church of the same name). The
virtuous Thomas retired to a nearby cottage with the misanthrope
Ducis after Dr. Tronchin recommended that he abstain from "all
cerebral stimulation." A perfect pretext for Chamfort's barbs (demonstrating once again his amazing ability to recover): "Who can be
counted on, these days?" he wrote to Thomas. "You're ordered to
observe the strictest moderation in the use of your mind, and now
Mme. Marmontel tells me that she received a 'charming letter, full of
wit' from you. This infraction of the rules has upset your friends. If
Mme. Marmontel had said simply, 'a charming letter,' I would have
said, 'that can be overlooked.' For how many times have we heard
it said of a new book or poem, 'It's a charming work.' On examination, the work illustrates the impropriety of the word 'charming,'
ordinarily used out of politeness. But 'full of wit!' . . . You are aware
how harmful it is for men to think; that for this reason there are
practically no men who think more than a hundredth part of their
lives; that yourself, for having thought only half your life, find yourself in a bad way; and now you not only think, but dare to be
witty."[7]

Thomas—whose *Epître au peuple* [*Epistle to the people*] was said to
have prefigured revolutionary ideas—was far from witty, but these
affectionate barbs hardly prevented him from receiving Chamfort
regularly. Thomas confessed the torment provoked by his obsession
with fame. "I don't need my contemporaries, but I need posterity."
"A fine product of philosophy," retorted Chamfort, "to be able to do
without the living, yet need those not yet born!"[8] These visits (carried out in the company of the young lawyer Hérault de Séchelles,
Marie-Antoinette's godson, a conventional writer and future terrorist) confirmed Chamfort's antiliterary convictions, at the moment
when the entire century—or almost—would turn literary. The former best pupil in France, the ex-tragedian of the realm, Chamfort
now wanted to be the first member of his generation to break with

the desire to write, with the posterity craze, with a sterility best described as incontinent.

Chamfort's life thus became restricted to the triangle formed by the houses of Boileau, Mme. Helvétius, and Panckoucke in Boulogne (a family chalet full of books and toys). The perfect setting for an anti-career. It was here, at this publisher's home, that Chamfort most staunchly defended his refusal to write. His mental equilibrium hinged on this paradox as well as on the affection of the young, good, and humble Mme. Panckoucke—herself daughter of a printer in Orléans—who befriended Chamfort right up to his death. He also enjoyed the affection of the child of the house, just eight years old, whose naive comments Chamfort found as refreshing as books on savages. Listening to the talk about writers published by Panckoucke, however—La Harpe, Suard, Delille, Morellet—Chamfort realized how small a vacuum his departure had left. As Sainte-Beuve would say, "There's no point in giving up society if society doesn't realize it." Paris would realize it, however. Chamfort rented a pied-à-terre on the Place Vendôme in order to make an assault on the only bastion worthy of his departure—the Académie française. Thus he would merit a biography revealing that one day he abandoned writing.

Chamfort, however, remained isolated. D'Alembert was openly hostile to this Philosophical renegade, and d'Alembert headed the Académie now that Duclos was dead. Chamfort himself felt that Voltaire's grand inquisitor represented the incarnation of the clan's abuses. A revealing exchange between d'Alembert and a porter can be found in the short dialogues concluding Chamfort's *Maximes*. (It serves as symbolic pendant to Chamfort's own conversation with a porter during a visit to this same d'Alembert at the start of his career.)

Porter: Where are you going, sir?

D'Alembert: To see M. de . . .

P: Why don't you speak to me?

D'Al: I address you, friend, when I want to know if your master is at home.

P: Well, then?

D'Al: I know that he's home, because we have a rendezvous.

P: That makes no difference; I'm always addressed. If I'm not spoken to, I'm nothing.

Chamfort thus presents d'Alembert as being no better than most aristocrats—as though the illegitimate son of the famous

Mme. de Tencin had led the battle for enlightenment only to recover his rank and exercise his privileges.

Consecration of the Antiwriter

Yet Chamfort was not dissuaded by this new battle between illegitimate sons.

He sat out the difficult election for Voltaire's vacant seat, then stepped down in favor of Chabanon (who threatened suicide if he lost), but finally declared his candidacy in 1780. He was ready to do anything—rumors, epigrams, etc. But his opponent, Lemierre, was immune to derision and reportedly sought ridicule because it made people talk about him. Powerless against the complacency displayed by the author of *La veuve de Malabar* [*The Widow of Malabar*], Chamfort tried for a second seat, contested by the comte de Tressan, who at seventy-four penned a "poem to my Fanny." Twice defeated, Chamfort accused the Forty of having rewarded "vice and ridicule."[9] "Why should M. de Chamfort complain about that," replied Tressan, "it means two more votes in his favor!"[10] Fortunately, a member of the Académie died in the early months of 1781. Chamfort's new rival was Bailly, an astronomer in search of a "hyperboreal" people who had invented the arts and sciences. D'Alembert found such hypotheses dubious; in addition, he was just a shadow of his former self following the death of Julie de Lespinasse. He therefore gave the Philosophers free rein.[11] Although Bailly was backed by the prestigious Buffon, who came out of his Montbard retreat to support his candidate, Chamfort became one of the "Immortals" on his third attempt, April 5, 1781. Mme. Helvétius and Mme. de Marchais celebrated Chamfort's victory, his revenge for *Mustapha*. The poet Roucher, an Auteuil regular who often received Chamfort at his home in Montfort-l'Amaury, asked rhetorically: "Why doesn't [the Académie] always elect Chamforts? Because there aren't any others."[12] Even La Harpe complimented Chamfort, after having tirelessly fought his candidacy; La Harpe nevertheless wrote to lawyer Boissy d'Anglas (who later became a member of the convention), "*La jeune indienne* wasn't sufficient title to admission, and *Mustapha* was a disqualification." Chamfort's reply to Roucher was, "I embrace you, Sir, with all my heart . . . though not in the hope of suffocating you, as suggested by the example set by others."

The day of glory arrived. White-gloved and beaver-hatted, Chamfort took his place in the French pantheon to the swish of gowns and clink of swords. The prince de Condé and his family were seated in the front row. Chamfort had awaited this moment for twenty years. He launched into a lengthy speech, a ritual homage to his predecessor, Sainte-Palaye, which provides almost clinical evidence of Chamfort's schizoid ambivalence. For Sainte-Palaye had focused on knights and chivalry, a subject that inevitably irritated Chamfort. Its haughtiness, its caste spirit, and its refusal to ally itself with any other class (a barely veiled allusion to the nobility) explained, in Chamfort's view, why it disappeared after having been feared by his compatriots. Chamfort cited only one exception to popular hostility to knighthood—Du Guesclin, whose coffin was followed by a tearful France—"and I mean the people!"[13]

This illegitimate descendant of the Chevaliers de Vinzelles nevertheless dwelled on those men devoted to God, war, tournaments, and women, and on the gay, bold, and amorous France of his ancestors. He shifted from enmity to eulogy, saluting Richelieu, Louis XIV, the literary "knighthood" now receiving him, and the prince de Condé and the "damsels" accompanying him. Nor did he forget Louis XVI, Marie-Antoinette and the child she was expecting—to the joy of a people ever able to love "its masters, perhaps the only people to cherish them constantly. . . . And were I to contribute not the expression, but just a respectful accent, of gratitude to the country's best wishes, I would add: May a son's smile reward the virtue of his august mother!" Three hours thus went by in a mixture of bizarreness and boredom. Only Rivarol noted the almost schizophrenic state of the speaker—"a cockscomb grafted onto poppies," he stated.[14]

Delighted at having turned the tables on *Mustapha's* assassins, Chamfort frequented the Forty (or rather Twenty, the bishops and dukes admitted by complacency being rarely in attendance). On October 21, 1781, he left with a group of academicians for Versailles to celebrate the birth of the queen's son, fulfilling Chamfort's prediction and finally giving the throne an heir. The delegation went from a dinner offered by Cardinal Rohan to the Gallery of Mirrors where Louis was enthroned. "You may assure my Academy of my protection," replied the king of France to the director's interminable congratulations. Chamfort was officially presented to the monarch before going to the bedroom of the sleeping infant who symbolized dynastic regeneration. "Perhaps one day, Monseigneur, you will be told that the Académie surrounded your cradle where, without knowing it, you received its homage."[15] Then, from one day to the next, Chamfort dropped out of sight.

10. LOVE, AND ONLY LOVE

M———, well known for his worldliness, would say that what had taught him the most was his ability to sleep, on occasion, with women of forty, and to listen to men of eighty.

    Chamfort

Chamfort dropped out of public sight because he had met Marthe Buffon—a woman who refused to be intimidated by him. They met at the home of the Panckouckes, though little else is known about her. The rare accounts describe the intensity of her gaze, her "fine figure," a mind "as youthful as at fifteen," and her inexhaustible conversation. Brought up in Sceaux, at the brilliant court of the duchesse du Maine (a boisterous tyrant who had sentenced Voltaire and Fontenelle "to wit's menial chores"), Marthe Buffon had seen everything and forgotten nothing. She and Chamfort apparently hit it off immediately. Even though the moralist's friends found her too talkative, she was one of the rare women able to answer him back. Weary and almost annoyed by the constant conversation surrounding her youth (which Chamfort found so fascinating), Marthe Buffon became more intimate with Chamfort following her husband's death in 1781. Chamfort opened his Auteuil house to her, arranging daily meetings. Complicity sprung up; habits were formed. After twenty years of emotional solitude brought on by the memory of the prostitute who had disfigured him, Chamfort dropped his mask. The bronze armor and "tortoise" shell fell along with it. Wariness collapsed in classic fashion: "Love is like an epidemic," he wrote. "The more you fear it, the more susceptible you are." At age forty-one, he finally succumbed to that fine sickness which could reconcile him with society.

He refused to speak of love, however, a somewhat shameful word at the time. "There could be none," he said, "because she was several years older than I"—the former libertine also had his pride (Marthe-Anne Buffon was fifty-three). "But," he explained, "there existed something more and better than love, since there was complete union on the level of ideas, feelings and attitudes."[1] Such equality and openness made him decide to live completely for this woman who seemed perfect—"relative to me"—and to create, far from high society and Auteil, an enclave that respected neither human laws nor conventions, a republic for two.

"When a man and a woman share an intense passion," he wrote, "it seems to me that, regardless of the obstacles separating them—husband, parents, etc—the two lovers are united *by nature*, belong to each other *by divine right.*" This affinity far outstripped his ideals of friendship, transforming the misogynist into a partisan of pure love.

Chamfort bade farewell to his friends, swore to return to Paris only in passing, and left with Marthe for her house in Vaudouleurs, near Etampes. He thus moved from a fashionable village to true nature. Fruit from the garden and a fire in the fireplace now moved him to poetry. A few books, walks in the Fontainebleau forest, and the company of Marthe Buffon provoked indescribable happiness. "Love doesn't allow its secret to be revealed," he said. "A man who knows it is incapable of divulging it, and he forgets it the moment his passion ceases, for the secret is nothing other than love itself."[2]

This was to be his most moving experience. Freed from rancor and from illness—a doctor had assured him that a mistress was worth a thousand drugs—he discovered life in a couple, emotional *dependence* accompanied by total financial independence. Marriage was never mentioned, apparently. But Aubin said he saw Chamfort love Marthe Buffon "as ardently as a mistress, as tenderly as his mother." With the pieces of his puzzle now in place, Chamfort decided to spent the rest of his days with Marthe:

Mes plus chers souvenirs, mes moments les plus doux,
Me laissent le regret d'avoir vécu sans vous:
J'ai connu des plaisirs et j'ai perdu ma vie.
Elle commence à vous . . .[3]

The sweetest of memories, most tender of times
Still leave the regret of having lived without you:
The pleasure I gained was at the cost of my life.
Which now commences with you . . .

But the fairy tale came to an end. In the spring of 1783, Marthe Buffon fell ill and, after two months of agony, died in Chamfort's arms. The six happiest months of his life came to a close—six months that seemed a mere "instant."

A friend hastened to bring him back to Paris in a post chaise.

There, cut off from the world, he relived all the stages of an emotion he thought he had banished from his life forever. "I've feared, I admit, I've feared your presence as much as I desire it," he finally wrote to the good Mme. Panckoucke. "I fear choking on seeing the person my friend loved best, about whom we spoke most often. . . . When I think that the very day, and probably at the very hour when I shall be at your place, she would be seeing you too. . . . I must stop, can write no longer."[4]

The Bellechasse Group

Moved by this tragedy, two of Chamfort's friends, the comte de Choiseul-Gouffier and the comte de Narbonne, dragged him to Holland, that Mecca of free trade and freethinkers, the most prosperous country in Europe. After a stopover at the prince de Ligne's chateau in Beloeil, the trio arrived in Amsterdam, which Chamfort visited mutely. The two counts organized a trip up the Moërdick canal on a yacht, but with no greater success. According to an aristocrat's account, however, Chamfort stood up and took Narbonne and Choiseul-Gouffier by the hand and said, looking straight at them: "Do you know of anything duller and dumber than a French gentleman?"[5] The two friends laughed, and Narbonne would laugh again in 1791 at this allegorical foreshadowing of the revolutionary Jeu de Paume oath. But the sunny spell did not last. Admiring the printer Plantin's tomb in Antwerp, Chamfort criticized France, accusing it of letting geniuses die of hunger.[6] The bitterness increased once back in Paris, symbol of the living death from which Marthe Buffon had saved him. The only period in his life he valued was over.

Seeing him determined to flee his past, Choiseul-Gouffier took Chamfort to the home of Talleyrand, Choiseul-Gouffier's childhood friend. There Chamfort would meet with Narbonne, with the brave and dashing duc de Lauzun (a suitor rejected by the queen, whom he subsequently detested), with the comte de Lauraguais (a brilliant and whimsical dilettante), and with Panchaud (a financier from Geneva). Unscrupulous speculators, partisans of an English-style monarchy and instant success, these young Turks immediately adopted Chamfort. "They thought themselves wits because they saw [him] regularly," claimed the comte de Moré.[7]

Chamfort became mentor to this group which dined "any old fashion" in a bachelor pad on rue de Bellechasse. "We talked a little about everything, with the greatest liberty," Talleyrand would later say. "This was in the spirit and the fashion of the times. For all of us it was pleasant and instructive, from the standpoint of a certain ambitiousness."[8]

The comte de Lauraguais was an exception, however. This author of a very strange *Mémoire par moi, pour moi* [*Memoirs by myself, for myself*] seemed to limit his ambitiousness to experiments on the firing of porcelain and the decomposition of diamonds, as well as to small volumes on racehorses, vaccinations, and the *Compagnie des Indes*. Born in 1733, with three sons by the singer Sophie Arnould (who had suggested that Chamfort was taking the *Mustapha* fiasco "tragically"), Lauraguais was known for violent outbursts earning him numerous *lettres de cachet* which he amusingly referred to as his "correspondence with the king." The comte de Lauraguais illustrates the amazing curiosity certain gentlemen had for science, medicine, the theater (he penned a tragedy), and even for the revolutions that studded the end of the eighteenth century: Paoli's uprising in Corsica in 1755, those in Geneva in 1768 and 1782, that of the usurper Pugatchev in Russia in 1773, and the American insurrection of 1775, not to mention the movements that would soon break out in the Dutch United Provinces and Austrian Netherlands. Observing history with the bemused indifference of his class, the dilettante count would thus follow his friend Chamfort into the whirlwind of 1789, along with the duc de Lauzun and the comte de Narbonne.

While Talleyrand's remaining guests were patently ambitious, Vaudouleurs had reinforced Chamfort's taste for the austere. "Suppose we throw him out the window?" suggested Talleyrand.[9] There was even a bit of Diogenes in this waif who held up Amsterdam's shipwrights as examples for Narbonne and Choiseul-Gouffier. This was obviously asking too much from an illegitimate son of Louis XV and a nephew of the great Choiseul. Not that Choiseul-Gouffier was the greediest of the group; he was a generous patron to artists, illegitimate children, and Greeks.

The good conscience Choiseul-Gouffier bought through his philanthropy, however, irritated the misanthrope. "You're easily contented on my account!" said Chamfort after Choiseul had noisily approved the proposed marriage between Chamfort and an illegitimate woman. This passing anger was merely the aggressive expression of an inexpressible mourning, for Chamfort would cite Choiseul-Gouffier (that "easy, loving and forgetful" friend accord-

ing to Talleyrand) as one of the people who had reconciled him to the
human race. Reconciled, he might have added, to a life he had been
ready to abandon.

The Lame Devil

Chamfort was equally fond of the only member of the Bellechasse
group who could rival him—Talleyrand (whom Napoleon would
much later describe as "shit in silk stockings"). Chamfort introduced
the cleric into the salon of Mme. Vigée-Lebrun, who left this portrait: "His face was graceful, his cheeks round and, although he was
lame, he was no less elegant and was referred to as a man of good
fortune." Great minds reportedly come together, but Talleyrand
was not yet at the peak of his talents. He became known in high society by the embarrassed "Ah! Ah!" which he had used in response
to a question by the duchesse de Gramont. "What do you mean by
that 'Ah! Ah!'?" continued the duchess. "I didn't say 'Ah! Ah!,' I said
'Oh! Oh!.'" And this comment apparently caused laughter. Chamfort
had carefully crafted "the cynicism of his [own] language to be a faithful picture of courtly behavior" (according to Chateaubriand),
whereas Talleyrand was just starting out. And just as Chamfort had
imitated Duclos, this young ecclesiastic agent set about copying
Chamfort's witticisms.[10] Of course, no one likes to cite their models,
least of all a Talleyrand who hoped that his personality would be discussed for centuries to come. Thus, in preening himself for his
Mémoires, the ex-bishop reduced Chamfort to the role of extra in his
own lightning rise, simply recalling several meals taken together at
the home of "some good woman." This self-sanctification evokes
another of Chamfort's aphorisms (also copied down by Talleyrand):
"Memoirs left by people in power . . . recall the story of the saint
who left a hundred thousand ecus for his own canonization."[11]

But history never repeats itself completely. While the art of conversation perpetuated itself through Chamfort and Talleyrand, society was changing. The prince de Ligne observed haggard, hurried
men discuss what they would do in the place of ministers and the
king. Social questions, disdained by the Enlightenment, began to be
raised—the Third Estate (commoners) was now recognized as being
intelligent. Comte Louis-Philippe de Ségur, who flattered himself in
his memoirs for having attracted Chamfort's attention, described
this change, due in part to the young aristocracy (whose leading
lights had left to fight for American independence). "All those who

occupied posts or responsibilities close to the throne were from another era, another century. We outwardly respected the old debris of an ancient order which we evaded by laughing over its behavior, ignorance and prejudices. . . . Freedom, whatever its language, pleased us by its courage; equality, by its convenience. It was pleasant to descend as long as you thought you could climb back up at will; and, without foresight, we simultaneously enjoyed the advantages of patricians and the delights of plebian philosophy."[12]

Talleyrand, Narbonne, Panchaud, and others circling around the Bellechasse group thus accelerated the shift from literature to politics, a conversion begun by Chamfort in Auteuil. Marthe Buffon's death had sapped his nihilism, and he had gotten into the habit of talking not only about independence but about trade and taxes. Shortly afterward, Abbé Morellet introduced him to the work of Adam Smith, the first free-trade economist (which Chamfort regretted not having read earlier in order to make money). He probably recognized the limitations of the "reformism" of Choiseul-Gouffier, who wanted to reroof his peasants' cottages with tiles instead of thatch, yet met with objection from the peasants because it would mean paying higher property taxes; Choiseul-Gouffier, meanwhile, was not above begetting himself to the Prévôt des Marchands (or "mayor") to see about having his own taxes reduced. Chamfort, after having long been a prisoner—even in the negative—of his literary obsession, finally saw that these liberal aristocrats and ambitious commoners offered the possibility of escape. He would encounter most of them on the front lines of agitation in 1787.

On the Ambivalence of Nobility

It was during this same period, however, that the maréchal de Ségur, Minister of War and father of Comte Louis-Philippe, announced that four degrees of noble lineage were required for officers wishing to serve in the army. This measure, often cited by revolutionaries as highly symbolic, in fact expressed the rise of aristocratic demands contemporary with and complementary to the rise of liberal ideas.[13]

Louis XVI was largely responsible for this phenomenon. Right from the first year of his reign, even as he was appointing Philosophers to his ministries (without much conviction, given his profoundly religious nature), he had recalled the noble *parlements* from an exile decreed by Louis XV as a result of their insubordination. Catastrophic from every point of view, this recall had given new hope to the *noblesse de robe* which was particularly vigilant over its privileges and took no delight in "slumming" (as demonstrated by Chamfort's real mother).

Far more closed than it had been under Louis XIV (who had ennobled numerous commoners), a major part of this ecclesiastic, judicial, and military elite now expected to recover the influence it had wielded under the regent earlier in the century. Spurred by Louis XVI's weakness, this aristocracy aimed to profit from the simultaneous decline of Enlightenment and despotism. It thus undoubtedly accelerated Chamfort's conversion. No one was more sensitive than he to the nobility's burlesque forms of snobbery. Choiseul-Gouffier recounted how, on leaving the Prévôt des Marchands, he ran into the comte d'Orsay, who had come to complain about a *reduction* in his taxes, lest this imply "any dishonor to his titles of nobility."[14] Chamfort detested this convulsive return to social "racism" on the part of a class that, ever since the decline of its military role, had hesitated between abandon and reconquest, suicide and revenge. It was every bit as ambivalent as he, judging by the example of the marquis de Montesquiou, who had just legally established his direct descent from Clovis and who would become an ardent revolutionary.

The probable cause of such ambivalence lay in the frustration of a class that had no real political role—apart from the ministers it provided—and which eyed with envy the parliamentary influence of the English nobility (regularly reinvigorated by the awarding of noble titles based on merit). This model explains the contradictory ambitions of Talleyrand's dinner guests, who were also guests of the duc de Lauzun during festivities at his "pleasure retreat" in Montrouge. They became the cadres for that aristocrat's revolution in which Chamfort would play, for a while, the role of paradoxical fellow traveler.

11. LONG LIVE MIRABEAU!
AND LONG LIVE THE CHARMER!

I can't resist the pleasure of rubbing the most electrifying head I've ever known.

Mirabeau

Mirabeau is just the flint I need for my musket.

Chamfort

This little revolution of 1782, like so many others, might have merely restored the old Chamfort, had it not been for the entrance that same year of the fascinating figure of Honoré Gabriel Riqueti de Mirabeau. Chamfort was diametrically different from this Provençal who dreamed of fame, fortune, and women, who raged like Hercules and repented like a lamb, and whose exuberant libido gave birth to exquisite erotic tales (in which nuns with "lewd little beavers" discovered bliss with their Mother Superior). Two personalities, one assertive and the other reactive; two provinces, one Mediterranean, the other mountainous—these two forces were irresistibly drawn toward one another.

For Mirabeau was also an illegitimate child, in his own way. Born with a twisted foot and with two molars already formed in his enormous head (his mother would nearly die giving birth), his father considered him an *ignoble* reminder of their origins. (Their oldest known ancestor was a cloth merchant. Mirabeau's father consoled himself with the observation, "Every race has its excrement.") Insulted, humiliated, and beaten by his father, Mirabeau was the last serf of a feudal lord who had freed his peasants, of a brilliant physiocrat known to many (including the moralist Vauvenargues) as the "Friend of Man." Fleeing such sadism—the Mirabeau and Sade families were related, moreover—the "plebeian count" racked up thefts, abductions, and duels. He slept with his sister, and forced an heiress from Aix to marry him by appearing nude on her balcony. He lost his remaining scruples after spending six years in prison; the historian Michelet would claim that he acquired the vices of the poor on top of those of the rich.

His release from prison at age thirty-one resolved nothing. He was threatened with a *lettre de cachet* by his father, and with a trial by his wife. His manners were heavy-handed, his compliments excessive. The enormous colored buttons of his clothing, the red gouges in his smallpox-scarred face (as though singed in hell), and the satyriasis that condemned him to a permanent erection all placed him on the fringe of society. This pariah recognized in Chamfort a social climber who could hoist him back into his class. Dazzled by Chamfort's contacts and his academician's chair, Mirabeau followed him from the Helvétius "hospital" to the Talleyrand bachelor pad with the energy that just twenty years earlier had been the prerogative of the Herculean *Adonis*.

Mirabeau, who was everything except common, also saw Chamfort as being of truly sturdy character during an era of fake Romans. Mirabeau was convinced that he himself was superior to everything that existed, yet inferior to what he should be, and he now incorporated Chamfort's image into this complex. "I left my cradle and swaddling-clothes too late," Mirabeau wrote to Chamfort. "Human convention strangled me for too long. . . . If only I'd had the good fortune to meet you ten years ago, my tread would have been so much firmer!"[1] Chamfort's opinions replaced a father's blows in Mirabeau's masochistic universe. The self-taught man placed himself at the feet of this teacher, whom he compared to Voltaire, Cato, Lucian, Epicurus, and Tacitus. Their relationship went from calculating to lyrical, almost loving: Mirabeau, who was punished for sodomy at school, confessed to having read Chamfort's letters with as much emotion as those from his first mistresses.

Mirabeau's adopted son, Lucas-Montigny, later tended to discount Chamfort's influence on his father (who held almost everyone in contempt, from his persecutors to his saviors). The influence nevertheless clearly emerges from their correspondence.[2] Chamfort was not only Mirabeau's elder by nine years but "a higher and older self from whom [Mirabeau] expected and awaited impulses," according to Nietzsche,[3] one of the first to have described their relationship in terms of Chamfort's influence on an entire generation. Mirabeau, a believer in superior personality, who was more aware of the force of his character than of his faults, saw Chamfort as the symbol of independence and success—for Mirabeau himself remained a slave to rebellion. "You are living proof that it is not true that one must bend or break," he wrote Chamfort, "that one can attain the highest consideration without a superstitious respect for society and

its laws."[4] Chamfort was practically a "natural" in high society, a reminder of everyone's origins, a superman (and the only man) for
whom Mirabeau would try to behave as well as possible. "There is
no situation of some seriousness where I don't find myself saying:
Chamfort would frown. Don't do that, don't write that; or *Chamfort will be
pleased;* and thus my joy is doubled or centupled." Mirabeau had
found someone to act as his conscience, his moralist, his Vauvenargues. Early in 1784, Mirabeau dropped the *"fils"* [the younger]
from his signature.

Chamfort did not believe too strongly in friendship. La Harpe
had made it suspect, and Marthe Buffon had rendered it bland.
"New friends made after a certain age . . . are to former friends
what glass eyes . . . are to real eyes," he observed. Mirabeau's irresistible friendliness and seductiveness, however, along with his insistence on placing Chamfort above "created beings," would change
everything. Suffering from his own singularity, Chamfort acquiesced to this noisy worship—and this complicity between rebels.
He had thought that he alone could survive at the level of lucidity
he had attained. "Almost all men are slaves . . . because they're
unable to pronounce the word 'no,' he asserted.[5] Yet Mirabeau
knew how to say no. Badgered by his sense of unfulfilled genius,
Chamfort lent Mirabeau the collection of aphorisms he had begun
writing in the utmost secrecy ever since the failure of *Mustapha*.[6] The
text had an instant impact on Mirabeau—"that sponge swollen with
the ideas of others," according to Rivarol. Twenty years of experience were passed on to the disciple, who discovered the harshest
agenda ever voluntarily adopted and henceforth claimed to be "of
one soul" with his best "and practically only friend." Thus the people's tribune, who would one day dazzle France, was nurtured on
Chamfort's unpublished work.

This "electrifying" encounter changed Chamfort, too. He realized, for example, that it was possible to shape people, that the
"public" did not represent all of humanity, that his rancor and misanthropy no longer sufficed. He had believed in a bygone paradise,
but neoclassicism, following science and Philosophy, turned out to
be incapable of changing things. So he turned to the future. Just as
he had taken a nom de plume twenty years ago, now—at age
forty—he launched his battle cry: "Human society must start
afresh!"[7] The idea would gain ground, would even become–for better or worse—the inspiration behind most revolutions up to the present. But it might have remained unformulated without Mirabeau's

megalomania. Man knows the movement of the planets, yet doesn't know how to conduct himself, Mirabeau would say to Chamfort. He knows how to grovel, but not obey; how to rebel, but not defend himself; how to love, but not become attached. The two men's lives—indeed, their century—suddenly changed register. They were conducting a private war against the whole world; they issued a public challenge to civilization. Soon posterity seekers would become interested in their contemporaries once again, would come to life in their own lifetimes. "Human society must start afresh!" This slogan, which no one took up at the time for fear of ridicule (yet which everyone would shout ten years later), launched the era in which being a revolutionary meant being *overly* ambitious. Chamfort, like a volcano in his native Auvergne, was becoming active just when America won its war against England.

Darling Child of the Ancien Régime

Yet this battle cry originated in the stately residence of one of the most visible of Versailles courtiers. For Chamfort had been living with the comte de Vaudreuil for several months, among paintings by Poussin, Rembrandt, and Hubert Robert, furniture by Boulle, Ming vases. Another contradiction in an unpredictable life, which Chamfort justified as follows: "He forced me to accept an apartment at his place."[8] Rather, Chamfort seized the chance to put Vaudouleurs behind him forever (whence Vaudreuil had come to rescue him), and to take up a life that now held about as much appeal for him as a "half-sucked orange." A long friendship thus commenced between "the most chivalrous, most magnificent"[9] man at court and the prophet of the Revolution. Chamfort swore to remain forever at rue de la Chaise in the Faubourg St. Germain neighborhood, next to this gentleman who was exactly his age.

      "Those who didn't live in the years around 1789 don't know how delightful life can be," Talleyrand said to Guizot. Vaudreuil knew. An impatient lover as well as unequaled horseman, actor, and dancer, this colonist from Santo Domingo had carved himself an empire in Versailles in only a few years, after having participated in the Seven Years' War. His mistress was the peach-complexioned, ivory-toothed favorite of the queen (who had her named duchess of Polignac and appointed her governess to the royal children). His best friend, Calonne, had become Comptroller General of Finances thanks to Vaudreuil's plotting. The king's brother, Artois, made his fortune available to Vaudreuil, Vaudreuil's own being blocked on the island by the American war. Marie-Antoinette sought him out for the idylls based on dialogues by Favart or Sedaine, performed in the theater at the Petit Trianon. "The Charmer," along with the Polignac clan, thus ruled over the pastimes of an Austrian who hated Versailles etiquette and had decided to enjoy the pleasures of private life. Vaudreuil's frivolity nevertheless masked a moodiness attributed to his poor health, and a pride that brooked no superiority (and which could even be "offended by equality"[10] claimed Besenval, a courtier). Gaining control over the queen—without ever controlling himself—and capable of Homeric anger against Mme. de Polignac (for being too impartial), Vaudreuil led the search for diversion at a hellish pace, exhausting the court. "Whoever has no character is not a man, but a thing," said Chamfort.[11] Vaudreuil was certainly not a thing.

Although he represented the perfect accomplishment of his class, the culmination of centuries of marriages and abductions, the apotheosis of aristocratic style (to which Mirabeau was an exception), Vaudreuil had no official role, save the derisory one of Grand Falconer of France (whose task involved receiving the gyrfalcons offered by the king of Denmark). But the fault lay not only with the king nor a court jealous of his privileges and condescending over his poor extraction.[12] "A learned man seeks for himself, a rich man endeavors to escape from himself," Chamfort noted.[13] Plagued by an ambition as vague as it was general, the Charmer (as Vaudreuil was known) compensated by becoming a patron to artists. He had not succeeded in being named duke, nor Gentleman to the Royal Children, nor even director of the king's buildings in place of his enemy d'Angiviller (who was then sketching plans for the future Louvre museum). So Vaudreuil set himself up as the center of an imaginary pantheon of writers. "He finds it fine, very natural, that one possess talent, merit, even loftiness, and that one be honored for such titles, even publicly [at court], whether or not one happens to be minister or ambassador," Chamfort confided to Abbé Morellet. The Charmer was avaricious at Versailles (where he constantly complained of having to live), yet would be the most generous and most sensitive of Chamfort's patrons as well as the salvation of his own family.

Yet Chamfort remained aloof from this redistribution. The memory of Angiviller, the fear of being considered a kept man, and an underlying desire to affirm his honesty before this unscrupulous Versailles courtier induced Chamfort to turn down all of Vaudreuil's offers. "I promise to borrow twenty-five louis from you when you've

paid your debts," Chamfort told him.[14] Vaudreuil insisted, convinced that "offering, giving, and accepting are all the same thing
between true friends." Chamfort begged off. "Please be assured that
I have no need of what I lack." Limiting himself to the superfluous,
Chamfort would attend the stately salons held on rue de la Chaise,
where every Wednesday Vaudreuil would pass out pens, pencils, and
guitars to his guests. Mme. Vigée-Lebrun dressed the Polignacs in
colors and the singer Garat wreathed them in notes, while Chamfort
taunted them with "strikingly resembling" portraits, since lost. But the
tone was so right that everyone applauded—especially Vaudreuil.
"These poets are madmen. But such beautiful lines, such beautiful
lines . . . " Chamfort would then go back up to his rooms, returning to
his Diogenes-like simplicity and reading tales to Mirabeau, the handsome comte d'Antraigues, or Talleyrand (who described such tales as
tedious in his *Mémoires*). "There he lived like an eccentric," recounted
Aubin, whom Chamfort also convoked to his "tub" on rue de la
Chaise, "to stand out all the more from men who seemed all alike with
their polite manners. . . . He was a kind of bear who acted tame only
during the show."

The Charmer Reddens

And the show was continuous. Celebrations and plays were given
at the Charmer's country home in Gennevilliers, where his friend
the comte d'Artois came to hunt. The king's brother (who would
one day reign as Charles X) was as frivolous and spendthrift as
Vaudreuil. Artois had his own "pleasure house," the Bagatelle, built
in only forty days. Along with Talleyrand, he was one of the regulars at Vaudreuil's chateau (today destroyed), and he suffered from
Vaudreuil's voraciousness. "I want . . . " Vaudreuil once began.
"Never has a Bourbon said I want," snapped Artois. Artois was nevertheless the first spectator to applaud the count on his little rosewood stage. Reputed to be the best actor in Paris society, equal to the
Comédie-Française actor François René Molé, the Charmer played opposite Mme. Dugazon at Gennevilliers, where he could forget his
mandatory duos with Marie-Antoinette, that "royally bad" actress,
at the Petit Trianon. Sometimes, reddening, he even launched into
his own verses, or read a little comedy for children.

　　While he was not the complete Renaissance man many gentlemen of the day casually aspired to be, Vaudreuil was nevertheless a
long way from the vapid courtier the Revolution would condemn.

He was as intelligent as possible in an environment where birth dispensed with the need to reflect, and he offered the following insightful criticism of the acting of his only society rival: "M. de Miromesnil tries to stagger; drunks try to stand up." He displayed early signs of an inferiority complex toward artists, at a time when his class held itself up as the model to be imitated by artists (going so far as to reject portraits felt to be of insufficient "likeness"). In addition to a strange affinity of temperament, it was this complex that united Vaudreuil and Chamfort (victim of a similar, if less fathomable, complex toward the aristocracy). This also explains the strangely peaceful coexistence between the "darling child of the Ancien Régime" and the illegitimate child awaiting the New—both were above their station, and the first sincerely thought he could make the second content.

The results of Vaudreuil's patronage were meager, however, unless Chamfort's maxims and anecdotes are included (rue de la Chaise provided Chamfort with numerous topics). The poet Lebrun would never publish the "masterpiece" he had been promising for twenty years (despite having added the name of the Greek lyric poet Pindar to his own). Vigée, brother of Mme. Vigée-Lebrun, mainly wanted to have a good time at Vaudreuil's residence, and he was content to write poems to the glory of his sister (winning himself the nickname "Figé" [stuck]). Ginguené, who had come to Paris from Brittany to publish his poem *Confession de Zulmé* and to write the libretto for *Pomponin*, an operetta by his friend Niccolo Piccinni, would produce almost nothing until his *Ode à Necker* in 1789. Only Hubert Robert and Joseph Vernet, painters famous for their ruins and storms, would be creative under the spell of the Charmer— excepting, of course, the dancers, violinists, and singers who were his protégés but who by definition left no trace. Paradoxically, the Ancien Régime's darling child was more effective as courtier than patron, intensifying Marie-Antoinette's attachment to Mme. de Polignac (Vaudreuil's mistress and distant relation) by skillfully thwarting access. He was also more successful as collector than patron, as suggested by the masterpieces currently in the Louvre.

Vaudreuil had excuses, however. Silenced by their own criticism, most writers published only *concetti*. Thus Ginguené, on the point of publishing "Lebrun-Pindare's" complete works following the poet's death, discovered dozens of epigrams by Lebrun directed against himself. Yet Ginguené had been Lebrun's friend and disciple prior to becoming Chamfort's, apparently around 1786. In the final analysis, it was Chamfort who properly fulfilled the role of "pro-tégé," reading his tales at rue de la Chaise, and winning a set-rhyme contest in Gennevilliers by composing a poem dedicated to Mme. Vigée-Lebrun (Vaudreuil's other mistress) using the four set words *fougère, hameau, bergère, chalumeau* [fern, hamlet, shepherdess, pipe]. It would be cruel to publish these "little nothings" here, but they were enough to keep Vaudreuil happy. He commissioned Chamfort to write a licentious and antireligious pamphlet,[15] then urged him to finish his poem on the Fronde—this was the only shortcoming of an otherwise perfect patron, for Chamfort found it "a little hard" to complete anything on demand.[16]

It was Chamfort who was henceforth able to put Vaudreuil to work, for he found that the liberal aristocrat had no "mote in his eye"—just "a little dust on his eyeglass."[17] Banking on Vaudreuil's contempt for a court that asked, on the birth of Jules de Polignac, "Is the child Vaudreuil's or the queen's?" and also counting on his un-conscious rivalry with the king (the count enjoyed provoking the king's early departure from the Polignac salon by setting the clocks ahead), Chamfort passed on to Vaudreuil the latest books banned by the monarchy. Nothing serious on the surface. But Chamfort's intel-lectual hold was patent, and some suspected that this planter who made slaves of Polignac, the queen, and even the king (according to Michelet), had just inherited a formidable counselor.

"If this play is performed, the Bastille will have to be demol-ished," Louis XVI is supposed to have declared on banning *Le mariage de Figaro*.[18] Chamfort then introduced Beaumarchais to Vaudreuil, who stated at Versailles, "*Marriage* is your only recourse!"[19] Chamfort repeated the operation with his former patron Breteuil, who had the king's ear. The queen, worked on by Vaudreuil, agreed in turn to bring her husband around. Thus on September 22, 1783, the court came to Gennevilliers to plant the bomb that would shortly blow up in its face. "You put yourself to the trouble of being born—nothing else!" Figaro tossed off to the Polignacs, who applauded. Chamfort was the only person to express reservations about a play which was "full of wit" but monstrous in its "triviality."[20] Finally, Chamfort gave Mirabeau's pamphlet, *Des lettres de cachet et des prisons d'état* [*On "let-tres de cachet" and royal prisons*] to Vaudreuil, who had it read to the king. Impressed at the extent of his own powers, Louis XVI ordered the closing of the keep at Vincennes. In 1784, the crowd paraded past this symbol "of former barbary," where Mirabeau once hud-dled. The incident, once again, was hardly decisive. Yet by unconsciously serving Chamfort, Vaudreuil hastened the decline of a Versailles that no longer courted the king but rather the queen, and where the mechanism devised by Louis XIV for all eternity now only clicked for a minority of courtiers.

Praising the Polignacs

Chamfort quite logically defended the tools of his subterfuge. These included the Polignacs, whose leader, Diane, admired Benjamin Franklin. "At the same time that he would tell us in a hundred pointed ways that people at court were idiots, insolent oppressors, lowly valets, greedy courtiers whose wives were so many tattlers and trollops," wrote Morellet, "[he] would speak of Mme. Jules, Mme. Diane and the duc de Polignac . . . and above all of M. de Vaudreuil—whose dining companion and entertainer he was—as infinitely worthy people of the finest character, possessing the best, most refined and profoundest minds."[21] Such enthusiasm also marked Chamfort's bucolic set-rhymes honoring Mme. Vigée-Lebrun, mistress to Vaudreuil and Calonne. This shepherdess was highly gifted in art and finance (famous for her sunny, flowery portraits of the queen and the Polignac den of females, she was showered with commissions from the Charmer—painting him five times—and with gifts from Comptroller General Calonne—there were rumors of diamonds camouflaged in candies); in her *Mémoires*, however, she regrets having invited certain guests. "There was one I always detested, as though anticipating the future: Chamfort. I nevertheless received him often, out of consideration for several of his friends, notably M. de Vaudreuil. His conversation was highly witty, but bitter and full of venom and utterly without charm for me; I found, for that matter, his cynicism and filthiness royally unpleasant. . . . M. de Vaudreuil had lodged him wonderfully at home and, being almost continually at Versailles, had a table set in his absence for Chamfort and those it pleased Chamfort to invite. He treated the man like a brother; and that man, when his revolutionary friends later reproached him for having lived in the house of a former noble, cowardly replied, 'What do you expect, I was Plato at the court of the tyrant Dionysius.'"[22] Did Mme. Vigée-Lebrun, whom Mme. de Boigen described as an "idiot," fully understand the allusion? It's unlikely. Dionysius of Syracuse, a patron of the arts, summoned Plato to his court to help him found the ideal Republic. This is obviously a long way from rue de la Chaise. But it was, during the Revolution, a way for Chamfort to justify his past; similarly, during the restoration, Mme. Vigée-Lebrun put her own in order, retrospectively populating the Ancien Régime with people above reproach— certain guests excepted.

Art without a Trace

Yet Mme. Vigée-Lebrun was not wrong on every point: never had Chamfort's conversation been so brilliant. He was at the summit of this art which left no trace. He now intimidated the class that had intimidated him. Mme. Roland claimed that he made people laugh and think at the same time, a very rare thing. Victims themselves applauded the "fireworks" that lit up their shortcomings with glaring clarity.[23] The aristocracy fought over this virtuoso who spoke ill of it with unrelenting inventiveness. "I saw him, so to speak, every day," noted the Swiss journalist Meister, who wrote for Grimm's *Correspondance Littéraire*. "He considered me a great friend, perhaps for having noticed that I listened more closely than others. Yet [I never] heard him repeat the same line or anecdote twice."[24] Only Rivarol and the prince de Ligne could compete with this champion talker who, not liking "mismatches," handpicked his audience. "Society people no sooner flock together, than they think their society high," would say Chamfort, who addressed himself, au contraire, only to those who *merited* it.

For he was everything except egalitarian when it came to conversation. He favored an elite based on intelligence and wit (his ultimate criterion), and actually achieved his dream of a veritable hierarchy. Chamfort imposed his injustice on the aristocracy—the best way, in his view, to cease being beholden to it. Through humor, one "avoids being compromised," he claimed. "It confirms our superiority over the things and people we make fun of." Yet Chamfort didn't feel that this particular superiority was iniquitous, because it was ephemeral, reversible, without real consequence; also because he had to constantly struggle to maintain it. "He was himself very careful to avoid ridicule; he considered it a misfortune to fall into it, and placed importance in avoiding it," stressed his friend Roederer. "He ascribed this foible to contact with high society: 'You cannot believe,' he would say, 'how much wit it takes to avoid ever being ridiculous.'"[25] And, it might be added, to avoid ever stumbling on the one battlefield (apart from bed) on which he bested the nobility.

Nobility not only weighed on his birth, it lightened his style.

Without the wit and contradictions of high society, without its vanity (that senile form of honor), Chamfort would have been less brilliant, less complex, less funny. It stimulated that mild contempt that encourages zest and brio. It enabled a writer hobbled by academicism to practice verbal nonconformism. And it made him laugh—at others' expense. The ridiculousness of high society confirmed his misanthropy, and he was grateful for that. It saved him from acrimony—all the while secretly nourishing his bitterness. He was invited to the party in order to spice the celebrations with a dash of doubt—a fleeting truth tossed off by the king's grinning fool. Chamfort's secret, according to Aubin, was "to think and say everything out loud, in front of those who cannot or dare not do either, and who are grateful to you for daring to do it for them."

Finally, aristocratic society enabled Chamfort to flee a literary scene compared to which the salons seemed a haven of kindness. Though he occasionally returned to the Académie, Chamfort in effect avoided his equals; this obviously included La Harpe, who accused him of living—or rather of "dying"—in envy. Chamfort in turn denounced La Harpe's "pride, venom and character," and in March 1784 waxed ironic about the performance of La Harpe's *Coriolan* given to benefit the poor:

> *Pour les pauvres la comédie*
> *Donne une pauvre tragédie;*
> *nous devons tous en vérité*
> *Bien l'applaudir par charité.*[26]

> On behalf of the poor, the Comédie
> Performs a very poor tragedy;
> Obliging us all, in all verity,
> To loudly applaud out of charity.

Suard, who had criticized the impurity of Chamfort's *Eloge de La Fontaine*, just as he criticized practically everything, also merited a dig: "The man's taste is distasteful." The war had become less violent, for Chamfort no longer wrote. But *Mustapha's* assassins remained vigilant against the ex-Philosopher. Only Marmontel, secretary to the Académie following d'Alembert's death in 1783, became an exception as a result of his cautiousness. This "fellow" found Chamfort amusing and admitted seeing him on occasion, "with precaution and propriety," not wanting to make an enemy of him. But the financial success of the clan's members underscored Chamfort's own failure, and he henceforth measured himself against them only in society. Conversation was the only art where he could dominate effortlessly and where his aristocratic contempt for work paid off.

For it was in high society that he was at his best, that he abandoned himself to pleasure. "Conversation is like a trip across water; we leave the land almost without noticing, and realize that the coast has been left only when it is already far behind," he noted.[27] Chamfort was not only a masked fencer lifting his adversary's mask with his sword, a salon vigilante putting everyone in their place without leaving his own, an urbane critic pointing out the unintelligibility of a line by Lebrun-Pindare (who would complain to Rivarol that "taste no longer exists in France"); he was also the dilettante who simply liked to pass the time, to travel via conversation. Although his oeuvre accurately conveys a certain harshness of character, the everyday Chamfort didn't drily recite maxims. He should be imagined improvising for hours at a stretch, happy to laugh and make others laugh, all the more amiable when appreciated. He should be seen seated against the paneling of the ground floor rooms at number 8, rue de la Chaise (the only ones still in their original state), recounting exchanges heard here and there: "M—— said to me, 'I've renounced friendship with two men; one, because he's never spoken to me about himself, and the other, because he has never spoken to me about myself.'" Another anecdote reveals the spirit of the times: "Beaumarchais, who let himself be maltreated by the duc de Chaulnes, without challenging him to a duel, received a challenge from M. de La Blanche. To whom Beaumarchais replied, 'I've refused better.'" As does this retort by a man known for the profoundness of his levity: "The dying M. de Fontenelle was asked, 'How's everything going?' 'It's not going,' he replied. 'It's going away.'" And then there's this comment on the gourmet who once served dishes exclusively *black* to guests dressed entirely in black: "M—— would say of M. de La Reynière, whom everyone visited for his cuisine, and whom everyone found very boring, 'He's edible, but indigestible.'"

Brilliance and Obscurity

That is the Chamfort we will never really know. He enabled the elite among the Ancien Régime and among his friends to pass delightful, fleeting hours. Which is why this misunderstood man was always invited back, even by hostesses such as Mme. Vigée-Lebrun who

scarcely appreciated his apparent "savagery." Which is why he enjoyed the unflagging friendship of dozens of his contemporaries.

Marmontel noted, as did Abbé Morellet, that Chamfort "had a
liking for certain important persons, whom he exempted from his
satire." Therein lies the key to his paradoxical behavior and his unavowed snobbism, which many saw as proof of his hypocrisy. Like
most superior beings, however, Chamfort was a "true liar." Once he
deceived himself by accepting the rules of the salon and the law of
the mask, he effectively believed, with the best faith in the world, in
the sincerity of his own antisocial statements. Just as he truly
thought he could completely dispense with literature and women
once they had wounded him, having repressed the memory of the
passion he once held for both.

Chamfort liked Vaudreuil, then; and secretly admired him for
what he represented—that nobility whose consistent happiness
Chamfort envied.[28] Chamfort was not jealous of upper-class
wealth—although he did experience that insidious jealousy toward
riches scorned, which this same upper class delighted in arousing.
He was struck, however, by its ability to be content with the pleasures of society, to accept the world *for what it was*. "In seeing and
experiencing the pain associated with intense feelings of love or
friendship, either through the death of the loved one or the vagaries
of life, one is tempted to think that dissipation and frivolity aren't
foolishness after all, that life is only worth what society people make
of it," he confessed.[29] This was a "bottom-line" policy for a moralist
at the peak of his society career.

Mirabeau, however, quickly saw the reverse side of this
brilliance—Chamfort said that he was one of those who best sensed
it. For while Mirabeau unreservedly admired Chamfort's *strength*,
he was tempted to exploit Chamfort's weaknesses as they became
apparent. Exasperated by Chamfort's slowness in writing the pamphlet that Franklin had commissioned from them (against the hereditary Society of the Cincinnati that America was considering establishing for the heroes of its War of Independence), Mirabeau took
Chamfort's invitation to be treated as an equal literally—in order to
become his superior. "You will do it 1°) because you are fond of me;
2°) because this work has been of some use," declared Mirabeau on
requesting Chamfort to correct *Des lettres de cachet*, which he wanted
to reprint.[30] Encouraged by Chamfort's suggestion, made in the
general enthusiasm, that they write a novel together, Mirabeau first
proposed a newspaper, then an account of the most "horrible"

crimes of the century, a treatise on philosophy and morality, and—already—the publication of their correspondence (that "monument to friendship"). The shadow of publisher Panckoucke henceforth loomed over their relationship.

Chamfort liked to be of service, and rendered it graciously, according to Ginguené; but he had sworn never to publish again. This puzzled Mirabeau, who had to sell his horses and furniture, pawn his half-mourning coat and his winter lace. "The young couple is starving!" he exclaimed on moving into modest furnished rooms on rue de la Roquette with the angelic Henriette de Nehra, his new mistress. But Chamfort had already given—and Mirabeau, the plebian count, had spent it all. Things became heated between the heir with no inheritance and the comfortably housed Diogenes. "The most cowardly of proverbs (*'Friends indeed . . . except in need!'*) is among the truest," complained Mirabeau.[31] "Be just before being generous," replied Chamfort,[32] who finally appealed to Vaudreuil. Thus the two prophets of revolution lived on the coattails of a courtier in debt up to his eyeballs.

Once this storm had passed, they would meet again over ice-cream in the Tuileries, lunch at the Bastille, or supper at the residence of the duchesse de Brancas. "I won't leave home," Mirabeau wrote Chamfort, " . . . unless fine weather, which is far from certain (I am writing at daybreak, and it rained last night) . . . induces you to come for a walk."[33]

All the while cursing his "lazy friend," this tireless Hercules swore allegiance once again. "I can never provide an exchange worthy of you (if you want to deal only with your equals you will be truly solitary); yet . . . while I had the misfortune to meet you so late, at least we will love one another for always." Mirabeau had become the affectionate disciple anew.

12. JULIE

There are more people who want to be loved than there are people who want to love.

Chamfort

Mirabeau regained the upper hand, however, as a result of an encounter with a twenty-two-year-old ex-dancer, Julie Careau. Blond, frail, and willful, Julie held a salon on rue Chantereine, off Chaussée d'Antin.[1] Abandoned by her mother, saved at seven from a fire at the Opéra by a gentleman who sent her back to be a chorus girl, briefed by a professional madam ("Maman Carotte"), thoroughly debriefed by a fleet of financiers, Julie ultimately received all those who, a few years later, would kill each other off in the name of higher principles—from Vaudreuil to Talleyrand, from Rivarol to Condorcet, from the baron de Breteuil to the painter David. The fate of such "girls" was strange. Although uneducated, they quickly became brilliant talkers. It was their job to make witty conversation—just as it was their job to place peacock feathers up banker Peixoto's derriere.[2] Back when Chamfort was a protégé of the duc de La Vallière, he saw the duke fall in love with little Miss Lacour at the drop of a sentence. She would yank off the duke's blue sash and order, "Kneel on it, old dukiduke!"[3] Before Chamfort fell ill, he could more or less identify with these courtesans, who were sassier than all the Encyclopedists put together. Such was the backdrop to Chamfort's arrival at the house on rue Chantereine, where Bonaparte would one day love Joséphine.

Yet Julie was not like other courtesans. Never made-up, never bejeweled, she dressed in white, amid white furniture. Compared to her rococo rivals, she incarnated the falsely austere taste of the reign of Louis XVI. A female friend claimed that, on meeting Julie, one had the impression of having always known her. To Chamfort she appeared to combine the simplicity of Marthe Buffon with the spice of Mlle. Guimard. Already dreaming of that complicity between illegitimate children which d'Alembert thought he had found with Julie de Lespinasse, Chamfort set about to recreate this good and naughty girl. "Apparently, love doesn't seek out real perfec-

103

tions," he wrote; "it even seems to shun them. It loves only those perfections that it creates or invents."[4]

Liaison Dangereuse

Julie, however, was well protected. Her last patron, the vicomte de Ségur (by whom she had a child), had left to take command of his regiment, leaving room for an Irish gentleman (by whom she had another child). And the Irishman himself was threatened by a pack of pretenders, including La Harpe. Chamfort was incapable of declaring his interest. Scarred by life and by his illness, the former Herculean Adonis retreated to Rosny, to a chateau owned by Archambaud, Talleyrand's brother. Chamfort dispatched Mirabeau to sound out Julie. Accustomed to bold action, Mirabeau obtained a rendezvous without difficulty. They spoke of this and that, of mutual friends, of Chamfort, in fact. While Julie felt that Chamfort had as much sensitivity and intellect as Voltaire, she found him too caustic, egotistical, too much a writer. That's just a mask he adopts toward those who are wicked! exclaimed Mirabeau. No, no, Julie still preferred the happy if illegitimate Abbé Delille to Chamfort. Such comments wounded Chamfort. Which made Mirabeau aware of his own power. The situation was henceforth in his hands.

This Hercules behaved in the finest French tradition—halfway between Vauban's military treatises and *Les liaisons dangereuses* (which Laclos had published two years earlier). Mirabeau drew up battle plans, set traps, plotted by letter. Julie was renamed "Lady-Ficulty" and Chamfort "the Auvergnat"—a novel in the making. He forced Julie to retreat on the issue of egotism, pushed Chamfort forward on that of love. She knows that you're unhappy far from Paris, Mirabeau told Chamfort, and would like to see you return. But Chamfort was impatient—probably suspecting that Julie preferred to go slow after the stormy relations with Ségur and the Irishman. Let me handle it, replied the plebeian count, "I don't think she can resist me for long." The second interview, in fact, went well. The Irishman was suffering from an attack of colic "which could well be his last," and Julie was in high spirits—"to the point of sauciness." She was amazed that she'd had no news from you, added Mirabeau triumphantly. Reassured, Chamfort gave Mirabeau a ten-page letter to read. It was astonishingly humble, as though love revealed a streak of weakness he had always repressed. Mirabeau seized on this to berate the Socrates who had intimidated him just six months earlier. "You are too rational to be imaginatively romantic; your imagination is too vivid and your heart too basically good to not be somewhat inclined that way. Thus I doubt that your philosophy has served you as well for women as for all other subjects."[5] Hurt, Chamfort demanded another nickname—Auvergnats were considered fools in those days—and claimed he was in perfect control of his feelings. Mirabeau dropped "the Auvergnat," and Chamfort became once again the philosopher who knew best concerning women, men, things, the country—and Julie was the person the most likely to make him happy.

Mirabeau, however, continued to lay down the law. Despite his verbal sycophancy, he insisted that a "fiction" was needed to overcome Julie's resistance—all the while affirming that La Harpe had not seen her more than once in two months. Chamfort thereupon wrote a poem that described Aspasia[6] embroidering for Socrates in her Athens salon:

> *Le philosophe, au comble de ses voeux,*
> *Sentit . . . , que sais-je, moi! ce que l'amour inspire*
> *Quand, par bonheur pour lui, le sage est amoureux.*[7]

> The philosopher, at the height of his power,
> Felt . . . , I knowest not! That which love inspires
> When, through good luck, the wise man is a lover.

The "novelist" cared even less for this poem and accused Chamfort of constantly appearing "subjugated" and won-over in advance. "I told you to alternate: a sweet and tender letter, with a little zest, one day; and then a refined, lively, spirited and mocking letter the following day. Lest she never be certain of her game. That's the a-b-c of love."[8] Already ashamed by the weakness he had displayed toward Julie, Chamfort was totally routed. Mirabeau, who again acted as stand-in for the final scene, dealt the deathblow. "She speaks freely of love and intoxication when there are others present," he wrote to Chamfort, "but never when alone with me; then she only spouts and imbibes cold water. [She is] . . . as removed from love as belief in the spine of Saint Pantaléon or the shorts of Saint Corléon is removed from the worship the deist . . . renders to the being of beings."[9]

So this "dancer"—who had studied under the maréchal de Soubise, the sugar merchant Beudet, and the vicomte de Ségur—stood unmasked. A tease, asserted Mirabeau, recalling that the

Greeks were right to consider women "as machines for babies and pleasure." A siren, replied Chamfort, abandoning his dream of equality and "complicity" between two illegitimate children. "Between [women] and men, there is . . . very little sympathy of mind, soul or character," he wrote. "This is proven by the small account women take of a man of forty."[10] The project to start society afresh thus began with a moving, almost senile attempt at a new personal beginning. As to Mirabeau, whom Julie held in boundless admiration, it is not quite clear how far he went. But his mistress at the time, the gentle and naive Henriette de Nehra, admitted that Mirabeau dined every evening at Julie's prior to his departure for London (where he fled to escape the legal action instigated by the Minister of Justice—whom he had insulted—as well as that instigated by his mother—whom he had swindled). Like Chamfort, Julie seems to have been taken in by the plebeian count's stratagems. When Mirabeau's letters were published, Julie commented, "Infatuated friends—Mirabeau at their head—gave me the flattering nickname Aspasia. That was at the time Chamfort was smitten by a terrible fever of love that I had sparked in him, without the least intention of doing so."[11] Chamfort met Julie ten years too soon. After the Revolution, she wound up resembling the image he projected of her. Abandoned by the actor François Joseph Talma, and subsequently dropped by Benjamin Constant, she came up with an aphorism worthy of Chamfort: "One should be able to start life over again. During the first performance, one doesn't know what one's doing."[12]

Black Hole

Evil fairies once again took over Chamfort's tale. In June 1784, his foster mother died. He hadn't seen her for fifteen years, but the passing of this woman who was "more impatient, at eighty-four, than I ever was," shook him. He owed her his pride, his education, and the little house that she left him in the village of Theix, huddled below his real mother's chateau. Floored by a double tertiary fever, transformed into a "heap of bile," he reflected on the women he had lost. "I inhabit their coffins, sending my soul to wander among theirs," he said. Thérèse Nicolas was the last remaining witness of his youth, while Julie would have been the first to witness his old age; he no longer had a rampart against death. Vaudreuil, Henriette de Nehra, and Rulhière filed by his bedside, but to no avail. By leaving for London, Mirabeau had deprived Chamfort of his energy. "I know myself by heart, and in the end you get tired of yourself," he confided to Abbé Roman, before bidding a "touching farewell" to Henriette de Nehra, who left to join the plebeian count in England.

Vaudreuil, whom he liked, had thrust him back into a society he disliked. In four years he had not resolved any of the questions that Vaudouleurs had put on hold. He had no money—and what else could he aspire to after forty? "Love is a source of pain," he wrote, "whereas sensuality without love is a pleasure that lasts only a few minutes . . . and the honor of being a father leads to a series of calamities; setting up a household is the trade of an innkeeper."[13] So this marvelous intellect, this "conscience's conscience,"[14] began to despair. Mirabeau in London remained without word and imagined the worst.

Weary of his meandering life—"I've traveled a thousand leagues on a sheet of paper"—Chamfort announced that he would be in Provence, "under a fine sky, in fine weather," by October 10, 1784. After that date, he swore, Paris would see him no longer. The prisoner rebelled against his warden. He left high society, that "bed of roses which he turned into a bed of thorns," as Sainte-Beuve would have it. But Vaudreuil mobilized Artois and the Polignacs, and a terrific, almost comic, battle ensued. "What struggles I have had with the sweetest and most devoted friends!" he wrote. "What is this invincible pride, this hardness of heart which makes me reject favors from a certain breed, when I . . . would like to do for them more than they can do for me?"[15] But the tragedy of *Mustapha* inoculated him against stipends and positions. He would never again be caught drinking "sugared arsenic" and living off a class that wound up costing more than solitude. It was not a question of sour grapes, as the Vaudouleurs incident had shown; he wanted to leave because his health was poor, his "sight was failing," and he had much to forget.

Chamfort's letter to Abbé Roman (a writer who withdrew to the Vaucluse region to compose his *Life*) expressed his rancor with rare insight. "It is certain, and believe me, my friend, I am not deceiving myself," he wrote when Vaudreuil announced a new position to him, "it is certain that I desire the non-success of a supposedly happy event, the necessary upshot of which would be to relaunch me in a career full of wretchedness and disgust, making me exist for a public I despise almost as much as the *literati* with their cabals, their slander, their absurd vanity, etc; making me either regret or pine for that fame which, thanks to the tone currently reigning in literature, is only an illustrious infamy designed to disgust a decent nature. Such are my feelings and ideas, which make me appear to be a bizarre being, so much have vanity and stupidity perverted every mind and soul. People are amazed that a man who is still regarded, in spite of himself, as being not entirely devoid of talent, does not want to undergo the fate commonly imposed on literary people— that of resembling donkeys kicking and biting before an empty hay-rack."[16]

Paper Exile

Although he was able to cross off the mediocre writer, Chamfort had a harder time resigning himself to being just an obscure, poor, and independent man. Two months later he wrote to Abbé Roman to announce once more his contempt for fame, which was all "smoke" for someone like himself who had now "judged everything." "I loved fame, I admit; but that was at an age when experience had not taught me the true value of things, when I believed that it could exist pure [and] . . . that, without being a guarantee of prosperity, it was at least not an obstacle to it. Time and reflection have enlightened me. . . . For, having attracted the hatred of a crowd of fools and ill-wishers ever since my initial success, without having merited it in the least, I consider this misfortune a great boon; it delivers me unto myself, it gives me the right to belong exclusively to myself. . . . I have become weary of being superfluous, a kind of addendum to high society; I have become indignant at the constant proof that naked merit, born without gold and without titles, is alien to men; and I was able to draw more from myself than I could ever hope from them. I now hate celebrity as much as I once loved fame; I have with-drawn my entire life unto myself; thinking and feeling are the final goals of my existence and my plans."[17] Now he merely wanted to be in Provence with his books—those friends who never betray, those superiors who never humiliate, those equals who open the doors to a pantheon of intelligence and art, the only *real* world for Chamfort.

   Yet he still felt the need to justify himself to another friend. This time it was an aristocrat—probably Choiseul-Gouffier, who had spent time with Chamfort prior to leaving for an ambassadorship in Constantinople. "I've always been shocked by the ridiculous and in-solent opinion, commonly held everywhere, that a writer who has four or five thousand livres of income is at the height of prosperity,"

he wrote the count, who was also a friend of Vaudreuil. "Having arrived more or less at this limit, I felt that I was affluent enough to live
alone; and my taste naturally inclined me to it. But since luck would
have it that my company was sought after by several persons with a
considerably greater fortune, it happened that my affluence became
veritable misery, as a result of duties which arise through associating
with a milieu I had not sought out. . . . I was considered bizarre,
extraordinary. Such protests are idiotic," he continued. "I excel, as
you know, in translating what my neighbor is thinking. Everything
that has been said on this matter really means: 'What! Is he not sufficiently reimbursed for his trouble and his errands by the honor of
seeing us, by the pleasure of entertaining us, by the delight of being
treated by us as no other man of letters is?' To which I reply: I am
forty years old. I've had more than enough of those petty triumphs
of vanity with which writers are so taken. . . . It is ridiculous to
grow old . . . in a troupe where one can not even pretend to a minor
part."[18] Throughout the summer of 1784, Chamfort announced to
everyone his decision to leave a city where he was known and received but where he still owned nothing. He would break with a society that might be pleasant "if people were interested in one
another." He would exile himself, despite knowing that he bore solitude no better than he bore society. He would abandon the exhausting role of living above his station to finally lead a *plebeian* life-style
without, however, pronouncing the word—the reaction of a man
who had sought to hide his background so thoroughly that it rightly
came back to haunt him.

For Chamfort was capable of recognizing only the objective factors forcing him to leave a world he had obviously overfrequented.
"'The difference between you and me,' M—— used to say, 'is that
you've said to all the masks: "I know who you are." Whereas I let
them think they fool me. That's why high society favors me over
you. It is a ball at which you have spoiled the others' game and your
own fun.'"[19] The same could apply to writers; Chamfort saw
straight through the moral and philosophical statements that
masked their fierceness and pride . . . without being able to see that
his own refusal to write did not exempt him from the same feelings.

Chamfort should be given the final word, however, for he ultimately hated the literary trade for valid reasons. "It has been noted
that writers on physics, natural history, physiology, and chemistry
are ordinarily men of a gentle, even-tempered and generally happy

disposition; but that writers on politics, legislation, and even morals, are of a sad, melancholic temperament, etc. The reason is simple: the former study nature, the latter society; the former con-
template the work of the great Being, the latter turn their gaze to the
works of man."[20] Chamfort could demonstrate lucidity even in his
blindest behavior.

13. FROM MORALIST TO VOLCANO

Chamfort—this wittiest of all moralists . . . a man who was rich in depths and backgrounds of the soul—gloomy, suffering, ardent—a thinker who needed laughter as a remedy against life and who almost considered himself lost on every day on which he had not laughed.

Nietzsche

It would take a whole book to explain to a quick-witted American all the meaning in one of Chamfort's epigrams.

Roederer

Chamfort's literary failure nevertheless haunted him, regardless of what he said. (He was one of the rare writers of the day who refused to consider his increasingly solid position in high society as definitive proof of his talent.) He obviously thought of those classical philosophers who never wrote a thing; he hoped that his ideas, his life, and his disciples would suffice to save him from oblivion, like Socrates. He "was constantly being printed," Roederer would say, "in the minds of his friends."[1] La Harpe popped up at regular intervals, however, to remind Chamfort of his sterility. Mercier nicknamed him "Champsec" [Dryfield], while Lebrun-Pindare accused him of constantly reworking "rickety verses." Chamfort began to justify himself via the aphorisms, anecdotes, and dialogues which, following the *Mustapha* fiasco, he noted down each evening on "square little scraps of paper" tossed haphazardly into boxes. These began to constitute an entire volume that recounted his rejection of competition, fame, and posterity as well as his disgust for writers, nobility, and a society so advanced it was falling to pieces. Sainte-Beuve claimed that these fragments "almost scorch the paper" by openly attacking a "sick" society where a minority enjoys more meals than appetite and the majority more appetite than meals. Where feelings are so discredited that sincerity embarrasses. Where everything is done to keep mankind feeble, making it easier to govern. Where entire portions of the self have to be anesthetized in order to survive, and a role must be played in order to exist. Where the bourgeoisie raises its daughters to be "compost" for a gentleman's property. Where the most dangerous thieves are the very people supposed to arrest them. Where justice, church, and might are in the hands of individuals who respect neither law, God, nor honor. Where going bankrupt is more highly thought of than having nothing. Where seven million people beg for charity, and where twelve million are in no position to offer any. . . . In this strong indictment, Chamfort for the first time dared to use "I," that pronoun hated by classicism, yet essential for getting at the truth. "The world can never be known through books," he wrote. . . . "Since such knowledge is the result of a thousand subtle observations which self-esteem forbids be shared with anyone, even a best friend. One is afraid of appearing to be someone concerned by petty things, although these petty things are very important to the success of the greatest undertakings."[2] He would henceforth write *against* literature, that unwitting ally of falsehood.

He nevertheless refused to unmask himself completely. Silence continued to surround his birth and his love life; to "I" and "Chamfort" he usually added "one" and "M——," a perfect melange of self and alter ego. "I" and "one" would converse, as though he wanted to rediscover the intimacy, the warmth, the truth of confessions made by the hearth. Chamfort covered his tracks, however: "M——" sometimes refers to other characters—Mirabeau, or a provincial intendant[3]—and is itself flanked by other anonymous letters—N, P, R—charged with the task of revealing Chamfort's most burning secrets, all the while conveying the intrinsic complexity of his personality.

But this game of hide-and-seek was not enough. Chamfort wanted to thwart the public totally. "I've thought of a sure way . . . to arrange it so that what I write exists, yet is impossible to use even if I am robbed of all my papers," he said. "The method I've invented gives me absolute control . . . for I have only to keep silent, and what I have written will die with me."[4] This mad decision is a logical one on the part of someone ready to disappear in order to remain his own man. The code or invisible ink he was alluding to was apparently of little use, for the fragments found after his death were completely legible, ready to confront posterity. Unless, of course, he was referring to the manuscripts that were later stolen. . . . [5]

Chamfort could now speak while writing. There were no more plots or outlines to concoct. He wrote "almost despite himself." Tragedy had revealed his lack of imagination, whereas the human comedy provided him with it. Neoclassicism had been an art within an art—Chamfort henceforth trusted only his instincts. Realizing that he was less a genius than a special case, half-admitting his own failure (a precondition to numerous successes), he gave his "bizarreness" free rein. Works "written with pleasure are often the best," he wrote, "just as love-children are the most beautiful."[6] This was a doubly personal book, then, as well as being "original"—a new criterion at the time.[7] He had just invented a process able to record all the comings and goings of his consciousness, like a *camera obscura;* the century, meanwhile, glimpsed an escape from the genres it had exhausted itself trying to revive.

A Lifetime's Work

Up to that point, Chamfort's "oeuvre" followed two lines. His comedies sought, in a light vein, to redress wrongs, whereas his eulogies and his tragedy sought to valorize virtue, honor, and brotherly love. He had fought vice with good words, falsehood with theater, pretense with pretense. Now he attacked the roots of evil—a theme much richer than goodness—by uniting his two approaches. He provoked indignation through laughter, awakened a sense of morality by showing it ridiculed, pushed the logic of the Ancien Régime to its limits. This was far more efficient than a sermon or a farce performed by an actress in a tiger skin.

Chamfort's *Maximes* cannot be understood independent of his life, for his life served as the catalyst, the complement, the companion volume to his oeuvre. Just as he had "bronzed" his heart in 1765, Chamfort subjected his style to the yoke of aphorism. In both instances, the process was similar. On the one hand, his highly sensitive nature banned all signs of weakness after having been wounded; on the other, his unavowed, nearly overwhelming curiosity for people (never did a misanthrope have so many friends and relationships) turned to disgust, his overextended diversity limited itself to maxims (after straying among the rules of drama and academicism), his indecisive literary personality exploited the *healthy repression* typical of aphorisms. He finally found the right *register.* The two Chamforts here become consubstantial, and their union means that his maxims are never an abstract experience but remain living testimony to what, in the final analysis, was the only "place" where he managed to live in isolation. Apart from Vaudouleurs, this represents his only successful exile. By shutting himself up in his room on rue de la Chaise to strike his "medallions," Chamfort avoided the dead-end of Auteuil, that cardboard village and phony countryside for weary Parisians. After having abandoned his trip to America and cut short his stay in Germany, he finally traveled above all in place—"around his room," as Xavier de Maistre would have it.

Unlike La Rochefoucauld, however, whose maxims perfectly fitted the classical mold, Chamfort did not consistently yield to the stylistic yoke. He liked to set down his intuitions, recollections, and the fruit of his reading in disorder. He cut his aphorisms with anecdotes, with details which relativized them and "humanized" them. "Love, such as it exists in high society. . . . " He left the wheat and the chaff together, in order to avoid the common "charlatanism" of moralists who convert their pessimism (or, less often, their optimism) into dogma. He did not produce an "oeuvre" in the strict sense of the term, rather he responded to a vital need to justify himself, writing to extend himself and to transcend the everyday. As opposed to La Rochefoucauld and Vauvenargues, he did not play the wise judge; he wrote in the hope—unfulfilled—of becoming wise, of curbing his passions (the way one wants to kill a horse one can no longer control, he said). He reflected, of course, but he primarily sought to convey the "spirit" of his times in its diversity, independent of any system. While on a formal level there are points in common between Chamfort and La Bruyère (who had openly denounced court and high society in the preceding century), on a historical level Chamfort merits comparison with only one other "moralist"—Pierre Choderlos de Laclos.

From Laclos to Rivarol

Laclos's *Les liaisons dangereuses* offered a vivid account of a period drawing to a close when the book appeared in 1782. It recounted the sexual and social Machiavellianism that culminated under Louis XV, in a geometric style respecting the coldness of prevailing cynicism. In spite of his refusal to publish, Chamfort probably shared Laclos's intuition that their half-century would be remembered less for its literature than for its mores and fashions, ideas and conversation. Both writers effectively captured the spirit of the Ancien Régime, only to turn it into a weapon—as though Chamfort had conquered the nobility only to destroy it, and Laclos pushed its Machiavellianism to perfection in order to drain it of its substance. . . . Chamfort, as skin-deep aristocrat, resided at Vaudreuil's in order to refine his analysis of the staged society, the count being a perfect product of that civilization. Chamfort, as gut-level plebeian, managed to touch readers by constantly throwing down the gauntlet, promising a duel with every phrase, claiming a nobility he did not possess.

The striking thing about that period is that the name "Buffon" means almost nothing today. Voltaire, though a looming figure, survives literarily thanks to his tales, his correspondence, and his *Dictionnaire philosophique*—his plays are no longer performed at all. Thomas, Abbé Delille, and even Lebrun-Pindare (who thought himself equal to the Greeks), have fallen into total oblivion. Bernadin de Saint-Pierre's *Paul et Virginie* is buried in literary textbooks. Rousseau alone is still read, almost in his entirety. His case apart, today's vision of the literary world during the reigns of Louis XV and Louis XVI populates it with unlikely cases: Diderot (Mme. Necker claimed that his role in the *Encyclopédie* and his plays— which he himself set above his novels and "dialogues"—wouldn't suffice to get him into the next century), Laclos (who, despite the splash made by *Les liaisons dangereuses*, remained a marginal literary figure), de Sade (considered by his contemporaries to be a sexual delinquent), Beaumarchais (whose success didn't shield him from harsh criticism concerning the impurity of his style), and, finally, Chamfort (who would die, nearly forgotten, in 1794, taking with him only the success of *La jeune indienne* and the failure of *Mustapha*). Not to mention Rétif de La Bretonne (author of the strange *Nuits de Paris* [*The Nocturnal Spectator*] or Louis-Sébastien Mercier,[8] copious scribblers known mainly for their literary incontinence. All survived by betraying the classical ideal, Chamfort being the only one to remain tangled in it for twenty years, breaking free at just the right moment to escape the literary vacuum made all the more complete by the Revolution. This was historical luck for a man who had not always had the good fairies on his side; it is also a fitting fate for a century whose megalomania equaled that of the following century, though with less power and inspiration (and less ponderousness).

From this standpoint, Chamfort could be compared to another moralist, Antoine Rivarol, who might even be considered Chamfort's counterpart. Although Rivarol's output is clearly thinner, his targets were the second-rate literary "dwarfs" who abounded following the decline of the *Encyclopédie*, and the foibles of an aristocracy reduced to playing out its own comedy. Chamfort's primary duel was with the class that consigned him to the status of *half-breed*. It is nevertheless striking that the monarchist Rivarol (whom the court felt had wandered too far from "good principles") also expressed, with fewer con-

tradictions, the same contempt for the society of falsehood as did
Chamfort. He, too, wrote his aphorisms in bed, then tossed them into
a big bag. On the fringes of the prevailing literary bankruptcy, the two
men decided to squander their verbal and literary talent. The comte
de Lauraguais described Rivarol as "a fire burning on water." He
could have said the same of Chamfort, as attested by those epigrams
attributed to both moralists, where the pragmatic gaity of the one
meets the despairing idealism of the other.[9]

"Tall and handsome, of noble manner and intelligent gaze . . .
Rivarol was the most presentable man of his day," reported the
baron de Theis. Rivarol's arrival in Paris in the late 1770s made an
impression. This son of a Bagnols innkeeper decked himself out
with the name of a famous geometrician (whom he falsely claimed
as uncle), became yet another protégé of Dorat (that "scribbler of
fans"), and quickly conquered the salons, which he abandoned
around 1785. Between those two dates, Chamfort had a friendly relationship with this southerner who was thirteen years his junior
(and who would struggle all his life to have the nobility of the
Rivarols recognized—an apparently justified, if lusterless, claim).
But these two conversational "superstars" were playing to the same
audience, and therefore remained at a distance despite having mutual friends—Abbé Roman, Lauraguais, Tilly, and Mirabeau.[10]
"Lions isolate themselves," said Rivarol. They both nevertheless left
their contemporaries with the same sickening impression of waste.
"Neither erected a true monument," noted Tilly in his *Mémoires*.
" . . . Chamfort perhaps didn't have the talent, although he possessed infinite wit and even more exquisite taste. Rivarol . . . was
prodigiously vain, which the instant success of daily conversation
flattered more conveniently than some uncertain and distant
fame. . . . Everything which happened in such rapid succession on
that bizarre stage thus vanished." And both writers were to remain
that way, in spite of everything. They differed only in their attitude
toward the Revolution.

Against All Posterity

Chamfort thus was rescued from oblivion by the Ancien Régime's
sense of wit—which his anecdotes render with almost photographic
precision—as well as by his criticism of that old order, given his unusual position and intense neurosis. Although he had reached the
pinnacle of society, he continued to consider it a foreign body, an

unnatural entity (unlike other authors who wrote to improve or entertain it). He observed it from exile, with the arrogance of a bastard belonging to no one, once he himself had created *Chamfort*. He symbolically remained both above and outside the social order, refusing to publish *or* to reproduce himself, not wanting to sanction, prolong, or immortalize that order; he perhaps resembled those proud elephants who refuse to bear offspring "in slavery," or those animals produced by cross-breeding, which nature renders sterile. "I have no wish to marry," he said, "for fear of having a son who resembles me. . . . Yes, for fear of having a son who, poor like me, does not know how to lie, nor flatter, nor grovel."[11] Chamfort's supreme ambition was to be an individual with neither antecedent nor sequel, to produce neither book nor child, to be beholden neither to the civilization of falsehood nor to the posterity craze.

This crucial point deserves to be stressed. Chamfort decided in 1784 that he would never publish his *Maximes et anecdotes*, and he stuck by this decision practically up until his death in 1794. His disciple Ginguené appropriately proposed that editions of his *Maximes* begin with a long preamble that opens with the question, "Why do you no longer offer anything to the public?" Written around 1790, as indicated by an allusion to the "theater of the nation" and to the "royal printing house," Chamfort's preamble lists the reasons for his silence with obvious ingeniousness:

> Because for me the public represents the height of bad taste and the obsession with denigration . . .
>
> Because I am urged to work for the same reason that when one sits by the window, one would like to see monkeys or bear-baiters pass in the street.
>
> There's the example of M. Thomas, insulted during his entire lifetime and praised after his death . . .
>
> Because I'm afraid of dying without having lived . . .
>
> Because I no longer wish to please any except those like myself.
>
> Because I have known almost all the famous men of our day, and have seen them all made wretched . . .

Chamfort thus accepted total oblivion, both as man and writer, until he decided that society could be totally made over. This is the radical and logical lesson to be drawn from his *Products of the Perfected Civilization*, the title given to his maxims (which is not unlike the titles used by the most secret and virulent critics of today's show-biz society, namely, the International Situationists). This man, who was considered bizarre yet who considered everyone else to be even more bizarre, imagined himself as the first member of a new race, that of free men. He was condemned either to die in a world of slaves, or to be reborn in a "republic" of citizens like that of ancient Greece.

All of that seemed far off, however, and Chamfort entertained no illusions—the monarchy could no longer be reformed. "Everything has degenerated so far that nothing can be improved," noted Georges Poulet in his brilliant article on the moralist.[12] The existing order had been in place for nearly a thousand years and reproduced itself effortlessly. Society was composed of rigid compartments, according to Chamfort, which men temporarily inhabit. "Those who occupy them are sometimes big, sometimes small, and almost no one fits in his place. Here we have a giant, bent and crouching in his nook, there we have a dwarf under a high arch."[13] The surrounding crowd awaits the first free spot, which it claims to deserve on the basis of birth or relations but almost never on talent. The Ancien Régime represented the reign of the anonymous, a deceptive system run by a false elite—"valets conspiring to remove their masters."[14] The Chamfort of the *Products* was not egalitarian, for he was convinced that "men become smaller when they flock together," and he remained largely in favor of individual solutions, even though society remained "a chess game which commoners must concede as soon as their turn begins."

Chamfort's collection of maxims draws no clear line drawn between Ancien Régime and Revolution. There are anecdotes that betray his complicity with high society—and maxims that condemn it. There's the Rousseau-style "no," and the hedonistic "yes"—two sides of an intrinsically mongrel world. "In ethics, as in physics, everything is a mixture," he said. "Nothing is simple, nothing is pure"[15]—like his own mixture of true novel and essay on phoniness, of witty snatches overheard and gems recopied, or original material and borrowings.[16] The world such as it was, impossible to live with, impossible to live without. He gave the ironic title of *Products of the Perfected Civilization* to this tome of human error—mistakenly retitled *Maximes, pensées, caractères et anecdotes* by the French publishers. A book without end, a repeated knock on the wall of prejudice, a pointless indictment—like all previous writing against the eternal and ever-changing civilization of phoniness.

Chamfort's idea of man *par excellence* was someone who realized

1782. Fireworks celebrating the birth of the Dauphin, son of Marie-Antoinette and Louis XVI (the king had wept at the premiere of Chamfort's tragedy, *Mustapha et Zéangir*). Watercolor by Nicolle, Musée Carnavalet. Photo: Giraudon/Art Resource, New York.

Nicknamed "Bébé" due to his diminutive stature, the critic Jean-François de La Harpe (*left*) was a protégé of Voltaire (*above*, drawing by Huber) and went from being Chamfort's best friend to his worst enemy. Mlle. Guimard (*right*, portrait by Fragonard), a dancer and courtesan, was mistress to Chamfort during his "Herculean-Adonis" days. Bibliothèque Nationale, E.R.L. Archives. Photo: Giraudon.

Prior to the Revolution, Chamfort was a protégé of the comte de Vaudreuil, "the most chivalrous and magnificent" of courtiers. Portrait by Vigée-Lebrun, Musée Jacquemart-André. Photo: Bulloz.

The comte de Mirabeau, known for his ugliness and his protean genius, was enthralled intellectually by Chamfort right up to the French Revolution. Bust by Lucas-Montigny, Musée Paul Arbaud. Photo: Roger-Viollet.

The Vaudouleurs residence, south of Paris, where Chamfort spent happy moments. Photo: J. P. Caracalla.

July 12, 1789. The people "liberate" the bust of Finance Minister Jacques Necker on display in the Curtius Waxworks at the Palais-Royal. Photo: Roger-Viollet.

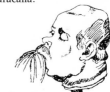

August 12, 1789. The decapitated and straw-stuffed head of Attorney General Joseph Foulon was paraded beneath Chamfort's windows at the Palais-Royal. E.R.L. Archives.

Pierre-Louis Ginguené was Chamfort's disciple and biographer as well as the first publisher of his *Maxims*. Ginguené later became a journalist critical of Napoleon's Empire. Bibliothèque Nationale, E.R.L. Archives.

Jean-François Marmontel, "easy-going" philosopher and fellow Auvergnat, accused Chamfort of being one of the key figures in the revolutionary "plot." Portrait by Saint-Aubin, Bibliothèque Nationale, E.R.L. Archives.

Chamfort taught Charles Maurice de Talleyrand the art of conversation prior to becoming Talleyrand's "prompter" at the Constituent Assembly. Portrait by Greuze, Musée de Saint-Omer, E.R.L. Archives.

Celebrating the "Fédération." On this, the happiest day of the French Revolution, Chamfort declared, "Let's preserve everything good from the old days, which were so bad." Pen-and-ink drawing by Sweebach, Musée Carnavelet. Photo: Bulloz.

April 1791. The funeral ceremony for Mirabeau in the church of Saint-Eustache. With Mirabeau's death the monarchy lost its trump card, the Revolution its "savior," and Chamfort his best friend. Drawing by Prieur, Louvre. Photo: Giraudon/Art Resource, New York.

Chamfort shot himself in the head after having been accused and imprisoned for applauding the assassination of Jean-Paul Marat. Etching by David, Bibliothèque Nationale. Photo: Giraudon/Art Resource, New York.

August 12, 1792. The statue of Louis XIV on the place des Victoires is toppled—and the monarchy along with it. Drawing by Prieur, Louvre. Photo: Giraudon/Art Resource, New York.

that it takes a little of everything to make up society—crooks and wise men, "actors" and "critics," the pure and the rotten—and who was free of illusion, able to laugh at his own outrage. Someone who was therefore more likable, more indulgent, and gayer than others. This is obviously an ideal, a portrait that resembles the "superman" venerated by Mirabeau rather than the sickly individual rejected by Julie. This "hedonistic" streak, however, was strongly present in Chamfort, testifying to a longing for mental equilibrium, if not happiness. "Give and take pleasure, without harming yourself or anyone else—that, I think, sums up morality," he claimed[17]—an agenda he was able to put into effect only once, at Vaudouleurs, that single ray of sunshine in his *camera obscura*.

Death as Cure

For elsewhere in this "book," the tone is fundamentally pessimistic, even despairing—God is accorded only a slim place. Chamfort "wouldn't have minded" believing in God, but wouldn't allow himself to do so, and never missed an opportunity to denounce priests as merchants of self-denial and obscurantism. Belittling the "Christian mob," Chamfort denounced the church as a sect that merely vulgarized the teaching of the stoics. He held religion to be a personal affair, a *secret* between the individual and the Great Being. And he condemned everything that obscured a faith he himself didn't share. "The king of Prussia had barracks built which blocked the sun from a Catholic Church," he reported. "Remonstrations were addressed to him. He sent back the petition with these words at the bottom: *Beati qui non viderunt et crediderunt.*"[18] But Chamfort was not among those blessed enough to be able to believe without seeing.

Similarly, he thought metaphysics ineffectual because obscure (it was all Basque to him) and philosophy doomed to failure. Just as Africans search for the souls of their dead "in the brush surrounding their villages" only to wind up admitting that the soul is not to be found, philosophers fail because there is no essence to be found either in man or in God.[19] Truth is like heaven—a fiction designed to keep beings alive and sedate their existence, a place which does not exist but "where one believes one would be happy if one went there." Philosophy, he continued, has "a lot of drugs, very few good remedies, and almost no specific cures"[20]—the observation of a sick man for whom sleep is the only sedative, death the only cure.

Chamfort was perhaps most radical in his vision of history. The outcome of thirty centuries of civilization was to deliver three hundred million living humans unto thirty despots, "most of whom are ignorant and feeble-minded."[21] Almost all of history is a series of horrors, he noted, in which each tyrant simply denounced the horrors of his predecessor in order to mask his own, consoling his people by telling them that their ancestors had been even more wretched. Although Chamfort reproached Christianity for having supplanted antiquity, he felt that no return was possible at the present time. Such hope amounted to "charlatanism," and he felt that any such attempt would be harmful, leading only to other horrors. For the human race is "evil by nature," and the masses (which Chamfort still conceived in terms of the public) even nastier and more contemptible. He who would become one of the most ardent revolutionaries could thus assert, several years prior to 1789, that "men are so perverse that the mere hope and even the very desire to correct them, making them reasonable and honest, is an absurdity, a romantic idea which is pardonable only in the ingenuousness of early youth."[22]

Chamfort, then, essentially had a single subject—his relationship as an individual to society, to its actors, to its illusions. This became an inescapable duel between passion and reason, man and woman, money and talent; it could not be transcended. Although Chamfort revealed the seamy side of a century that produced the most felicitous elite ever known, he had neither utopia nor ideal city to propose. Like all great critics, he drove his subject home so often that he became wed to it. In 1785, his "ideology" could still be summed up as himself, a very civilized savage. Gathering impressions, anecdotes, and proper names, he remained an intellect inhabiting world and history, a consciousness trapped between salon and Revolution. He never asked himself for what, or for whom, people exist; he did not question human origins (just as he remained silent on his own). An implicit answer to such questions emerges, however—Nature. Life being the only certitude, nature alone explained human presence in the world. It impelled people to reproduce, despite the incompatibility between the two sexes, the two races. "Nature intended . . . ," Chamfort would often say. "Nature appears to use men for her own designs, with no concern for the tools used, much the way tyrants dispose of those they have used."[23] Here Chamfort is perhaps at his most original, for the eighteenth century generally perceived nature as good, harmonious, and generous, whereas he saw nature as a dreaded mistress, a demiurge who skillfully doled out reason and passion to humans in her laboratory, in order to insure that her work would endure. For irresistible instinct was required to force the species to reproduce under tyrannical conditions. By giving men "a completely indestructible taste for women" despite their contempt for females,[24] and by blindly pushing women (he might have said his mother) to risk their honor, position, and freedom out of love for a man who would impregnate them (thereby swapping "a few moments of convulsion" for "an entire year of illness"), nature established a domination of humankind as perfect as it was both coveted and invisible. This thesis inspired Schopenhauer's misogynist, organicist morality, and also explains Chamfort's refusal to reproduce. Here again he rejected the law of the fittest, the logic of birth, just as elsewhere he resisted all forms of despotism—even those of his own invention. Here again he demonstrated pessimism in the face of everything, during a century historically endowed with miraculous optimism. Here again he was practically alone in asserting, "Such is the wretched condition of men that they are obliged to seek consolation for nature's evils in society, and consolation for society's evils in nature."[25]

The Mind Reverts

Chamfort was received poorly in France because there was something too Italian about him, suggested Nietzsche, who was wrong for once. Rather, Chamfort's despair surprised a country content with itself. By refuting everything (and practically refuting himself), Chamfort broadened the field normally explored by French moralists. True enough, he typically denounced courtiers—"those poor people enriched by beggary"—and a society "where you have to let yourself be taught lots of things you know by people who don't." Classic moralists merely condemned stereotypes (the financier, the hypocrite), while La Rochefoucauld denounced the abstract ruses of self-pride. Chamfort, however, in addition to making an inventory of the soul, attempted to take stock of civilization. He drew inspiration from everything (like Lauraguais and a good number of gentlemen at the time who were curious about everything), applying zoology to society and history to heaven. "In politics . . . nothing is as unfortunate for the people as reigns which last too long. I hear that God is eternal—which says it all."[26] This was his testament—

and perhaps humanity's, too. Chamfort's conciseness fascinated the endlessly rambling Mirabeau, and prompted Balzac to refer to Chamfort and Rivarol as, "Those people who put whole books into a witticism, while today, we're lucky to find a single witticism in an entire book."[27] Which explains the success of this "instant oeuvre" (almost entirely directed against the "civilization of the instant"), of this autobiography by a man who did no more than think and feel (and revealed no more than his critical gaze), of this masterpiece that would efface forever the memory of a mediocre writer.

In 1784–1785, when many of his *Products* were penned, Chamfort was at the height of his misanthropy, his individualism, his pessimism. The very intensity of these feelings provoked a movement in the reverse direction (as did, to a lesser extent, the rising clamor of liberal demands and the "electrifying" contact with Mirabeau). Chamfort was of reactive temperament, reacting all the more strongly against himself. He never remained set in his ideas, nor let his hatreds rest. The libertine became an ascetic through disgust for his own desire, whereas the misogynist *reverted* into the bashful lover twenty years later. The illegitimate offspring became a skin-deep aristocrat, then *reverted* to solitude (or to an advocate of exile, at least). The posterity seeker renounced fame, and the natural child rejected nature, as if Chamfort himself were the site of an endless chemical reaction, the formula of which escaped him. The individualist spoke of "starting human society afresh"; then, at the slightest difference with Mirabeau, he reverted to his gilded self-sufficiency under Vaudreuil's wing.

Similarly, the "theorist" of nature as tyrant reverted again; not into an advocate of benign nature, but of a new reign which would do away with all the laws of blood, of history, of aristocracy, of church, of the human race. Obscurely, Chamfort's project became one of breaking with the genealogy of evil, the weight of the past, the fatalism of the world—once again the project of an illegitimate child. Whereas his cynicism had been a reaction to his original puritanical streak, the misanthrope now reverted to idealist. Chamfort wanted to start the world over at zero. He would counter nature's evil laboratory with a good laboratory able to manufacture men endowed, like himself, with an instinct for liberty. He would create a new Adam, rediscover the original energy of the Creation which *natural* man possessed.

Chamfort was highly reactive in almost all spheres and would thus be a revolutionary in all domains, whether political or private, and for reasons that differed from those of Mirabeau. This latter wanted to liberate individual energy, talent, and intensity, but only in the context of a "conventional" historical order. Mirabeau's direct, unsublimated temperament underwent constant and ever-changing expansion, and he sought to balance his plebeianism with the authority of a king (failing his own authoritative leadership). Chamfort's schizophrenic temperament was subject to explosion followed by contraction, then by further explosions, and he would constantly re-launch the revolutionary mechanism in the confused hope of recasting nature, of abolishing every tyranny. Whereas Mirabeau's excessive ambition spurred him to remake the social order, Chamfort's excessive despair spurred him to remake the human race.

As Georges Poulet has pointed out, the twenty-year old Chamfort already thought himself a genius who could "renew mankind," like some meteor that chanced to pass near the Earth and would rejuvenate nature by disrupting it. But that young genius aged and degenerated into a man of talent who had failed in his redemptive mission. This ruin provided the debris with which the moralist illustrated his work. Aware of this implacable decline, which he confusedly identified with that of civilization, Chamfort began to hope for an apocalypse, which took the common metaphorical form of a volcano. Once again, this expectation of something unnameable and violent—a catastrophe designed to purify men and make them start afresh—could be detected as early as 1768. That was the year Chamfort presented his *L'ode sur les volcans* [Ode to volcanoes], which disconcertingly evoked the simultaneous destruction of slave and tyrant by the redeeming lava.[28] Less dangerous than war, tyranny, or man himself ("man forever the most destructive of scourges"), the volcano incarnated Chamfort's millennialist ideal, his hope in a secular flood—a response to the original sin which spawned his misanthropy.

The Volcano's Twin Slopes

Destroy everything and start afresh, drown blood in lava, supplant wicked, ancestral man by a new and fraternal being—such was the aspiration Mirabeau sparked in a man who thought he had left intense pleasures, great loves, and grand projects behind, all the while perceiving the usefulness of this ebb in passions. In an intriguing association, he observed, "Great men produce their masterpieces once past the age of passion, just as the soil is most fertile following eruption of volcanoes."[29] Only an explosion could regenerate a society that stifled talent, a human nature become inherently evil. Only a catastrophe could enable humanity to rebuild on healthy foundations (just as the *Products* rescued their author from sterility). Even prior to neoclassicism, Chamfort had sought to rediscover the energy of the original man "when, awakened from nothing by the voice of the creator, he sat alone in the midst of the world."[30] Now he expected the future to offer nothing more nor less than a re-Creation, both for himself and for others.

For the moment, however (and Chamfort, like his contemporaries, lived above all for the moment), civilization imposed its laws. Chamfort expressed resistance only through his character "M——," who displayed Chamfort's qualities and shortcomings—to excess. This ideal self was composed of a little bit of Mirabeau and a lot of himself. When Mirabeau and events were no longer present to trigger Chamfort's internal chemistry and natural volcanic activity, his supreme goal was simply to be himself, to be free, to remain independent, to resist society's every attempt at subjugation.

It is disconcerting to find the moralist and the "prophet of apocalypse" side by side in the same book, even if these two versions of himself had been gestating for a long time. One is ironic and elitist, the other furious and plebeian. The first was satisfied with his own wry smile and misanthropy, the second already wanted to destroy what he denounced. The former was a worldly animal who implicitly acknowledged the nobility's ephemeral genius, all the while condemning it explicitly; the latter believed savages and Americans to be free and happy, insofar as nature permits. On one side a cynic was convinced that happiness comes from adapting to the world as it exists, while on the other an extremist dreamed of cataclysm.

In 1785, a "dialectical" relationship thus existed between the individualist (that misanthropic, skin-deep aristocrat who delighted the most virulent reactionaries) and the believer in the flood; between the apostle of complete pessimism and the radical who repeated the comment first made by either Duclos or Diderot—"I would like to see the last of the kings strangled with the guts of the last of the priests";[31] between the elitist and the politician (who predicted that the English booted out of America would resettle in French and Spanish colonies in Latin America, thereby spreading the concept of human rights which would in turn provoke the birth of republican constitutions from the Tierra del Fuego to the Rio Grande, and the expulsion of colonial powers from the entire continent);[32] between the despairing soul who regretted that nature had instilled "an irresistible taste for life" in man and forbade suicide (as did priests and kings), that ultimate recourse against *every* tyranny, and the millennialist hoping for the rebirth of mankind. As early as 1785, the choice was between liberty or death.

Yet these two individuals (who could be called Vinzelles and Nicolas) remained prisoners of an egotism encompassing their contradictions. For Chamfort never sought the formula behind the chemical reaction he embodied. He never attempted intellectual self-integration. He refused, as a discerning moralist, to develop a personal ideology. As he stressed right from the first fragment of the *Products*, his maxims have no universal value, they must be read and *interpreted* in terms of the trajectory that elicited them. Each individual reacts differently, for individuals are not the fruit of a single principle but rather the outcome of numerous possibilities, an unstable collection of unrealized potentialities. The ancient Greeks noted that "man is born many, but dies one." Which is why these *Products* are more than a work in progress, a "forthcoming book," an unfinished volume. In 1785, Chamfort's double nature—his personal puzzle—was at its zenith; it afforded him a blind spot from which to observe the world with extreme lucidity. Which is another key to his success.

From "Superman" to Rancor

Some people reinvent their life, others repudiate it. There are compulsive liars (such as Chateaubriand, Malraux, Céline) and repudiators (such as Chamfort). The process of repudiating what one loves, then coming to love the product of such negation (even setting it up as an ideal), leads to the "true liar," that man of rancor described by Dostoevsky (*Notes from Underground*, with masochistic sensuality as a plus), Nietzsche (*The Genealogy of Morals*) and Max Scheler (in his book *Man of Ressentiment*, published in 1912). Chamfort's life could be summed up briefly as an initial passion (admittedly ambivalent) for fame, women, literature, and the aristocracy, followed by relentless criticism of them all. "The slave revolt in morals begins by rancor turning creative and giving birth to values," wrote Nietzsche, "the rancor of beings who, deprived of the direct outlet of action, compensate by an imaginary vengeance. All truly noble morality grows out of triumphant self-affirmation. Slave ethics, on the other hand, begins by saying *no* to an 'outside,' an 'other,' a non-self, and that *no* is its creative act."[33]

Several years earlier, in *The Gay Science,* Nietzsche had written forthrightly and enthusiastically of Chamfort's "easily understandable *rancor.*" This apparent contradiction will be taken up later, but it should be immediately pointed out that the French moralist probably inspired part of Nietzsche's theses on this type of human, the "invention" of which was sparked by his reading of Dostoevsky. It is hard not to think of Chamfort and his patron, the comte de Vaudreuil, on coming across this passage in *The Genealogy of Morals:* "When a noble man feels resentment, it is absorbed in his instantaneous reaction and therefore does not poison him. Moreover, in countless cases where we might expect it, it never arises, while with weak and impotent people it occurs without fail. It is a sign of strong, rich temperaments that they cannot for long take seriously their enemies, their misfortunes, their *misdeeds;* for such characters have in them an excess of plastic curative power, and also a power of oblivion. (A good modern example of the latter is Mirabeau, who lacked all memory for insults and meannesses done, and who was unable to forgive because he had forgotten.) Such a man simply shakes off vermin that would get beneath another's skin."[34]

The passage alludes to neither Chamfort nor, obviously, Vaudreuil. The reference to Mirabeau nevertheless suggests that such an association respects the spirit, if not the letter, of the concept. It is hard to see how the moralist differs from the man of rancor, led by implacable logic to invent an evil enemy, the principle of the "Evil One." From there he projects, through imitation and antithesis, a "Good One": himself! This is perhaps the defining feature of "M——" in the *Products,* whom Chamfort sets up as an ideal in contrast to the "perfected" civilization and nobility. He is perhaps the very type of man unable to put an end to anything, in contrast to that "blond Teutonic beast" (a concept Nietzsche employs several times) whose devastating energy puts an end to everything that hinders his vital rise to power.[35]

There is no point in dwelling on the ludicrous—and odious—aspects of passages that denounce the long-meditated influence of Judaism as well as the more recent one of those "sickly and effete creatures whom Europe is beginning to stink of today," in which Nietzsche perceived the ethnic resurgence of a "black-haired" type, a "pre-Aryan population" that blond domination had long muzzled.[36] It is here, however, that the German "moralist" locates the origins of rancor—which ultimately produces humility, Christian love, the sterile revolt of the slave, bad conscience, an attraction to weakness, socialist humanitarianism, the "abstract love" of beings, etc. Nietzsche, more Manichean than ever, winds up proposing the following tautology (the first term of which is false, by the way): the aristocratic spirit has no need of slaves to exist, whereas impotent slave mentality is derived from the negation, not of power, but rather of an "effigy" of the aristocracy.

While Chamfort's self-poisoning hypersensitivity and bitterness, along with his penchant for the secretive, the hidden, and the *indirect*, undoubtedly mark him as a man of rancor,[37] he escaped this classification through his energy, his "volcanic activity," and above all his egocentrism. For Chamfort, in 1785, was republican out of self-love, out of the certainty of his superiority (and not inferiority) over a class more or less consciously seeking new legitimacy through art, conversation, and "talent." He was sure to best it in those areas it came to consider essential (as did he), and he would therefore become more "aristocratic" than others. Similarly, Chamfort contradicts this other definition of the ideology of resentment: "To not seriously 'want' what it pretends to want."[38] As will be seen, Chamfort truly desired the downfall of the nobility—even though it was the idea of nobility that motivated his revolutionary commitment right to the end, to his own detriment.

Nietzsche could hardly accuse Chamfort of Christian humility or humanitarianism stemming from guilt, and he therefore could not expressly refer to him in *The Genealogy of Morals*. The sick philosopher, more German than ever in spite of himself, knew the logic of resentment too well and had read Chamfort too well to overlook the fact that Chamfort, like himself, was born to "a life of anonymity and battle" which would nevertheless contain "moments of re-emergence into the light, when one tastes the golden hour of victory."[39] The reversible nature of Nietzsche's vision (like that brought to bear on Chamfort) enabled him to admire Chamfort for his "superhuman" influence on Mirabeau almost at the same time that he instinctively sensed Chamfort to be a man of rancor. "He hated the Revolution," said Mme. Overbeck, Nietzsche's patronness. "He resented Chamfort for getting mixed up with people involved in the Revolution and didn't want his own name to be cited next that of Chamfort."[40] This is early testimony to the constant literary dialogue between these two exegetes of personal contradiction.

Like Chamfort, Nietzsche called civilization into question. According to him, the historical origins of bad conscience, guilt, self-hatred, and love of others—therefore of rancor—lay in the internalization of an aggressivity stemming from the transition, in distant times, from individual war to collective peace, which gave birth to society.[41] Rancor is thus not only a negative value, it is also the product of small warrior peoples subjected to vast pacified empires, and of individuals who harbor deep within themselves an instinct of human life and death that predates the adoption of civilization's controlled, inhibiting violence. The point to be stressed here is simply that these two "overcultivated" moralists shared a nostalgia for "natural" man in all his splendor—even if Chamfort's idea of "savageness" closely resembled the pastels collected by Vaudreuil, whereas the terrible militaristic frescoes painted by Nietzsche reveal a nostalgia for the narcissistic omnipotence enjoyed by the leaders of primitive hordes.

The Attraction of Hindu Castes

Max Scheler also "granted" certain attributes to *The Man of Ressentiment*. "A strong feeling of impotence and incapacity, accompanied by intense and painful depression"—this sounds like Chamfort— "and also of fear, anguish, of shyness in terms of any expression or activity liable to reflect the repressed feeling"[42]—which sounds a lot less like our man. Although Chamfort effectively repressed the causes of his illegitimacy and his illness, and although this denial created "a source of infection ready to spread," it was his wounded certainty of *superiority* (over the aristocracy, over women) that led to his rancor. And, in his case, repression did not lead to "shyness," to say the least.

Certain symptoms described by Scheler nevertheless apply to the former Hercules Adonis. By sublimating his wounds into a general if eminently reversible aggressiveness against nobility and the second sex, Chamfort provoked a chain reaction in himself which effectively "colored" his "vital energy." Such an individual, claimed Scheler, is no longer "comfortable in his body, for he contemplates it with that sad feeling of *distance* and objectivity underlying much of dualist metaphysics (neo-Platonism, Descartes, etc). . . . Often enough, these painful internal sensations are strong enough to modify the very direction of feelings. They thus turn against the subject himself, and become self-hatred, disgust for oneself, the desire to take revenge on oneself."[43] There we have Chamfort in a nutshell.

The clinical examination of our moralist continues (he was,

moreover, truly ill and must have wanted to get better).[44] "As soon as a man of resentment no longer manages to justify, to understand, to realize his being and his life in terms of positive values of power, health, beauty, freedom, unbridled scope of being and life . . . his sense of values imperceptibly shifts to arrive at the conclusion that, 'all of that means nothing.' He thus decides that only those aspects contrary to reality are necessary to human salvation—poverty, suffering, pain and death. Through this 'sublime vengeance,' as Nietzsche called it, resentment plays a truly creative role in the history of moral judgments."[45] Similarly, rancor had an influence on the Revolution, via Chamfort's harnessing of Mirabeau's vital energy; yet the Revolution, like all great historic (as opposed to political) groundswells, was carried along by life-giving forces which matched those of death.

Scheler remains more coherent—or more prudent—than his mentor, even if his attempt to establish a Nietzscho-Christianity seems particularly dangerous. Although he notes that "the slave who has a slave's nature, or who feels himself and knows himself to be a slave, feels no bitterness" (pointing out, in contrast, that women, Jews, the elderly, domestic servants, and the proletariat—the list is comic—are particularly prone to rancor), he suggests several ways to alleviate resentment—parliamentary democracy, a free press, trade unionism. From there to revolution is just a small step that Scheler, the good Christian, refused to take. He made this interesting comment, however: "The amazing explosion of rancor against the nobility and its lifestyle at the time of the Revolution would be absolutely inexplicable (as would its development) if that nobility hadn't been invaded by bourgeois commoners (who bought the estates of nobles and then assumed their titles and names) and eroded by marriages for money (Sombart estimates that more than four-fifths of the 'nobility' were commoners)."[46] Rightly understood, then, this means that it was the massive presence of recently adopted (or "illegitimate") nobles that triggered the explosion of 1789.[47] Extreme proximity within the social hierarchy, when confronted with extreme distance within the symbolic hierarchy, is, therefore, an optimum condition for historic upheaval, as Scheler recognized. "There would be little rancor in a democracy which, socially as well as politically, tended toward equality of wealth. History also shows that little rancor would exist within a society organized according to the caste system as it existed in India, for example, or in any clearly differentiated social system."[48]

Chamfort thus occupied a "tricky" position, that of the middle ground created by the decline of strictly hereditary nobility and the rise of commoners, where the criteria of birth encountered that of talent. Given the unlikely adoption of an Indian caste system, he was, therefore, logically (if the term can be applied to Chamfort) a potential follower of the other system. He nevertheless suffered, in flesh and blood, from this strange historical tug of war. Similarly, the typically ambitious man of 1785 could "logically" be both a candidate for ennoblement and a budding revolutionary. Nobility was no longer legitimate enough to be respected, obeyed, or even tolerated, and the bourgeoisie was not yet prestigious enough to be tolerable. The year 1785 was a pivotal one in which many an inferior could imagine himself above his superior, while this latter, following Vaudreuil's example, extended a hand, not knowing whether to step down or clamber higher.

Max Scheler concluded that rancor stemmed from a chronic comparison between the self and others. Everything in Paris during the reign of Louis XVI (who himself felt inferior to his forebears) encouraged Chamfort's sense of rancor, in addition to his own temperament and personal history. He was not alone, as things would have it; the feeling was shared by Brissot, by Marat (who wore a gentleman's sword ever since he had been doctor to the comte d'Artois's guards), and by Danton (who would use the noble signature d'Anton). Chamfort was even, in a way, emblematic of such friction, of that irritated contact sparked by the negation of aristocratic life forces. An excess of such negation, when combined with ambition, energy, and—in Chamfort's case—pessimism, would ultimately give birth to the ineluctible affirmation of commoners' talents, as perfectly formulated by Mirabeau: "The time has come when men must be judged by what they possess in that little space behind the forehead, between the eyebrows."[49]

14. HALF COCKSCOMB, HALF POPPY

The intensity of absolute pleasures, as metaphysicists say, diminishes with time. Yet time apparently increases relative pleasures; and I suspect that this is the artifice by which nature has been able to bind men to life.

Chamfort

Peop le judge themselves by what they disdain as much as by what they attain, and Chamfort was exemplary on this score. But the crisis following Julie's "betrayal" and the death of his adoptive mother wore him down, as did a summer spent ruminating over things. "The contemplative life is often wretched," he admitted. "It's important to act more, think less, and not watch yourself live." In October 1784, therefore, he accepted the post of principal secretary to Mme. Elisabeth, Louis XVI's sister, as Vaudreuil had urged. He apparently had no second thoughts about this volte-face. Things had changed—to his advantage—so he had changed; a man "who never bends when it is in his interest to bend, inevitably winds up with nothing at all to lean on, having no other friend than an abstract being called virtue, who will let you die of hunger." It was not an easy decision to make, however. "Those people should provide me with 20,000 livres of income,"[1] he said on receiving one-tenth of that sum to run the library for the king's sister. He consoled himself by slipping several incendiary works among that very Catholic flock in Montreuil—works which Mme. Elisabeth forbad her ladies in waiting (mischievously nicknamed Fury, Bombshell, and Demon) to read.

It is intriguing to see a "fox" like Chamfort set among the sheep populating the paradise surrounding this saintly princess. Louis XVI feared his sister would retire to a convent; Diane de Polignac tried unsuccessfully to exploit her goodness; and some people, even today, would like to see her canonized (Mme. Elisabeth having been guillotined during the Revolution). Chamfort was now working for a truly *symbolic* sum, royal stipends being paid with a delay of three years due to the treasury deficit and to the escapades of Marie-

Antoinette, the Polignacs, and Vaudreuil. Nevertheless, one can imagine how stimulating it was for the moralist to discover the way a court worked—even if Montreuil offered only a miniature, rustic version of Versailles (which was still off-limits to commoners).

Forgetting both his planned exile to Provence and his financial paranoia, Chamfort henceforth demonstrated manifest gratitude toward his patron. "Independently of my new position, my relationship with M. le comte de Vaudreuil has become such that there is no longer any question of my leaving the area. It is the most perfect and tender friendship imaginable," he wrote to Abbé Roman, to whom he obviously owed some explanation. "I'm unable to put the details in writing; but I submit that, outside of England where these things are simple, there is practically no one in Europe who could understand such a strong attachment between an isolated man of letters seeking even greater isolation, and a man of the court, possessing the greatest fortune and the greatest favor. When I say attachment so strong, I should say so tender and pure; for . . . this is a question of friendship, and that word says it all."

Chamfort has often been accused of ingratitude. True, he would amply prove his lack of historical gratitude toward the aristocracy (which hardly treated him generously at birth). But he was rarely ungrateful on a daily level, in personal (and not class) relationships. D'Angiviller, Condé, and Vaudreuil thus received his most moving letters, and this was not simply courtly flattery. Beneath his dread of the "evil patron" and his visions of an apocalyptic flood, he harbored a nostalgia for the "good father," an obscure search for a lost noble paradise. On being appointed secretary, he claimed he was "unjinxed," as though released from an *evil spell*.

Chamfort's modest Auvergne education had left him with limited financial imagination. His idea of money was close to barter, to primitive exchange, to a "natural" contract. Thus his embarrassment, his shame almost, when gifts presented to him exceeded his means, leaving him unable to reciprocate. And thus his joy at owing Vaudreuil only the ultimately theoretical sum paid by Mme. Elisabeth. One of his fragments reveals this fear of not being up to the aristocracy, which increasingly indulged in conspicuous excess, magnificent gifts, and the spirit of ostentatious one-upmanship. "The lover, too well loved by his mistress, seems to love her less, and vice versa. Are feelings of the heart like favors? When one can no longer hope to pay them back, one becomes ungrateful." The comparison with love illustrates the importance Chamfort placed on the issue. It was the fear of not being equal to their generosity that made him mistrust certain patrons, comparing them to Satan buying the submission of souls (at lofty prices) for the pleasure of watching them struggle in his hands. The Charmer not being Satan—he would even pay to *be influenced*—Chamfort this time enjoyed their relationship without undue dread.

Mirabeau, long without news of Chamfort, learned of the "resurrection" with relief, and of the appointment with annoyance. You're abandoning the friends who love you, you've sold yourself without even being paid, effectively argued the plebeian count from London, describing at length his disappointment in the liberal English system, all the while demanding for the hundredth time the pamphlet attacking the Society of the Cincinnati which Benjamin Franklin had commissioned from the two of them. Thus Chamfort, who wrote rarely, went back to fleshing out the drafts of a "theory all his own"—Mirabeau *dixit*—the force of which had struck the American ambassador when the two friends had read a first version of their text to him in his house in Passy in July 1784. This theory obviously concerned the nobility, and Chamfort had never disguised from Vaudreuil the fact that he considered nobility to be a fundamental obstacle between talent and power (just as the clergy constituted a barrier between the believer and God). It therefore deserved to disappear. If men are evil, society makes them "even more evil," for society was not a decadent version of nature but an entirely artificial creation. While the monarchy was not to be repudiated, the aristocracy, church, and magistrature were complete concoctions and could be totally dismantled. This conviction, echoed by Mirabeau, obliged Chamfort to find a *political* middle road between individualism and apocalypse, between M—— and the renewal of the species.

This was hardly the first pamphlet directed against the nobility. It had been attacked for its near monopoly over the clergy, magistrature, and army, and for its medals and sashes—"those seeds of loathsome vanity," said Chamfort. But it had never been openly accused of gang "murders" and of "lowering the human race." Benjamin Franklin worried about the emergence of an aristocracy within the young American republic. Chamfort pointed to the "vermin" undermining France and the Old World. But, faithful to his promise to never publish again—as well as to his old cautious streak—he let Mirabeau sign the pamphlet.

Individualism versus Nobility

What was it that made the nobility a "breed" apart, ruling over men like mankind over animals? It was the belief in blood. Heroism and virtue were supposed to be hereditary, and increased over time, to judge by titles. Chamfort thus noted that his contemporary, the prince de Turenne, was "more noble" than his ancestor, Louis XIV's illustrious marshal. This was a widespread preconception—even the skeptical still believed it pertained to themselves (including Mirabeau, who remained very attached to his title of count). Chamfort countered with the observation that there was no more relationship between a noble and his ancestors than between Cicero and Rome's cicérones. A knight of the Cincinnati, eight generations later, would have only 1/512 part of the blood of the hero of the American Revolution, the rest coming from his other ancestors—probably including "knaves, royalists and prostitutes." There was, therefore, no pure heredity but only mixtures, *bastardy,* individual destinies. This corresponded to the Christian concept of the soul as the sum of values proper to each human being. Franklin was hardly exaggerating when he predicted, at Mme. Helvétius's place, that the face of the earth could be changed simply by applying Christian principles to politics. Such an application was behind the French Revolution, the way modern individualism stems from Anglo-Saxon protestantism—the paradox being that the aristocracy of the day accelerated this movement by also preaching uniqueness and talent.

Individualism was a constant trait with Chamfort. His illegitimacy and his skittish disposition exacerbated this trait, and only Rousseau was more intensely individualistic. It was a logical counterpart to Chamfort's misanthropy, a defensive reaction to human aggressiveness, yet it was also the expression of a particularly intense social and financial frustration. Such frustration became more and more widespread at the end of the Ancien Régime. Chamfort was not the only one to denounce an order where a minority of "asses" denied the best horses access to the tournament. There were dozens of ambitious young men (including certain aristocrats) who saw no prospects in a literary field that was prodigal yet spent, nor in a political field without institutions. The appetite of this generation of 1780 was stimulated by the cult of fame stemming from academic infatuation with antiquity, by the American example in which French officers were covered with laurels in a matter of months, by the general impatience spurred by the civilization of the moment, and by the symbolic frustration of a bourgeoisie enriched by the peace reigning since 1763. Such impatience was demonstrated not only by Mirabeau and by Talleyrand's guests, but by people like the future revolutionary Jacques Pierre Brissot, a young and brilliant lampoonist Chamfort met in the plebeian count's wake. Born in Chartres, soon possessor of a fake noble particle and a frenzy of projects, Brissot "de Warville" keenly resented the barriers erected by the nobility (he would even admit to being jealous of the king). There was also the comte d'Antraigues, a thirty-year-old gentlemen from Languedoc who was highly influenced by Rousseau and Chamfort. Antraigues was an ambitious and versatile bluffer who was feudal lord on his manor but backed republican ideas in Paris after having been excluded from court on grounds of insufficient nobility. And then there was Clavière, the banker banished from Geneva after the abortive antiaristocratic revolution of 1782, who was also linked to Mirabeau.[2] Chamfort, therefore, became a highly personal spokesman for these "commoners," whose demands would soon turn France into a country of twenty-five million individualists. His *Considérations sur l'Ordre de Cincinnatus* [*Considerations on the Society or Order of Cincinnati*] supplied, in 1784, considerable leverage by calling into question not only the "hereditary" legitimacy of the nobility but also its historical legitimacy—the nobility's final justification for domination once its military role had lapsed.

Gauls versus Franks

For the nobility pretended that it descended from the Franks who invaded the land in the fifth century. A dubious pretension, rarely expressed out loud, but which Chamfort took literally in order to evoke the "thirty thousand armor-clad oppressors who, lance in hand, trampled eleven or twelve million Gauls under their horses' hooves"[3]—a victory that enabled nobles and the ennobled, thirteen centuries later, to remain exempt from taxes (taxes being tribute paid by Gauls). Chamfort was occasionally accused of chauvinism, but he was motivated by a sincere affection for his country, language, and culture (though not for Frenchmen), and thus he could drive home his point: "the kingdom's privileged population of seven hundred thousand still behaved "ethnically" and economically like foreigners—almost like colonizers.

Nor did he merely indict the nobility in the name of an emerging nationalism (a word still brand new). He condemned it in the long run. All its institutions, he said, were based on force "all the more oppressive for completely residing in things and almost always independent of people." Such "determinism" left little room for reform and sparked a call for "the only, true nobility," one based on reason and virtue. Thus the "republican" was born, indifferent to opinion, fame, and money, existing only for *himself* and ready to die for *himself*. Chamfort's influence can be detected throughout this treatise and motto—"Liberty, virtue and country above all"—which Mirabeau embellished with commentaries and passages lifted from Turgot and Franklin. The class that pretended to treat its peasants as sons—and treated certain of its sons as peasants—had just discovered two privileged enemies. The revolt against bad fathers—the counterabandonment—was approaching. Chamfort had penned one of the first openly republican pleadings of the Ancien Régime. Mirabeau wrote to Chamfort from London: "Failing reforms which I will try to facilitate, by writing and any other means, Louis XVI will be the last French monarch."[4] These would remain, to the letter, their respective positions during the Revolution.

The *Considérations* met with a certain success, although the Society of the Cincinnati had meanwhile won Franklin over by dropping its hereditary clause (with the exception of its French section, to which Mirabeau's brother belonged). Appearing simultaneously in London and Paris, printed in two thousand copies in each instance, the pamphlet was criticized for its lack of rigor, all the while enjoying undeniable success. Mirabeau, the only one to sign it, was also the only one to profit from it. Now widely known, he instructed Chamfort to lay the groundwork for his return to Paris, yet at the same time attacked Joseph II, Marie-Antoinette's beloved brother, in a new lampoon.[5] The difficulties he created for Mme. Elisabeth's secretary were just beginning. Early in 1785, Mirabeau dragged his valet before the London courts, accusing the man of having stolen a few shirts. But the judge forced the plebeian count to admit that the Voltaire-d'Alembert correspondence had also disappeared; it was Chamfort who had allowed Mirabeau to read the original manuscripts, belonging to the prince de Condé, unaware that Mirabeau would have it secretly recopied in order to sell. Chamfort had thought himself safe from the notorious kleptomaniac, but now he was disillusioned. Worse, fragments recopied from the collection of aphorisms Chamfort had lent Mirabeau would be found among the count's London papers.[6] The cup was running over. Geniuses might be wonderful in books, but Hercules was all flesh and blood. Yet another request for money finally convinced Chamfort. On finding his letter in shreds, Mirabeau said, "I'll wager it's the only one of mine he's torn up."[7] This sordid ending revived memories of Julie. "Intense and delicate friendship is often wounded by the wilting of a rose," admitted Chamfort. Other reasons may have been behind the abrupt cooling in their relationship—Mirabeau constantly writing of "my *Considérations*," overwhelming Chamfort for letters of introduction to English notables signed by Vaudreuil or Franklin, begging him to get his lawyer friend Target elected to the Académie on the basis of the compelling argument that "Target has done better than to produce bad or mediocre books; he has produced none at all." The lawyer was, in fact, elected. Or again, Mirabeau used Chamfort's name in the preface to highly questionable attacks against Beaumarchais.

The moralist complained to Brissot of the thefts he suffered and discovered that exasperation with Hercules was general. The financier Clavière, also charged with preparing the count's return to Paris, wrote to Chamfort that "I think that I would be hard pressed to defend the count against someone who might follow his conduct step by step, for he ultimately ridicules those from whom he seeks patronage."[8] Henriette de Nehra returned to Paris ahead of her lover, to pave the way, but was met with howls of outrage. Mirabeau was a genius at rounding up his flock, but nothing was to be done— the charm had broken. Chamfort was no longer on the list of best friends the count drew up in 1787 for Henriette, the moralist having been replaced by Talleyrand.

Mirabeau's Eclipse

Literally drained by the incident, Chamfort performed a second volte-face. On October 21, 1785, he accepted the honorary post of interpreter-secretary to the Swiss and Grison Regiment. At Calonne's request, the king added two thousand livres to Chamfort's annual stipend for *Mustapha,* in August 1786. Having become one of the best pensioned writers of the kingdom, he assiduously attended the Académie, which appointed him chancellor. "Before being immortal, I want to know if I'll live," he would say to justify his literary retirement. Henceforth comfortable, he entered society again— abandoning it always made him desire it once more. Affluence healed the wounds of a career begun too early and abandoned too swiftly, and he even made a fuss on seeing Bernardin de Saint-Pierre move to a disreputable neighborhood. "I simply located myself where I've been classed for a long time," replied the author of *Paul et Virginie* bitterly. Having arrived at mid-life—or so he believed—Chamfort granted himself a respite. "To scorn money is to dethrone a king," he asserted.[9] The year 1786 marked a discreet restoration, and an apparent stability following his successive grief and failures.

"He was then happier than he had ever been in his life," recounted Ginguené, who was also present at Vaudreuil's residence. "Free from every yoke and every duty, he could still choose between the solitude which no one dared disturb . . . and a select society, composed of people able to appreciate him and delight him, whose faults and silliness he found less unbearable since he had acquired the privilege and even made it an honor to satirize them. His mornings were divided between his studies and his old friends, whom he had never seen and cultivated as assiduously as in this period of favor when he was practically besieged by many new friendships."

He didn't seem to realize, however, that Vaudreuil, whom he wanted to "convert," had financially rallied Chamfort to the old order. The pendulum was swinging back toward the center. The Philosophers' clan was on its death bed and could no longer even find candidates for election to the Académie. Curiosity in the sciences became farcical as believers and nonbelievers alike were "magnetized" by charlatans such as Mesmer and Cagliosto. In a sign of the times, Chamfort saw the famous Mlle. Lacroix present the mystery of her "visions" at the residence of the princesse de Wurtemberg (the future empress of Russia) in the company of his most faithful enemy, La Harpe.

Political and social confusion was as complete as it had been when Chamfort first entered society in 1763. Ideas and talk remained virulent, but in fact people were falling back into line (with the exception of Brissot, who henceforth took up the vacant post of rebel). Beaumarchais was richer than ever, Mirabeau was preparing to leave for Germany on a semi-official assignment, Talleyrand would soon become an advisor to minister Calonne (who, like his friend Vaudreuil, wanted to surround himself with sharp minds). Chamfort himself sat on an opera jury chosen by the king—all the while admitting his ignorance in the matter and secretly advocating the downfall of the civilization of the mask. Never had the Ancien Régime so little resembled its textbook caricature, in Paris at least—princes, the bourgeoisie, and "bohemians" mixed and mingled, discussing politics from dawn till dusk, without worrying about the excessive etiquette typical of the 1760s. "High society was worn-out," admitted the prince de Ligne. The constant escalation in disguises had given way to an inflation of ambition, gravitating around ministers and liberal aristocrats. In 1765, the marriage of talent and nobility had been apparent in only a dozen salons. By 1785, it was the rule just about everywhere. "Chamfort the volcano" entered a dormant period, finding himself in a paradoxical situation. He was beholden to princes, yet republican in his soul; he believed certain illusions were indispensable, yet he no longer had any; he felt passions were more useful than reason, yet he avoided excitement. He reconciled what would soon become irreconcilable.

Metamorphosis, Act I

Everything might have continued thus if it hadn't been for the awareness of a vacuum at the head of the monarchy. Louis XVI had neither the arrogance nor the cruelty required of his role. Too frumpish to get on well, too honest to pretend, all the weaker for dreading his weakness, Louis fled his autocratic duties by hunting and playing locksmith, allowing his ministers to acquire overwhelming influence. Power is maintained by setting the terms of debate, by cultivating an obsession with authority—whereas Louis XVI gave in to the caprices of others. Aristocratic and liberal demands piled up on his desk; forced labor and torture were abolished. But most well-known writers enjoyed royal stipends, and so demands originated mostly from the nobility and from literary bohemians. "Sire," said the old maréchal de Richelieu to the king, "under Louis XIV no one dared to say a word, under Louis XV everyone spoke in hushed tones, and under Your Majesty everything is said out loud."

As an indirect consequence, the court became more "feminine." The Polignacs' friends gathered together to milk ewes near the Petit Trianon, saying "sensitive" things to one another in tiny voices. The queen dressed up as a barmaid during festivities. Courtiers began driving their own carriages, and the king was seen getting down from his carriage to extricate a cart horse from the mud. Versailles, which had always tortured nature by pruning shrubs in triangles and spirals, now covered the walls of the Hameau with imitation straw, under Hubert Robert's direction. This decadent court remained under the sway of a tinsel version of Rousseau, until the political version of Rousseau came to sweep it away. At the center of this cardboard kingdom was That Austrian Woman, to whom

Calonne would say, "If what Your Majesty desires is possible, consider it already done. If it is impossible, it will soon be done."

The "Necklace Affair" brought things to a head. It was discovered that Cardinal Rohan, a Versailles regular (where he had received the newly elected academician Chamfort), let himself be driven bankrupt by swindlers in the hope of entering into the queen's good graces through the gift of a magnificent diamond necklace. Marie-Antoinette, though innocent, became the prime target in a scandal that thoroughly discredited the monarchy. Having decided to reassert royal authority, she brought the period of frivolity to an end. Vaudreuil, who had defended Cardinal Rohan (as did a large part of the aristocracy), fell into disgrace. Rohan himself, the unwitting tool of the swindlers, was dragged before the courts at the insistence of the baron de Breteuil. The king, who had never liked Vaudreuil (nor falcon hunting), approved. Vaudreuil's death knell sounded with the death of a creditor, followed by the bankruptcy of the financier Saint-James, with whom Vaudreuil had placed his money. The Treasury demanded the nine hundred thousand livres loaned Vaudreuil by the comte d'Artois, and he was banned from the court for excessive gambling—and for having too long obliged the queen to share her favorite.

This return to moral order, however, came too late. Public opinion was struck by the fortunes poured into chateaus, festivities, and gowns. Bankruptcy threatened, and Calonne suggested imposing an egalitarian tax and creating provincial assemblies—a sort of English-style minirevolution that would decentralize France, win middle-class loyalty to the crown, and purge those whom the minister had been pampering just a few months earlier. Chamfort backed this compromise (and would continue to praise Calonne right up until 1792). He decided to lobby the heads of the regime, and once again discovered the social skill that had been so lacking with Julie. He convinced his former patron Breteuil, who had gone from being a liberal to being an ultrareactionary, to support reduced powers for the king's provincial intendants, without mentioning their abuses. Instead, Chamfort pointed out to Breteuil that they forced the greatest gentlemen in their provinces to address them as "Monseigneur."[10]

While he counted on the snobbery of the nobility to undermine the king's power, and on the king to undermine that of the nobility, Chamfort remained skeptical about the possibility of imposing a tax on the privileged class. A "lively" difference of opinion with

Vaudreuil resulted. Chamfort was already warning him of the risks of violent eruption. But the Charmer stood by Calonne, who was his last hope. This was the first cloud on the horizon of that "perfect" relationship that had withstood all the attacks in the *Considérations sur l'Ordre de Cincinnatus*.

In February 1787, the king convened the notables to discuss Calonne's proposed reforms. An alliance was forged between the minister and "English" liberals such as Talleyrand,[11] who wrote to Choiseul-Gouffier: "The people will finally count for something, my friend." But Chamfort swiftly proclaimed this a sham, since the majority of notables belonged to the elite of the kingdom. The reaction of men already baptized *Notables* by the clubs in the Palais-Royal was thoroughly predictable. They completely rejected the reforms, resulting in Calonne's exile on April 8. "They ignored him when he started the fire, but punished him when he sounded the alarm," observed Chamfort.[12] This crack got around, obliging Chamfort to deny authorship of an anonymous pamphlet favorable to the minister.[13] Vaudreuil kept one step ahead of the game by leaving for London on May 3. His post of Grand Falconer was abolished, officially leaving him with fourteen thousand livres of income—the same as Chamfort. Vaudreuil put the house on rue de la Chaise up for sale, along with his Gennevilliers manor and his paintings. The Polignacs laid low, Versailles tightened its belt, and the political clubs were closed on Breteuil's order. Marie-Antoinette had to leave a performance of *Athalie* in February when the crowd applauded the tirade denouncing tyranny and calling for the fall of that "cruel queen." Louis XVI seemed to have the situation under control for the moment, but the preceding three months had given substance to dreams of the "flint" and the "musket." Chamfort committed himself totally, viscerally, to what was not yet called the revolution, and he abandoned a queen who had disavowed him in 1785 by backing Maisonneuve's theatrical revival of *Mustapha et Zéangir*.

15. THE PALAIS-ROYAL POWDERKEG

Whoever is not a misanthrope at forty has never loved mankind.

Chamfort

There is no perfect misanthrope—you may think you're one, but your fervor belies it.

Droz, to Chamfort

Chamfort was one of the men who most desired, anticipated, invoked and cherished the revolution.

Barras

Vaudreuil's return to Paris proved painful. Abandoned by his class, the man who had argued "*Marriage* is the only recourse" became bitter himself. Chamfort tried to win him over again, but the gulf between the prophet of the Revolution and its first victim was widening. The best that Vaudreuil could do in return, according to Ginguené, was "to not hate" Chamfort. Chamfort is supposed to have laughingly suggested to seven "rascals" dining with him on rue de la Chaise, that they "whip" Marie-Antoinette, who had secretly come to see Mme. de Polignac.[1] The anecdote can be taken for what it's worth; the point is that the queen's two former protégés no longer spoke the same language. Coexistence could have become unbearable, added Ginguené, but Vaudreuil left for Rome before it did, and, by common agreement, Chamfort abandoned the mansion on rue de la Chaise with all its servants—that luxury for which he just was not cut out. Four years of stability ended with his move to the Palais-Royal district, where he installed himself at number 18, Galerie de Montpensier, in the spring of 1787. Here the crowd was vulgar and overexcited, in total contrast to the Saint-Germain neighborhood. The Palais-Royal, inherited by the duc d'Orléans—the richest man in France—had become a city within the city following the real-estate operation that ringed the grounds with three arcaded galleries. The galleries housed restaurants, a theater, jewelers, bookstores, furnished accommodations, and eventually a circus. There was the waiterless Café Mécanique where the curious watched drinks rise to tables in hollow shafts worked from below. There was the famous Café de Foy (where Desmoulins would raise the call to arms in 1789), and the Café de Chartres (now the Grand Véfour restaurant). There were gambling houses—craps, lotteries, thirty-one—and a pool in which a seal reportedly played the mandolin. There were the Chinese baths where one could take "rising and falling" showers. There was the Curtius showcase, which displayed wax busts of famous men. There was also a store that carried that recent invention, the raincoat. Under the arcades, or in the shadow of the garden's chestnut trees, strolled swarms of streetwalkers—Chouchou, Zéphire, Aurore, Amarante, Violette, Zélia, Giroflée, la Bacchante—as though the Regency, born in this very palace of the dukes of Orléans, had come back to prostitute itself in force. Experts discussed the respective attractions of Carline (who "injected pleasure with extreme rapidity"), the Valmont sisters (the four of whom could be had for eighteen livres), and Betsi (a mulatto with "a charming little gem"), according to the *Almanach des addresses des demoiselles de Paris* [*Almanac of addresses of young ladies of Paris*]. Shyer ones could go see pretty Zulima, a flesh-colored mannequin that could be undressed (for a fee) at the "Tartar Camp" stand. When the gardens opened in 1784, the duc d'Orléans was referred to as the first member of the royal family to have sunk to the bar trade. By 1787, the crowds were so thick, in spite of the prices charged, that an apple dropped from the second floor would not have hit the ground. One aristocratic monopoly had come to an end: two years before the fall of the Bastille, pleasure was taken by storm by Parisians determined to have as much instant fun as Vaudreuil.

But Chamfort was familiar with all that. He had, of course, a regular gaming table and a stool at the Café du Caveau (where writers and speculators met under the bust of Gluck), but nothing more. "I am like a salamander [i.e., impervious to flames]," he said when warned against the dangers of loose women.[2] He preferred to comment on events with the newsmongers who gathered under the Tree of Cracow in the middle of the garden. Like them, he approved of the sale of the Crown's chateaus, as decided by the king. He was outraged that no noble signed the memorandum proposing—already—the abolition of their privileges. He applauded the reduction of royal pensions—including his own for *Mustapha*. When the clubs were closed, he shifted to the Lycée, the institute founded by the comte de Provence in order to popularize chemistry. There Chamfort explained to his fashionable audience (which included the future "terrorist" Barère) that France had been living without a constitution for centuries.[3] Mme. Elisabeth herself received pamphlets sold in the arcades put up by the duc d'Orléans, who hoped to dethrone his cousin Louis XVI and thereby give the Palais-Royal its true vocation. He therefore encouraged the agitation of Parisians frustrated by a century of monarchic exile to Versailles. Chamfort's choice of a new home may have been a coincidence, but it seems more like fate—no one can resist a revolution taking place in his own backyard, especially if it means releasing the incredible tension Chamfort had been accumulating for years.

The Aristocratic Revolution

Though the Palais-Royal was becoming more of a political forum than an amusement park, certain subjects remained taboo for Chamfort. He had no comment on the abolition of the Polignacs' posts, and he defended the comte d'Artois against the charge that the count had said to a notable backing the Third Estate, "Are you trying to make commoners of us?"[4] Yet there was one slogan, that of the aristocratic revolution, which met with unanimous approval—"France must be debourbonized." This explains why the "English" left-wing associated with Calonne was discredited, and why the newly convened *parlements* were so popular (they had been summoned to pass reforms they didn't want, yet earned an antiabsolutist label by asking that the States General be organized). It was the triumph of a magistrature undone by Louis XV and reinstalled by Louis XVI, which dreamed of recovering its old glory.

Might the Revolution have been aristocratic, like the Fronde a century earlier? In 1787–1788, such a hypothesis was not unthinkable. There were numerous layers of nobility under the Ancien Régime, and Chamfort had known only the most cultivated, the richest, the most liberal. Yet the local gentry and even the highest ranking nobles in the provinces (from which he descended via his mother), along with the elite at court who had been bored for years in their mansions flanking the chateau at Versailles, considered the fall of Vaudreuil and the Polignacs a personal victory. The same was true of the fall of the handsome Lauzun, the duc de Guines, and all those suitors who, even though rejected, flattered the queen's narcissism. These ranks of nobles, including the poorest and the oldest, had been denied positions, incomes, and honors for so long that they saw rebellion by the *parlements* as the just deserts of a queen who thoroughly ignored the throne's oldest and most faithful pillars.

The Revolution, then, might have taken another turn. But the love affair between bourgeoisie and artisans on the one hand, and the *parlements* on the other, did not last. For the *parlements* sparked dissension by referring all reform to the States General. The third estate, victimized by the last convening of the States General back in 1614, demanded the same number of delegates as the clergy and nobility combined. "Debourbonization" suddenly took a back seat, and the movement that had started by defending Cardinal Rohan's innocence now changed direction. Positions were no longer drawn in terms of despotism but in terms of the Third Estate. "Next year you'll be behind the carriages, and we'll be inside," shouted the crowd at the noble promenade at Longchamp. Apart from the liberal upper aristocracy (which, like Mirabeau and Chamfort, had its own conception of the Revolution, and part of which would remain faithful to it up until 1793 or even 1794 for the writer-lawyer Hérault de Séchelles), the other layers of the nobility began to resist a Third Estate that was "usurping" their movement. Conversely, after those first few months when the *parlements* skillfully represented everyone's frustrations, the Third Estate displayed consistent aggressiveness toward the aristocracy, reserving its admiration for the liberal fringe alone (the faction that led to the renouncing of feudal privileges on August 4, 1789). Henceforth, the nobility would unite, becoming that single class perceived by Chamfort, who detested its self-proclaimed superiority (all the while making exceptions of his friends, who generally supported the Revolution, and his former patrons, who all fought against it).

As early as 1788, then, Chamfort was in tune with those French who felt superior to everyone and who could no longer bear to be automatically considered inferior to nobles (as he had been, on entering the salons). Having long lived in rancor, Nicolas once again dominated the skin-deep aristocrat—representing the first change of identity triggered by the Revolution. The time had come to "de-Frank and de-christen"[5] in the name of fraternity, to unite against those false fathers denounced in the *Considérations*. Chamfort was born too early—or too late—to produce a major literary work, but he

arrived just at the right time to change the world. Mirabeau, whom
Chamfort had been seeing again since early 1788, helped complete
this transformation.[6]

Farewell to the Charmer

Chamfort himself was amazed by this change. Just three years earlier he would have laughed on discovering "some absurd injustice."
Now he waxed indignant in front of a young Breton whom
Ginguené, a distant relation, had just introduced. The young man—
pretty as a girl and shy as a lad—was none other than François René
Chateaubriand, who still aspired to write like Dorat, that "scribbler
of zephyrs." Chateaubriand found Chamfort to be "a talker with a
unique and inimitable tone of voice, full of cold fury and insolence."[7] By discussing the court and Rousseau, the logic of vice and
the contradictions of virtue, Chamfort wound up "politicizing" the
young Breton whom he took along to meet Mme. Helvétius, and
who was seen in a café open-mouthed with admiration before
Chamfort. "Happy moments when he consented, with a select
group of friends, to sup with my family," said Chateaubriand.[8] He
watched with pride as Chamfort took a lively interest in Lucile, his
sister and muse, that violent personality frightened off by men and
by life, who would soon become paranoiac (like the Revolution itself) and who was described as "having her brother's genius, yet
free from a writer's debasement."

But the most startling thing was Chamfort's lively interest in the
smallest economic and monetary details, in the *real world* that the
Revolution would have to erect on the ruins of that imaginary world
peopled by the artistic and intellectual pantheon which had held
sway over him for so long (particularly through its negation). His
destructive rage and fantasies of exile became concrete projects; he
wanted to rescue France from bankruptcy and finally establish himself in the country he had long criticized. This was the essence of his
answer to Vaudreuil who, out of touch after a year in exile and feeling "vaporish and bored by everything," asked Chamfort to write a
satire on the Third Estate. Chamfort objected:

> This is not the time to employ the broad strokes of Swift or
> Rabelais, when we are perhaps nearing disaster. For what's at
> stake? A suit opposing twenty-four million men to seven
> hundred thousand privileged people. . . . You think that you
> are being attacked personally, that we want to attack you.

Not at all. A great nation can elevate and admire a few
distinguished families, three hundred, four hundred, more or
less. . . . But, can it in good conscience carry seven hundred
thousand privileged people who, in terms of taxes, in terms of
money, have the same rights as the Montmorencys and the
most ancient knightly families? . . . Don't you see that such a
monstrous state of affairs must be changed, or that we will all
perish together—clergy, nobility, third estate? . . . There is talk
of the danger of the third estate acquiring too much influence; some go so far as to pronounce the word democracy.
Democracy! In a country where the people don't possess even
the smallest fraction of executive power! . . . Where the most
unbridled luxury and the most monstrous inequality of wealth
will always leave too great a distance between one man and
another! . . . So many false pretexts, so much ignorance or,
rather, dishonesty! Why not clearly admit, as some do: "I don't
want to pay?" I entreat you not to judge others by yourself. I
know that, if you had five or six hundred thousand livres of
landed income, you would be the first to scrupulously and
rigorously tax yourself; but . . . don't the Breton gentry
claim that it is not in their power to abandon their effective
privileges, that it is their children's heritage? . . . And you
want me to write! I dare assert that if the privileged were so
unfortunate as to win their case, the nation, thereby crushed,
would become . . . in respect to its assembled neighbors, what
Portugal is to England: one big farm. . . . If, to the contrary,
what must almost infallibly happen does happen, I can see
only prosperity for the entire nation. . . . If I were asked to say
in all sincerity which class of men I think will most profit from
the revolution in the making, I would answer that this
revolution will be profitable to all in proportion to already
existing superiority. I except the clergy, for whom neither you
nor I am anxious, and government ministers . . . but they will
not lose their taste for the trade, and anyway one cannot
prevent all accidents. That is how I see this unique and
incredible crisis. I wanted to make this profession of faith so
that, if by chance our opinions are found to be too different, we
might never again dwell on the subject. Our opinions have
differed more than once, without our hearts ceasing to
comprehend and love one another—that's the main thing; or
rather, that's everything.[9]

Did Chamfort still hope to convince Vaudreuil to go to work for the Revolution, just as this latter had once convinced Chamfort to go to work for the court? Undoubtedly. Did he really think it would enrich Vaudreuil? Probably, given that the count no longer had anything. And last, was he banking on the count's resentment against the court, the queen, and the baron de Breteuil (head of the Austrian Committee who had pressed Marie-Antoinette to dismiss Vaudreuil out of jealousy, and whose ambitiousness now pressed her to adopt a firm stance against the Revolution)? This, too, is possible. But Chamfort's plea came too late. Absolved by Marie-Antoinette, Vaudreuil and the Polignacs were already battling against Necker's return to the ministry. All Vaudreuil's confidence in Chamfort then melted, according to Ginguené. And their friendship ended on December 13, 1788, with these words from Chamfort: "I am speaking to you from the depths of my sanctuary, as I might do from the tomb, as the most tenderly devoted of friends, who has loved you only for yourself, free from fear and hope, indifferent to the all distinctions separating men."

The Chamfort Riddle

In fact, Chamfort no longer trusted the nobility. Vaudreuil was the exception that wound up proving the rule of the *Considérations:* no class can escape its role. That of the Third Estate was to replace birth by merit, to replace a society resembling a library where books are classified according to their size with a society where books are classified according to their value. Chamfort had held on to this conviction since his school days, and it was perhaps the only one he never betrayed. Which is why he wept with joy when Necker— whom the king had recalled—announced that the Third Estate would be granted twice the usual number of representatives to the States General. This also explains his subsequent metamorphosis, or rather his evolution. He felt that his own rise under the Ancien Régime prefigured the rise of the Third Estate, just as his long-held patriotism prefigured the hostility of "citizens" toward aristocratic cosmopolitanism. Since he had always kept silent about his birth, Chamfort would say nothing about the hidden inspiration behind his rebirth, even though he wished for a revolution of openness. As a good disciple of Rousseau, he even mistrusted elected representatives, and envisaged total openness between the power and the people.[10] Everything indicates that he experienced the events of 1789 not as a rupture but as a transition.

His attitude is obviously easier to explain than to justify. For the revolution was also for him an opportunity to definitively rid himself of the middling writer, the protégé of influential people, the man of rancor, the obsessed and nihilistic egotist—the "old man" (or "old type," in Nietzsche's words). He could emerge from his *cave* in the hope of becoming part of a community finally able to give the world a *meaning*. Through this assimilation of ideas, Chamfort also succeeded in transcending his own personal case. He had real moments of freshness, generosity, and enthusiasm, in which his ardent and reactive energy once again reverted to positive energy, to vital force. This makes it interesting to see how others later exploited his case to settle their own scores. Chateaubriand used Chamfort as the mirror image of his own evolution. "I was always amazed that a man who knew so much about men could espouse any given cause so intensely," he wrote as early as 1797 in *Essai sur les révolutions [An Historical, Political, and Moral Essay on Revolutions, Ancient and Modern]*. "Didn't he realize that all governments resemble one another, that republican and royalist are just two words for the same thing?" Chateaubriand nevertheless wound up making the distinction himself, just prior to the restoration of the Bourbons. The mature Chateaubriand indignantly repudiated the young Breton who dared compare Chamfort to a Greek sage, claiming that he had been blinded by "literary fame" at the time. Chateaubriand would explain from "beyond the grave" that Chamfort "was unable to forgive mankind the accident of his birth."[11] Case dismissed. For a while at least. "I am convinced that for Chateaubriand—son of a freemason father and a devout mother, himself a converted Philosopher—the influence of his youthful ideas . . . and literary friends was very important and lasted into . . . the liberalism and even republicanism of his final years," wrote his biographer, George D. Painter, in a letter to this author. "In the final analysis, it was all the same to me," Chateaubriand would say one day.

The question of Chamfort's birth remains crucial, of course. Nietzsche (who still thought Chamfort to be the illegitimate son of a noble canon) expressed amazement that the moralist could commit himself to such a cause, yet alluded to Chamfort's easily understandable rancor and his sacred vow to venge his mother. The author of *The Gay Science* detected a "hatred" of the father and of "all nobility [based on] blood," which stem from very real facts. Chamfort's birth coincided with famine. He grew up in a milieu that had no hope that some historian or biographer would recount its deeds, yet yearned for someone to take an interest. This explains Chamfort's determination, like Rousseau, to set "the spectators on stage." Hence his obsession with emending history. Stendhal, who understood this, was one of the few people in the following century who did not accuse him of ingratitude.

For ingratitude is the condition of any power asserting itself against another power to which it has been subservient—the bourgeoisie against the nobility, the monarchy against feudalism, Christianity against Judaism. Sainte-Beuve (a bachelor himself) claimed that Chamfort's rejection of the "joys" of marriage wound up embittering him. Perhaps. But not all those bitter women who backed the revolution were sterile. The author of *Causeries du lundi* [*Monday-Chats*] also claimed that Chamfort was out to get a regime that considered him a minor poet. Then why would a genius like Hugo have continued to rage against the Second Empire? There was surely a disparity between Chamfort's intelligence and his talent, between his head and his hand. But 1789 can't be reduced to a literary problem. "The poor are the Negroes of Europe," claimed Chamfort,[12] who had once slaved away as a ghostwriter. The people aspired to abundance, a wish inscribed on pottery in 1789 in hopes that such plates would be filled. They also believed in the promises of happiness that eighteenth-century France held out for everyone. They no longer wanted to be passive victims; they wanted to try their own luck. They could no longer bear the interminable winter of work when confronted with a class always on vacation. Obscurely, they wanted to concoct their own riddle, like all those who govern. It is possible that Chamfort was blind to all that; perhaps he really only wished to kill off the "old man" in himself. Nothing could be less certain, however.

For Chamfort was uncontestably sensitive to the plight of the people, through the prism of his own illegitimacy. One of his aphorisms betrays this intellectual and emotional identification. "Given equal wit and enlightenment, it would seem that a rich man can never understand nature, the human heart, and society as thoroughly as a poor man. For every time the former can invest in pleasure, the latter has to console himself with reflection." This aptitude for reflection made the people a key tool in Chamfort's utopia, which entailed freeing mankind from everything degrading and establishing new ground rules. The fatalism of birth and the authority of fathers were to be replaced by fraternity, that horizontal genealogy. This was to be the basis of the new human contract, the formula that would free the species from the imperatives of society and allow it to blossom. Yet this concept also appears to be the political expression of friendship, that total sharing of consciousness he always longed for. The secret energy behind Chamfort's political commitment stems from his youthful Rousseau-like idealism as much as from his rancor.

Right from the start of the Revolution, however, his past came back to haunt him. Late in 1788, he was accused of being the author of *Mémoire des princes de sang* [Memorandum by princes of the blood]—written, in fact, at Condé's instigation—which waxed indignant about threats to "the inequality of fortunes." Along with Mme. Vigée-Lebrun, Chamfort's name appeared on a list of "horrid reptiles to be purged," which made the rounds of the Palais-Royal.[13] He didn't bother to respond, but signed, along with Mirabeau, a petition calling for the direct election of delegates to the States General.[14] The two friends were joined by numerous writers affiliated with the Ancien Régime. These writers were beginning to speak up, but they still saw the growing movement as a conclusion to the cultural revolution begun in 1750. The Third Estate nevertheless counted Chamfort among its candidates, he being presented as a poet who, "amidst the revels at the court of a prince, always concerned himself with politics and defended the people."[15] This is obviously exaggerated, but the strange itinerary of the prince de Condé's chief secretary (which Chamfort still was, in title) required an explanation. At age forty-nine, he began a political career totally devoid of ambition—fame remained inadmissible ever since the failure of *Mustapha*.

Deputy, or . . .

Along with Mirabeau and Talleyrand, Chamfort joined the Club of Thirty. Founded by Espréménil (a "left-wing" magistrate), Abbé Sieyès, financiers Panchaud and Clavière, and the writer-lawyer Hérault de Séchelles, this club prepared for the first four-round democratic election France had ever seen. And for which Chamfort officially declared his candidacy. Four-fifths of all adult males were to elect their representatives—"deputies"—to the States General, and Chamfort was charged by the Thirty to establish contacts between the provincial clubs and Paris, while Laclos, who had become an advisor to the duc d'Orléans, drafted a model of the *Cahier des doléances* [List of grievances] which was distributed throughout France.

Chamfort barely had to blow on the coals—fires broke out everywhere early in 1789. All of France voiced its complaints, and things came to blows in Brittany. Mirabeau triumphantly concluded his Marseille campaign just as Chamfort was launching his own in Paris. He worked up and down the Palais-Royal, listening "avidly" to the people and assessing their determination. At the Académie, he had a welcoming speech replaced by a dissertation on the Third Estate. "He could no longer sit still," said Ginguené, while Sélis wrote, "He henceforth had just one single idea, one single wish— the people's party, the triumph of the people's party." Up at dawn to meet with leaders, he already appeared to be one of the stalwarts of a revolution that still lacked a doctrine.

For in spite of what followed, the Thirty was no Central Committee. Unlike 1917, the Revolution of 1789 was improvised by *individuals,* even if that improvisation was orchestrated. Robespierre and Marat still claimed to be true-blue monarchists, and even radicals were merely calling for a Regency. Camille Desmoulins said that there weren't ten partisans of a republic in all of Paris. Chamfort was, therefore, clearly ahead of his times. Republican in his very soul, favorable to an economic *and* social revolution—like his "disciple," the comte d'Antraigues—his comments were appreciated by the Thirty. (The club changed the day its members dined together so that Chamfort could attend sessions at the Académie.) His republic, however, still resembled the ones he studied at Grassins. It was to history what neoclassicism was to literature—an idea he liked mainly for its sobriety (just as many liked the monarchy mainly for its pomp). It presupposed perfect conditions, a refined atmosphere, an open-minded populace. But facts were stubbornly otherwise. The population was 70 percent illiterate and unaware of the Enlightenment. It was minus 2°F in Paris, the wheat had been hit by frost, and famine threatened to turn the citizens into wild animals. Who wanted to hear about a Senate during one of the coldest winters France had ever seen?

On closer inspection, it turns out that Chamfort still distrusted Frenchmen; he considered them a cross between "dog" and "ape," with their contempt for law and their respect for force. He suspected that they had grown accustomed to their chains during thirteen centuries of monarchy—somewhat the way Edmund Burke argued that a revolution born of despotism would return to despotism. But Chamfort preferred to set aside his doubts and, for the first time, suppress his misanthropy, that usually chronic condition. "Proving that men are incorrigible is no way to correct them," he said, wagering on the slow education of the people. A colossal task for which he laid the groundwork by "democratizing" his epigrams (thus making his first sacifice to the Revolution). "The nobility, say nobles, serves as intermediary between king and people. True, just as the hound serves as intermediary between hunter and hares."[16] This quip became a "slogan" which made the rounds of Paris. Although the republic was not yet in sight, Chamfort could herald it by launching his digs.

Here again, however, he shunned the limelight. He stayed in the wings of the Revolution, letting others voice his words. The tactic worked, according to the comte de Lauraguais, that dilettante present at the "Talleyrand" dinners. Lauraguais reported a conversation the two had early in 1789.

> "I've a lot to tell you," began Chamfort.
> "Good, what has befallen you?"
> "Befallen, huh! . . . what can possibly fall to *us?*"
> "Well, then, what have you done?"
> "Ah, that's something else again, I've come to talk to you about that," replied Chamfort. "I've just finished a piece."
> "What, a book?"
> "No, not a book, I'm not so stupid. Rather, it's perhaps the best work that can be produced these days, because it sets everybody talking and leaves no time for meditation. . . . "
> "So what's the title of this work?"
> "As you'll see, the title is the work itself; for it sums up the content. Thus I've already made a present of it to my puritanical Sieyès. . . . Here it is: *What is the third estate? Everything. What does it have? Nothing.* Do you find any boring passages in that?"[17]

Chamfort had just come up with the title of the most famous and most widely sold pamphlet of the French revolution, which he saved from ministerial pulping by registering it for a prize at the Académie. This title became a conversational tic, with the Third Estate butting into every sentence. (Although Sieyès had watered it down by adding: "And what does it want? Something.") Thousands of "Gauls" discovered that they were a race apart from the Franks—

whom Sieyès proposed sending back to the Germanic forests—and read the words "national assembly" for the first time. Chamfort dropped some of his mistrust of the French as well as some of his misanthropy.

The Chamfort of early 1789 was a shadowy, influential, hard-to-grasp figure. He advised Mirabeau, yet was tactful toward the king, in view of elections. Since he lived in the Palais-Royal district, he was accused of being in the pay of the duc d'Orléans. But he also hobnobbed with the Protestant bankers backing Necker, in Artaud's gambling house. Some saw his hand behind the comte d'Antraigues' *Mémoire sur les Etats généraux* [*Memorandum on the Estates General*], the first pamphlet to directly attack the royal function, in which the hereditary nobility was presented as "the most horrible scourge that heaven, in its wrath, could inflict upon a free nation." Suspicions were further aroused by Chamfort's sudden disappearance from the election proceedings—no one realized that he had fallen sick again, exhausted by the infernal pace of the campaign. "Fever, insomnia, languors, skin rashes, baths, medicine, that's what occupies his miserable life, in the hope that spring will give him the strength necessary to digest the herbal juices prescribed for him," wrote the marquis de Cazeaux to Roederer. On this score, the Revolution still had not healed the "old man," who thereby failed to be elected deputy—just as earlier he failed to enter the diplomatic corps. In any event, Chamfort preferred to act indirectly, remaining in the shadows.

. . . Conspirator

Such mystery, in fact, was to his liking. It was part of his character, a fate he artfully adopted. The elections over, he even poured forth secrets—he had reportedly anticipated everything, including the fall of the monarchy, just as he had outlined the rest of his life at age twenty. "We have our secret doctrine and our public doctrine," Delisle de Sales reported him as saying.[18] And Marmontel painted Chamfort as a prophet in an account written eight years later.[19]

> "One day, we found ourselves alone at the Louvre after a session of the Académie. 'So,' he said to me, 'you're not a deputy?' [Marmontel had also been an unsuccessful candidate.]
> " 'No,' I replied, 'but I'm getting over it.'
> " 'Indeed,' he responded, 'you're excellent at edifying, but hopeless at destroying.' "

Marmontel assumed that Chamfort was aware of Orléanist intentions, since he was "friend and confidant to Mirabeau, one of the faction's leaders." He pressed Chamfort for an explanation. " 'You frighten me with talk of destruction,' " continued Marmontel in his Auvergne accent, " 'it seems that we're going farther than the nation intended. . . .' "

" 'Well!' retorted Chamfort, 'Does the nation know what it wants? It will be made to want and say what it has never conceived of. . . . The nation is a big flock seeking pasture, and shepherds with good dogs can lead it where they will . . . and, in tracing out a new path, we have every reason to want to make a clean sweep.'

" 'Clean sweep?' " stressed Marmontel, " 'of both throne and altar?'

" 'Both throne and altar will fall together; they are two flying buttresses holding one another up.'

" 'You're announcing an undertaking which would seem to present more obstacles than means to success.'

" 'Believe me, the obstacles have been anticipated, the means taken into account.' "

Chamfort's avowed "plot"—as reconstructed by Marmontel—supposedly relied on the weakness of the king and the strength of the Third Estate. Thanks to the Thirty, the provinces were to rise up on a signal given by the Dauphiné region.

"He acknowledged that a good many home-loving citizens in their houses, stores, offices, and workshops might find such plans too bold, disturbing their peace of mind. 'But if they disapprove, they will do so only timidly and quietly,' he said, 'whereas there is an entire class determined to impose itself, for it has nothing to lose from change. The most powerful motives for rioting now exist—scarcity, famine, money. . . . You've heard eloquent speakers from among the bourgeoisie, but you should realize that such orators at the tribune are nothing compared to all those Demosthenes who, for an ecu a head, proclaim havoc in public squares, in gardens, on docksides. . . . Now that's what I call eloquence. We've just tried a little experiment in the Faubourg St. Antoine, and you wouldn't believe how little it cost the duc d'Orléans to have honest Réveillon's factory sacked. . . .'[20]

"'So,' I said to him, 'your experiments are in fact crimes, and your militia are bandits.'

"'They have to be,' he continued, '. . . respectable people are weak, self-centered and timid; only scoundrels are determined. Having no morals is an advantage for the people during revolutions. . . . Mirabeau is right: Not a single one of our old virtues is of use to us—and the people don't need any, or else they need virtues of another caliber entirely. The main principle is that everything necessary to the revolution, everything useful to it, is just.'

"'That may be the principle followed by the duc d'Orléans,' I replied, 'and he's the only person I can see who can lead these people in revolt, yet I admit that I don't have a high opinion of his courage.'

"'You're right,' he said. 'Mirabeau, who knows him well, says that counting on the duke would be like building on mud. But he has shown himself to be popular, he has a commanding name, and millions to spread around. . . . And if he lacks courage, we'll provide it; for intrepid leaders will emerge from among the people themselves, especially as soon as they've rebelled and think themselves criminals. For there's no going back when retreat means the scaffold. . . . But,' he added, 'I see that my ambitions grieve you. . . . Do you really think that revolution is just a bowl of cherries?'"

How much truth is there in this account? A great deal, yet none at all. It reveals the violence of 1789, plus Chamfort's contradictions and his cynicism (not to mention that of Marmontel, who backed a well-fed France). The last traces of Chamfort's misanthropy can also be detected, expressed under the Ancien Régime as follows: "Men are governed by using the head. A kind heart is useless in a chess game." Also revealed is Chamfort's taste for catastrophe, volcanic eruptions, and floods. It is nevertheless hard to believe that he proclaimed such low methods so loudly (at a time when the ministry was being accused of having manipulated rioters in the Réveillon affair, a thesis Chamfort would defend in his *Tableaux de la Révolution* [Historical Pictures of the Revolution]), or that he considered sparking a famine which already existed. In playing the sorcerer's apprentice, Chamfort probably wanted to impress Marmontel, the Philosopher who had murdered *Mustapha* only to retire on his comfortable income, and who now believed the world was too old be made over.

By exaggerating deeds, 1789 also exaggerated egos, and Chamfort could claim certain rights over a movement he had predicted. The intense atmosphere of conspiracy obviously appealed to him— "Vigorous natures thrive on extremes," he said.

But had a "faultless system" really been drawn up? Chateaubriand asserted that the Revolution "hung on" a plan known only to "a few insiders. . . . I learned the secret from the very lips of the famous Chamfort, who let it slip one morning when I went to see him." The romantic writer explains that the insiders had perceived "with genius" that it was pointless to hope for democracy without a complete revolution "in morals."[21] Apparently Chateaubriand only half-believed such revelations. The only detail he offered on this system which supposedly influenced the Jacobins and their English counterparts was that it aspired to "an unheard-of purity of government and conduct." Chateaubriand would moreover wind up by retracting his statement in a later edition of *Essai sur les Révolutions:* "I gave these blackguards too much credit; they had no genius." Marmontel, however, really thought that 1789 could have been avoided if the ministry had believed him when he went to report Chamfort's comments. "There's no lack of dupes," Talleyrand would say, "only a lack of mountebanks."

Reactionaries at Versailles were just waiting for an excuse to demand that the States General be canceled, however, and such talk also disturbed the Thirty, who had become the Thirty-Six. Abbé Sieyès opened the Valois Club, showcase for a revolution which already needed cooling-off. Chamfort followed the entire enlightened community into the luxurious premises in the Palais-Royal to await the meeting. There were gaming tables and an office for the press (undergoing galloping expansion). Partisans of the three main factions—those of Calonne (including Vaudreuil himself), the *parlements,* and the Thirty-Six—debated together "like the English parliament." Leaving the eighteenth century to its "extravagance" of a revolution, Chamfort shut himself up for a week to write a poem dedicated to himself. The Revolution had not yet abolished contradiction, that privilege Chamfort indulged in so heartily.

The Jeu de Paume Oath

The respite didn't last long. In early May, Chamfort set up in a little house on rue Sainte-Elisabeth in Versailles, in order to follow the States General. The opening ceremony was marked by the humiliating dress the Third Estate was ordered to wear. Mirabeau, already the center of attention in the Salle des Menus-Plaisirs where the deputies met, hired Chamfort to be the anonymous author of the *Journal des Etats généraux* (Chamfort would in turn hire Ginguené, who "became haughty" according to Chateaubriand). Although Mirabeau and Chamfort both resolutely demanded that the three orders vote collectively (since voting by order would guarantee a majority to the nobles and clergy), the "flint" and the "musket" nevertheless had their divergences. Mirabeau, split between his penchant for rebellion and his respect for authority, favored a populist system headed by a strong king, replacing "monarchy as superstition by monarchy as religion"—in which Mirabeau hoped to become the *eminence grise*. Whereas Chamfort feared getting bogged down (as the Fronde had a century earlier, pushing the bourgeoisie into the arms of the monarchy). He wanted to act quickly, profiting from the agitation to make irreversible gains. Mirabeau had been unsettled on seeing the delirious mob kiss the wheels of his carriage in Marseille—but then, excess was the order of the day. "At the moment when God created the world," wrote Chamfort, "the movement of chaos must have made chaos appear more disordered than when it lay in undisturbed disorder. The same thing applies here, when the confusion of a society reorganizing itself gives the appearance of excessive disorder."[22] Reassured by what he knew of Louis XVI and his disintegrating court through Vaudreuil and the Polignacs, Chamfort began the month of May with amazing confidence and with his republican schemes still intact.

On June 16, Abbé Sieyès resolved the impasse by suggesting that the three orders meet together as a National Assembly, endowed with legislative powers. Mirabeau opposed this blow to the king, who was already weakened by the death of the Dauphin whom Chamfort had "baptized." "I know of nothing more terrible than the sovereign aristocracy of six hundred people," declared Mirabeau. But the duc d'Orléans backed Sieyès, followed by numerous clerics, and Mirabeau was obliged to go along. Those "assembled" were forced to occupy the *jeu de paume* (rackets court), and they solemnly swore to continue meeting until a constitution was drafted. Chamfort and Mirabeau were both present in this royal gymnasium where the Revolution pulled off its first show of strength. A majority of the clergy then voted to join the assembly. This was solemnly celebrated in a church in Versailles, where Chamfort wept along with ten thousand spectators—an "enchanting sight, new on earth," he said.[23] The king's attempt to intimidate the deputies led to Mirabeau's famous phrase (purportedly inspired by Chamfort): "We are here by the will of the people, and we will leave only at the force of bayonettes." This time, the plebeian count truly merited his nickname. Vaudreuil encouraged the queen to reply with firmness to this "sacrilege" against the sovereign. Two years after their separation, Chamfort and his former patron squared off via intermediaries.

Louis finally legalized the National Assembly, but at the same time called up his most loyal troops (on pressure from Breteuil and Condé). Thirty-five thousand men formed a hermetic barrier between Paris and Versailles. Two companies of French guards immediately mutinied, rejoining the Palais-Royal to applause. Chamfort returned to Paris to follow the revolution he would chronicle in *Les tableaux de la Révolution française* [*Historical Pictures, Representing the Most Remarkable Events Which Occurred during the Early Period of the French Revolution* . . .], published in 1791 with Prieur's famous engravings. Mirabeau, back in Versailles, was already trying to approach the king through his new friend, the comte de La Marck, whom he asked to "[l]et it be known at the chateau that I am more disposed toward them than against them." One hundred thousand people then gathered under Chamfort's window before breaking into the prison at the St-Germain-des-Près Abbey, where eleven mutineers had been taken. The doors were broken down by blows from "axes, picks, and hammers." The prisoners were led triumphantly to the Palais-Royal, where they were fed and housed in the Théâtre des Variètès Amusantes [Music Hall]. The incident, noted Chamfort, gave the people a sense of power and enabled Paris to seize the initiative once again.

France was henceforth split into two camps, farther apart than two foreign countries, according to Chamfort. The first was drawing up a list of enemies—with Breteuil, Artois, Condé, the Polignacs, and Vaudreuil at the top of the list. The second was mobilizing its army, which sparked wild rumors (the Assembly would be mined, Montmartre packed with cannons). Louis XVI then abruptly dismissed Necker (who would be punched by the prince d'Hénin), and named Breteuil at the head of a reactionary government. Reduced to gritty, bitter bread, the people took alarm at the announcement of an encampment of ten thousand men. Chamfort wrote to the maréchal de Broglie, provocatively offering to write a derisory chronicle of his "glorious campaign." Chamfort was hardly impressed by Broglie's

intimidating maneuvers, having met Besenval, the colonel charged
with containing Paris, at Julie Careau's place. "A weak and corrupted courtier," acknowledged Chamfort, but "neither cruel nor
barbarous." The Palais-Royal neighborhood confirmed such optimism by responding to the call to arms made by Desmoulins from a
table at the Café de Foy. The date was July 12, and Chamfort jovially
commented, "Things are going well, and I think that we'll pull off
some heady act."[24]

Insurrection

Insurrection began several hours later with the demand for the rein-
statement of Necker (whom Chamfort had never liked). Accosted by
the Palais-Royal crowd, Chamfort went to close the theaters as a sign
of mourning, forcing "dukes, marquesses and counts" to file out between two rows of "undistinguished, indeed unknown" citizens, in
a highly charged atmosphere. Strangers stopped to talk to one another, while others went to Curtius's wax museum to "deliver" the
colored bust of Necker, which was covered with a black veil and carried in a reliquary to cries of "Hats off!" The procession moved down
the boulevard du Temple, strolled along rue Saint-Honoré, and
found itself at the place Vendôme confronted by the Royal-
Allemand regiment. Parisians, who had bolted during the Fronde
uprising, now advanced in closed ranks. A doctor brought down a
cavalryman as the demonstrators passed by in icy silence. But at the
Tuileries, a detachment of dragoons killed the man carrying the bust
of Necker. "More stunned than frightened," the crowd took refuge
in the gardens, pursued by the prince de Lambesc, who struck
down an old man with his sword. It was a Sunday, and strollers
hurled chairs at the soldiers. Chamfort admitted that this "atrocity"
by royal troops "powerfully served our cause." Composed up till
then mainly of idealists, agitators, and the starving—and based on
arguments advanced by the liberal, upper aristocracy—the Revolution now broadened. "A middle-class Parisian who, the day before,
would have shuddered at the very idea . . . became a mortal enemy
of the ministers and the court."[25] The "ogre" Lambesc succeeding in
creating a holy alliance between the poorest, the richest, and a middle class which up to that point had made itself small.

The night which followed was the hottest that Chamfort had ex-
perienced ever since the "blessed" days of Louis XV and Mme. de
Pompadour. Foreign regiments occupied the Champs-Elysées, and
Paris rose up against Breteuil, who reportedly threatened to burn

everything down. Hussars were lynched and brought piecemeal to the Palais-Royal, which had become a warehouse for "crime and its punishment." More French guards went over to the people, followed by children lighting their way "with zeal and with joy." Church bells sounded the alarm, "bandits" and the unemployed entered the fray. Houses were on fire, a city tollhouse by the architect Claude Nicolas Ledoux was burned to the ground, the Saint-Lazare monastery was sacked. Firemen intervened as groups armed to the teeth patrolled without orders. Paris went to sleep "without king, without government, without police." These events, though "scarcely recounted the next day," according to Chamfort, provided an "inexhaustible subject of conversation" once calm was restored.

But the capital awakened with the determination to organize itself, even though certain moderates, like Abbé Morellet, were already disavowing the movement. A militia of forty-eight thousand men was formed—the National Guard, which La Fayette would command—to defend liberty and property. The royal repository was sacked and weapons seized ("from the poison arrows of Savages" to Du Guesclin's [fourteenth-century] sword, presaging the "triumph of humanity over chivalry," claimed Chamfort).[26] Barricades went up all over town, groups milled around the Palais-Bourbon where Chamfort once resided. By that evening Paris had its own emblem—the red and blue rosette—its own army and its own government (the electors designated for the States General). The Third Estate no longer depended entirely on its deputies—that was the astounding discovery of that July 13. Citizens declared themselves independent, just as Chamfort had done earlier. From that day onward, the detested "public" became the redeeming "people."

For Parisians had exceeded Chamfort's wildest hopes. He heard them shout "No more money" to the burgher who wanted to pay the "citizen" who had saved his life. He heard spontaneous orators deliver "shafts of classic eloquence." Pillagers even spared the Crown jewels, considering them to be the property of the Nation. Prévot (i.e., mayor) Flesselles, who annoyed Chamfort with his temporizing ("My children, I am your father, and you will be happy . . . "), finally fell out of favor. Only the king remained popular, for he was said to be misled by his entourage—an attitude "maintained throughout the revolution," acknowledged Chamfort.[27] On the morning of July 14th, the committee of electors sent a delegation to the Bastille, which governor De Launay received at breakfast. The most famous day in history was about to unfold.

16. THE BASTILLE

Moments of crisis produce a redoubling of life in men. In a society which is dissolving and recomposing, the struggle between two spirits, the collision of past and future, the mixture of morals old and new, form a transient arrangement which leaves not a moment of boredom. . . . Mankind, on vacation, takes to the street.

Chateaubriand

H elvétius's house in Auteuil served as an appointed stopping place for Chamfort during his comings and goings between Paris and Versailles. There he would inevitably encounter Cabanis (the widow's adopted son, a doctor from Brive who was treating Mirabeau), often find Abbé Morellet (who already disliked the Revolution), occasionally meet Abbé Delaroche (who wrote the preface to Helvétius's *Oeuvres* and whom Chamfort had met twenty-five years earlier at Mme. Saurin's salon), and from time to time see Abbé Sieyès. But the most eagerly awaited visitor was Mirabeau, who dropped by after Assembly debates to compare notes with Chamfort. They engaged "in a tiresome intercourse of compliments" according to Dumont, one of the members of the Geneva committee which worked day and night for the plebeian count. "We noticed that he was always more extreme after having seen Chamfort,"[1] continued this "Mirabelle"[2] who resented the "musket's" ability to destroy their moderating influence on the "flint" in a matter of hours, even though Chamfort never managed to weaken Mirabeau's monarchist leanings. The two friends henceforth scheduled regular meetings—at Mirabeau's place in the morning, at the Assembly during the day, and at Auteuil in the evening. It was at Auteuil that Chamfort first heard the news. In the presence of Count de Volney (author of *Les Ruines*) and Abbé Delaroche, he listened to the account given by Cabanis, who by chance had been at the Bastille. "Volney exulted, Chamfort shouted, and Abbé Delaroche wept with emotion," wrote Jules Bertaut.[3] They did not yet know that the attackers suffered ninety-eight dead and that De Launay, Flesselles, and numerous defenders were massacred. In the enthusiasm, Abbé

Delaroche left to rejoin the victors, who danced at the Palais-Royal that evening around heads and hearts impaled on pikes, singing:

Ah! il n'y a pas de fête
Quand le coeur n'y est pas.

Oh! You can't truly celebrate
if the heart isn't in it.

At which point the oldest and most powerful monarchy in Europe capitulated. The next day the king (who had entered "Nothing" in his diary for July 14) went to the assembly along with his brothers Provence and Artois to announce the withdrawal of the troops. Chamfort returned to Paris with the deputies, come to congratulate the capital for having saved them from probable dissolution. "Egotism seemed annihilated," he said, on seeing the contributions pile up on the electors' desks throughout the night, while pikes were being manufactured even in the churches.[4] Eighty thousand armed Parisians threw flowers before Talleyrand, Sieyès, and the others accompanying them to City Hall where Bailly, the discoverer of "hyperboreal" people and Chamfort's unsuccessful rival for a seat at the Académie, was named mayor of Paris. The archibishop suggested a Te Deum to the crowd, which insisted that he don a civic wreath. The prelate, on the arm of a gunpowder distributor, then led the procession to Notre-Dame, where Chamfort prayed as a good citizen. Talleyrand, named Bishop of Autun a year earlier, hammered his clubfoot along the streets leading to the Bastille. Mirabeau and Beaumarchais each gave a swing of the pickaxe into the fortress, while Chamfort lingered with the demolition crew headed by Palloy (who would sell off *his* stones from the Bastille right up until the Consulate period). With nightfall, however, the crowd became aggressive again. When someone noticed Chamfort's "dressy" clothing (the silk stockings, sword, and buckle normally worn by writers), he was pulled aside and threatened with hanging. He ran, arriving late for his dinner engagement—yet smiling. "They took me for an aristocrat," he said to Barras, a young gentleman from Provence who had been frequenting Chamfort in recent months. "Oh! How well things are going!" He was so happy that he would inform any remaining supporters of the Bastille: "It is getting smaller and more beautiful all the time."[5]

The fortress, of course, held only seven prisoners (including one madman and four counterfeiters). But its fall resounded throughout Europe and beyond. England applauded the leap taken by a France considered backward on the political and agricultural level, and which it hoped would adopt its own liberal system. America backed the rebellion of a country that had supported its own Revolution. Kant, in Königsberg, changed the course of his daily walk for the first time. Congratulatory embraces were exchanged as far away as St. Petersburg, where another revolution would start one day. The king then recalled Necker and advised the comte d'Artois and the Polignacs to vanish abroad. Duchesse Jules left with her husband and son for Basel. The baron de Breteuil left France for Solothurn, his government having lasted for one hundred hours. Vaudreuil, one knee to the ground, bade farewell to the queen, who wept; escorted by a regiment, the "most chivalrous" man in Versailles left for a second exile, this one to last twenty-five years. He and Artois hastily passed through Chantilly to drag the prince de Condé along in their flight (under the jeering gaze of Grouville, Chamfort's replacement as secretary). Everything having been decided at the last minute, Condé was nearly thrown in the Oise River by peasants and Artois had to disguise himself as a postillion to complete the trip. His patrons gone, Chamfort remained among a "people of brothers" which received the king at the Chaillot gate on July 17.

The reception, initially aloof, warmed up at City Hall. The heroes of the Bastille, enjoying a total victory and basking in a military glory previously reserved for the aristocracy, celebrated the arrival of Louis XVI in the company of a million Parisians. The king wore the red and blue rosette, to which was added the white symbolizing the kings of France. "Then those swords and lances which, two hours earlier . . . had formed a vault of steel over the head of the monarch . . . were respectfully lowered before him," commented Chamfort.[6] This was the second investiture of a king crowned too young—yet too old to have benefited from a regent, as had Louis XIV and Louis XV. After a nine-hour march, he fully realized the extent of his popularity and his solitude.

The Prophet Was Right . . .

The eighteenth of July marked a pause. Chamfort reflected on those dazzling events, on the new order knocking at the door. Whereas Vaudouleurs had seemed a mere "instant" to him, "thirty years" seemed to elapse in the preceding twenty days. "It is with much pleasure that I receive my diploma as prophet from your hands," he confided to Mme. Panckoucke. "It is worth more than that of sorcerer, which was awarded to me by several of my friends. But women are always kinder and more polite than men. Moreover, since prophets are no longer cut down and witches no longer burned, I can enjoy the honors of my farsightedness in full safety. But, in truth, you only had to get close to the colossus to perceive that it was hollow and rotten, shiny on the outside but worm-eaten on the inside. Its fall was so sudden that confusion will reign for some time yet; but we'll make out."[7]

Everything happened so fast that everyone continued to act as though nothing had changed, thus warding off fear. At the Académie, Chamfort presented a charity case to Marmontel, in almost comic counterpoint to his dire prophecies. Hundreds of aristocrats left, to the delight of Parisians who nevertheless worried at seeing these sources of income dry up. Chamfort responded with an anonymous gift of a thousand ecus to the Revolution, "his hard-won savings from twenty years of privation and work," pointed out Abbé Morellet.[8] This symbolic transfer marked Chamfort's determination to commit himself completely. But unlike Chamfort, who asked Panckoucke to make the *Mercure de France* "a little more republican" (". . . that's the only thing that works now," he added, to convince the savvy publisher), many thought the Revolution was already over. The smothering heat, which slowed everything, seemed to confirm this opinion.

The Palais-Royal returned to its usual ways—soldiers drank to victory, the latest shows were discussed. "Here the tale of a murder, there a vaudeville song; propositions for debauchery next to a stand proposing political action."[9] Yet there were also "shabbily dressed" citizens already tapping on the panes of the Artaud Club, saying, "The Nation wants to know what's happening." On the evening of the twenty-second, the bloody head of Foulon appeared in the glow of the garden's lanterns, to the sound of drums. "Make way for the people's justice!" shouted the crowd before the remains of this attorney general, who supposedly advised the starving people to graze on grass. Foulon was indeed a reactionary, but Chamfort thought such a comment "unlikely." He was horrified by the scalp stuffed with straw, by the icy silence of the crowd, by the brandishing of Bertier's heart. The blood of Bertier—Foulon's son-in-law, an intendant in charge of supplies—was drunk to the health of the Nation. The killers' impunity provided Chamfort with a glimpse of the "overthrow of all social order"—a sight he would never forget.

Calm, when it returned, remained uneasy, for such crimes had made liberty suspect, order desirable. The Assembly was envisaging repressive laws. This threat alone sufficed to bring Chamfort around. He pointed to the crimes committed by the monarchy for centuries and offered this laconic statement: "Reduce the people's suffering, and you'll reduce its ferociousness." The Assembly itself recanted when Mirabeau referred to the "abominable end" of the attackers killed at the Bastille. According to Chamfort, this comment was one of the greatest services Mirabeau rendered to the Revolution. But the specter of anarchy loomed again in the provinces during the days known as "The Great Fear," when men sacked everything and women hid in the woods in fear of invading brigands or returning emigrés. In fact, the emigrés were convinced that their return was just a matter of days. Chamfort's former patrons already dreamed of revenge, and Breteuil was awaiting the signal—which would never come—to seek foreign help. Chamfort responded, however, with his forced optimism. "The revolution will make its way around the world."

"Yes," came the ironic reply, "head by head."[10]

Feudal Hara-Kiri

In order to appease peasant wrath, the deputies (mainly those from the nobility) met during the night of August 4. This unique event saw an elite group of men outdo one another to scuttle their own privileges, just as earlier they had scrambled to obtain them. Dukes raised their voices over those of marquesses to propose still more sacrifices, more restrictions on their ancestral rights, further abdication of dovecotes, woods, feudal jurisdictions. It was the most stunning—and final—testimony to that prodigal sense of potlatch proper to Vaudreuil's class, even if one has to be very rich (or, on another level, very poor) to be so generous. It was the product of twenty years of ambivalence, during which the aristocracy hesitated between suicide and reconquest. Which is why Chamfort remained wary. The nobility's prestige, enhanced by such sacrifice, might enable it to seize the initiative once again. Admitting the fine gesture, he nevertheless put the following words in the people's mouth: "I must be wary of [my representatives], because I was forced to choose them from among the classes interested in deceiving me. I

will monitor everything, and will rely only on myself."[11] Nothing
was to halt the rise of the "new" nobility prophesied by Chamfort in
his *Considérations* and baptized at the Bastille.

Events would reassure him. Despite the nobles' hara-kiri, the
seizure of weapons continued. The cannon from Chantilly chateau
were brought to Paris—"a good haul," said Chamfort—and a million peasants, rifles in hand, took advantage of liberalized hunting
rights. The people were aware that the "feudal colossus" had merely
staggered, observed Chamfort (noting once again the accuracy of his
own instincts). The Assembly regained the initiative by passing the
Declaration of Human Rights, drawn up under Sieyès. On September 5, the Palais-Royal was cleaned out, and the agitator Sainte-
Huruge arrested. Chamfort withdrew to Auteuil, where Abbé
Morellet was once more subjected to his "skillful intellect." Mme.
Helvétius kept silent in order to avoid siding with one or the other of
her friends. Mirabeau joined Chamfort there, still hoping to dominate a weak king in order to strengthen him—just as Richelieu had
done—but becoming increasingly snared in the web of his own
schemes.

For the "People's Tribune" had just performed a volte-face. He
was angry with Necker for descrediting him in the eyes of Louis
XVI, had been accused in the Assembly of being lukewarm toward
the events of August 4, and was aggravated by the queen's contempt for him. Marie-Antoinette had claimed, "We will never be so
unfortunate, I believe, to be reduced to the painful extremity of
resorting to Mirabeau." Somewhat like Vaudreuil before him,
Mirabeau took revenge by widening the gap he was constantly offering to bridge. He invited Chamfort to join the *Courrier de Provence,*
where Chamfort's impatience with Necker and the Assembly clearly
emerged, muted by the respect due the king. Forgetting their respective positions—monarchist and republican—"the lion and the
cat" (as Rivarol described them) were once again on the same wavelength. In their wake appeared Camille Desmoulins, Robespierre's
former fellow student at the Louis-le-Grand school, and a partisan
of radicalization. Chamfort praised the precociousness and "burlesque extravagance" of Desmoulins, who loved Mirabeau "like a
mistress." The would-be Richelieu was now wagering, perhaps, on
a Regency. And Chamfort, perhaps, was pressing the duc d'Orléans'
entourage to undertake a show of strength. This "conspiracy," in
which our partisan of open government was reportedly implicated,
merits a closer look.

Baker, Baker's Wife, and Baker's Boy

The events are well known. On October 1, at a regimental banquet in Versailles, tipsy guards trampled the blue-white-and-red rosette underfoot, in front of the royal family. This raised the specter of a "Saint-Bartholomew's massacre" against patriots. Which led to calls for another round of revolutionary measures (responsibility for which the *Courrier de Provence* placed squarely—and in advance— on "a ribbon of a certain color"—the queen's). The timing was right; ruined by the emigration of their customers, butchers, wigmakers, and woodworkers were wandering around, unemployed. It was the women, however, who gathered on October 5 to demand bread, and to undertake an armed march on Versailles. A delegation was received by the king, who promised to sign the Declaration of Human Rights and to send provisions to Paris. But thousands of demonstrators remained in front of the chateau, and at dawn charged up the marble staircase and into the chateau. Six guards were killed. The queen, surprised in her sleep, barely escaped the pikes. Several hours later the royal family—"baker, baker's wife, and baker's boy"—left the inviolable temple of the monarchy and headed, discountenanced, for the Tuileries palace in Paris.

The attack went off so easily that questions were raised. Mirabeau was reportedly seen on the afternoon of the fifth, sword in hand, haranguing men disguised as women. The duc d'Orléans, also in drag, purportedly pointed out the queen's bedroom to the attackers. Theories of an Orléanist plot made the rounds, in imitation of dynastic conflicts during the Fronde. "The suspicion aroused by the conduct of M. le duc d'Orléans acquires a new degree of certainty with each passing day," wrote the bailli de Virieu, minister of Parma in Paris. "A great many of the most zealous courtiers are convinced that the duke listened to the advice of ambitious people like Lauzun, Mirabeau and Chamfort, sparking his desire to assume the regency."[12] Versailles now had an explanation for the fall of the "worm-eaten colossus"—a prince had been manipulated by several turncoats from the Ancien Régime who cynically placed themselves at the service of the people.

But the evidence is slim. The investigatory proceedings conducted by the public prosecutor painted a picture of two confused days. Testimony was contradictory, pirandello-like. Another Virieu—this one a deputy—supposedly overheard Mirabeau speaking of a vacant throne. The women, invading the Assembly, asked for "old lady Mirabeau." Sieyès, often accused of being in the Orléans camp, reportedly said on learning that Versailles had been sacked: "I know, but I don't understand at all—that's moving in the wrong direction." A century later, Taine would accuse Chamfort of having contributed both his savings and his mistresses to the riot.[13] Yet Chamfort had already pointed out, "The revolution is the result . . . of causes going back centuries." He cited the most recent causes, such as the pressure of public opinion during the previous two reigns and France's backing of America, which led the royal presses to print out most of the Declaration of Human Rights well before it was promulgated by the Assembly. "The Revolution is the work of no one man," he continued, "it is the work of the entire nation."[14] Chamfort would defend this idea tirelessly, yet he continued as advisor to the most influential men of the Revolution. He was split between his historical "determinism" and his penchant for exceptional individuals—for "geniuses."

Mirabeau's attitude during those critical days remains unclear, however. After having denounced a conspiracy himself—the thief who cries theft—he said of the duc d'Orléans, "He wants to, but can't. That eunuch could never carry out the crime. We needed a dummy, and that c—— would have done as well as any other."[15] Were the lion and the cat thinking of a malleable regent? Did Laclos—another major suspect, and the duke's dinner companion—want to apply the lessons of *Les liaisons dangereuses* to politics? If so, these "market-place Machiavellis," as Taine called them, mistook their hopes for reality.

For the events of October 6 backfired. The king emerged ever-popular, and the Constituent Assembly got cold feet after having let Mirabeau convince it to meet in Paris. Six hundred out of thirteen hundred deputies asked for a passport, and one hundred and twenty resigned. Mounier, who had been behind the *Jeu de Paume* oath, left; moderates would date the Terror from that day. The comte d'Antraigues, Chamfort's former "disciple," also departed, unable to watch his violent republicanism being put into effect. Mirabeau then realized that nothing could happen without Louis XVI, to whom he forwarded a plan. "He wanted him to leave Paris," Chamfort told Helena-Maria Williams, "going first to Rouen and then to Le Havre. . . . The king would have called upon the entire National Assembly and all Frenchmen . . . to join him there to promulgate the Constitution."[16] This revolutionary plan strangely resembles those of the court. Chamfort, however, remained firm, claiming that October 6 had achieved its goal—Paris henceforth controlled the king. There would be no more courtly conspiracies, and perhaps there might even be flour. Instead of enforcing order, the Assembly would pass laws. All of that, he felt, was worth a few excesses. "Courtiers and those who lived off of the horrible abuses crushing France repeatedly say that the abuses could have been eliminated without destroying what was destroyed. They'd also like to see the Augean stables cleaned out with a feather duster."[17] Chamfort, admittedly, was not one of those "compassionate" people saddened by beheadings yet unmoved by empty bellies. As he had pointed out several years earlier, soil is never more fertile than after an eruption.

17. NORMALCY

Theologians, ever faithful to their goal of duping mankind, and
government henchmen, ever faithful to their goal of oppressing it,
gratuitously suppose that the great majority of men are condemned to the
stupidity brought on by purely mechanical and manual labor. . . . But
suppose that just one quarter of the time and effort taken to dull these lower
classes were used to enlighten them; suppose that instead of putting a
catechism of absurd and unintelligible metaphysics into their hands, they
were given one which contained the basic principles of human rights and
responsibilities . . . One would see that nature not only created men to
live in society but has also given them all the good sense necessary to create
a reasonable society.

   Chamfort, 1790

Paris finally got to meet its deputies (those who left having been replaced). There were no longer two revolutions—one at Versailles, the other at the Palais-Royal—but a single show which drew every gaze. This took place in the "Salle du Manège" adjoining the Tuileries palace, where the Assembly now met. Chamfort was reassured by this marriage of "Forum" and "Senate"—the first step toward open government. He would encounter two of Mirabeau's collaborators, Maret and Méjan, in the public galleries (where daughters of ministers and aristocratic heiresses rubbed shoulders with lower-class women who passed the time during arid discussions by knitting). Chamfort attended these unique performances, for which lines formed as early as eight in the morning. Seats were not numbered, and so people even camped all night in front of the Manège prior to major debates. Deputies occupied the long and narrow hall (with its appalling acoustics) while "eating, gesticulating, chatting," according to Chateaubriand. The ultrareactionary members of the clergy and nobility sat apart, sniggering over an institution they contested.

   Yet most of the deputies in the Constituent Assembly were competent, hardworking, and sincerely dedicated to the reconstruction of the nation, thus overcoming Chamfort's Rousseau-inspired skepticism. The somewhat abstract republic he advocated—even in its violence—gave way to support for these "sages" who spent two years reviewing all the laws governing France.

During this time, they also invented the notions of "left-wing" and "right-wing." Opponents of the August 4 abolition of feudalism were seated on the right. They were called "aristocrats," but not all of them were nobles. Among the staunchest was Abbé Maury, a priest known for his vulgar speech and "lower-class" bearing. Near him sat Mirabeau's brother, nicknamed "Tonneau" ["Tubby"], a booming speaker and heavy drinker who was less convincing in his praise for the values on which France was built. The plebeian count himself commented, "In any other family, my brother the viscount would be considered a bright but bad boy; in my family, he seems a fool, yet well-behaved."

The right also included "Monarchists," moderates who favored an English-style revolution, with two strong houses balanced by the king's right of absolute veto. Malouet became their spokesman following the departure of Mounier (who was already attempting to stir revolt in the Dauphiné region). Some of the greatest aristocrats nevertheless sat on the left with bourgeois deputies comprising the "Patriot Party," which had its own hero (La Fayette), tribune (Mirabeau), intellectual (the young lawyer Barnave), and club (the Jacobins, almost exclusively composed of deputies, founded by some of the original members of the committee of the Thirty-Six). Another surprise was that the "patriots" adopted a tone more hidebound than that of their adversaries. Some of them took up the uneasy poses of neoclassic tragedians mimicking the Roman republic, and many still used the bombastic language of *Mustapha et Zéangir* (which had premiered in a nearby hall twelve years earlier). The galleries protested—"The Declaration of Human Rights won't feed us," claimed the women involved in the October events. But the Assembly preferred to provide them with symbolic satisfaction, decreeing that Louis XVI was no longer King of France, but rather King of the French (to which the king acquiesced, in an antiroyalist gesture worthy of Chamfort). Chamfort would meet up with Maret and Méjan most evenings at the Hotel de l'Union on rue Saint-Thomas-du-Louvre, where they had set up the office of the *Bulletin de l'Assemblée Nationale* and where the young lieutenant Bonaparte would later stay.[1] They dined swiftly, the night being devoted to transcribing debates, for which Maret invented a method of abbreviation. Chamfort left the journalists to their documents and ended the day in the company of the poet Ponce Denis Echouchard Lebrun-

Pindare. These two former protégés of Vaudreuil would poke fun at the deputies the way they used to poke fun at the Polignacs. And now hundreds of citizens could do likewise, to Chamfort's grand satisfaction, for the king in the Tuileries palace and the Constituent Assembly in the Salle du Manège were henceforth subject to the people's "scrutiny."

Another test of strength occurred following the October 31 mob massacre of the baker François, who had refused to surrender his last loaves to the crowd. At Mirabeau's suggestion, the Assembly adopted martial law, followed by a three-tier election system based on wealth (Rousseau would not have been entitled to vote). The left congratulated itself, however, on having disenfranchized a million peasants and valets too easily influenced by their masters. Mirabeau, Talleyrand, and Chamfort then united to attack France's largest fortune—that of the clergy. Chamfort wrote that the churches "seized the land while promising the skies."[2] The three friends worked in relay, with Talleyrand, well-placed as a bishop, providing figures for the transaction which was to save France from bankruptcy and the Revolution from irrelevance. Backed by Mirabeau, the lame devil moved on October 10 that all church property be transferred to the nation.

Pressured by the jobless, the Assembly worked out a compromise. Church land worth three billion livres virtually fell into the state coffers, to be used as guarantee against state-issued scrip. "Self-interest itself recommends becoming a citizen,"[3] declared Chamfort, more pragmatic than he was six months earlier, when such egotism seemed "annihilated." He now played the parliamentary card via Mirabeau and Talleyrand, in order to legalize July's accomplishments and thereby replace an organic society with a world conforming to a text—the Constitution. Henceforth, Reason would govern History just as neoclassic rules were to govern literature. Reasoned acceptance of the new order would replace submission to the old, thanks to an education Chamfort envisaged as being both moral (to avoid producing egotists) and prudent (to avoid producing martyrs). Chamfort's conversion to legalism, however, placed him in a paradoxical position. Although he was wary of the deputies' mounting power, he played the role of prompter to the least honest among them (Mirabeau and Talleyrand) for over a year. Alongside the monarcho-populism of the former and the radical Anglophilia of the latter, Chamfort would do battle against clerical obscurantism, judicial archaism, and ministerial despotism, in order to extend the Enlightenment to all. The day of the beheaders was over, that of parliamentary intrigue was dawning. Yet the rallying cry was the same: reduce the people's suffering in order to reduce their ferociousness. Chamfort entered another "dormant" period as the flood temporarily subsided.

The Prompter

The Constituent Assembly would work fast. The ancient *parlements* were recessed, and the king's authority was disputed in matters of justice, the military, and administration. The king began to resemble a paper tiger, and the monarchy's trappings fell away, just as Chamfort had predicted. The new regime was about to issue its own money in the form of scrip (another of Mirabeau's significant contributions, noted Chamfort), and France was to be divided into eighty-three administrative *départements* at Sieyès' suggestion. The only black mark was that the Assembly awarded compensation to the clergy. Chamfort retorted in *Le Moniteur Universal*:

> Courage, allons mes chers Français,
> Economisons sur les frais
> De la seconde maladie
> Dont nous ne guérirons jamais.[4]

> Be brave, oh ye French
> Let's save on the expense
> Of a second illness
> From which there's no deliverance.

Chamfort would reprint these verses in the *Almanach des muses* of 1790 (in which Chateaubriand published his first poem),[5] not out of spite but because he considered the Constituent Assembly's measures to be legitimate retribution for abuses committed under the Ancien Régime.

Chamfort may have been satisfied, but the lion fulminated. Mirabeau was first rebuffed by La Fayette (to whom he proposed forming a strong-armed government), and was subsequently unable to prevent the Constituent Assembly from declaring deputies ineligible to become ministers. Motivated by jealousy, the measure effectively put an abrupt end to Mirabeau's march to power (he who had announced, on leaving the Vincennes prison, that he would be minister once he was no longer fit to make love). Mirabeau returned to the charge on the issue of the eligibility of deputies to accept salaried positions in the government. Chamfort helped him in this battle, which opposed Mirabeau to Barnave for the first time. Barnave, the left's rising star, and the handsomest man in the Salle du Manège, intervened so rapidly and violently that the lion remained speechless. Despite the myth, Mirabeau was a thoughtful speaker who detested French bombast and "operatic outbursts." He gave his brother the floor (who criticized the count out of personal jealousy) and went to meet Chamfort on the steps of the gallery. "Articulateness is a fine talent on condition that it never be exploited," prompted Chamfort, pointing to Barnave. Mirabeau picked up the phrase, and returned to the podium to begin his reply. "I've long said that articulateness was one of nature's finest gifts, on condition that it never be exploited; and what I have just heard scarcely makes me change my mind."[6] Despite this verbal rescue, Mirabeau suffered another setback. Yet Chamfort once again served as "flint" against the left, just as Hercules was the "musket" against the right—the Revolution having reversed their roles. Desmoulins pointed out that in ancient drama one actor recited the text while another performed the action. This provided a perfect "job" for Chamfort, who dreaded the limelight but loved being influential from the wings.

Another leading figure provided Chamfort with a frame of reference. This was the "puritanical" Sieyès. He was born in Fréjus, was one of Talleyrand's follow students at the Saint-Sulpice Seminary, and was as virginal in love and rambling in speech as of the virtuous Thomas. A proud and often ill man (his semibald head was covered with flaky scales), touchy but principled, Abbé Sieyès was the most important theorist of this first Assembly. Chamfort held him in great esteem—which was reciprocated, according to the royalist press (the only source of personal "gossip" about the patriot camp)—due to their shared desire to see the aristocracy vanish forever, and their shared conviction that the Revolution should adopt a radical, moral stance. Chamfort, as pointed out above, hoped that a new species of "free man" would emerge. Sieyès, on the other hand, elaborated the theorem that "purported historical truths" (meaning the ineluctuable nature of arbitrary power and obscurantism) "are no more real than purported religious truths." Both men wanted to replace Catholicism with a social religion under the authority of a secularized Christ. Sieyès and Chamfort represent an aspect of the year 1790 overshadowed by the scheming of Mirabeau and Talleyrand.

"Sound politics is not the science of what is, but of what should be. Perhaps one day these two will converge," suggested the twenty-seven year-old Sieyès (whom Mirabeau called Mahomet). Chamfort experienced his habitual split, now caught between cynicism and idealism, between parliamentary action and ideological abstraction, between skinny Sieyès and fleshy Mirabeau. The details of his relationship with Sieyès remain cloudy, however, for most of the letters Sieyès wrote during the Revolution have disappeared. This gap in the archives is all the more unfortunate since this taciturn abbé—who also liked to act behind the scenes and who hastened the Revolution thanks to the pamphlet for which Chamfort provided the title—played a decisive role in the drafting of the constitution early in 1790.

The prompter then hit full stride. Assisted by Sieyès, Chamfort drafted an assessment of the first months of the legislature, which was read by Talleyrand in a speech to the Assembly on February 11, 1790. His goal was to demonstrate to conservatives that the series of laws passed since October 6 represented solid accomplishments which were already part of history, and to encourage them to continue reorganizing France by creating a civil clergy and a free legal system based on a jury of peers.

"The National Assembly had the courage, or rather the good sense, to think that useful ideas were not exclusively destined to decorate the pages of a book," Chamfort had the bishop say[7] (the latter hid his pectoral cross a little more each day). Never had he so well handled the chamber where Louis XVI had just come to take oath, and which henceforth held most of the power. "What do you have to fear?" Talleyrand asked the deputies. He was normally as tepid in public as he was sparkling in private. "Nothing, nothing but a fatal impatience—continue a few moments longer, on behalf of liberty! You have alotted so many centuries to despotism!" Initially a republican, Chamfort pursued the Revolution as a moderate parliamentarian behind Talleyrand (who had learned the duc de Choiseul's secret of success—put others to work).

The Constituent Assembly was nearly unanimous in its decree that his "Address to Frenchmen" be read in all the churches in France. The reconciliation between the Christians of the Ancien Régime and the Romans of the new era thus began. There was to be a return to normalcy. Chamfort brushed aside William Pitt's warning that the French were merely passing through a period of liberty. "The revolution has been nearly consummated," asserted Chamfort.[8]

The Volcano Falls Dormant

Chamfort could thus be objectively aligned with La Fayette, the moderate leader of the patriot party, hero of the American war, and commander of the national guard created in July 1789 to restore order and to protect Paris from court machinations. Goals still differed, of course, since La Fayette sought an "American-style" unanimity which would reconcile king and people, Tuileries and Palais-Royal, monarchy and Paris. Concretely, Chamfort felt closer to La Fayette than to Barnave, that herald of a full, middle-class revolution. This was a question of generation, habits, and milieu—Chamfort had little in common with Barnave, a product of the Grenoble middle class, and had a certain reason to understand the language and style of La Fayette, born into the high liberal aristocracy in Auvergne and son-in-law to the duc d'Ayen (that grand seigneur who had feted Chamfort during his triumphant stay at the Barèges spa in 1779). Abandoning Barnave, who wanted to set the Revolution on the path to economic and social change (and who had the then-rare ability to analyze history in terms of classes), Chamfort tactically aligned himself with La Fayette, who had emerged as the major victor of the events of October 6, enjoying a popularity that pained Mirabeau. The republican had truly cooled.

Once the spasm triggered on October 6 had passed, Chamfort took up certain former habits. *La Jeune indienne* was performed as a preamble to Marie-Joseph Chenier's *Charles IX* in a benefit for the Cordeliers Club (which pronounced this rococo trifle sufficiently patriotic). The Panckouckes convinced Chamfort to write for *Le Mercure de France* (which he had refused ten years earlier), where he shared the literary column with his two oldest rivals, La Harpe and Marmontel. The paper's political reporter was still the monarchist Mallet du Pan; this baroque, almost unbelievable mixture of contributors was symptomatic of the lull—and was good for sales. Thanks to these four former protégés of Voltaire (Mallet du Pan had also started out among the Philosophers, then attacked their theories one by one), *Le Mercure* boasted eleven thousand subscribers and three times as many readers, becoming "the cleverest and most widely read paper" of 1790—another example of publisher Panckoucke's special genius. Although the Palais-Royal crowd preferred the brasher (and, above all, more inventive) sheets which proliferated at the time (from Hébert's *Père Duchesne* to *L'Ami du Peuple*, a periodical Marat edited during the long baths he took to assuage his skin disease), Chamfort still believed in the effectiveness of his articles (in which women remained that "gentle sex," three months after their active role on October 6). "What amuses me most," said Chamfort, "is that . . . thanks to the editor of the political section, the entire aristocracy subscribes, and on receiving M. Mallet du Pan's genuflections for its money, it also receives my slaps."[9] Le Mercure would enable that public that obsessed Chamfort to remain against the Revolution while remaining within the Revolution, and also enable Chamfort himself to mix with nobility one last time. Rivarol would then take up the pen: "Formerly, a number of articles in Le Mercure could lead a poor man to the Académie; currently, one has to be a member of the Académie to write an article for Le Mercure—this is a rather naive idea of Revolution."[10]

Chamfort and Rivarol, as brilliant as they were literarily "sterile," and more intellectually aristocratic than all the nobility put together, had been on the same wavelength in 1784. Out of contempt for the monarchy, Chamfort sided with the people. Rivarol, however, out of contempt for the people, sided with the monarchy. The States General had effectively transformed Rivarol into a provocative royalist, one who differed from Louis XVI and from the emigrés insofar as he also favored pluralism and liberty. One day he would advise the king to assume leadership of the Revolution in order to contain and subsequently overcome it, and the next day would advocate a counterrevolution (or rather a violent antirevolution). Rivarol was consistent on only one point: Louis XVI should be king.

Rivarol delighted in personal attacks, which he disguised as outraged defense, and considered Chamfort to be his "citizen" counterpart, his patriot twin. He edited Les Actes des Apôtres [Acts of the apostles], a periodical unique for its kind, in which false information and ludicrous allusions sketched an imaginary revolution. Rivarol indirectly accused Chamfort of forsaking both the humor typical of "their" class and the skepticism associated with Voltaire. On this point at least, Rivarol was right. Chamfort's written style, in Le Mercure and elsewhere, was no improvement over his output under the Ancien Régime. The irony of a skeptic like Rivarol, on the other hand, was well adapted to antirevolution, which he preached as the "logical" sequel to his earlier criticism of philosophical, social, and literary myths prior to 1789.

Rivarol's Barbs

Many of Rivarol's attacks in *Les Actes des Apôtres,* however, remain unfair. Chamfort was obviously not one of those literary dwarfs who, in Rivarol's opinion, were primarily responsible for the Revolution by having converted their bitterness into ideology. Whatever the complex reasons behind Chamfort's patriotism, his commitment stemmed from more than the simple failure of *Mustapha* (as illustrated by the existence of his *Products*). Similarly, the people of 1789 (whom Rivarol, in his *Journal Politique National,* described with appalling cynicism as being perfectly well-fed) had other reasons for rebelling than the duc d'Orléans' putative attempts to prevent supplies from reaching Paris.[11] Nor did Chamfort frequent Vaudreuil for his money, nor abandon him following his bankruptcy. Moreover, by secretly turning his savings over to the Revolution, Chamfort "brilliantly" demonstrated his deeper nature—that of a man fundamentally inegalitarian in terms of intelligence but displaying the attitude of austere mountain or island peoples when it comes to money. He in no way wanted to be thanked or acknowledged for his gifts. "When I have done some good and it becomes known, I feel myself punished, instead of . . . rewarded," he said. He who had never wanted to beg, did not now want to perform charity. Chamfort wished to replace Christian charity with social justice, and he behaved accordingly toward both rich and poor, even if his mania for secrecy inevitably masked his better qualities.

Rivarol knew too much about Chamfort, however, to abstain from mocking his patriotic credentials. Nicolas was already a "democrat at age thirty-eight," joked Rivarol, recalling that Chamfort had found the memoirs of Henry of Prussia "not bad for a prince." Nicolas had not just laid the groundwork for 1789, continued Rivarol in another issue of *Les Actes des Apôtres,* he literally liberated France and Turkey thanks to *Le marchand de Smryne* and *Mustapha;* Nicolas never acted out of self-interest—Vaudreuil and the Polignacs were in fact *his* protégés, etc. Rivarol would henceforth dog Chamfort step by step, with the same ferocity as had La Harpe under the Ancien Régime.

Such attacks, comprehensible only to those privy to aristocratic circles, revealed royalist exasperation with the consensus established by the speech Talleyrand read. This victory brought reproach upon the clergy's Judas as well as Vaudreuil's betrayer, for the two men were accused of being in the pay of Jews. A royalist pamphlet described Chamfort as being "constantly attached to the Bishop of

Autun, equally calculating and a better writer, [a follower of] the party which pays and seeks to demean those who can no longer pay. That, I think, is what is known as a statesman."[12] Such accusations were partly true for Talleyrand, the "lame devil," who considered himself a "bad boy" and who would in fact be enriched through the nationalization of church property. Jean Orieux's 1970 biography of Talleyrand alludes to spoils amounting to half a billion francs. "He'd sell his soul for money, and with good reason," commented Mirabeau following an argument with Talleyrand shortly before the Revolution, "because he'd be swapping his manure for gold."

But such accusations against Chamfort were completely unfounded. For he never sought to profit from the Revolution and, *pace* Rivarol, never abandoned his old patrons for new ones. "The proof that Chamfort was not ungrateful," noted Roederer, "is that he remained attached to friends divested of their extravagance, just as he had when they were endowed with it." Friendship, in this respect, was his sturdiest principle.

The Assembly rejected such accusations by electing the bishop its president at the end of February, whereas Chamfort became chancellor of the Académie. Backed by Mirabeau, the two friends counterattacked. Chamfort published article after article to obtain the permanent nationalization of the church and thereby return to the "glorious days" of Christianity when the apostles were Jewish, poor, and married. "Misanthropy, hard-heartedness, egotism and several anti-social drives naturally stem from the avoidance of marriage," he declared—not without cheek—to refute priestly celibacy.[13] He subsequently demanded citizenship for the forty thousand Jews in Alsace and Avignon. Denouncing not only anti-Semitic prejudice but also the belief held by certain devout Jews that God wanted them to be unhappy, he indignantly continued, "Jews are men. . . . And philosophers, men of genius, have been obliged to write books just to prove it!"[14] Envisioning a hybrid utopia for every religion, he prayed for the day when, leaving an Assembly presided over by a Jew, he would see a Catholic divorced from a Lutheran marry an Anabaptist, subsequently going to dine with a priest "who would introduce us to his wife."[15] So down with celibacy, that last obstacle to the great melting pot from which a new mankind should emerge, and up with the Hottentots, where father slept with daughter and brother slept with sister, yet everyone awoke "with a pure heart."[16]

A Ghost of His "Old Self"

But the utopian philosopher had to come down to earth. For the attacks increased, just when the consolidation of the Revolution was at stake. The fourth volume of the *Livre rouge* [*Red Book*], listing royal stipends, sold in tens of thousands of copies to a people avid for financial revelations, reminding them of Chamfort's long career as a "venal" writer. "Those who employ [him] in politics or secret affairs are sure of success," asserted the author.[17] Rivarol then defended Chamfort—the better to incriminate him: "Honest Chamfort . . . has proven that he sold himself only to the sovereign, that today the nation is sovereign, and that consequently he must sell himself to the Nation."[18]

Associated with the most opportunistic members of the Constituent Assembly, Chamfort began to pay for his role as *éminence grise* just as the Revolution was taking an increasingly moral turn. He nevertheless owned up to such contradictions. He argued that Mirabeau and Talleyrand were tools of History, even if they thought that they were manipulating it, just like the irreprochable Sieyès. As to himself, of course he had changed, he said, but that was precisely the point of 1789. The "old self" denounced by right-wingers was now only a ghost sometimes conjured up to play that role dear to revolutions—a witness of the past. Yes, he knew "people in high places," Chamfort intimated, but while his patrons bought his intelligence, his intelligence ultimately paid off. Yes, he had rubbed shoulders with the maréchal de Richelieu, a libertine who died in 1788, the symbol of an unpunished class. But Richelieu served Chamfort as a negative hero, like Laclos's Valmont in *Les liaisons dangereuses* who exploited his talent and privileges to the "utmost," perfectly executing his selfish designs. Now Chamfort could reveal behavior that merited sanctions more serious than mere ridicule. "Despotism plots its own downfall a long way off through madness, idleness, gaity,"[19] he wrote in *Le Mercure*. Which also explained, perhaps, his presence in Vaudreuil's household.

Chamfort would not return to the issue, for the byword in that spring of 1790 was to avoid all provocation. It was easier to pass laws than to implement them, and the Constitution wasn't even finished yet. The Jacobin Club (to which Chamfort had been one of the first writers admitted, though it is not known whether he attended regularly) nevertheless followed Barnave in rejecting the status quo.

Chamfort, along with Mirabeau and Talleyrand, thereupon joined the Société de 1789, the club started by La Fayette on April 12, 1790, to unite all those constitutionals hostile to both monarchists and Jacobins. The Society proclaimed itself to be "Against reaction and against insurrection." Admission was limited to six hundred and sixty paying members, and the club tended to propose laws favorable to Louis XVI. Like "puritanical" Sieyès (touchstone for the committee drafting the constitution), Chamfort thought it was possible to permanently separate the king from his entourage, at the cost of major concessions toward his person designed to mask his loss of power. Optimism abounded during the initial meetings. Enlightenment ideals were invoked, for the Society also believed in the infinite perfectability of "social art." Chamfort, who a year earlier had been caught up in the rhythm of rioting, now sat down with Condorcet to study the "science" that would inevitably render men happy.

Condorcet's Enlightenment

As intellectual as Abbé Sieyès (whose proposed jury system had just been unanimously voted down . . . it was said that deputies would have had to understand it before they could adopt it), Condorcet was one of the rare Philosophers to commit himself totally to the Revolution. The marquis de Condorcet was a member of the Academies of Science and Letters, had long been linked to d'Alembert, Julie de Lespinasse, and Voltaire (to whom he confided his poor opinion of *Mustapha et Zéangir*), and was, like Chamfort, a member of the Society sponsored by the comte de Provence. He and Chamfort had become closer following the demise of the Philosophers' clan, with Condorcet inviting Chamfort to the Hôtel de la Monnaie on the Quai Conti. Endowed with a prodigious memory and a truly encyclopedic curiosity, Condorcet was able to converse about lace with women and about calculus with men, had written eulogies to Linnaeus, Jussieu, and Benjamin Franklin, plus a treatise against the enslavement of blacks (under the pen name Schwartz), and had invented a method for determining the probability of future events based on the observation of past events. Yet Condorcet had been deeply affected by the failure of his attempt to go into business early in the reign of Louis XVI, when the Throne and the Enlightenment were enjoying their honeymoon. "Insolence toward those unfortunates who lack bread is infamous inhumaneness which will not endure for long," he wrote as early as 1780, echoing Chamfort's indignation at a gentleman who commented, on being solicited by a pauper, "Although we give them nothing, these people always ask." Condorcet was a convinced advocate of constitutional monarchy, enjoyed an international reputation, and viewed history as a tale of endless progress, from the adoption of agriculture to the acquisition of languages, from the invention of the state to the discovery of freedom. He was sincere and passionate, possessed a superhuman capacity for work, but was intimidated by crowds—d'Alembert described him as "a snow-capped volcano." Though not a deputy, Condorcet contributed on every issue. Like Chamfort, whom the royalist press described as Condorcet's "shadow," the marquis was just then experiencing favorable political conditions for his projects and his unshakeable optimism.

It is hardly surprising that Condorcet and Sieyès influenced Chamfort, whose revolutionary personality was as shifting as his literary identity. For both men provided ideological justifications for the reformed misanthrope, that partisan of a "volcanic" cataclysm who now supported a moderate constitution. They convinced him that politics was a "science" able to organize mankind rationally rather than a trigger for millennialist dreams. Although aristocrat and priest, respectively, they cleared Chamfort of Mirabeau's and Talleyrand's plots by converting him—superficially—to a precocious positivism, according to which the age of metaphysics would give way to that of universal Enlightenment.

On May 12, 1790, the Société de 1789 celebrated its incorporation with a grand dinner in its premises at the Palais-Royal. The hat was passed prior to sitting down to dinner, and toasts were made to nation, law, and king, and to writers who paved the way for the Revolution through their work—notably Sieyès's *What Is the Third Estate?* The abbé himself proposed a toast "to the finest Constitution, to the United States of America, and to patriotic Frenchmen." The crowd below, meanwhile, shouted in protest on seeing chandeliers aglow and on hearing the clink of glasses. But the deputies showed themselves at the windows, and calm returned.

On June 17, Chamfort returned to celebrate the first anniversary of the National Assembly, along with one hundred ninety members of the Society (including Mirabeau, Talleyrand, Abbé Sieyès, Bailly, and the Corsican hero Paoli). The feast was sumptuous, and this time they had taken care to invite a delegation of women from the marketplace. Sixty musicians played clarinets, oboes, and horns.

"There was an entirely celestial harmony," observed the journalist Gorsas. The young Chateaubriand was also there, "dumb" with admiration before Mirabeau's "tales of love" and "plans for withdrawal, with which he enlivened dry conversation." Mirabeau admitted his "sovereign contempt" for individuals insensitive to the people's misfortunes . . . as well as for his personal enemies in the patriotic camp. "He looked straight at me with eyes full of arrogance, vice and genius and, flatly placing his hand on my shoulder, said, 'They'll never forgive me for being superior!' I can still feel the imprint of that hand, as though Satan had touched me with his fiery claw," commented Chateaubriand in *Mémoires d'outre-tomb* [*The Memoirs of François Rene, Vicomte de Chateaubriand*].

A Herculean Salary

While the banquet was disbanding to the sound of oboes, a rumor was making the rounds. Started by the extreme left and picked up by the *Livre rouge*, it accused Mirabeau of open treason. Was Chamfort aware of the contract negotiated by the lion, in which the court assumed Mirabeau's debts and paid him a million livres? Probably, at least in part. For Mirabeau did nothing to hide his new lifestyle, having set up in a mansion on rue de la Chaussée-d'Antin rented from Julie Careau, complete with eleven servants and carriages adorned with his coat of arms. Chamfort did not seem too troubled, however; the Revolution needed the king to put a brake on royalist agitation and to prevent potential foreign intervention. Similarly, Mirabeau could not survive without the Revolution—he would even tell the court that to clear his name he would have to appear more virulently revolutionary than ever. Whatever the case, Chamfort knew Mirabeau well enough to realize that his very opportunism precluded treason. "Those who always want to see a single design behind extraordinary destinies, from the first step to the last, demonstrate a fundamental ignorance of men and things," Chamfort would say, the comment being equally true of himself. "The cleverer a man is, the more he adjusts his advance to the means which chance offers him, and which are not usually those he had foreseen or anticipated."[20] Mirabeau would describe himself as "bought but never sold," to which Chamfort added:

> . . . *Vengeur des peuples il sert, par son génie,*
> *L'humanité, l'Etat, peut-être tous les rois.*[21]

The people's avenger, his genius serves
Humanity, the State, and perhaps all kings.

Tactical considerations as well as political conviction induced Chamfort to discourage Mirabeau from drifting too close to the king (whom the count now venerated as his savior) and queen (whose political spouse he hoped to become).[22] Chamfort seized the occasion offered by the debate over who had the right to declare war, a debate sparked by a conflict between England and Spain which threatened to involve France (allied to the Spanish throne by the Family Compact). Discussion was heated, with the right fearing a warmongering Assembly that might vote to spread the revolution abroad, while the left accused Louis XVI of seeking an excuse to overthrow the Constitution. Partisan of revolution in a single country, Mirabeau threw all his weight behind the option of leaving the initiative for war with the king—with the implicit backing of the Société de 1789. But Barnave rallied support for the rights of the Assembly, and Chamfort urged Mirabeau to compromise. On May 22, the people's tribune entered the Salle du Manège to threats from fifty thousand citizens. "Yesterday the Capitol, today the Tarpeian Rock," shouted Volney, one of the Auteuil regulars. Mirabeau amended his motion to give joint rights to Assembly and king—a motion adopted after being amended yet again. The following day, Chamfort met Sieyès in the 1789 club. Sieyès was annoyed at being increasingly ignored by the constitutional committee and had kept silent for several weeks (described as a "public calamity" by Mirabeau in a speech on May 20, begging Sieyès to speak up). Sieyès now admitted that he was worried. The "moderateness" of the current law still provided the Jacobins with too many good arguments. Chamfort promised Sieyès that he would have Article 9, concerning foreign alliances with France, amended. "Nothing in the world would be more honorable . . . than an explanation coming from yourself, made by your own decree, in the goal of making it popular," wrote the prompter to Mirabeau that very evening. "For this, you must attend the opening of the session. . . . If, for some reason I haven't anticipated, you are prevented from making the motion yourself, indicate this same to me so that I can find someone as of tomorrow morning to assume it; for I attach the greatest importance to not leaving any doubt about such an article. . . . The Assembly does not want to leave the king the right to compromise the Nation in affairs with other peoples."[23] The next day, Mirabeau proposed that a special committee be formed to revise diplomatic treaties made by the Bourbons. Robespierre backed it, the Assembly assented, and the exportation of both revolution and reaction were outlawed. Mirabeau was henceforth less likely to be lynched.

The Nobility's Swan Song

This slim victory confirmed the Sociéte de 1789's supremacy over Barnave's Jacobins. But suspicions of corruption redoubled when a long civil list for the king was passed. Chamfort was able to right things by doing away with all titles of nobility: Highness, Monseigneur, Duke, Excellency, Knight, Eminence, names of estates or provinces—all those hated signs of heredity were abolished along with coats of arms and livery. Aristocrats had to prove themselves anew, under new names, just as young Nicolas had done twenty years earlier on adopting Chamfort. The nobility, which had survived all other sacrifices, now lost its magic. Even those who participated in abolishing feudalism on August 4 resisted, justifying Chamfort's earlier anger, when he had written:

> Perdre bons marquisats fit moins pousser de cris
> Que perdre le beau nom de monseiur le marquis,
> Une jambe est coupée, et c'est le bas qu'on pleure.[24]

Losing good marquisates raises less outcry
Than losing the name of marquis:
A leg is cut off, and the stocking is mourned.

In addition to vindicating these verses from the Ancien Régime, Chamfort now savored the revenge he had desired for thirty years. The time had come when names would no longer take the place of men, when words would no longer replace things. Louis XVI was rechristened Capet, La Fayette became Motier. Mirabeau, whom Chamfort had called "my dear count," became his "dear friend." Furious at having to use his family name, Riquetti, the tribune first took revenge on his valet—"I do hope that I'm still monsieur le comte to you!"—and then went to meet the queen at Saint-Cloud on July 3, in the greatest secrecy, promising her that he would save the monarchy. As to Chamfort's "valet" (as the royalist press dubbed Grouvelle), he explained in the Journal de la Société de 1789 that completely abolishing inequality would probably mean that sons should no longer bear their father's name. Although he dropped the "de,"

Chamfort was one of the few "aristocrats" to keep his name. True enough, Nicolas would have been difficult to use, for it was the name of one of the notorious assassins of October 6, nicknamed "Big Beard." So the writer's signature became S.R.N. Chamfort, although the royalist press continued to make frequent allusions to his namesake, prior to nicknaming him "Hide'n Seek Nicolas."

No one listened when he demanded private cells for prisoners—"those unfortunate victims of society"—and the opening of a home for abandoned children, many of whom died of cold during winter. Visibly moved, he vainly stressed that five million Frenchmen were on the brink of starvation, and that misfortune's only remedy was further misfortune, since most of the indigent died young. By adopting the civil constitution of the clergy, the Assembly nevertheless partly rewarded his efforts. "Equality, indulgence, tolerance, humility—that's the doctrine of Jesus Christ!" he cried.[25] Talma nevertheless had to appeal to the deputies on July 12, through Mirabeau, to receive authorization to marry Julie Careau in church—actors were still denied the sacraments. But bishops were henceforth chosen by electors, as were magistrates. Eight months of all-out reform and compromise with the king led to this civil organization of the clergy, a watershed in the reorganization of France. Chamfort won his parliamentary game, at the cost of several insults. Convinced of Louis XVI's weakness and goodness, he allowed that the king was virtuous. "The Bourbons can't be ennobled," he had said to Vaudreuil in 1788, "but they can still be made illustrious by giving them citizens as subjects." At that point he still believed, as did most the third estate, that there was a future for a minimal monarchy, civic equality for all, plus one—the king. France was already preparing to celebrate the first anniversary of this new order, ushered in by the fall of the Bastille.

18. SHATTERED DREAMS

The only history worthy of attention is that of free peoples. The history of peoples subjected to despotism is just a collection of anecdotes.

Chamfort

How fine were feelings then!
How grand we felt, how free . . .

The princesse de Salm referring to 1790

*C*hamfort now enjoyed his sunniest moments as a revolutionary. Paris was going all out in order to be ready in time for the provincial units arriving to celebrate the anniversary. Fifteen thousand workers erected stands along the Champ-de-Mars. Carthusian monks pitched in alongside "shameless" girls, and the duchesse de Luynes was seen pushing a mahogany wheelbarrow. "Neither you nor anyone can imagine the enthusiasm generated here by the celebration for the 14th," wrote Beaumarchais to Salieri, Mozart's rival. ". . . Everything is joy, song, dance."[1] The crowd sang:

Celui qui s'élève on l'abaissera,
Celui qui s'abaisse on l'élèvera,
Ah ça ira, ça ira, ça ira . . .

He who raises himself we'll lower,
He who lowers himself we'll raise,
All will be fine, 'll be fine, 'll be fine.

On the morning of July 14, 1790, Chamfort took a seat opposite the altar where Talleyrand was to say the mass, a charade the bishop reportedly rehearsed with Mirabeau at M. de Saisseval's residence, having forgotten the liturgy.[2] But rainstorms beat down on the Champ-de-Mars. Some people prayed, others accused God of being an "aristocrat," and Chamfort took shelter under a canopy. The parade of the *Fédérés*, provincial units armed with bayonets, began at ten o'clock. The deputies, shielded by umbrellas, took their places in the grandstand in front of the Military Academy. At noon, the royal family arrived in a carriage, and the king was seated on a throne adorned with golden lilies. "Down with the umbrellas," shouted the wildly enthusiastic crowd, which couldn't see a thing. Chamfort glimpsed a drenched Mme. Panckoucke. Talleyrand, meanwhile, went up to the altar surrounded by two hundred priests, a choir of one hundred children, and his two abbés, to whom he said, "Whatever you do, please don't make me laugh!" The bishop managed to remain impassive throughout the ceremony—just as he remained impassive throughout the Directorate, the Empire, and two restorations. The Fédérés took an oath to the new Constitution, and Louis XVI did the same after having been spurred on by La Fayette. Even the queen was acclaimed. The sun came out, brilliant, to warm up the five hundred thousand Frenchmen there to swear allegiance to King and Nation. Chamfort then crossed the Seine to return to the Palais-Royal (the only two victims of the day's events, in fact, were drowned in a ferry crossing).

This sacred union, the atmosphere of concord and peace, and the crowd's joy led people to believe in the utopia preached at the Palais-Royal—the eighteenth century would truly benefit everyone. "Let's preserve everything good from the old days, which were so bad," said Chamfort.[3] From below his window he could hear cries of, "Abolish all royal stipends." Chamfort, the "venal" writer, replied to the good Mme. Panckoucke, "I say, 'Abolish whatever you wish, I will change neither principles nor feelings. Men used to walk with their heads, now they walk with their feet; I am content; they will always have failings, even vices, but they will have only those that are natural.' "[4] That evening he discovered Marmontel and his wife in tears. To their son, Chamfort said, "Come, my little friend, some day you will do better than us; someday you will weep for your father on learning that he had the weakness to weep for you at the idea that you would be less rich than he."[5]

Chamfort was a happy revolutionary at this point. He earned a living as a journalist with *Le Mercure*, he was prompter to Mirabeau, the plebeian count, and to Talleyrand, the lame devil, and was confidant to both "puritanical" Sieyès and visionary Condorcet. He hewed a middle path between intrigue and uprightness, pragmatism and utopia. He acknowledged certain "leaders," but also had his own disciples. These included Ginguené, a Breton writer eight years his junior (who had met Chamfort at Vaudreuil's and, being a literary and political purist, now worshipped Chamfort and the late Rousseau), the young Grouvelle (son of a Paris goldsmith, married to the daughter of a druggist, and Chamfort's successor as secretary to the prince de Condé in Chantilly, where he composed an opera on *Plums* prior to writing on Montesquieu), and Roederer, a highly visible deputy from Lorraine (who was tall, thin, serious and a hard worker, yet lively and subtle, the very model of a young parliamentarian drawn to the Revolution through a mixture of sincerity and legitimate ambitiousness). Roederer arrived from Metz at the end of 1789 and actively participated in all debates the following spring, despite his mediocre eloquence, speaking out on the abolition of religious orders, on replacing the justice of traditional *parlements* by a jury of peers, and on the civil rights of actors, blacks, and Jews. He was by far the most competent of Chamfort's friends, capable both of serious literary analysis (as he would prove with Chamfort's aphorisms) and solid political and economic reasoning. Roederer broadly followed Chamfort's political trajectory; he was commended by Mirabeau as early as 1789, was linked to Talleyrand, admired Sieyès, and was appointed president of the Société de 1789 in August 1790.

Rain

But nothing lasted under the revolutionary sun. The very success of the Fédération ceremony sparked the wrath of reactionaries. The prince de Condé called for a coalition against the "French disease [another name for syphilis]," and armed thirty thousand men (including, in an unsettling coincidence, four of Chamfort's relatives on his mother's side). Agents of the comte d'Artois were stirring up the south, and in August twenty thousand royalist guards gathered at a chateau in Jales. Sensing the danger, Mirabeau criticized the prince de Condé in the Assembly but with a violence that seemed suspicious. A second wave of revolutionaries now rose up against La Fayette and his allies. La Fayette had been the major beneficiary of the Fédération ceremony, but he was also responsible for the bloody repression of a soldiers' mutiny in Nancy. The Société de 1789 was denounced as a haven for "modern Machiavellis" and as a symbol of the appropriation of the Revolution by the rich. Dozens of affiliate clubs in the provinces switched to the Jacobins, as did Mirabeau and Condorcet. Talleyrand himself quit because, as the *Actes des Apôtres* mockingly claimed, "M. Nicolas (better known by his former name of Chamfort) took advantage of his confidence to persuade him that Abbé Sieyès had far more wit than he." Chamfort, as the prophet of the new faith, nevertheless refused to quit a club that met next door, where he played daily chess games surrounded by an audience that delighted in his "witticisms." Along with what remained of the Fronde-like elite—the duc de Lauzun and the marquis de Montesquiou—Chamfort preferred to prolong the utopia of the Fédération at the Louvre apartments of Mme. de Flahaut, Talleyrand's mistress. According to *La Chronique Scandaleuse*, Mme. de Flahaut complained to Chamfort of the lame devil's greed and the "ridiculous duration of episcopal preening." A child joined this final act played out in the Louvre—Charles de Flahaut, Talleyrand's illegitimate son whose own son, Morny, would one day become a minister under Napoleon III.

Just as he had been a republican too early, Chamfort was a royalist too late. For Louis XVI supported the priests who objected to the nationalization of the clergy, one of the causes behind the resistance brewing in the Vendée region. The king had been humiliated when the Paris *sections*, or districts, voted against his ministers—so, one year after Mirabeau, he discovered the art of two-timing. His chapel filled up with nonjuring priests, and he now seriously considered heading east. This compromised the chances for a constitutional monarchy, which might have succeeded had Louis firmly backed it. Chamfort then realized his mistake: the "dear" king who was to have reconciled the old and the new orders turned out to be a monarch like the others, an evil father, a Frank-like Clovis, his original predecessor on the throne of France. The revolution, stripped of its "strongest rampart" against foreign invasion, was left bare. The swiftness of this turnaround staggered the prompter. "I have learned that Chamfort, disgusted with the world and indignant (so I am told) at everything that's happening, wants to withdraw from the world and bury himself in a haystack far from the capital. That would prove to me that he smells counter-revolution, and the chap has a good nose," wrote Vaudreuil to the comte d'Artois on September 26, 1790.[6] Chamfort acted, however. Like Sieyès, he quit the Société de 1789 to back Mirabeau's offensive against La Fayette. The plebeian count tried to draw the king leftward by suggesting a "secret ministry, sheltered from the storm," to be composed of "very modest and very reliable [men], whose only power is their intellect."[7] He was perhaps considering Chamfort for this shadow cabinet, designed to get around the law that disqualified Mirabeau from serving as minister. But the plan, like most of the tribune's schemes, came to naught.

Chamfort then began moving leftward again. He was hardly alone, for there was rampant maneuvering in late 1790. Mirabeau competed with the Orléans clan to win control of the Jacobins against La Fayette, who was still trying to infiltrate them in late September. At the December meeting, Mirabeau cried, "May my fellow members surround me!" But he gathered only thirty members against Robespierre, one of the mainstays of the club. Chamfort then took refuge in the "Emigrés de 1789" club, composed of "energetic patriots" (according to Ginguené, who says no more about this compromise solution).

Farewell to Plutarch

For the first time, the Revolution was moving too fast. The convoluted plotting of a protean Mirabeau exhausted Chamfort (accustomed to being split merely two ways). Civil peace and the Assembly—that great invention of the first half of 1790—suited Chamfort better. Secretly uneasy with all the "clubbiness," Chamfort took refuge in his books. He wrote in *Le Mercure* that he could "be accused of a lingering weakness for Greek and Latin . . . due to old models that a few idle people still take pleasure in reading. Yes, alas! I am one of these idle people."[8] He was discovering that his times cared more for a single, scathing motion at the Jacobin club than for all of Plutarch. Anti-intellectualism was on the increase, and writers were accused of having committed themselves to the Revolution too late. Actors, on the other hand, retained their popularity and prerogatives; Chamfort joined a delegation of writers who appeared before the Assembly on August 24 to claim their unwon rights, arguing that writers had laid the groundwork for "the grandiose events" of 1789. This harked back to the period when Beaumarchais organized his gatherings.

But there were more serious affairs. Education had still not been reformed, and villages remained in a state of "stupor" which worried Chamfort. The sons of privileged families quit school to join the clubs, from which they could threaten school directors. An overly cultivated generation threatened to give way to an uncultivated one. The people must be enlightened, said Chamfort, "most especially when they have become most powerful."[9] He attempted to forget his legislative disappointments by compiling a library for Mirabeau.[10]

But here again Chamfort was ambivalent. He opposed a plan to reform the Académie française with the excuse that any change could destroy a body hostile to change—"and what would become of the dictionary?" he asked in *Le Mercure*. At the same time, he surreptitiously wrote a pamphlet against the Forty as part of the plan for national education Mirabeau was to present to the Constituent Assembly. Schizophrenia or duplicity? Both, probably. Chamfort continued to attend the Académie up until February 1791. In order to spy, some said. But probably out of perversity, since Abbé Morellet noted that there he defended the "truly atrocious" decrees of the Assembly with great alacrity, ahead of La Harpe, Condorcet, and Chabanon, and to the great annoyance of Suard, Marmontel, and Abbé Delille.

Chamfort really wanted to debunk the Forty himself—an old academic tradition. On learning of the proposed reform from Mirabeau, he wrote, "I suspect that, had I known of this project before taking up bow and arrow against the Academies, I would have deigned to nod and extend a hand. But since my task is completed . . . in a few days more I'll fire off my little bundle."[11] Events forced the tribune to postpone his speech in the Assembly, during which time Chamfort stressed his political shift and sharpened his "bundle." "All I've been able to think about for the past two months is setting fire to all this old academy furniture," he wrote to the Academy in Angers, which wanted to make him an associate. "Down with all classes and cliques, down with all the universities. . . . That's my refrain, and Mirabeau's refrain, and in a few days you will hear the noise and crackling. . . . Happiness and fame for all."[12] This was a new twist for Chamfort, who had never advocated the equality of intelligence—it was his first appearance as a sansculotte.

Even prior to his election to the Académie française, there were signs of his hostility toward this symbol of a detested trade. Moreover, it was just like Chamfort to denounce the literary aristocracy, too, thereby renouncing his own "feudal privileges." But after twenty years of yearning feverishly for admission, it seems strange that he should be the first to strangle the institution. The undertaking was all the more dubious in that the Académie was already in its death throes. The populace had forgotten the avant-garde role played by the Académie under Louis XV, and called for its abolition right from the fall of the Bastille. It was attacked in the Assembly and in the press (by Palissot, an enemy of the Philosophers who had gone over to the extreme left). Marat described the Académie as a menagerie which consumed the bread of forty ménages. Abandoned by the public, it no longer even bothered to replace deceased members. Only the literary ardor of La Harpe and Suard could convince the deputies in August to not strangle it financially—Chamfort being paradoxically present during the session in which the Académie drafted its riposte.

Chamfort's motives were complex. Like the nobility on the night of August 4, he wanted to reacquire virtue, conjure away his post-Fédération malaise, and refute the accusations made in the *Livre rouge*. His pamphlet thoroughly negated his acceptance speech, and thereby sounded the death knell of what remained of that "old self" who, rejected by the Philosophers, had offered an extravagant dedication to the queen; the bell tolled for the author of *Mustapha* as well as its murderers. Carrying out this obsession, Chamfort guided Mirabeau to the podium in order to liquidate a whole period of his life. As in a dream, and with a sort of suicidal joy, he gave in to iconoclastic pressures, in anticipation of the puritanical order envisioned by Rousseau. Chamfort began to rearrange his own past, vaunting lower-class credentials where he once claimed title to nobility.

Metamorphosis, Act II

The winter of 1790–1791 was marked by this evolution. "Recently, Nicolas Chamf . . . was heard disgorging loathsome things against the queen in a rather decent café," wrote *La Chronique Scandaleuse* in February 1791.[13] "The listeners refused to follow. Nicolas, determined to do her harm, tried to say good things about her—but his listeners remained unmoved. Finally, determined to arouse the café against this queen, Nicolas suddenly got it into his head to say that she had been his benefactress. At which point there was one great outcry against her, and everyone agreed that she fully deserved her misfortune." This anecdote, probably doctored by Tilly (editor of *La Chronique Scandaleuse*),[14] provides a good description of Chamfort's metamorphosis. Several days later he participated in a dinner with La Fayette—a political opponent with whom he had rubbed shoulders just six months earlier in the Société de 1789. This hero of the American War of Independence, seeing his popularity fade, confided his nostalgia for the days when he served "Papa" Washington. Chamfort then leaned over to his neighbor and whispered, "If he goes back to Philadelphia to see Papa Washington, and if Papa learns of the stupid things his son has been doing over here, there may well be a whipping."[15] Paris, which had never appreciated the lavish receptions given by La Fayette for the Société de 1789, laughed over this crack for four days. Chateaubriand, like Ginguené, also witnessed Chamfort's leftward drift, and increasingly "sharp" discussions divided the two. "Personal politics bored me," wrote the author of *Memoires d'outre-tombe*, all the while admitting that the revolutionary populace enabled him to overcome his shyness. "My true life was in higher spheres." Dropping men who were too partisan for his taste (but who nevertheless continued to associate with his sister Lucile), Chateaubriand then decided to leave for America to seek the Northwest passage.

The second act of Chamfort's metamorphosis was now fully underway. Mirabeau, aided by Cabanis and Condorcet, had completed his plan for a national education system, and Chamfort's bundle of vitriol, titled *Des académies* [On academies], was included along with proposals for public schools. The lion and the cat set the month of April 1791 for its presentation to the Constituent Assembly, all the while setting up their library in Mirabeau's house (described as resembling "the boudoir of some little mistress"). But Mirabeau—who remained a sort of political pariah even during his brilliant ascendance—was completely exhausted by his machinations to get around the decree barring him from becoming minister. He was constantly coming and going between the Assembly and the Jacobin Club, between the "Royal Cattle" and Desmoulins, between emissaries from abroad and tavern patriots. Mirabeau spoke from the podium one more time, on Monday, March 28, to defend the fortune of his friend La Marck, who owned major mines in the north. He subsequently collapsed, however, and withdrew to Marais, his estate near the Porte d'Argenteuil. Chamfort went to Mirabeau that very evening. They inspected the construction work and visited the temple to Liberty that workers were erecting at the end of the park. Mirabeau livened up on contact with his "musket," regaining a "most naive" gaity. On the road back, he declared himself recovered. "I'm not sure I should be too pleased about it," he told Chamfort. "For surely you would have done a good obituary on me?"[16] And thereupon he passed in review all the stages of his life with obvious satisfaction.

The Lion's End

The next day, however, Mirabeau's condition worsened. It may have been due to uremia, or to amorous excesses committed several days earlier in the company of a courtesan and a ballerina. Whatever the case, the tribune was just a shadow of his former self. His heart was congested, his muscles stiffened (he would die with an erection). Crowds invaded rue de la Chaussée-d'Antin, bringing him medicinal remedies like James's powder and cinchona [Peruvian bark]. On the second floor, Dr. Cabanis attended to the sick man (whom some suspected of having been poisoned), accompanied by faithful friends. "There was Chamfort, Frochot, La Marck," recounted Chaussard.[17] The end approached. "Lift my head, you won't always hold the likes of it," Mirabeau said to his valet. Of La Marck, he inquired, "My dear connoisseur of fine deaths, are you satisfied?" Delegations multiplied, Barnave himself coming to salute his rival. Abbé Maury, the right-wing orator, also made the trip, while Mirabeau gave his deputies the speeches he hadn't had time to present, including "Des académies." Talleyrand appeared on April 1 to inherit the plebeian count's political mantle—"a confessor truly worthy of the penitent" it was said. On April 2, after having scrawled the word "sleep," the forty-three-year-old Mirabeau expired. The monarchy had lost its last card, the Revolution its apprentice dictator, Chamfort his best friend. The schizophrenic Chamfort watched this Proteus vanish, the man who had stolen from him, copied from him, and deceived him, yet who just several weeks earlier had gone all out to salvage Chamfort's remaining stipends. Entire portions of Chamfort's past crumbled with Mirabeau, that noble pariah, that rebel he had trained, that people's tribune who had adopted Chamfort's theories prior to discovering his own genius. They had lived through the best of the Ancien Régime together as well as the best of the new. They had their "idyll" with the queen and their marriage with the people. During those ten years of disarming admiration and perverse affection, Chamfort was never bored. During those ten years he played the role of Socrates or secretary, yet always that of friend. During those ten years they spent an hour together almost every day, from Vaudreuil's mansion to Julie's house. And even during the most questionable periods and the most flagrant disagreements, they remained faithful in their hatred of social "charlatanism." Mirabeau, that magnificient scoundrel, that authoritarian rebel, that man ready to do anything for money (even good, claimed Rivarol), left a vacuum that Chamfort would never fill. The Revolution henceforth would feel like the day after.

On April 4, the funeral procession left Julie's house, over the

door of which Talma had the following lines by M. J. Chénier inscribed:

L'ame de Mirabeau s'exhala dans ces lieux;
Homme libres, pleurez, tyrans, baissez les yeux.

Mirabeau's soul rose up from this place;
Weep, free men—tyrants, lower your gaze.

On reaching rue Montmartre, the procession was followed by
an enormous crowd. People climbed trees and rooftops to witness
the lion's last journey. It was headed by several detachments of cav-
alry whose trumpets and drums were draped in black crêpe.
Batallions of the old and the young, with women dressed in black
and white, fell into step behind the ministers, the entire Assembly,
the duc d'Orléans and his son (the future Louis-Philippe, king of the
French), Chamfort and Cabanis (henceforth friends). Sixteen soldiers carried Mirabeau's coffin, others a cushion on which rested his
heart, topped by a count's coronet. The office of the dead was performed at the Church of Saint-Eustache, where Abbé Cerutti gave a
funeral oration for this rather special Christian, and where more
than two thousand soldiers fired a salvo in honor of the deceased,
seriously wounding several spectators.

The magnificent burial, Gossec's music, and Mirabeau's induc-
tion into the Pantheon marked the end of an era. The generation of
1780—Chamfort, Talleyrand, Laclos, Lauzun—watched as the generation of Barnave (aged thirty) and Danton and Robespierre (both
thirty-three) came to the fore. The Revolution passed imperceptibly
from the hands of renegades from the Ancien Régime into those of
provincial lawyers. The Assembly, freed from a crushing weight,
paused to catch its breath. Only Marat dissented. "People! Your
most dreaded enemy has just died!"

19. THE ACADÉMIE DISMEMBERED BY A MEMBER

Chamfort was of taller than average height, a little bent, and his pale face had a sickly pallor. His blue eyes, often cold and veiled when at rest, flashed with lightning when he became animated. Somewhat flared nostrils lent his physiognomy an expression of sensitivity and energy. His voice was supple, its modulations following the movement of his moods; and during the latter part of my stay in Paris, it had taken on a harsh tone.

Chateaubriand
Essai sur les révolutions

Now, Gods, stand up for bastards!

Shakespeare
King Lear

With Mirabeau gone, Chamfort published *Des académies* under his own name.[1] The detail is significant, for this testament to their friendship was in fact the first "book" that Chamfort had published since the resounding failure of *Mustapha et Zéangir*. He took little care, however, to justify his academic past under the Ancien Régime. He simply observed that, in the absence of any support from society itself, it was normal for intellectuals to take refuge in special "societies." This was a feeble alibi, but why bother defending academicians at a time when all "true orators" were in the Assembly? as Chamfort pointed out. And who would resist the humor of his conclusion, originally intended for the deputies—"Spare the Académie a natural death, gentlemen. Give its supporters, if any remain, the consolation of believing that, but for you, it would have been immortal."

Mirabeau, however, played one last trick on Chamfort; he had long ago revealed Chamfort's text to Garat, a friend of Suard's (who then warned the survivors of the *Encyclopédie*). Thus blows rained down the instant *Des académies* appeared. Protests came not only from old rivals such as La Harpe and Suard but also from friends like Talleyrand, Condorcet, and Chabanon. A publisher printed Chamfort's acceptance speech of 1781 at the front of his pamphlet, and a participant in the 1756 interschool Competitive Exam reminded Chamfort of his enthusiasm for medals. "The Académie never produced a masterpiece?" asked Abbé Morellet in a pamphlet.[2] "If M. *de* Chamfort had Corneille or Racine's genius, would it have prevented him from producing a better tragedy than *Mustapha et Zéangir?*" Philosophers ultimately colluded with the king to limit the Enlightenment? Then why had Chamfort merely come up with "bawdy stories" when the struggle was at its height? D'Alembert was a coward? Then why did Chamfort frequent him? The Académie was a simple product of the monarchy? Then why did he attend so regularly for ten years? Acceptance speeches are comic exercises in mutual flattery? Then why did he defend them in his own speech, delivered in 1781 before the prince de Condé? And so on. "Courageous when convenient," concluded Abbé Morellet in disgust. But the real moral of this debacle was that Chamfort always wound up detesting what he had desired.

People were no longer interested in this anachronistic debate, however. It had been outdistanced by the revolutionary language of papers such as Hébert's *Le père duchesne* (familiarly addressing readers with "Hello," or exclamations of "Damnation"). Even the royalists favored the closure of an institution they had long considered too political. Abbé Morellet's pamphlet, all five hundred printed copies, went unnoticed. The publisher finally pulped it, anxious at having printed the name of Condé without an accompanying insult. Chamfort replied a year later—to someone else's attacks *against* the Forty. "Vulgar insults," he would write in *Le Mercure*,[3] all the while praising the boldness of his own eulogies to Molière and La Fontaine, and the role of the Académie under Louis XV, who reportedly considered abolishing it. Chamfort's contradictions stagger the imagination.

Acts III and IV

The king's flight to Varennes opened the third act of Chamfort's metamorphosis. Louis attempted to reach Montmédy disguised as a valet; his arrest en route made the throne wobble. The cities of Clermont and Bayonne demanded his removal, and the first truly republican mob hit the streets in Paris. The royal family was forced to return to the Tuileries palace, accompanied by Barnave and Pétion, but Chamfort, like Condorcet, now abandoned all illusions of a constitutional monarchy. Two years earlier, Chamfort had said, "Despite advice and warnings, royal power is marching blindly ahead towards its own fall."[4] Chamfort the republican reappeared, this time with no Mirabeau to moderate his mistrust of the king.

The Assembly temporarily suspended Louis XVI, and then played for time to avoid choosing between the various alternatives to monarchy. Chamfort was involved in a number of attempts to overthrow the regime, according to the royalist press. He was accused, for instance, of planning a republic with Condorcet and Brissot, in exchange for a seat in the Senate. Elsewhere, he was reported as present at meetings to install a *deciumvirat* with Barnave, Lameth, Duport, Talleyrand (the latter asking that Chamfort be given a post of secretary). But Barnave was seduced by the queen on her return from Varennes, and Talleyrand was already making ministerial suggestions to the king. As to Condorcet, he was too intellectual; Brissot, too new. Only one strong figure could have truly taken advantage of the situation—but he was dead.

After hesitating between Regency and republic, the Assembly decided to rewrite the Varennes incident: the king had been *abducted* by disloyal officers. Barnave and La Fayette, enemies in 1790, now found themselves united in call for a constitutional monarchy. "One more step toward equality means the destruction of property," warned Barnave. Chamfort then joined the Jacobins, which Barnave had left to found the Feuillants with La Fayette, a club that adopted the moderate ideals of the Société de 1789. There was a strange switch in positions between the writer turned radical and the politician become moderate, between Mirabeau's friend and his rival (Barnave becoming, in turn, adviser to the royal couple).

The term "Jacobins" originally referred to the holy order occupying the monastery located on rue Saint-Honoré. But the monks were replaced by the deputies, writers, and journalists affiliated with the left wing of the patriot party. It remained a "bourgeois" group, however, in the image of Robespierre. This handsome, slender deputy from Arras, carefully powdered and dressed in elegant striped vests, still considered the club in 1791 as the guardian of grand revolutionary principles, from the right to vote to the abolition of the death penalty. Mirabeau, true enough, had seen beneath Robespierre's formality and compared him to "a cat which has drunk vinegar." But Robespierre was now as surprised as Chamfort to discover this former monastery (located a stone's throw from the Salle du Manège) suddenly surrounded by two thousand men from the populous districts, who were fed up with the Constituent Assembly's wait-and-see attitude. The tension mounted between the two camps—the Feuillants (where Chamfort still had friends), and the Jacobins (where his enemies formerly met). The events of July 16, 1791, ultimately triggered the final act of his metamorphosis, signaling his return to volcanic activity.

At dawn, Jacobins Brissot (republican) and Laclos (Orléanist) drew up a petition calling for a referendum on the king's removal. Members of the Cordeliers Club, even more radical than the Jacobins, then tried to amend the petition by eliminating any allusion to a Regency. The motion was rejected after four hours of debate which sorely tried the club's maniacal legalism. Chamfort applauded Robespierre for the first time, when the deputy attacked the "corrupt" majority in the Assembly and referred to the Jacobins as "the people's true representatives." Late that evening, Chamfort was elected to the club's Correspondence Committee, whose task was to prevent provincial chapters from going over to the Feuillants.

That night, however, the Assembly restored executive power to the king, on the condition that he approve the Constitution. The Jacobins withdrew their petition, but the Cordeliers maintained it. On Sunday, July 17, people from the populous neighborhoods streamed to the Champ-de-Mars to sign it. Two men found hiding under the altar were accused of spying and had their throats slit. Bailly and La Fayette advanced at the head of twelve hundred guards, waving the red flag indicating martial law. The twenty thousand demonstrators dispersed, singing and heckling the troops. Shots were fired, and the troops charged (heading into a nearby park, where Condorcet's wife and daughter were nearly killed). Officially, fifty deaths were announced; unofficially, there were fifteen hundred. Blood had been shed on the very spot where the Fédération had been celebrated. A red line now divided the Revolution in two.

On hearing of the massacre, Chamfort headed over to rue Saint-Honoré. "Drawn by an irresistible force, despite my illness and suffering," he wrote, "[I] ran to the Jacobins, arriving the twentieth or thirtieth. . . . I'm not sure of the number, but the room was empty."[5] Opponents of the constitutional monarchy had been shaken by the surprise show of force, heralding a mini-Terror which induced Danton, Marat, and Desmoulins to flee Paris. Emissaries were dispatched to question witnesses to the massacre, and Robespierre went to the podium. "I am alarmed at the damage they want to inflict on us," he said between clenched teeth. "The people still manifested a sort of energy, so it was necessary . . . to deprive them of this proud attitude which so frightens their oppressors."[6] But the clank of weapons interrupted Robespierre's revelations concerning the Assembly. Chamfort and the other members hastily left the monastery. By eleven-thirty, La Fayette's troops completely controlled the premises.

Those two days caused Chamfort his "first pain as patriot," wrote Ginguené. He was trapped between populace and Feuillants, abandoned by Talleyrand and Sieyès (who preferred monarchic government "which culminates in a point" to republican government "which culminates in a platform"), and now found himself alone. The center and moderate left united around the monarchy, while the right demanded that the Constitution be revised. "This is a vile coalition which will cost us the blood of five hundred thousand Frenchmen," cried Chamfort. For the first time, he was drifting toward illegality. He sensed the threat posed by an Assembly ready to call a halt to the Revolution, yet felt isolated within the already isolated left. At a time when the majority was king, Chamfort discovered himself to be a painful minority.

Bitter Fruit

In 1789, Chamfort had slipped Sieyès the famous title, *What Is the Third Estate? Everything. What Does It Have? Nothing. . . .* To which the abbé added, *What Does It Want? Something.* The risk that this could lead to a sellout was now pointed out to Chamfort, who replied, "Then I'd hang myself."[7] But he wouldn't have to. The Assembly, dreading further "aggravation," restrained from crushing the lower-class neighborhoods and closing the Jacobin Club. The club then counted its survivors—six hundred affiliated chapters out of twenty-four hundred. Outright dissolution was considered, but Robespierre's prestige carried the day. Chamfort made every effort to bring provincial affiliates—most of them who had left to join the Feuillants—back into the fold. He discovered the world of circulars, meetings, printers—the dreary side of activism. A purge was made, enabling his friend Roederer to join the Committee of 72, which spearheaded the revival. Penitent deserters began to come back by August 3, and provincial chapters returned to the fold. This was a victory for Chamfort, who spoke from the podium on August 10. Tempered by this experience, the Jacobins adopted their steely personality, and Chamfort "bronzed himself" anew.

But he was now fifty-one and unable keep up. He yielded his seat on the Correspondence Committee to Fabre d'Eglantine (the poet who later named the months of the revolutionary calendar). "True, the country hadn't yet been saved," he wrote, "but the steadily growing crowd . . . seemed to guarantee victory." He left the club for good once elections to a new Assembly were announced. "More courageous in the face of danger than in the face of chatter," commented Ginguené, with apparent justice. By late September, the Jacobins had recovered six hundred provincial affiliates.

This recovery rekindled right-wing aggressiveness and contempt for Louis XVI's weakness. From abroad, Vaudreuil, Calonne, and the comte d'Antraigues (Chamfort's former "republican" disciple, now head of the counterrevolutionary spy network) considered installing a substitute monarchy in Lyon, in the name of the comte d'Artois.[8] Leopold II confirmed Austria's readiness to intervene. The royalists indulged in provocation everywhere—in Chambéry, a dog wearing the royal white rosette attacked a patriotic dog. Chamfort and Laclos were accused of having asked the Jacobins to "crush all parties" and anyone who "dared speak or write."[9] Overwhelmed, the Constituent Assembly itself anticipated civil war. Two events, however, reduced the tension. The king signed the Constitution (revised in his favor); Austria and Prussia signed the Pillnitz agreement, which was so vague as to remove the threat of immediate foreign intervention. The Cordeliers Club reopened, and Louis XVI was no longer under house arrest in the Tuileries palace. A single stroke of the pen blotted out his flight to Varennes and the massacre on the Champ-de-Mars.

This was a bitter pill for Chamfort. His efforts had merely benefited the king, who was publicly applauded at a performance of *Castor et Pollux*. The deputies absolved those who perpetrated the massacre—"everyone freshly emerged from the people takes arms against them," claimed Chamfort.[10] Two years of revolution seemed to have produced an elite determined to abolish privileges in order to "pick up the pieces."[11] Chamfort discovered that the liberal revolution was just a disguised version of the ideas promoted by the "advanced" aristocracy he had frequented back in 1780. Nor had the people shown themselves to be superior to the deputies. They had been unprepared for the Varennes incident, and their immaturity had led to acceptance of the king's return. Gunned down on the Champ-de-Mars, they had left it to the Jacobins to fight back. "The National Assembly gave the French people a constitution stronger than they are," wrote Chamfort,[12] thereby disavowing Sieyès's highly theoretical guidelines (Mme. de Staël claimed that Sieyès would have preferred to deal with a species other than mankind). "Like animals who can no longer breath above a certain altitude, the slave dies in an atmosphere of liberty,"[13] Chamfort had asserted earlier. He was on the point of believing it again.

The doubts expressed back in 1788 were, in fact, well-founded. Without free public education (finally instituted only under the Third Republic), the Revolution would amount to nothing. This conviction was shared by Condorcet, who played a decisive role on the Public Education Committee later set up by the Legislative Assembly. Until the Declaration of Human Rights was universally known by heart, the new elite would rule over the disparate masses of the populous neighborhoods (masses industry would unite in the following century under the name of proletariat). Chamfort now spoke to Talleyrand of a "children's catechism"; Talleyrand took up the idea in the "Report on Public Education" he delivered to the Constituent Assembly in September—one of the lame devil's rare disinterested acts during the Revolution. This would be the prompter's last "speech" to the Assembly, and his most alarmed. It was a sorry conclusion to the Constituent Assembly, whose crucial and lasting impact Chamfort tended to overlook, in spite of his own contribution to it.

To prevent a similar drift in the new legislature (known as the Legislative Assembly), Chamfort ran for election. The royalist press renewed its attacks, and Marat took up his crusade against the election. "So we'll see our electors, in the pay of the court, continue to fill the nation's Senate with all those double-faced men with great dexterity and lungs—such as Chamfort, that cheap sycophant to Condé, whom he generously abandoned the moment he saw him relieved of his fortune."[14] Chamfort never recovered from this accusation—wrong, moreover—by Marat, who hated academicians since that day in 1783 when the Academy of Science derided his experiments on fire and light, shattering his dream of outdoing Newton. Chamfort was defeated in the Paris primaries by Brissot and disappeared from the electoral scene (as did Beaumarchais, whose name no longer sparked any interest). The Legislative Assembly would drift along without him.

The election went to the moderates—two hundred sixty Feuillants, one hundred thirty-six Jacobins, and a vague center. The Revolution paused for breath. France—as Chamfort himself admitted—was an "exhausted patient."[15] The Constituent Assembly disqualified its own members from running for the legislature, out of Rousseau-like purity, which meant that Robespierre and Sieyès withdrew to the provinces for a while. Chamfort took advantage of the calm to leave the Palais-Royal and move to 83, rue Neuve-des-Petits-Champs. Reduced to his *Mercure* salary and to royalties from *Tableaux de la Révolution*, he let his servant go and hired a housekeeper whom Sélis described as "very attached and respectful, but strict and penny-pinching." Chamfort advised his local district committee of the move and prepared to lead the modest life-style of a revolutionary. Ginguené had an apartment two floors up, where Chamfort dined in the evenings. Ginguené—who also wrote for *Le Mercure* and who was very attached to both the Revolution and to his wife, Nancy—was therefore treated to the best of Chamfort. "Perhaps few men could exude as much charm as he in intimate company," said Ginguené. Number one among the disciples then surrounding the writer, Ginguené was too fragile for the Roman breastplate bequeathed by his "master." Described by Guizot as somewhat provincial, touchy yet upright, this drab and humorless shadow was nevertheless the solid friend Mirabeau had not been.

20. DOING AWAY WITH THE SELF

He became repentant with a violent passion, and this led him to put on the clothes of the mob, as his kind of hairshirt. He had a bad conscience because he had not taken revenge.

Nietzsche
The Gay Science

After two years of legislative maneuvering and personal plotting beyond the grasp of the populace, 1792 marked a return to moral issues. The disappointing outcome of 1791 convinced Chamfort that everything had to start over at zero, that the tawdry past had to be left behind, that the Revolution had to be *incarnated* rather than built. As Marx and Engels pointed out, if man is shaped by circumstances, then the circumstances should be shaped humanely. But individuals who attempt to reform "circumstances" inevitably reproduce the defects of their own upbringing. For there is never a pause in the human race, to the great dismay of revolutions. The ceaseless flow of acts, speeches, and quarrels means that the pivotal generation responsible for changing the world can never be "purified." It passes on the flaws in spite of itself.

Ideally, republican principles could be taught to the sons of citizens, providing everyone with what the Grassins school had offered Chamfort. This generation, once educated, could then undertake the true, grand revolution. In reality, however, one had to deal with politicians "corrupted" by the past, tainted by the spirit of *Les liaisons dangereuses* and the vices of the perfected civilization, or by a last-minute conversion to liberal values. This situation provoked a radical, almost religious reaction in Chamfort, inducing him to adopt his most rigorous agenda to date.

He decided that his renunciation of literary feudalism was insufficient, and thus proceeded to strip away his last titles, the remains of his aristocratic skin. "He passionately monitored all excesses, even his own," wrote Roederer.[1] "He fulminated against stipends until he no longer had a stipend . . . against all idolizing, servility and courtesy until there no longer existed a single man who dared try to please him, and against extreme opulence until he no longer had any friends rich enough to propose a carriage or invite him to supper. . . . 'I won't believe in the revolution,' he often said in 1791 and 1792, 'as long as I still see coaches and gigs overturning pedestrians.'"[2]

Chamfort's style prevented him from communicating with the populace, so he changed it. The voice changed, dress and hair evolved, the metamorphosis took place with noticeable thoroughness. The writer who had been mistaken for an aristocrat the day the Bastille fell could no longer be distinguished from a common sansculotte. Chamfort thus succumbed to a new and insidious form of social "charlatanism." *La Chronique Scandaleuse* revealed, "We encountered him the day before yesterday, at nine o'clock in the evening, in the gutter of the Rue Neuve-des-Petits-Champs, composing, declaming and gesticulating like a fanatic."[3] The republican author of the *Considérations* lost all self-consciousness. Naked as Adam, he predicted the end of all buying and selling, commanding and obeying. He was now closer than ever to Rousseau, for whom everything was fake and unhealthy, including beauty, nourishment, feelings, pleasure. He renounced the remaining pretenses which enabled him to survive and rejected the immoral theater of the world. Chamfort had gone from ill-humored accomplice of the Ancien Régime to enthusiastic victim of the new one.

"He ultimately raged against frivolity, wittiness, and even literature, until all his acquaintances, concerned solely with civic issues, were indifferent to his writing, his comedy and his conversation," continued Roederer. "He grew impatient on hearing his *Marchand de Smyrne* praised as a revolutionary comedy. He even waxed indignant [about it]." Having purged his needs, Chamfort now purged—like the Jacobins in 1791—his friends. Culture was limited to ceremonies staged by David and to plays by Molière rewritten in patriotic terms.[4] The French Revolution, influenced by Antiquity, Christianity, and America, represented a watershed in human history, where books would be less useful than equality, work, and "strong and simple" morals.[5] History and literature, those elitist and narcissistic preoccupations, could even be harmful (it was pointed out that ancient philosophers had never managed to prevent despotism). The Revolution would become its own art, its own stage, its own audience. By establishing physical fellowship and by *making* history, the Revolution would offer instant glory to all.

Chamfort glorified the spirit of sacrifice everywhere. His friend Chabanon had cheered the rebellion of blacks in Santo Domingo which had led to his own ruin, so Chamfort devoted an article to Chabanon in *Le Mercure*. La Harpe rejected two of Ginguené's articles in December 1791, so Chamfort resigned from *Le Mercure* in solidarity, thus losing his main source of income. This impolitic decision was guided by a higher, almost sacred, moral code. "I am everything, others are nothing—such is despotism, aristocracy and their supporters. I am the other, the other is me—such is the people's system and its supporters."[6] He wanted to become morally untouchable, his outer shell of altruism recalling the armor he had donned under Louis XV. The individualist became a "sharer," the cynic dropped his remaining masks, the egotist renounced the obsessive *self*. He now said *we* at every opportunity. At fifty-two, the superman admired by Mirabeau had become a candidate for republican sainthood. There was a powerful resurgence of that extraordinary plan to start humankind afresh following a cataclysmic flood, which Sieyès and Condorcet had successfully converted into a rational project. But once again, the volcanic Chamfort only wreaked havoc on himself.

Despite anti-Christian statements, Chamfort's "rebirth" strongly resembles a conversion, itself the apostasy of his true origins. For the resentment flowing from political powerlessness led him to yet another manifestation of "self-hatred." Unable to perform the true, grand revolution, Chamfort adopted the ascetic ideal, which Nietzsche compared to "pious debauchery." The rejection of his past and the wholesale sacrifice of his own history represented a magic equivalent for the inaccessible return to "natural" man. The other spark behind Chamfort's eruption of altruism involved becoming a nobody, in order to finally become someone whose flesh and blood would no longer carry any trace of social division. After dreaming of the equality of the few within the liberal aristocratic milieu, then of liberty for all within the Nation, he now hoped for equality in universal anonymity. After wanting to enrich everyone in 1788 (including Vaudreuil), then transferring money from the clergy to the people in 1790, Chamfort now became a pauper all by himself.

This new metamorphosis—one of the most spectacular during the entire Revolution—provoked royalist fury. As a cynic, Chamfort had comforted the royalists' poor opinion of "patriots." As a model of morality, he became a convert to be eliminated, a Saint Paul of egalitarianism. They had feared him under the Ancien Régime; no longer fearing him, they detested him. His fall outraged them, as though it deprived them of the pleasure of punishing him. An anonymous pamphlet accused him of aligning humanity with his own illegitimacy and failure,[7] of being a "wandering zombie" seeking to spread his affliction, someone who was "useless in life" and jealous of happiness and who wanted to impose equality when he himself was of unequaled ingratitude. The anonymous author warned Chamfort: "The men, women, and even children led astray by you will hound your corpse." Meanwhile, Marat also attacked this fellow sufferer, who just five years earlier had sprawled in Vaudreuil's mansion and who, despite his current frenzy of sacrifices, remained unknown to the activist sansculottes running the Paris district committees (and was even more anonymous to the rest of the French people, over 80 percent of whom were still peasants). Chamfort never really knew to which social class he belonged and had groped among various revolutionary ideologies, but now he finally glimpsed a way to end such wavering: he would get closer to the people, perhaps take their place, regain the role he had temporarily dropped in 1791—that of history's special representative.

War

War distracted everyone's attention, however. Once the emigrés had called for desertion, Brissot called for war, and war became the key issue of the second revolution. The Assembly wanted to force the king to choose between royalist Koblenz and patriotic Paris, the Girondin faction dreamed of liberating Austrian-controlled Brabant, and the Parisian sansculotte districts wanted to spread the "French disease" abroad. Even Louis XVI thought that a conflict (which he expected to be catastrophic) would give him the opportunity to intervene as savior. Everyone wanted war, except for Chamfort and a Jacobin minority led by Robespierre. Chamfort still hoped that the Revolution would "travel round the world"; in 1790, he had even suggested that Africa be colonized by prisoners and the unemployed in order to spread it. But the time wasn't ripe, for the Minister of Foreign Affairs (De Lessart) and top military leaders were hostile to the people, while the civil service was infested by royalist clerks. Chamfort "laughed pathetically" on seeing the patriotic party bank on such doubtful troops. Since the enemy was clearly within, he advised remaining wary ("[Wariness] is to the revolution what jealousy is to love," claimed Robespierre). Chamfort even feared victory more than defeat. The comte de Narbonne, who had formerly dragged him to Holland and was now the Minister of War, advocated (along with the Feuillants) a limited conflict against the emigrés, which would provide Louis XVI with easy prestige. Chamfort knew, via friends who were "highly informed on affairs in the Netherlands," that in such a case Austria wouldn't budge. ". . . For a month they've been telling me four days in advance of what turns out to be verified by events," he added. Chamfort was a pacificist by negation: "The Feuillants are fools, the Jacobins are madmen."[8] He suggested waiting. "I suspect that all this is a problem with no solution, a confused and troubled tragedy, the resolution of which depends on some deus ex machina out of Euripedes."[9]

Chamfort was nevertheless completely isolated. The people preferred war to wariness. Brissot, who wanted to prove that Louis XVI was colluding with foreign elements, admitted, "My only fear is that we *not* be betrayed." Such thinking escaped Chamfort's rational comprehension, and here he showed striking lucidity. Even Condorcet would declare that "France will take up arms with regret, yet with fervor." Once again in the minority, Chamfort now paid for his sacrifices. "Chamfort has only three months to live," wrote the royalist broadsheet *A Deux Liards, à Deux Liards Mon Journal*.[10] The bourgeoisie of 1789 split over the short war proposed by Narbonne and the pacifism preached by Barnave, thereby losing the initiative. The lower classes were forbidden to gather by the Assembly but rose up against price hikes and the scarcity of sugar. So the right also felt that the enemy was within. "The Huns are among us," wrote Mallet du Pan. "Fanatics from your region are causing you a lot of bother," Chamfort wrote at that time to a deputy (probably Condorcet). "But the disgust with which formerly decent schemers and rogues inspire me here, fills my soul with an even more melancholy feeling."[11]

The queen then had Narbonne dismissed, fomenting a crisis for her own ends. The Assembly, spurred by Brissot's warrior mystique, ordered the massive manufacture of pikes. De Lessart was hauled before the high court and was replaced at Foreign Affairs by General Dumouriez, who promised war.

"Nobody likes armed missionaries," warned Robespierre. But the Revolution ignored the "wary." Outwardly calling the shots, Brissot had Roland appointed to the Ministry of Interior and Clavière to Internal Revenue. Thus the Gironde faction, in existence for less than six months, found itself in power.

By convincing the Constituent Assembly to declare its own members ineligible for reelection, Robespierre paved the way for a

Legislative Assembly full of inexperienced deputies. All those in the patriot party still attended the Jacobin Club, but even prior to the debate on war differences in attitude (rather than policy) became apparent. The "Girondins" led by Brissot and Vergniaud believed in a certain idea of happiness based on liberty, civic equality, and individual talent—perhaps because they were excellent speakers and hailed from sunny climes. The deputies that Robespierre would unite under the "Montagne" banner were mostly jurists and lawyers, too, yet they were less optimistic and less affable. They exploited the least weakness in the conduct of the war by the Girondins—whose federalism, based on Swiss and American models, made the mistake of weakening a highly centralized nation. Robespierre and company also fanned the growing jealousy of sansculottes in Paris. The conflict at this point was barely perceptible, however, and, while Girondins held all the strategic posts, the governmental strongman was the ambitious, bold, and highly supple General Dumouriez. In 1765, Dumouriez had proposed one plan suggesting the annexation of Corsica and another granting it independence. His secret plan now was to limit the influence of the left by adopting its policies, in hopes of one day reconciling everyone through his own commanding presence.

Siding with the Gironde

Another incident brought war nearer. In March 1792, the cautious Leopold II died and left the Austrian throne to his son Francis II. The new emperor, a warmonger like his aunt Marie-Antoinette, rendered Chamfort's arguments obsolete. The revolution could now only conquer or perish, and it opted for war. On a motion by the king (as required by the compromise Chamfort had suggested to Mirabeau), the Assembly voted for war on April 20; and the Revolution remained at war right up until the fall of the Empire. Six hundred thousand volunteers presented themselves to liberate the Brabant and conquer the Austrian Netherlands. The seven recalcitrant deputies were totally isolated, and most ambassadors were replaced. "M. de Chamfort is being mentioned for the Ratisbon diet," wrote Le Mercure.[12] This would have been a strategic post, given emigré counterdiplomacy conducted there by Breteuil, but Chamfort was never summoned to confront his former patron.

In Chamfort's opinion, the Gironde's merit lay in placing "popular" ministers in the king's government. It also promoted a revolution able to question its own ends, thereby halting the slide toward self-destruction. Chamfort, however, did not associate the Gironde with fine Assembly speakers such as Vergniaud, Guadet, and Gensonné, spokesmen for deputies mostly born in Bordeaux and Marseille. Rather, his Gironde was composed of its theorists and instigators, who would swiftly link up with major journalists and what remained of the Parisian "intelligentsia."

Chamfort's Gironde was the one headed by Brissot (whom he had met in 1784 in Mirabeau's entourage), coordinated by Cabanis (Mirabeau's personal physician), backed by Roederer and Condorcet as well as by Lauzun (the queen's former gallant) and Clavière (the financier with whom Chamfort had prepared the plebeian count's return from England). This Gironde reunited men who had spent ten years preparing and sparking the Revolution.

Other contacts were made at the Nine Sisters' masonic lodge, many of its members having joined the Gironde. But the Gironde inherited Mirabeau's confusion as well. It declared war in the name of peace and inaugurated the guillotine in the name of human rights (since it made death mercifully swift). "The Country" became a goddess charged with translating an expanding "French culture" into action (on the model of a global "Roman culture"). This somewhat hollow rhetoric found no echo within political clubs (the Gironde remaining a strictly parliamentary organization) and dampened Chamfort's enthusiasm. He would occasionally back Robespierre and the Montagne faction, often regretting the dissension between the two groups. The Gironde nevertheless revived a man made sick by clubs, and who was neither deputy nor journalist. It appealed to a citizen who could no longer make a place for himself between the Constitutionals (whom he disowned) and Marat (who hated him), a prompter who was unemployed following Mirabeau's death and Talleyrand's departure for London. Chamfort was just recovering from his attack of self-sacrifice; he became a "Girondin" more through personal affinity than through political choice. Such affinities, however, meant a lot to a group that would shortly be accused of cronyism.

This critical juncture provided the setting for yet another episode in Chamfort's twenty-five-year-long conflict with La Harpe.

Politics had nothing to do with it; the two men had followed more or less the same trajectory, from moderate columns in *Le Mercure* to renewed attempts to defend the cause of playwrights, with stints in the Jacobin club. Despite their disagreement over the fate of the Académie, Chamfort even considered Bébé to be a good patriot (who, it is true, claimed he was unable to think unless he was wearing a revolutionary red cap). La Harpe's rejection of Giguené's articles and Chamfort's resignation from *Le Mercure* were grounds enough for a new outbreak of war. Late in 1791, La Harpe solicited subscriptions in the hope of starting a paying course on literature (like Chamfort, he was bankrupt when royal stipends were abolished). "La Harpe's mind is going begging," commented the advocate of total pauperization. "Chamfort has that of a thief," retorted Bébé, not forgetting (with good reason) the rumors of plagiarism that dogged *Mustapha*. Early in 1792 the two mongrels were sinking their teeth into one another again, under the bemused gaze of the royalists. Chamfort accused La Harpe of still owing ten sous to the "fruit-lady" who plucked him newborn from the gutter, while La Harpe accused Chamfort of never having paid his wet-nurse. That, at least, was the version given by *Le Journal-Pie*, a counterrevolutionary paper that summed up "their irreconcilable hatred" in its own way: "Chamfort fully understands that La Harpe is talented, but he won't admit it; La Harpe knows that Chamfort is intelligent, but he denies it. So that on the one hand intelligence is jealous of talent, and on the other, talent is jealous of intelligence." As could have been predicted as early as 1763, the more tenacious of the two would be La Harpe, who continued to attack Chamfort even after his death. Beaumarchais used to say of La Harpe that "if wounded, he would bleed bile."

The Journalist Routed

The war—the real one—swiftly turned catastrophic. The poorly prepared troops were decimated. Entire companies went over to the enemy, and the duc de Lauzun (who, along with Chamfort, had been one of Talleyrand's regular dinner guests), now a general under the name of Biron, beat a retreat at Mons. Once again, Chamfort had been precociously right—military commanders did not really want to win. Unable to buck the army, the Gironde had one of its own men appointed Minister of War. And out of rivalry with Dumouriez, it charged La Fayette with regaining the offensive—a tactic straight out of Mirabeau. Dumouriez approached Chamfort, among other Gironde sympathizers, and on May 1 appointed him editor-in-chief of *La Gazette de France*. "The editor I've chosen will provide patriots with a solid guarantee of the soundness of my principles and the purity of my intentions," wrote the general, who in fact needed to provide such guarantees, even though his policies happened to be more coherent than those of the Gironde.[13] Chamfort's editorship of *La Gazette* effectively meant left-wing support for the bellicose Dumouriez. The paper had been founded in the seventeenth century by Théophraste Renaudot, France's first journalist. Its seventeen government censors, who had successfully masked the fall of the Bastille from readers, were let go. The publication was placed under the aegis of the Foreign Affairs ministry, became a daily, and recruited better contributors. Talleyrand, on unofficial mission to London, was named editor of the English desk.

But *La Gazette*'s budget was bled dry by secret operations undertaken by Dumouriez and Roland (Minister of the Interior), each of whom had a network of agents in France and Belgium. Victimized by this ministerial rivalry, Chamfort was obliged to make unwilling "and therefore disasterous" cutbacks.[14] *La Gazette* disintegrated into factions, became depressed by the rout, found itself short of handlers, and lost subscribers. Talleyrand no longer received his copy, and editors fought over proofs. Moreover, only royalists noted the leftward shift of the paper edited by Chamfort. *A Deux Liards, à Deux Liards Mon Journal* wrote, "He congratulates himself on seeing Jacobins at the head of the Post Office. . . . Poor fool! Can't you see that nobody wants them anymore!"[15] These attacks—accompanied by outlandish rumors of his imminent departure for Koblenz (wishful thinking on the part of the right, which couldn't stand Chamfort anywhere)—could not mask the obvious fact that the academician Chamfort was unsuited to turn a ministerial publication into a firebrand. It was increasingly edited by an orthodox Girondin, Lebrun-Tondu.

Dumouriez's scheming exacerbated Chamfort's disenchantment. The general remained in contact with the right through his mistress (Rivarol's sister), in hopes of one day emerging as a unifying strongman. In May 1792, Bonnecarère, Dumouriez's close associate and Chamfort's immediate superior, was accused of dishonest dealings by the virtuous Minister of the Interior Roland. On June 4, an "Orléanist" plot was decried in the Legislative Assembly, the plotters being Dumouriez, Bonnecarère, Talleyrand, Lebrun-Tondu, and Noël (another journalist at *La Gazette*). The deputies laughed at the revelation, but it spurred Chamfort—barely out of his puritanical phase—into resigning. "Time is short and the house is burning," he wrote to the ministry, complaining of the total disorganization of his offices. The Gironde, discredited by the military defeat, was removed from government by the king. On the same day Chamfort confirmed his resignation, made public on June 16. That was the day Dumouriez, who had hoped to profit from the situation, was himself forced to resign. Chamfort's time at *La Gazette* was as brief as the Gironde's reign.

The incident confirmed Chamfort's old suspicions. The government had done nothing, for ministers were mere guests in the "worm-eaten" Tuileries palace, whose owners were in league with Austria. Once in power, the Gironde discovered it was *powerless*, as had Chamfort at the newspaper. Defeat brought austerity to the fore again—"the Country is a being to which sacrifices must be made," wrote Roland, the Girondin to whom Chamfort felt closest (and who had created a scandal by arriving at a King's Council without buckled slippers). Seeking some breathing room, the Brissot faction bypassed Robespierre and appealed to the Parisian districts, offering La Fayette as scapegoat. From the front, La Fayette was pressing the Assembly into a show of strength. But the populous outlying neighborhoods (with the tacit support of the Paris Commune) stole the march on everyone on June 20, 1792. They forced their way into the Salle du Manège and then invaded the Tuileries palace with the verbal support of several Girondins, including the former minister Clavière. Encountering no resistance, the mob got as far as the Oeil-de-Boeuf salon, where the king was in discussion with three of his ministers. Mme. Elisabeth was mistaken for the queen and let herself be insulted by the intruders without letting on, even though she was not fond of her sister-in-law. Louis XVI was forced to don a red cap and drink wine from the bottle. Marie-Antoinette was discovered in the Council Chamber, where the people stared at her as though she were some strange animal. The king stood firm for once, maintaining the Feuillant ministers appointed to replace the Girondins. On returning from America, Chateaubriand found Chamfort and Ginguené "delighted by the events of June 20th." They would soon be disillusioned.

Fear

The Girondins were the big losers of the day. The king had been subjected to indignities, like a suffering Christ. The Assembly, humiliated, called for revenge. La Fayette returned hastily from the front and paraded through Paris on horseback, while the queen still held out hope that Prussian and Hessian troops would arrive. Chamfort, fearing a coup d'état, lay low. But he lived near the palace. "Anxiety over the Tuileries conspiracy prevented him from sleeping," wrote Dumont, one of Mirabeau's former collaborators. "He thought he was on a mine which would explode any minute." The Gironde, strong when victorious but feeble under attack, trembled.

Louis XVI, obsessed by the fate of Charles I of England (the absolute monarch beheaded by Cromwell) and plagued by nightmares, nevertheless allowed the queen to reject the show of strength suggested by La Fayette (whom she detested). Prussia's entry into the war ruined the king's last chances. On July 7 Abbé Lamourette successfully moved that the deputies all embrace one another as a sign of reconciliation, and on July 11 a proclamation announced, "The Country is in Danger." Brunswick, as head of the foreign coalition, threatened the "total overthrow" of Paris. This sent patriotism soaring to delirious heights. France kissed and made up, finding its scattered sons again (but losing Chateaubriand, who emigrated to Belgium). The first campaign had nevertheless taught Chamfort a lesson, and he now urged that the army be purged. "He knew both the official measures and the inside story," wrote Helena-Maria Williams, the English poet who had arrived in early August. "Thus he was seriously worried about the future. He approved of me, me with my somewhat naive enthusiasm of the time; but he often warned me that I should remember that I was not destined solely to see liberty triumph."[16] He sensed that the Revolution was fighting for survival.

On August 3, however, forty-seven out of forty-eight Paris districts voted to oust the king. The popular militia marched in from the provinces, singing *La Marseillaise,* and the Paris Commune overtly organized insurrection. Tamed by the events of June 20, the Gironde negotiated with the king in an attempt to recover its ministries. Robespierre and Danton seized this opportunity to appeal to the people. Time was running out for the king.

21. THE MONARCHY'S DEATH THROES

These days, Chamfort's great grandson would be a bolshevik.

   Echo de la France (May 1944)

When militant sansculottes sounded the alarm during the night of August 9, Chamfort was ill and remained at home. The next day's event would be recounted to him by his friend Roederer. Roederer, who had been present during the June 20 sacking of the Tuileries palace, was once again present in his role as syndic (i.e., administrative head) of the Seine Department. He theoretically had authority over the police, but in fact had little control over the Paris Commune, which that night had been replaced by the Insurrectional Commune. Since dawn, Roederer had been trying to convince the queen and Mme. Elisabeth that it would be pointless to resist. The commander of the defending forces was summoned to City Hall, where he was killed and tossed in the river. So Roederer himself, dressed in green, reviewed the troops. He read the law authorizing them to quell riots—in a tone discouraging them from doing so. Louis XVI, suffering from lack of sleep, poorly coiffed, and advancing like a sleepwalker, was greeted by cries of "Long live the King!" from the Swiss guards, while the artillery company shouted "Long live the Nation!" From there the king reached the terrace of the Feuillant monastery, where the crowd recognized him and shouted abuse—"Down with the fat pig!" The pallid king turned back to his soldiers, but all he could say to them was, "I like the National Guard." Refusing to fire on their "brothers," the cannoneers jammed their weapons and joined the crowd. Roederer advised the royal family to retreat to the Salle du Manège. The king consulted with the queen, who balked. "Sire, all of Paris is on the march," insisted Roederer. The king finally gave the order to "March," demonstrating authority only in retreat. Greeted by Gironde orator Vergniaud, the royal family was installed in the loge reserved for the paper *Le Logographe*. They were occupying these few square feet in this shrine to popular sovereignty when they heard the first cannon shots ring out.

Despite the resistance put up by gentlemen commanded by an eight-four-year-old maréchal, the assault succeeded. And degenerated. Swiss mercenaries were castrated, and the journalist Suleau wound up with his head on a pike. The attackers suffered four hundred dead but inflicted six hundred on the defenders. Grouvelle, on duty in his district, made his debut as commissioner and grave digger. "There were corpses there just awaiting his orders," said Chamfort, "which is what happens when executive authority forces sovereignty to take recourse in revolutionary power."[1]

While the night had been "horrid," the day's events paid off this time. The king was held hostage, and the army fell under the surveillance of the commissioners. The Paris Commune obtained the powers to police the city, Narbonne went into hiding, and Beaumarchais was arrested for weapons dealing. Roederer was accused of having ordered the Swiss to fire and was hidden by Lebrun (Chamfort's former schoolmate at Grassins, and a future consul) until he was cleared. This first Terror was built on the ruins of the monarchy. The Assembly had to share power with the Commune, and the Gironde had to share ministries with Danton.

The events of August 10 freed Chamfort from his fear of a coup d'état. The king had been neutralized, and the Legislative Assembly voted for the election (this time by universal suffrage) of a convention which would recast the Constitution. The dramatic outcome was once again imposed "from above," leaving Chamfort a mere spectator. "Without being gay, I'm not exactly sad," he wrote two days later. "This doesn't mean that calm has returned or that the people have not again this night hunted down all aristocrats, including journalists sympathetic to their cause; but one has to make the best of untoward events of this sort." He could point to several noble gestures: the National Guard rescued a hundred Swiss mercenaries from massacre. Roland and Clavière were once again part of the government, with Grouvelle acting as secretary (three years after having been secretary to Condé). Although Lebrun-Tondu had wrested *La Gazette* from him, Chamfort was happy to see Lebrun-Tondu named Minister of Foreign Affairs. He was nevertheless worried by a people "who had talked about their sublime Constitution for three years, but who are now going to destroy it and who, in truth, have managed so far to organize only rebellion. . . . Although," he added, "that's better than nothing."[2]

Visiting Toppled Kings

When Chamfort went out on August 12 to view the battlefield, the weather was fine and the corpses were gone. Arriving at place des Victoires, he found that the statue of Louis XIV had been pulled down. At place Vendome, he and hundreds of other onlookers circled around bronzes of this same Sun-King and his horse, brought down on David's orders. No one uttered a word on behalf of the absolute monarch who still reigned at the beginning of the century and who was still admired just twenty years earlier. Arriving at place Louis XV (now place de la Concorde), Chamfort continued as far as the Tuileries. "It was a spectacle hard to imagine," he wrote. "The people filled the gardens, as they might do at the Prato [i.e., the Prater] in Vienna or the gardens in Potsdam; the crowd inundated the apartments stained with the blood of their friends and brothers, pierced by cannon balls."[3] Some rummaged through the queen's furnishings, others tried on the king's clothes. The people installed itself in history, making one of Chamfort's oldest dreams come true. Yet only Catherine de Medici, another foreign queen, was denounced, as though Marie-Antoinette no longer existed. The Florentine sovereign's influence on the weak Charles IX and on the Saint Bartholomew massacre was decried, and the past was discussed with an attention to detail hard to believe today. "A man in rags told the anecdote about the Duchess of Marlborough's gloves and bowl having caused a war," recounted Chamfort. "But he was wrong, they resulted in one war less." The writer, however, no longer wanting to be taken for an aristocrat as he had following the fall of the Bastille, kept quiet. "Moreover, the mistake was so slight and the intention so good," he added, commenting on the anecdote to a friend (probably Sieyès, who had been maintaining a nervous silence for over a year).

Yet the Capet dynasty had been so lucky, so successful at hanging on throughout eight centuries, and so skillful at leading the Revolution's finest elements astray (from Mirabeau to Barnave to Chamfort himself) that the monarchy's downfall left Chamfort dazed. It was hard to believe that the king, queen, and Mme. Elisabeth (from whom he had just received, by disturbing coincidence, back pay of five hundred livres on the day of the attack) had been forced to leave the Tuileries palace. "Would you like to know how many centuries opinion has evolved in the past two months?" he wrote to this same friend. "Remember the symptoms I mentioned of the French obsession with royalty, which I proved by the ease with which the Jacobin dancers under my windows switched from the tune of *Ca ira* to the tune of 'Long Live Henry IV!' Well, that tune is now banned, and at the very moment I am speaking, that king's statue is on the ground. . . . It required nothing less than the current court to perform such a miracle; but finally it managed it— may it be praised!" This happy ending even inspired the following joke: "I've been told that you've been mentioned as tutor to the prince royal," Chamfort wrote to his correspondent. "But there's one problem: How will you know which trade to teach your pupil?" Several hours later, the king and the "Austrian panther" were im- prisoned in the Temple.

Victory lent Chamfort wings. The fall of the Bastille had conse- crated freedom, and now the events of August 10 announced equal- ity for all *minus* one—the king. Ridden of unfair competition, the republic no longer made people afraid. Citizens changed their name from Leroi ("King") to Laloi ("Law"), and decks of cards dropped their jacks (or "valets"). This second revolution banished "traitors"—Barnave was brought before the High Court, La Fayette delivered himself to the Austrians. The cry raised ten years ago had finally been heard: society was really going to start afresh. Chamfort would no longer be alone in personally creating the new man. Any enemy of the Revolution was now a personal enemy.

"He often got out of hand," wrote Ginguené. "He reformulated popular opprobrium with energy and originality, [having gotten] into the habit of speaking out in clubs, of supporting his opinion to excess."[4] Abbé Morellet confirms such behavior. "He looked on the burning of chateaus and the cruel laws against emigrés and those who stayed, I wouldn't say with joy, but with a great deal of toler- ance, considering them at the very least as necessary evils."[5] A revo- lutionary tribunal was formed to judge aristocratic crimes relating to August 10, with the families of emigrés being held hostage. While the events of June 20 had been unpopular, those of August 10 were well received, and the provinces backed Paris against Brunswick's manifesto. As the guillotine was being oiled up, Chamfort admitted, "These days you have to be cruel out of humaneness."[6]

The Rolands' Librarian

This time Chamfort was more enthusiastic than Helena-Maria Williams. The two were invited to the Bituabés,[7] an elderly, delightful, and fervently pro-Robespierre couple. There Chamfort drank to victory. "He was still young, she was pretty, he was French and a poet," wrote Thiébault, who added, "Never was he more brilliant."[8] Helena-Maria Williams asked Chamfort's opinion of Abbé Delille, and he replied, *"Un moulin à vers"* [A word mill]. Asked about the state of volunteers at the front, he composed this rhyme—his final antiliterary effort, his first patriotic outburst:

Troupes guerrières
Sur vos drapeaux
Placez ces couplets:
Paix aux chaumières,
Guerre aux châteaux.

Valiant soldiers
Emblazon your banners
With this best of mottoes:
Peace to cottages,
War on chateaus.

In recompense for such enthusiasm, Roland offered Chamfort the directorship of the Bibliothèque Nationale. Chamfort declined, his friends insisted, and the farce began again. "Accept it, friend, and settle into a post which is to your taste and which my wife and I envy you," Roland wrote to Chamfort. "Think about it and come sup with me one evening, we will talk about it again. I am the minister of money, you the minister of intelligence."[9] On August 19, Chamfort wound up agreeing to share the post with Carra, one of the leaders of the August 10 events whose paper, *Les Annales Patriotiques,* was read widely in the army for its strong stance. The two men shared the director's apartment at 49, rue de Richelieu as well as the eight thousand livres of income. This was a "severe cutback" from pre-Equality salaries but represented a step up for our moralist. Roland's wife, Manon, claimed that her husband had never met Chamfort prior to appointing him.[10] This is unlikely, however, in view of the above letter from the "French Franklin," who already had shown himself to be a rigorous civil servant under the Ancien Régime and who tirelessly rallied a maximum number of journalists and important supporters to the Gironde cause. It is nevertheless true that Chamfort saw above all Mme. Roland, the dominant personality within the couple. Beautiful, extremely sensitive and serious, envisioning a Gironde geared more toward Sparta than toward Bordeaux, this daughter of an engraver on place Dauphine grew up in the religion of Rousseau and Plutarch. Mme. Roland was by turns mystical, Cartesian, Jansenist, stoic, deist, and revolutionary, but was always wholehearted and passionate. She was the idol of the young Girondins, the soul of a party she received twice a week in the greatest simplicity, seated at a table covered with papers and pamphlets (a salon her enemies from the Montagne faction and the Commune would soon denounce as a temple of luxury and vice). Nicknamed "Queen Coco," and known more for her character than her conversation (though speaking with a purity that made her language ring with a "type of music"), Mme. Roland received Chamfort at home and at the ministry more for his intellectual qualities than for his librarian's responsibilities. The hour of sacrifice was over; it was time that intelligent work begin.

Chamfort, however, barely had the time to take up his post. For August 10 had provoked new desertions of officers and divisions from the ranks. Longwy was surrounded by the Prussian army (the best in Europe), and the front was overrun by advancing Austrians (battle-hardened in recent campaigns against the Turks). The rout nevertheless provoked a new patriotic outburst, even among the "intelligentsia." Church bells were melted down, and Carra demanded "pikes, pikes, and more pikes" across all eight pages of his paper. Already anticipating the government's retreat to Blois, Roland gave Chamfort the responsibility of spreading yet another "French disease" among the enemy—dissension within the ranks.

Words Mightier Than Bullets

Discreet by nature, Chamfort's propaganda campaign remains little known.[11] Chamfort was nevertheless the perfect choice for this shadowy war. He had been struck by the role played by desertion among royal troops during the initial successes of 1789. Poor pay and a handful of newspapers slipped into the barracks had been enough to topple the monarchy. And no one was better at seducing the enemy than Chamfort. Maret and Colchen (two civil servants in the Foreign Affairs Ministry who headed Belgian spy operations) informed him of Brunswick's overconfidence and of the dysentery ravaging the troops. Chamfort thereupon devised clever propaganda playing on both positive and negative attitudes. Convinced that "the time is coming when foreigners will wish to become French," he suggested publishing the letter of a German deserter who described his new life in France in idyllic terms. At the same time, posters relying on the extreme "stupidity and ignorance" of the Austro-Prussians were to be put up near the front, in which deserters were promised pensions based on their rank and payable to their wives in case of death. Such measures were against the law, but the "minister of intelligence" enjoyed the confidence of both Roland and Lebrun-Tondu. Did the government execute Chamfort's proposals? We don't know. But, in fact, desertions within enemy ranks increased in September 1792. Some archive may one day bring to light this counteroffensive (the first victorious one in four months), revealing its exact role in a psychological war already waged by Vaudreuil on behalf of the princes' army in order to demoralize the patriotic ranks. It is nevertheless easy to imagine Chamfort's pleasure at finally being useful as a writer.

Such success explains his amazing confidence even as Paris was quaking before the enemy advance. He was dining with Lebrun-Tondu on September 2, when the fall of Verdun was announced. The minister's guests paled, but Chamfort remained unflustered. Enjoined to explain himself, Chamfort replied, "Yes, you're right, they say there are Prussians around."[12] His confidence was mistaken for indifference at a time when indifference was criminal. At that very moment, Danton was calling for "Daring, yet more daring, and more daring still," galvanizing the convention and the volunteers leaving for the front.

Hours later, the mob attacked those arrested on August 10. A hundred and fifty priests in the Abbey and Carmes prisons, accused of wanting to open Paris to the Prussians, had their throats cut. The massacre continued in the Force, Conciergerie, and Chatelet prisons, and again at the Abbey, where three hundred prisoners died under various types of torture. The killings—organized by the Paris Commune, encouraged by Marat and tacitly approved by Danton—lasted until September 6. It took Roland and Brissot over twenty-four hours to protest. Chamfort kept silent. "I dare not suggest that he approved [the events of] September 2nd," wrote Abbé Morellet, but Ginguené admitted that Chamfort "came to terms with cruel scenes."[13] Chamfort didn't want anything to hobble the republic, which had yet to be proclaimed—the idea had obsessed him for too long to be sacrificed at the last minute. Mme. Roland was more lucid. She rebuked the minister of intelligence for his "excessive confidence" when she learned that the Paris Commune had targeted her husband. "You're taking things to extremes," replied Chamfort, "because, placed in the midst of the commotion, you think such action is widespread. . . . Those people are discrediting themselves through their own excesses. They can't undo eighteen centuries of Enlightenment."[14]

Just as war had saved him from self-destruction, the September massacres appeased Chamfort's aggressiveness. The time had come to withdraw into the hushed atmosphere of the Bibliothèque Nationale. The massacres over, he had to swear before his local district committee that he had signed "no petition against the people,"[15] then took charge of a staff almost unchanged since the days of the Ancien Régime. Men who had worked there for thirty years were fired, some abruptly, in conformity with Roland's austerity program. Two employees who refused to take the civic oath (requiring citizens to be ready to die to defend liberty and equality) were sacked over the protests of a colleague, who was himself fired. The twenty-one members of the noble titles section quit, whereas Bounieu, "a famous painter and excellent patriot," was hired.[16]

A House of Books

After the purge came changes. Nonspecialists were granted access daily, instead of being limited to just two hours, three days a week. Artisans and workers—those who were literate—could henceforth consult humanity's resource material. Working hours were nearly doubled and pay was reduced, but the enthusiasm of the new arrivals compensated for the firings. Thanks to the director's intensive conservation policy, the "B.N." became a place of republican pride, proof that the Revolution could do things just as well as the monarchy. Louis XVI's library was confided to Chamfort personally, as was the classification of the collections belonging to Angiviller and Talleyrand (the latter having "revolutionarily" emigrated in September). Chamfort housed objects from the Royal Depositor and books from the Tuileries palace, including those of Mme. Elisabeth. This was perhaps an indirect reaction to the massacres. The past was systematically rescued, thanks to Abbé Barthélemy, whom Chamfort had met at the Choiseul residence in Chanteloup, and who had headed the B.N.'s medals department for years. Gold objects from Sainte-Geneviève Church (seventeen thousand in all), treasures from the Saint-Denis mausoleum, and the prince de Condé's medals—all threatened with melting down—made their way to the library on the rue de Richelieu, as did mounds of precious stones and rubies.[17] In anticipation of looting, the B.N. became a veritable thieves' den. Barnabite manuscripts and Elzevir editions from Saint-Germain-des-Prés were "nationalized," as were manuscripts from the Sorbonne. Chamfort himself filed the new entries. Not a single missal—not even one of La Harpe's pamphlets—would be thrown away! "Leibniz used to say he had never come across a book which was totally useless," Chamfort pointed out.[18] Thus genealogies—the pride of aristocrats—were saved from paper recyclers, despite Roland's orders, because Chamfort felt they might be useful to commoners claiming rights over a given piece of family property. Running a finger over the dusty books, the librarian remained, at the end of the day, the sole guardian of the world's memory. The fever of iconoclasm had passed.

But cutbacks ordered by Roland and delays in payment hampered Chamfort's efforts. Carmontelle's watercolors (representing most of the salon habitués Chamfort had encountered under the Ancien Régime) and the collection of revolutionary writings assembled by d'Ormesson, his predecessor, got away from him. Chamfort was overwhelmed with work when Carra left for Chalons, but he showed himself to be an efficient, authoritarian administrator of almost maniacal integrity. With a budget less than half that of pre-Equality days, he managed to double the library's collection and to make himself respected (he was even truly liked by Van Praet, the rigorous and urbane Belgian scholar who had enrolled in the Jacobin Club in 1790 but who had been just as good a curator of prints under the monarchy as under the republic). On rue de Richelieu, Chamfort was far from the tempest. His hatred of literature was dead—but so was literature. Beaumarchais, La Harpe, and Laclos no longer wrote, having been imprisoned, drafted, or radicalized. Literature had been superseded by journalism. Chamfort, the contented anti-writer, reigned over the books of the past. His world was reduced to a library . . . which was paradise for this great reader.

France finally proclaimed itself a republic in September 1792. The utopia spawned at the Grassins school finally emerged. The birth of free men replaced the birth of Christ as the starting point of time, and the months comprising Year I of the new era (which would be used in France up until the Empire, forming a parenthesis between the nineteenth and twentieth centuries) were given evocative names such as Germinal, Thermidor, and Fructidor. Dumouriez's victory at Valmy removed the threat of foreign invasion, and the first Terror came to an end. Fabre d'Eglantine suggested that children be named after nature's fruit—cabbage, apple, pear—instead of after the church's saints. As in 1790, Chamfort found himself waiting for a new constitution which was to establish a "natural" social contract. Brissot declared, "Where there is no more tyranny to bring down, there should be no more strength in insurrection." The "Septembreakers," the Montagne faction, and the Commune backed down. Chamfort settled into the new order, supporting continued progress within safe borders. Having witnessed the disorder reigning in the B.N. over the past three years, he shifted imperceptibly rightward.

The time of sacrifice had certainly come to an end. The "fanatic" was now a boss, concerned about his employees' wages. Poorly paid himself, he drafted a petition against a law on literary property which reduced writers to a "state of vexation" unknown under the Ancien Régime. He would have "blushed to speak thus, only three months ago."[19] But now he was a conscientious director confronted with concrete problems. He began to criticize the "sudden" patriotism of all those who wanted to paper over their former zeal for the Ancien Régime. And he arrived at that watershed that so intrigued him when he detected it in La Fayette and Barnave—the moment when violent revolution is abandoned.

Normalcy Anew

His voice was heard again in salons. On Sundays, he went to young and lovely Helena-Maria Williams's place on rue Helvétius (now rue Saint-Anne), where he met Vergniaud, Brissot, Bernardin de Saint-Pierre, and Bancal des Issarts (a young Girondin whom Mme. Roland had recommended as a lover to the English poetess in order to rid herself of a suitor). Chamfort, who had expressly asked to meet Williams and who had outdone himself at the Bituabés' in order to impress her, no longer debated political issues (his opinions generally ran against the Montagne faction) but spoke rather of his "scientific" view of the difference between the sexes. "It appears that women have one brain compartment less and one heartstring more than men. Men require special organization in order to make them able to put up with, care for, and caress children."[20] The soundness of this idea struck Helena-Maria Williams, the last woman to be courted by Chamfort.

There was also the good, indispensible Mme. Panckoucke, who had become as natural a revolutionary as she had been a Philosopher. She received the writers published by her husband—

along with the last ambassadors remaining in Paris—at her residence near place Maubert. She continued to declare special affection for Chamfort, who had in fact done nothing to enrich her husband. The national librarian thus saw the couple's daughter again—now married to the publisher Agasse—whose comments had so amused him during his literary exile in Auteuil. Thanks to this salon, where he had shined for nearly twenty years, Chamfort still paid homage to friendship, to conversation, and to the undying memory of Marthe Buffon (whose best friend had been Mme. Panckoucke). "Let's preserve everything good from the old days, which were so bad," he said during the Fédération celebrations. He nearly managed to.

Then there was Mme. Roland's loft on rue de La Harpe, where Chamfort had become a regular. "At first I found him too talkative," wrote Queen Coco. "I reproached him for that superfluous and domineering type of speech that our men of letters commonly adopt . . . but I ultimately pardoned him for speaking more than others, because he amused me more."[21] Since Chamfort was more familiar with "plotting, personalities, politicians and that ilk than any of his contemporaries," Mme. Roland made him one of the mainstays of her little committees, along with Condorcet. While he stayed away on those evenings when the Gironde outlined its policy, he participated in the overall project of encouraging the emergence of an elite based on talent.

As a culmination to this return to normalcy, Chamfort found his way back to rue Chantereine where Julie Careau, now republicanized and married to the actor Talma, helped Paris maintain its status as capital. The setting had changed since the vicomte de Ségur and the Irishman had departed; furnishings were now "Greek," the walls were covered with yataghans and trophies recalling Talma's great roles, and the bedrooms housed two additional children. Although a fervent supporter of the Gironde, Julie nevertheless remained the perfect hostess. "She discussed all the difficult political and philosophical questions with equal lucidity . . . all the while keeping pedantry and frivolity at bay . . . as Aspasia had formerly done with Alcibiades, Pericles and Socrates," claimed Arnault, a rue Chantereine regular.

There the courtesans of the Ancien Régime met the "beaus" of the new régime (Girondins such as Vergniaud, Guadet, and Gensonné). The painter David and the inevitable La Harpe also took tea with Julie, who had received them as early as 1785. This patriotic fin-de-siècle was now spending the last of the *louis* it had earned between the sheets of Louis XV's financiers. Guests like Etienne Méhul (composer of the patriotic *Chant du départ*) and Marie-Joseph Chénier (author of *Charles IX*) mused long into the night how far Voltaire would have gone, or Rousseau. Talma himself had long since fallen asleep in the "national" outfit David had designed for him, while Chamfort left on tiptoe. Yet the skin-deep aristocrat had entered the lists once again, astride that almost miraculous psychological equilibrium of the years 1786 and 1790. Rediscovering the style of *Products of the Perfected Civilization*, Chamfort effectively became an authentic Girondin.

He might have gone on this way for a long time, proclaiming Fraternity to his employees, and sharing his enthusiasms with Mme. Panckoucke, with Maria-Helena Williams, with Manon Roland the Spartan, and even with Julie Careau the Athenian (who had so wounded him earlier). Enjoying the privilege of having been among the first to condemn privileges, he dropped his "collectivist" agenda of 1792, just as he had successively abandoned his tyrannical agenda of 1765 and his neoclassic resolutions of 1772. Chamfort constantly rewrote his projected destiny, the better to shed overly constraining prophecies and to avoid dehumanizing himself. Now he had found his true social place among the revolutionary elite, halfway between his period of sacrifice and his Ancien Régime extravagance, both of which were merely adopted existences. High society having lowered itself to his requirements, Chamfort now felt it to be almost fair. It was his turn to have—like Vaudreuil before him—"a little dust on his glasses," his turn to play at an "aristocratic" revolution.

22. A BAD DREAM

The moment he abandoned one illusion, his imagination gave birth to another, like those rose bushes which produce roses in every season.

Chamfort, referring to himself

Chamfort's quaking made everyone quake.

Tilly

The scales fell from Chamfort's eyes on October 16, 1792. That was the day Julie entertained Dumouriez, the victor at Valmy. The entire Gironde turned out to greet the general (with his forty-eight guards), who was treated to a performance by the comic mimic Fusil. Chamfort completed the court staged by Talma, in which even Brissot (the Gironde leader) was eclipsed by the triumphant general.[1] As the very pretty Mlle. Candeille was singing at the piano, the haiduks guarding the door were suddenly shoved aside. It was Marat who burst in, accompanied by Bentabole, chief interrogator at the Comité de Sûreté Générale (i.e., the investigative police established by the convention on October 2). General Santerre, in charge of security that evening, immediately shouted Marat's name. This produced the sudden flight, according to Marat, of "several masks it would be interesting to know." With a Madras handkerchief on his head, from which "locks of greasy hair"[2] escaped, Marat violently harangued Dumouriez over the punishment meted out to two batallions of volunteers who slit the throats of Prussian deserters—or emigré nobles, according to Marat. Dumouriez turned his back, while the Chevalier de Saint-Georges, a mulatto officer, brandished a threatening fist in the direction of Marat. "This house is a hotbed of counter-revolution," shouted Marat to the transfixed audience on his way out. The air would have to be "purified" with perfume before the party could resume.

"Major conspiracy discovered by citizen Marat," cried hawkers for *L'Ami du Peuple* the next day. Marat's paper denounced at least one conspiracy per day, however, so the plot supposedly being hatched on rue Chantereine to assassinate "The People's Friend" was hardly credible. Dumouriez's presence in a house where "the fate of the Nation" was being decided nevertheless worried a regime haunted by the fear of its own overthrow, just three months following that of the king. Chamfort, recently a partisan of an "open" revolution, now found himself accused of being one of the "masks" among the "nymphs" and "fairies" on rue Chantereine. These dancers, actresses, and singers—such as Julie Candeille, Vergniaud's mistress—were suspect not only because of their Gironde politics but also because they embodied that policy of feminine whimsy and pleasure that had reached its zenith under Louis XV. Revolutionary misogyny (of which Napoleon would be the culminating caricature) thus indirectly targeted Chamfort, who had been among the first to denounce women as being emblematic of a civilization of masks (though his own misogyny had always remained rather theoretical).

Paris, now under the sway of the Montagne faction, had given Chamfort only one vote during the first round of elections for the Convention when he ran against Hébert (editor of *Le Père Duchesne*) and Jacques Roux (leader of the radical Enragés movement). The Revolution was henceforth being played out between a mere few hundred Parisian actors. The former "fanatic" was henceforth considered bourgeois and received threats in the name of the poor, of soldiers, and the unemployed. Fratricidal war had begun.

For neither the Montagne nor the Commune accepted this second return to normalcy. Hesitating, however, before the economic repercussions of a true social revolution, they offered the sansculottes a scapegoat—the Gironde. Yet the Girondins, remained confident, given their majority in the Convention, the recent conquest of Savoy and Nice, and Dumouriez's new victory at Jemmapes. Chamfort even saw his "Peace to cottages, war on chateaus" given as watchword to the troops occupying Belgium, following a speech Cambon gave to the Convention on December 15, 1792. Unfortunately, Roland supported a completely unregulated market, thereby becoming the favorite target of the extreme left, even though his honesty was as unimpeachable as Robespierre's. In order to check his fall in popularity, Roland took a page out of Chamfort's book and suggested that the chateaus of emigrés be demolished. But both men saw their positions further weakened when the iron trunk in which the king had kept his secret papers was finally opened. These documents revealed Mirabeau's constant two-timing, Roederer's ambivalence, Talleyrand's various propositions, and so on. Roland was accused of having removed documents that compromised his party, and the name of Mirabeau became equated with infamy. As the danger became more tangible, the minister of "intelligence," like the minister of money, sought an aggressive response.

Whereas the Gironde was calling for a national referendum on the king's fate, Chamfort backed the Montagne faction's proposal for an immediate vote within the Convention—that, at least, is what he would claim when denounced as a counterrevolutionary. This does not necessarily mean that Chamfort favored the execution of Louis XVI, simply that he favored an immediate, therefore less-considered, decision. Nevertheless, after a confusing, two-round vote marked by switches among numerous Girondins, the death penalty was pronounced by a single vote—that of the monarch's relative, the duc d'Orléans, rebaptized Philippe Egalité. Grouvelle (Chamfort's "valet"), as secretary to the Council, then left for the Temple prison. There, accompanied by Justice Minister Garat and Foreign Affairs Minister Lebrun-Tondu, he read the sentence in a "weak and trembling" voice to Louis XVI[3] who was duly guillotined on January 21, 1793.

We don't know how Chamfort—author of a tragedy that had once made the king weep—reacted to the execution. It would nevertheless seem that while Chamfort was horrified by crimes committed before his eyes (like that of Foulon), he remained relatively indifferent to those executed "cleanly"—in the name of republican principles and with the approbation of Sieyès. By 1793, Chamfort saw Louis XVI as merely the golden calf of an antediluvian reign swallowed up by history. Exhibiting neither hate nor pity, Chamfort simply observed, "Ministers brought on the downfall of royal authority, just as priests had done for religion. God and king were published for the stupidity of their underlings." Whatever the double-dealing and failings of a king obviously not cut out for his job—Stefan Zweig claimed that Louis would have made a better craftsman—this hardly enhanced Chamfort's stature.

Nor did such aggressive posturing do any good. Once Louis XVI was out of the way, hatred focused on the Gironde. Accused of complicity with England, Roland left the political stage. The Brissot clan allowed their best minister to leave, and Mme. Roland closed her salon. "I would have continued to see Chamfort with pleasure. . . . He was as virtuous as Ninon [referring to a famous courtesan under Louis XIV] was honest,"[4] she said. She added that this already meant a lot, given the corrupt climate. But England's entry into the war on February 1, 1793, left Chamfort open to the same accusations leveled against Roland. England "would prefer to suck our blood rather than spill it," Chamfort had said earlier, based on his London informers, Maret and Talleyrand.[5] Like Mirabeau, Chamfort had always been partisan of an Anglo-French alliance. The prophet Chamfort, steadfastly pacifist, had made the wrong prediction for once. The Commune snatched the battle standard from the Gironde, Chaumette inciting the people to "frenchify, municipalize, and jacobinize" all of Europe as far as Moscow. Chamfort was now associated with a party on the decline.

Rupture

He nevertheless still had a few cards up his sleeve. Roland's successor at the Ministry of the Interior, Garat, belonged to the Gironde, and Chamfort had known him when he occupied the room at the Suard residence which later fell to Condorcet. But radicalization continued apace. "Ideas which were previously considered dangerous . . . have become almost trivial," wrote Chamfort.[6] At this point, the Gironde committed the error of rejecting proposals made by Danton (who was vulnerable due to his weakness for Dumouriez, but whom Mme. Roland had always detested). With the Montagne faction on the rise—it held eleven out of twelve seats on the Comité de Sûreté Générale—everyone turned against Brissot's party, from recent Jacobin converts to the "toads" sitting in the Convention's "marsh" (where they were accused of wallowing in the center). Attacked by his former "brothers," Chamfort defended himself tooth and nail. "This Barère is a brave fellow; he always rushes to aid the strongest," said Chamfort of the terrorist deputy who in 1789 had applauded his lectures at the Lycée near the Palais-Royal. "Your Pache is an angel," Chamfort confided to an admirer of the radical mayor of Paris, who in fact owed his start to Roland, "but in his place I'd own up."[7] Yet Chamfort's fund of confidence, which had so amazed Mme. Roland, was running low.

Civil war then broke out in the Vendée region, triggering a chain reaction. Lyon, followed by Marseille, Bordeaux, and Corsica rebelled either in the name of the king, of Brissot, or of England. The Gironde's federalism was accused of destroying the unity of a country that had always managed to retain a certain cohesiveness despite the feudal claims of Burgundian dukes, despite provincial resentment, despite a diversity of languages and the difference between a gothic north and a romanesque south. Dumouriez now prepared to march on Paris, ostensibly to halt the looting (done by his own soldiers in the name of "war on chateaus") but in reality because his position had been weakened by several defeats in Belgium. The enemy was once again within, and the capital mobilized itself. Directed by Varlet and tolerated by Pache, gangs burned Girondin presses on March 9. The journalist Gorsas had to leave his printshop pistol in hand—the second Terror, the real one, was beginning. "Let us be terrible to dispense the people from being so," cried Danton, who had the revolutionary tribunal restored. The republic was preparing to consume its own children.

Chamfort would not even have time to register disappointment. The call for denunciations and the guillotine shocked him. "It was in his nature . . . to go into extreme states," wrote Helena-Maria Williams.[8] Steadfast in his "delirous" love of freedom, Chamfort refused to submit. The events of March 9, which had not resulted in a single death, spurred him to break the silence maintained since the September massacres. "He wanted to create fear, not create suffering," said Roederer, who added that "he thought it necessary to appear terrible to avoid being cruel." *Appear* terrible, not *be* terrible (as Danton advocated). More likely, Chamfort simply felt that what was tolerable for his enemies until the republic had been proclaimed was intolerable for his friends. The Revolution, right up to the fall of the monarchy, had been "a fight to the death between masters and slaves," and Chamfort did not think that the distinction between "Frank" and "Gaul" could ever be blurred. Despite the secret propaganda war *he* conducted against the armies of the foreign coalition, despite the bloody end of the two brothers in his tragedy *Mustapha et Zéangir*, Chamfort never dreamed of treason or fratricide within his own camp. His sense of "humanity" had led him to "arm awful men with violent maxims,"[9] and to back the death penalty after having called for its abolition in 1791. Humanity, unfortunately, was no longer on his side.

Smug judgments made two centuries later, however, are inevitably misleading. No one prior to 1789 had tried to change things so drastically. Vaudreuil would justify himself under the restoration by saying, "We were all novices, we'd never seen a revolution."[10] Illegality and violence began with the stoning, in May 1788, of two royal representatives in Rennes, and most royalists endorsed such tactics by cooperating with the regime that emerged after the fall of the Bastille. The death of hussars at the hands of the mob on July 13, 1789, created more stir than the invention of the guillotine. Does this suggest that the only unsullied people were the Polignacs, who left on the sixteenth? After Foulon was murdered, Barnave asked, "Was this blood really so pure?" The entire Revolution relied on such rationale—with increasing conviction.

Both royalists and Jacobins indulged in Hiroshima mathematics: a hundred deaths now would avoid a thousand later. The former were defeated because they were unable to convince a king opposed to bloodshed of the need to launch a "total" civil war. The emigrés, who backed Brunswick's manifesto which promised a reign of terror once victorious, were no more upset by the September massacres than was Chamfort. The French Revolution was a series of power ploys, denounced sometimes out of principle, usually out of self-interest. Liberal revolutionaries sanctioned the killings of October 6, 1789, as well as those on the Champs-de-Mars, not to mention those of 9 Thermidor (when Robespierre was brought down). The poorer sansculottes would surely have prolonged the reign of the guillotine, out of self-interest as well as out of ideology. In a revolution almost everyone favored at one moment or another, it is hard to determine where the unacceptable begins. The fall of the monarchy was, a priori, no less legitimate than the long struggle of the Capets against feudalism. The conditions in which Louis XVI was imprisoned were similar, originally, to those of the Bastille. Escalation may have sullied the Revolution, but it also kept it going. The only real brake on escalation was attrition, which wore down the likes of Barnave and Mirabeau. Chamfort succumbed to it in March 1793. Judged by the monarchy's yardstick, he would have merited prison, by that of the republic he envisioned, a veteran's pension; and by that of today's democracy (based on the human rights the king endorsed only under pressure), a symbolic sentencing. The violence committed during the Terror equals just a few hours of a Napoleonic war, and Chamfort was guilty for just a few minutes.

Trying to judge Chamfort on his record is like trying to solve a Chinese puzzle. He was pampered by Vaudreuil but was really happy only in his "republic" at Vaudouleurs. He rebelled well before 1789 against a voracious clergy, sham justice, and a dizzying concentration of land and wealth, yet he was a revolutionary out of resentment as much as by conviction. He could be ungrateful yet sincere, hedonist yet disinterested, cynical even in his idealism; he loved the idea of "the people" more than the people themselves, but he was ready to sacrifice everything to prove the opposite and to mask his very real love-hate relationship with the aristocracy. Chamfort believed in a free, rational, and fraternal humanity—after having proclaimed his misanthropy for twenty years. Now, however, he wanted out.

The Challenge

Chamfort went straight from shock to dejection. Anticipating the worst, he soon spoke to Barras, a deputy who had become influential within the Montagne faction after starting out as a moderate. Barras suggested that Chamfort accompany him to the Alps, where he was being sent on mission as government representative. "Alas, were I only given permission," replied Chamfort. "If you take care of securing it from the Comité de Salut Public [i.e., the national security commission later dominated by Robespierre] I'll joyfully leave Paris, where my life is in danger."[11] The passport issued, Chamfort packed his bags. But several hours later he returned to see Barras (who subsequently headed France during the Directorate). "My friends have dissuaded me from making the trip; they think there is perhaps less danger here in Paris than on assignment with Barras." According to Barras, Chamfort feared armed conflict in the south, not a denunciation—a revealing detail given Barras's role in crushing the Gironde. But the anxiety shown by a man who had been so brave on the ruins of the Bastille seems to have truly moved the future "Leader of the Corrupt." It would be their last meeting.

Chamfort quickly subdued his panic. He had decided to stick by his Girondin friends rather than patrol the borders. Chamfort closed ranks with Garat, the minister to whom he reported, and assembled his certificates of residence and patriotism, along with four moral witnesses, in order to renew his citizenship card at the neighborhood Surveillance Committee (one of twenty thousand committees set up across France). Sébastien Roch Nicolas, known as Chamfort, 1.73 meters, brown hair, short nose, and broad forehead, would enjoy the title of "French citizen" for a little while longer.[12]

The turning point came in April 1793. On April 3, Dumouriez went over to the enemy to avoid arrest, effectively shelving the military coup Bonaparte would finally pull off on 18 Brumaire (November 9, 1799). Danton, seeking to clear himself, denounced the would-be Caesar's Parisian acquaintances and demanded that Lebrun-Tondu reveal the whole truth about expenditures made in Belgium to demoralize enemy troops. Chamfort thus found himself on the front line along with Lebrun-Tondu, facing a Montagne which now backed total economic revolution. On April 6, the government formed by Danton and the Gironde was replaced de facto by the Comité du Salut Public, which included Barère and Cambon. Hérault de Séchelles asked Chamfort (with whom he had once visited the virtuous Thomas) to use his "caustic claws"[13] to popularize the law that threatened counterrevolutionary pamphleteers with death.[14] Chamfort's refusal was scathing. To which Hérault replied, "You'll regret that."

Several days later, Chamfort was summoned to appear before the Comité de Sureté Générale. Entering the Tuileries palace via the Marsan pavillion, he was led through a long planked corridor to the former Brionne residence, where the committee then convened. He waited for two hours. Marat bustled around everywhere, and Robespierre passed without recognizing Chamfort. But Chamfort was let off without further trial. Unintimidated, he openly ridiculed the two rulers of the day. Ginguené described this as, "So many crimes which were noted."

The Cat Who Drank Vinegar

Many Girondins, however (including Condorcet), still hesitated to directly attack the Montagne, from whom they differed only as to means. "It requires good sense to hate one's enemies,"[15] noted Chamfort, who was not intimidated by Robespierre. He had seen Robespierre ape Mirabeau in the early stages of the Constituent Assembly, only to stammer before the amused deputies. Chamfort rescued the Jacobins along with Robespierre, and he knew that Robespierre had been a republican only since June 20 and that he had remained in hiding on August 10, 1792. These lapses led Chamfort to ignore Mirabeau's warning: "The man is dangerous, for he believes everything he says." Chamfort's mistake was to have known Robespierre too soon. Robespierre invested the clubs with his own moral anguish and succeeded in identifying himself with the Revolution. He was the only one of all those leaders under thirty to escape the flaws of his age, perhaps the only one who was never really young. Robespierre could thus impose his authority and charisma on the sansculottes, to whom Chamfort had merely offered foreign chateaus to sack. Chamfort should have remembered what he had written in the *Considérations:* "The poor are the true commoners in a Republic."[16] Although Chamfort was a prophet of the Revolution, Robespierre—whom David was already comparing to Christ—*was* the Revolution. Chamfort may well have been a follower of Rousseau and a republican before everyone else, now he was just a writer linked to the Gironde, a descendant of Voltaire facing an "incorruptible" Robespierre determined to avenge Jean-Jacques. "The Philosophers . . . sometimes decried despotism, yet they were in the pay of despots," wrote Robespierre. "Sometimes they wrote books against the court, and sometimes dedicated their books to the king."[17] Paranoics' intuitions are often valid—unlike their behavior.

On closer inspection, it turns out that those who "judged" Chamfort (Robespierre and Marat in particular) were nurtured in the fold of the Ancien Régime (just as almost all the leaders of the counterrevolution professed, back in 1780, certain liberal ideas which led to 1789). Robespierre was a protégé of the church, had a scholarship to the prestigious Louis-le-Grand school, and was a diligent member of the Amiens Literary Academy; he hardly sprang naked from the revolutionary waters, even if his integrity is rarely questioned today. Nor was Marat virginal, to say the least. He had once been doctor to the comte d'Artois' guards (a post also held by Marthe Buffon's husband), and had published hysterical attacks against the Philosophers around 1789, not to mention his pro-monarchy articles up until 1790. Chamfort became a classic scapegoat, exemplifying the latent threat hanging over all those active in a revolution subjected to increasing paranoia, inclined to see plots, traitors, and "masks" everywhere.

May 31, 1791, sounded the death knell of Chamfort's patrons. The Gironde failed in an attempt to indict Marat, and threatened—but only verbally—to crush the Paris mob. It then collapsed under combined counterattacks by Robespierre and the Paris Commune. Roland managed to flee to Normandy, but his wife was imprisoned in his place. Eighty thousand sansculottes showed up on June 2 to blockade the Convention which, thus terrorized, voted to arrest the twenty-nine Girondin deputies. Brissot and Lebrun-Tondu let themselves be taken, while Barbaroux and Louvet fled to Calvados to rouse the region. Clavière, the sole survivor of those who had dined on rue de Bellechasse, went straight from the Ministry of Finances to the dungeon. Thus the "republican" eighteenth century drew to a close with the cult of virtue and the Supreme Being triumphing over happiness, talent, and the individual. The Convention gave in without resisting, less valiant than Louis XVI during the first invasion of the Tuileries palace; it assumed its new role in the very hall where *Mustapha* was first performed, in which they now met. This would be neoclassicism's final victory—for the Revolution, as Saint-Just noted, was on ice.

The Bibliothèque's Marat

Once the Gironde went down with its journalists and theorists, Chamfort entrenched himself in the Bibliothèque nationale and the "intellectual" neighborhood bounded by rue de Richelieu, rue de Chabanais, and rue des Petits-Champs, where most writing had gone on prior to 1791. "The more I study mankind, the more I see how little I see," he admitted on August 10, in a flash of melancholy. [18] The tyranny of the Paris Commune put the moralist back in the saddle—he whose skepticism concerning human sentiments had never completely disappeared. Deprived of speech, Chamfort adopted the weapons of "subjected peoples"—quips and anecdotes. Of Marat's policy, he commented, "It preaches the brotherhood of Cain and Abel." When it was pointed out that he was repeating himself, Chamfort admitted, "You're right. His brotherhood is really that of Eteocles and Polyneices." [19] On June 21, Pache ordered that "Liberty, Equality, Fraternity or Death" be painted on all walls. Chamfort suggested that this be replaced with "Be my brother or I'll kill you." A telling crack, yet one which found no echo. Chateaubriand, however, would find "or Death" daubed everywhere on his return to France in 1800, which meant that the motto "Liberty, Equality, Fraternity" had truly taken root—seven years too late.

For such precocious antiterrorism was limited to Chamfort and Carra (recently returned from Chalons) and to their influence on several employees at the library. Elsewhere, fear won out. Abbé Sieyès no longer dared to appear at the Convention, and Condorcet took refuge at Mme. Helvétius's house in Auteuil. Friends of the twenty-nine Girondin deputies no longer slept at home; Roederer hid out at Pecq, where he would henceforth remain. Chamfort's "valet," Grouvelle, managed to be appointed French envoy to Denmark—Mme. Roland spared no words in denouncing his cowardice, self-importance, coldness, and incompetence. "These men, steeped in vanity, with neither character nor virtue, whose wit is mere jargon, whose philosophy is just a show, and whose feelings are shammed, seem to me to be moral eunuchs, whom I hold in contempt and hatred more cordially than certain women disdain and detest others," she wrote in her *Mémoires*. It was at this point that *Le*

Père Duchesne organized the witch-hunt against "all those knaves appointed by old Roland."[20] The noose tightened around Chamfort and Carra (who was accused of switching from the Montagne to the Gironde on August 10, after having suggested placing the duc de Brunswick—current leader of the foreign coalition—on the throne of France). Employees left the Bibliothèque Nationale in the face of additional work imposed by the return to mandatory deposition of all publications, and given the feebleness of wages, which even Chamfort himself felt to be "discouraging."[21] Yet no one at the Bibliothèque protested when Chamfort exclaimed, on hearing that Charlotte Corday had assassinated Marat on July 13, 1793, "King Marat is dead!"—no one, that is, except the "patriot painter" Bounieu, whom Chamfort had hired. Paris responded by parading massively before the corpse, David himself having masked its pustules with makeup. "The People's Friend" lay nude under a blue-white-red flag in the Cordeliers monastery, receiving the homage of District Committees, the Commune, and the sansculottes, while his bathtub was displayed at the place du Carrousel. The century that had most loved high society canonized the man who did the most to destroy it.

A countercult was immediately established at the Bibliothèque Nationale. Charlotte Corday had become Chamfort's model, his saint, his Joan of Arc. Having arrived from Caen knowing no one, rebuffed twice before managing to approach Marat, she performed the one act of which Chamfort would have been proud. She was tragedy come to life, venging the Gironde's Mustaphas. Chamfort read and reread her letter to Barbaroux—"the most sublime work ever to issue from this earth"—swearing to keep it always on his person. To the judges who would interrogate him, he replied: she didn't kill, she rescued the "packet" of twenty thousand heads demanded by Marat. She didn't betray the Republic, she saved it from a monster who was wreaking havoc on it. Unlike the men of the Gironde, she showed herself to be equal to the greatest heroes of antiquity—the tyrant-slayers. "Her remains will be venerated within twenty years," predicted Chamfort at the Bibliothèque. Such a statement was tantamount to offering himself in sacrifice to Charlotte.

Four days after Charlotte—Corneille's granddaughter—was executed, Chamfort was accused by a library employee of advocating criminal behavior. Tobiesen-Duby, the accuser, described Chamfort as a parasite of the Ancien Régime and a tyrant under the new, and claimed that he had insulted Bounieu, had called Tobiesen-Duby "factious" and threatened him with dismissal, and had also given a "grand dinner" for Montagne deputies in order to subvert them.[22] There followed a "report on members of the Bibliothèque" in which all the employees except Bounieu and Tobiesen were candidates for purge. X was an "underhand" aristocrat, Y was "enfeoffed," Z snickered during district meetings. So-and-so mourned all the "beheadings," someone else had "pliably" groveled before dukes. One department head was described as a "little Fayettist," another as a counterrevolutionary "whippersnapper," and even the lowly warehousemen were "aristocrats." The letter reached Chrétien, a café owner sitting on the jury in the Corday trial, who read it to the Commune and to district commissioners.[23] The library employees then gathered in the main reading room to discuss the situation. Renewing their confidence in Chamfort, they appointed him to defend them case by case, Carra having already been indicted during the Girondin purge on May 31. The director went to testify before the district committee in early August. The accusations were so preposterous that he was let off.

Chateaus and Prisons

Chamfort seems to have been reassured by this confrontation and by the support of his staff. Long a republican, he was at any rate certain of having greater credibility than his employee and accuser. "I won't leave the Bibliothèque until the Prussians come to drive me out," he exclaimed.[24] Garat was still Minister of the Interior (thanks to an alliance with Danton), and Chamfort neglected his own defense to take up that of Carra, for whom he found a lawyer— Tronson du Coudray, who also defended Marie-Antoinette.[25]

Chamfort's accuser, Tobiesen-Duby, merits a few words. A "star" of the Terror's secret proceedings, Tobiesen-Duby had "inordinate ambition" according to his colleagues (who detested him), yet had languished in the Prints Collection for ten years.[26] His was the classic image of an informer. Not a year went by when he didn't ask to be transferred to the Books Department and to be allocated an official apartment, when he didn't fawn upon his superiors (only to denounce them to their successors), when he didn't try to get ahead by invoking his father's name (already employed by the Bibliothèque), or that of Brissot or Mme. Roland. When Chamfort arrived,

Tobiesen requested a raise of twelve hundred livres for the nth time. Chamfort granted a raise of four hundred, which was quashed the very same day by Roland, the "minister of money." But Chamfort earned five times as much, and Tobiesen had a family to support. Tobiesen then joined the Correspondence Committee of the Jacobin Club, on which Chamfort had sat in 1791. Several days before Marat was murdered, Tobiesen had already denounced the "counter-revolutionary interviews" taking place in the office of the director of the Bibliothèque.

On August 10, 1793, Chamfort left for Fontainebleau with Delisle de Sales, one of Diderot's old friends. "We conversed without agreeing, which is common enough," reported Delisle, "yet without ceasing to esteem one another, which is somewhat more rare."[27] En route, the two friends learned that the Academies had been abolished. Chamfort noisily approved, even if the abolition owed more to David's report than to his own pamphlet published two years earlier. Chamfort also approved the announcement that Louis XVI's lawyers would be tried. Delisle objected, and the two men parted near the Vaudouleurs manor, with Delisle heading on to the chateau of his friend Malesherbes. But a storm also obliged Chamfort to take refuge at the chateau of this former minister—a member of the Académie française—who had defended the king during his trial. The conversation centered on the decree, the Forty, and Racine, in surreal counterpoint to the tempest. The two men were arguing about those dukes and cardinals elected to the Académie without ever having written a line, when Malesherbes's son-in-law announced the arrival of a Revolutionary Committee from Fontainebleau. Malesherbes, a former patron to the Philosophers, turned to Chamfort and said, "You must come see me in prison, former colleague, we still have to debate the resurrection of the Academies." Chamfort then stepped between Malesherbes and the sansculottes, whose mere arrival sufficed to change Chamfort's mind. "Friends," he said, "you are mistaken, this old man is not on your list of outlaws; you know of my burning patriotism, and I will answer for him with my own head. Return to Fontainebleau. I, on my side, will go to Paris to enlighten the government's conscience; within three days you will know whether the owner of this chateau should remain free, or if I must share his sentence." The sansculottes left, and Chamfort returned to Paris where he obtained a reprieve for Malesherbes, probably through Garat's intercession.

Convinced of the aberrant nature of most of Tobiesen-Duby's accusations, Chamfort was less concerned about defending himself. He displayed the confidence typical of other crucial moments in his life, yet proved to be as poor a tactician on his own behalf as he was an effective defender of others.

For everything marked Chamfort as a "counter-revolutionary," from his hostility to Marat to his links to Sieyès (whose silence increasingly resembled panicky fear, yet whom Robespierre accused of acting behind the scenes, of "directing and clouding" everything, of creating factions in order to benefit from the disorder—in short, of being a "brilliant mole"). More serious was the fact that the accusations against Chamfort were making headway. Tobiesen had Gombaud-Lachaise transmit them to the all-powerful Comité de Sûreté Générale, as well as to Drouet, whom he knew (Drouet had had the king arrested at Varennes.) Gombaud-Lachaise, as a "veteran soldier" and editor of the *Bulletin de la Convention* (good references for an informer) went one further on August 8 by accusing "the secretary to 'His Rotten Highness the Prince de Condé' "—the very phrase Marat had used—of dining with the Minister of the Interior. "Not that I want to indict the Minister," explained this fine soul, "but this just shows how the snake tries to insinuate itself, through twists and turns, into Garat's very breast. I am myself a witness to his unpatriotic comments, of his moaning over present circumstances. I will be his accuser. My frankness, my thirty-two years of honorable service, and the truth I profess will be my shield. Let him appear, that I may confound him. In the name of the Republic, there shall be no half-measures! Return to the dust those beings made for it, and give patriots the satisfaction of seeing their enemies reduced to total non-existence."[28]

Once again, the outcome was dictated from above. Robespierre demanded that the civil service be purged, and on August 16, 1793, the Comité du Sureté Générale decided to fire the entire staff of the library—with the exception of Tobiesen-Duby[29]—and to replace them with "avowed patriots." On the twentieth, Garat had to resign from his ministry after having been denounced by Collot d'Herbois. With his last card gone, Chamfort took ten days to reply to the Committee and to the Commune. And by refusing to dissociate himself from Charlotte Corday, this writer described as "stinking of slavery" implicitly proved his accusers right. He was arrested at dawn on September 2, the anniversary of the 1792 massacres, and led to the

Madelonnettes prison with most of his employees (except his friend Van Praet, who managed to hide out at a bookseller's). Shortly after, La Harpe was incarcerated at the Luxembourg prison for having criticized Robespierre. The journey to the end of the night had begun.

23. HIS OWN EXECUTIONER

I asked M. R.——, a man of great intelligence and talent, why he in no way surfaced during the revolution of 1789. He replied, "Because for thirty years I found men so nasty, in private and taken one by one, that I could not hope for much good from them, in public and collectively."

Chamfort

I am the wound and the knife.

Baudelaire

The attractive name of "Madelonnettes" referred to a sordid prison near the Temple, which until August 10 had been reserved for whores and counterfeiters. Enormous hounds barked in the courtyard, and guards were posted near a lightning rod which sported the revolutionary red cap. Each cell had four rows of three vermin-swollen straw mattresses. Built for two hundred, the prison overflowed with new inmates drawn from the aristocracies of talent and federalism as well as the aristocracy of the Ancien Régime. New arrivals slept in the hallways, and even on the stairways—the doctor ordered that they be given fifteen minutes of strenuous exercise before each meal. On the menu were beans, maybe a few potatoes. Meat went untouched, since it was suspected of coming from the bodies of those guillotined. The toilets overflowed, and the resulting miasma provoked epidemics of plague and smallpox. Vinegar was poured on red-hot shovels in an attempt to purify the air; for Chamfort, who choked even in the clubs, it was torture. Deprived of baths, medication, and air, it took him back to the worst days of a disease that had plagued him for thirty years. His distress was also moral, however. Even the Ancien Régime itself had not dared infringe on his independence in this way. Chamfort was enraged at being exposed to the pity of aristocrats, of being imprisoned with thieves after having sacrificed all his savings in the euphoria of 1789. Immured in his innocence, this authentic revolutionary refused to admit that he was guilty of "non-conformity" to the anti-Gironde struggle in the same way that the ministers and magistrates next to him were guilty of nonconformity during the antimonarchy battle. Condemned to the "tyranny" of cellmates he hadn't chosen, Chamfort attempted to hang on to the only thing he hadn't sacrificed—his freedom.

The librarians had nevertheless been well received. Inmates arranged their cells, and the "prison kids" took care of the old and the sick. Royalists helped Girondins, and the rich shared their packages (obtained thanks to the indulgence of concierges). This generated mutual cooperation which some later fondly recalled. Never had equality been so fine as in the jails of the egalitarians—but Chamfort wasn't having any of it. The former sharer was the most wretched inmate in that sad brick prison the queen could see from her window in the Temple.

The first hours of detention are always the toughest, he was reminded, but to no avail. For how many months or years would he remain there? How far could such perversity go, depriving freedom's prophet of freedom? Who would clear him of Tobiesen's accusations? Not even the release of Abbé Barthélemy late that night did any good, for the head of the Bibliothèque's medals collection probably benefited from his advanced age and from the immense success of his *Voyage du jeune Anacharsis* [*Travels of Anacharsis the Younger in Greece.*] Unable to sleep, Chamfort wrote his third letter to the Comité de Sureté Générale.

The arrival of the actors from the Comédie Française the next day, September 3, reduced the tension a little. Sentenced for having identified with their roles in Neufchâteau's *Pamela*, the actors (who had performed *La jeune Indienne* again the previous winter) were greeted with cheers by the prisoners who lined up in double rows, hats off. But the news was bad. Toulon had fallen into the hands of the English, and there was talk of more preventive massacres among the prison population. Fear mounted, and some inmates readied the opium pellets hidden in the buttons of their sleeves, just in case. . . . Chamfort spent another sleepless night in the filthiest jail in Paris, into which had crept the government's "stool pigeons." The most anxious inmates paced up and down the corridors, candle in hand.

The next day, however, the Comité de Sûreté Générale ordered Chamfort's release. Prison overcrowding and the moderateness of certain Committee members had carried the day. Yet those forty-eight hours in prison—a lark for the times—traumatized Chamfort. He swore he would never go back. Two other librarians joined him in newfound liberty: Abbé Barthélemy's nephew, and Desaunays.

The three men were led to lodgings belonging to the Bibliothèque, at number 18, rue Neuve-des-Petits-Champs, where they lived under the watchful eye of a gendarme they had to feed and house.

Informer's Sense of Honor

That very day the *Journal de la Montagne* printed another letter from Tobiesen-Duby. "I will prove, at his pleasure, that no more than six weeks ago he said to a good republican that if he hadn't looted and killed, and wasn't a Jacobin, he wouldn't get a certificate of good citizenship."[1] Four days later, the accused replied to the editor of the same paper. "Chamfort an aristocrat! All those who know me laughed, and laughed a little too heartily as far as I'm concerned, because I was in Madelonnettes prison. Aristocrat! He for whom the love of equality has been a constant, dominating passion, an innate, irrepressible and automatic instinct! He who brought to the theater, more than twenty years ago, the play *Le marchand de Smyrne,* which is still regularly performed, and in which nobles and aristocrats of every sort are sold off cheaply, and finally shown to be worthless! He who wrote against the Academies." A thin alibi for one who admitted that he rarely went to district meetings, and who not long ago grew impatient on hearing his *Marchand* described as revolutionary. Chamfort then resigned from the Bibliothèque, to await the Nation's verdict and prove his good faith. "Let's tell the truth and have done with it. M. Duby desires a post, although he claims the opposite in his note. I am resigning mine as of this moment, that it might be given to him; but it will not, and he will have slandered to another's advantage."[2]

Things might have rested there if it hadn't been for Tobiesen's fury. The Bibliothèque's Marat wanted not only Chamfort's job but his hide. Tobiesen used the podium of the Jacobin club to accuse Chamfort again of persecution and moderateness. Meanwhile, the Terror's intelligence agents were accusing Chamfort of keeping Marie-Antoinette's books in the event of a counterrevolution.[3] Threatened by a new law concerning suspects, which practically equated accusation with proof, Chamfort bought and distributed a hundred copies of the *Journal de la Montagne* in which his reply appeared.[4] Having fallen into the exhausting cycle of self-justification, the man once so fond of "we" was now trying to save his own skin.

The nightmare began again on September 23. "What does this strange privilege signify?" asked the informer, indignant at the presence of a gendarme at the side of Chamfort and the other two librarians. "Either these men are suspects or they aren't."[5] A man of honor, Tobiesen offered the Comité de Sûreté Générale an option: "Prison for him, or for me." On October 9, Chamfort had an open letter posted all over Paris, one week after the Convention announced that forty-six Gironde deputies would be tried. "Come to the Bibliothèque, citizens, and see for yourselves that Tobiesen-Duby has done nothing for the last five years but weave a web of intrigue."[6] But no one was interested in the petitions of a social climber, and no one remembered the republicanism of the *Considérations*, nor Chamfort's stint at the Jacobin Club in 1791. Chamfort nevertheless carried on, dismissing the allegation of being an "old chateau aristocrat," as charged by Tobiesen. "He tries to link me to Roland—me who, as is publicly known, maintained only those relations required of my position. And did I seek this position? . . . Do I know Minister Roland, even by sight? He claims I am linked to the Gironde, of which I never saw a single member except in rare, unforeseen and chance encounters. Here I publicly challenge. . . ." Absurd challenge, since he had been seen at Helena-Maria Williams's place with Bancal des Issarts, not to mention Mme. Roland or Julie. Such protests only made Chamfort that much more suspect.

The Terror drove every defense to side with the prosecution, and Chamfort affirmed his "absolute" opposition to the Gironde's major policies,[7] swearing to remain faithful to the republic "one and indivisible," even if it meant twenty years of prison. Which was a way of claiming to be more righteous than that "Tartuffe of integrity"—Tobiesen. "All you true Jacobins who, not knowing him, admitted him among you . . . all you upright and pure men who want accusations to be a means of punishment and repression against aristocrats and traitors, but [not] a weapon in the hands of schemers to be used against republicans, come to the Bibliothèque." No one came. The tattered posters carried this final plea: "I only ask that you *open your eyes and see.*"

Chamfort had once been more lucid. "Those who enter into long written justifications before the public," he used to say, were like dogs barking at a poste chaise.[8] In lying by omission and trying to prove his revolutionary fervor, Chamfort was barking for nothing. Merely tolerating the Gironde was already punishable by prison, and being a director was suspect in a revolution taking an increasingly radical turn. The Terror created a nobility of those who *shed*, rather than shared, the blood of others. Members were recognizable by their double-barreled names: Billaud-Varenne, Fouquier-Tinville, now joined by Tobiesen-Duby and Gombaud-Lachaise. Chamfort was not part of that. He had clearly wished for a rapprochement between the Gironde and the Montagne, but events decided otherwise. The moral of his moving poster is perhaps to be found in Cardinal Retz's observation: "You have to contradict yourself many times to remain with your party." Or, it might be added, to remain at liberty.

Unable to start society afresh, the Terror destroyed those around it. Helena-Maria Williams was incarcerated by a nation for which she had abandoned everything. Condorcet went into hiding. On October 30, the Girondins inaugurated the mass tumbrel, Carra not even having the right to the lawyer Chamfort had found for him. Bound with leather straps, the library's codirector fell beneath "the national razor" two weeks after Marie-Antoinette and two weeks before Bailly (Chamfort's rival for election to the Académie, who had testified on behalf of the queen at her trial). Finally, on November 1, Mme. Roland appeared. This "great leader" of the Gironde defended its policies and, once upon the scaffold set up on what is now place de la Concorde, cried, "Liberty, oh liberty, what crimes are committed in thy name!" Whereupon her husband, hiding near Rouen, took his own life under an apple tree. Cabanis, formerly Mirabeau's doctor, distributed poison to his entourage. Paris, which the Terror's agents described as being perfectly calm, rang hollow like a vault. Purged of two hundred thousand suspects, France was in the hands of Jacobin Zéangirs. Chamfort increasingly resembled an emigré from within.

Chamfort's Sense of Honor

Although his posters equivocated, Chamfort spoke openly in front of his gendarme. When told that Parisians were abandoning the theaters, he commented, "Tragedy no longer has the same effect once it roams the streets."[9] People spoke of Girondins such as Barbaroux wandering famished in the southwest of France, hiding in cellars and attics. "The Revolution is a lost dog that no one dares collar," observed Chamfort, who had once hoped it would "tour the world."[10] Laying low in the confines of his official accommodation, he resisted ministerial orders to "vacate the premises." But on November 15, the gendarme suddenly announced that Chamfort was to return to prison. Chamfort polished off his soup and coffee, left the table where his colleagues were finishing dinner, and ordered his housekeeper to prepare his belongings. Then, as though getting himself ready, he shut himself up in his dressing room. The time had come to make good his word. He took a pistol from its hiding place, put it to his temple, and fired. But the recoil diverted the bullet through the right eye. "Astonished at being alive,"[11] he grabbed an ivory-handled razor and slit his throat. But the blade slipped, he had to try again, pressing harder. Taking up a second razor, he slashed his chest, thighs, and calves, digging deep. Then he locked himself into another room where he collapsed with a shout. The housekeeper ran up, pounded on the door (under which a river of blood already flowed), and went to get her husband. Who then pounded on the door himself before going off to get help. At the third try, this time by an employee of the Bibliothèque, Chamfort himself finally unbolted the door. He surged forth "like a ghost" and then staggered back into the room. The man fled, shouting, and the housekeeper and her husband returned to find their master lifeless on the sofa. The couple carried him to his bed, staunched his wounds, and thoroughly scrubbed rooms and razors.

But first, the law. Someone left to get a policeman, who referred the matter to the district commissioner. The commissioner arrived with a clerk to take down the gendarme's statement. Then, going over to Chamfort's bedside, they finally called a doctor. "And thereupon we asked the said Chamfort his family name, first name . . ." Impatient to explain himself, he answered the question, "By whom were you wounded?" with, "By myself . . . having horror most of all of going to rot in prison . . . and satisfying nature's calls in the presence of, and in common with, thirty people."[12] He reasserted his innocence, his patriotism, and his determination to live free, then carefully reread the entire statement. While the gendarme took Chamfort's two colleagues off to prison, the legal officers left to interrogate the housekeeper and her husband. Three surgeons then arrived to examine Chamfort. The prognosis was pessimistic. The nasal wall was shattered, some of the twenty-two wounds were deep, and his larynx protuded through the slit in his throat. Unable to locate the bullet in his head, the doctors ordered that the victim not be moved, at the risk of a mortal hemorrhage. Chamfort had won—he would not return to prison. Under the Ancien Régime, he had observed, "Kings and priests, by condemning the doctrine of suicide, wanted to insure that our slavery would endure." By tolerating his self-destruction, the new regime represented a step forward.

The Mummy

News that Chamfort was dying nevertheless spread throughout the neighborhood. Mme. Ginguené arrived in tears, followed by a crowd of curious onlookers. "My dear friend," Chamfort said to her, "you see what we patriots are reduced to. I feel sorry for your husband, I feel sorry for you. For me, it's all over. My only regret is having lived too long."[13] Meanwhile, Ginguené himself arrived to discover, horrified, the dying man wrapped in bandages, a mummy in red and white. "His pillow and sheets were also stained with blood; the little of his face that could be seen was still covered with it." Chamfort dictated his final wishes to his biographer, explained his act, grew weary. "Dumb" with admiration and distress, Ginguené took Chamfort's hand, thinking his final moment had come. But Chamfort spoke again. "That's how to escape these people. They pretend I missed, but I can still feel the bullet in my head, where they won't go looking for it."

At this thought, however, Chamfort sat up. "What do you expect? This is what it means to be clumsy—you don't succeed at anything, not even killing yourself." Then he recounted once again how he shot out his eye, slashed his throat and chest without reaching the heart. "Finally, I recalled Seneca, and in honor of Seneca I wanted to open my veins. But Seneca was rich, had everything he wished, a good hot bath, in short every convenience. And I'm just a poor devil, with none of that. I've hurt myself horribly, yet here I still am. But I've got a bullet in my head, that's the main thing. A little sooner, a little later, that's all." At which point his gendarme returned. "So, where did you take them?" Chamfort asked. "To the Luxembourg prison, citizen." "Oh, Luxembourg. I thought we had to return to Madelonnettes; if I'd known it was to be the Luxembourg, maybe I wouldn't have killed myself. Anyway, I was still right to do what I've done." The local district officers and the justice of the peace then parted, leaving four sansculottes with him to prevent any new attempt. "Two will be enough for my needs and far too many for my means," commented Chamfort, since a sansculotte cost a hundred sous per day. His wish was granted.

Then, like a comical interlude to this tragic episode, the new head librarian burst in. Lefebvre de Villebrunne was also author of eighty small volumes on medicine, and he complained to those present, "But M. de Chamfort hasn't read my article against suicide! It has had enormous success. In it, I prove *primo* . . . and *secundo*, I prove . . ." This prolife advocate then left as he had come, without asking about Chamfort's condition. The onlookers then left the room, and Ginguené parted discreetly, confiding his friend to the sansculottes. Chamfort dozed off under the gaze of his housekeeper, speechless with emotion.

The news astounded Chamfort's entourage. Mme. Roland had admired the firmness of his principles, but she feared that, as a good child of the Ancien Régime, he had more wit than character. Thus she wondered how far he would go to defend these very principles. "Would he sacrifice his peace of mind, his little pleasures and his life to see them triumph . . . ? I rather think he'd adjust."[14] Not only did Chamfort not adjust, he unhesitatingly followed the motto of 1792—"Liberty or death." Far from the aristocratic indifference exhibited by those guillotined, Chamfort imitated Charlotte Corday's fury in killing Marat. As though, given the impotence of words, he wanted to shock a period that had dispossessed itself of everything, including the calendar.

Pointless pride, said Barras in his *Mémoires*. "Could anything worse than death happen to him? It's always worth holding out for luck."[15] In fact, Chamfort would probably have been saved by the Thermidorian end to the Terror. But nothing—not even republican rhetoric—could have forced him to confide the end of his biography to the executioners. Charlotte Corday broke the monopoly of terror; Chamfort took the monopoly upon his own person. While his suicide, with its Roman echoes, conveys the unbearable tension during that winter of 1793, it also represents the revenge of liberty over equality, a return to the "me" during the reign of the familiar "thee," the rebirth of an individualism more rugged than ever. Chamfort wanted to owe his death to no one but himself—just as he had assumed a new name in order to owe his life to no one but himself. He committed suicide to escape the Terror carried out in Robespierre's name, just as he had destroyed himself literarily to escape that other terror conducted in the name of Racine. He employed his only available recourse against the tyranny of society and nature. This day truly marked the end to his hopes of seeing a new human race emerge. Having failed in his millennialist project, the "volcano" expended his final energy in destroying himself.

24. ...FROM THE DEAD

Chamfort was the most bilious of the literary people I knew in Paris; stricken with that malady which produced the Jacobins . . . he betrayed the trust of the houses to which he had been admitted. . . . His wit and talent could not be denied, but it was wit and talent of no issue. When he realized that he amounted to nothing even under the Revolution, he turned the hand he had raised against society against himself. In his arrogance, the red cap appeared to be but another type of crown, sans-culottes became another kind of nobility whose grand lords were Marats and Robespierres. Furious at discovering inequality of rank even in the world of pain and tears, condemned to be just a villein *in the executioners' feudal system, he wanted to kill himself to escape the high priests of crime; but he failed— death mocks those who beckon it and who confuse it with nothingness.*

Chateaubriand
Memoires d'Outre-Tombe 1841

The reasonable ones survived, the passionate ones lived.

De Gaulle, quoting Chamfort, Christmas Message, 1942

Flanked, like a hero, by his two sansculottes, Chamfort received his first visitors. The good Mme. Panckouke brought linen, with which Mme. Ginguené bandaged him. No one held out much hope. But Chamfort clung to "what survived of himself," frightfully disfigured and practically one-eyed, "an object of horror to those for whom he was no longer an object of pity," according to the dramatist Arnault (one of these who frequented Julie's salon).[1] With a certain indifference, Chamfort consigned his manuscripts to Ginguené, the faithful friend who now read him newspapers. The news, however, only confirmed the soundness of his suicidal act. "Nor was there any risk of being tossed into that dump of a Pantheon," Chamfort commented.[2]

On his friends' insistence, Chamfort sent for a doctor. Though the operations produced terrible suffering—Dr. Brasdor would ultimately return sixty times—Chamfort didn't complain. After two weeks, the festering had ceased. He began to read with his left eye (formerly the weaker), translating Greek epigrams and writing poetry. Several days later he was fit enough to go out. "The slenderness of your frame, the fineness of your features, and your resigned and even somewhat sad demeanor . . . will always lead your friends to underestimate your strength," Mirabeau had once told him, and Mirabeau had been right. At Chamfort's request, the Comité de Sûreté Générale agreed to remove one of the sansculottes. The remaining guard, a tall man who was a trained valet, shared meals and conversation with Chamfort. Flattered to be treated as an equal, the guard ignored instructions. "Good Lord, I'm not spying on you," he said to Chamfort's old friend Sélis, who remained wary. "I just happen to enjoy it." Robespierre himself spoke less freely than Chamfort in front of his jailer, who hoped to guard Chamfort for as long as possible.

With Chamfort recovered, Ginguené organized a gathering. "Allow me to introduce my sans-culotte, who is a lot less sansculotte than me," began the resurrected man. He spoke to each of his guests, thanking them for their assistance. "I haven't come back to life, but rather back to my friends," he told them. Weak in the knees and with a black band over one eye, he amazed them by his simplicity and warmth. "The men who hated [him] most . . . couldn't have seen him without being touched," wrote Ginguené.[3] Chamfort then left on the arm of his Antigone.

The Philosopher

"Rid of myself, I'd do just fine," Chamfort used to say under the Ancien Régime. This was now practically the case. Having successively done away with the lover in 1765, the writer in 1780, and the ideologue in 1793, he was finally at peace with himself, and nearly healed. The wounds released the bile which had plagued him for thirty years, and the pains in his bladder and stomach disappeared. He gained weight, lost his yellow pallor, regained some color. He admitted to Colchen (one of his "informers" in the Ministry of Foreign Affairs): "The horrors I see make me constantly want to try again."[4] But his heart wasn't in it. In killing the sick man, he had finally become a philosopher. He could now say, like Valéry's Monsieur Teste, "I loved myself, hated myself, and then we grew old together."

"Little by little, he resumed some of his former habits," wrote Ginguené. Keeping to the streets near the Bibliothèque (practically unchanged to this day), Chamfort visited his remaining friends and received his puritanical Sieyès (who had become almost invisible). This was his way of rejecting the Terror, that evil that forced everyone to focus on himself. Overcoming his disgust, Chamfort laconically commented on the series of executions carried out on the first anniversary of the king's death. "Well done! The Convention offers a free show!"[5] Faithful to the Revolution he had predicted, organized, and finally incarnated, Chamfort watched as it went beserk. If he had any regrets, he didn't show them. He had already taken them out on himself, by killing the little Marat he once harbored. He felt that the events of 1789, 1790, 1791, and 1792 were unavoidable after so many generations of fatalism. Once calm was restored, the Republic would provide France with lasting laws. The Terror was only a parenthesis in the reign of liberty. Chamfort's prison stint, of course, offered striking proof that he was no longer, and never had been, truly egalitarian. Yet for nothing in the world would he be caught saying again, as he had during the Ancien Régime: "Men are so perverse that the mere hope or even the mere desire to correct them, to see them become reasonable and honest, is an absurdity."[6] The applause that greeted the guillotine had no effect, for the people had vanquished his misanthropy once and for all. Or at least that's what he continued to declare. Only Arnault refers to Chamfort's secret shame at having been duped.

Ginguené wanted to "occupy him with something useful," so the two men drew up plans for a review. Aware of his role in annihilating literature, Chamfort wagered one last time on reason and rationality. Backed by the protestant Jean-Baptiste Say (the first French theorist of free enterprise), Chamfort brought together a team of journalists drawn from the entourage of Mirabeau and Mme. Helvétius. The upshot was *La Décade Philosophique,* Chamfort's first posthumous publication, a review that intellectually paved the way for Thermidor and defended Enlightenment ideals right up until the Empire. The publication, which had the indefatigable Mme. Helvétius for patroness and the loyal Ginguené for editor, was haunted for years by Chamfort's style and personality. *La Décade* ultimately viewed the regimes that followed the Terror as the lesser of all evils. Its main contributors were Roederer and Abbé Sieyès (who effectively ended the Revolution by supporting Bonaparte's coup d'état on 18 Brumaire), Grouvelle, Garat, Daunou, and Destutt de Tracy. (Destutt founded the science of Ideology, which studied the origin of ideas[7] and the laws governing them as well as their relationship to language; certain aspects of this movement were taken up by Marxism.) *La Décade Phi-*

losophique published Chamfort's first maxims as well as the biographical articles written by Sélis, Chamfort's oldest friend. As to Ginguené, he and the Ideologues constituted an academic opposition to Napoleon.

But Chamfort was never fated to be happy for long. Evicted from the lodgings on rue Neuve-des-Petits-Champs by his successor, he moved to a mezzanine apartment on rue de Chabanais, right near the Bibliothèque. He wrote his name and age on the patriotic blue-white-red panel in the entrance, and decided to ask that his guard—become "guide"—be dismissed. He accordingly wrote to the people's representatives on January 18, 1794: "Reduced to poverty which I bless by a revolution which I bless even more, ill and imposing every possible privation on myself, I am selling my furniture piece by piece, including my books."[8] With a heavy heart, the sansculotte went off. Chamfort was free to survive in the few square feet he rented from M. de Chabanais, the main landlord on the street. Seven years after having left the Vaudreuil mansion, his kingdom had become a single room with window overlooking the street, plus a little alcove on the courtyard.

"I feel livelier than ever," he said, "what a pity that I no longer care about living."[9] The situation seemed hopeless indeed. Two heads fell per day in Paris, while in the provinces deaths numbered in the hundreds (mounting to tens of thousands in the Vendée). The Revolution claimed it no longer needed intellectuals, and the Terror now threatened citizens suspected of being suspect. Saint-Just would shortly proclaim: "Subtlety of mind and character is a major obstacle to liberty." France was establishing its own version of Sparta, hard and cold as a razor. Condorcet hid out on rue Servandoni, where he demonstrated impressive conviction by writing his *Esquisse historique des progrès de l'Esprit humain* [*Outlines of an Historical View of the Progress of the Human Mind*], a masterpiece of Enlightenment philosophy. Although Chamfort remained loyal to the cause, his aspirations (and perhaps his anxieties) shifted. Sélis caught him with Liebniz's *Theodicy* and Locke's *Reasonableness of Christianity,* as though Chamfort wanted to reinforce his revolution with revelation. Disturbed—but too proud to admit it—he consoled himself with these tomes on deism and tolerance, in which everything is for the best in the best of all worlds. This incredible serenity, following decades of misanthropy, was another way of refusing to grant the Terror the victory of despair.

Yet his financial decline continued, inexorable. In March he sold a bed, a small bathtub, a bust of Voltaire, and two hundred and thirty bound volumes. His collection of *Le Journal Encyclopédique*, in which his first articles had appeared, left for the auction room. At the age of fifty-four, he borrowed money for the first time. Five pieces of furniture, a few engravings, and thirteen volumes of Greek plays remained his most valued belongings. At which point he learned that Condorcet, wandering famished from house to house, then denounced at an inn due to the size of his omelette, committed suicide on March 29 with the poison Cabanis had given him.

No Flowers, Please

Nor did Chamfort have long to live. In closing up the wounds, Brasdor had forgotten to leave drainage slits. Infectious fluids once again spread throughout the body, provoking a fierce inflammation of the bladder. Chamfort lost his appetite, couldn't sleep. Alarmed by Chamfort's pains, the Ginguenés summoned Desault, one of the greatest living surgeons (who also treated Robespierre and the young Louis XVII in prison). But the specialist prescribed the wrong remedy and then decided, too late, to operate. During a slight improvement, Chamfort spoke again to Ginguené of his manuscripts, and settled part of his debts. He fainted as night fell. The next morning—Sunday, April 13, 1794—after a second attack, the faithful friends watching over him put a mirror to his lips. Colchen closed the eyelids—Chamfort was dead.

"The Terror [was] . . . so widespread that it represented an act of courage just to accompany him to his final resting place," wrote Ginguené, who felt that few were worthy of being invited to the funeral.[10] Most of those invited, however, showed up. The law reduced the official cortège to a bare minimum; it comprised the faithful Ginguené, puritanical Sieyès, worthy Colchen, and learned Van Praet (one close friend, the former Mohammed of the Revolution, plus two civil servants . . . far less than Mirabeau's procession). But the atmosphere was dignified, and many wept. Despite the more or less official closing of churches, Ginguené wanted to "religiously" fulfill all the "holy obligations"—Locke's *Reasonableness of Christianity* apparently had an impact. On the cover of the file listing Chamfort's estate is written "Les Innocents Charnel House."[11] But that cemetary had been closed in 1786, so his remains are probably in the catacombs, where Ancien Régime cemetaries were dumped. The author of *La jeune indienne* and *Mustapha et*

Zéangir having been practically forgotten, Chamfort's death was as clandestine as his birth. It merited just a few lines in the papers (Danton, Camille Desmoulins, and Hérault de Séchelles, guillotined a few days earlier, had been granted no more space—the Terror created equality in death, if not in life). Two weeks later, the loyal Ginguené joined poets André Chénier and Roucher in prison. The poets would be guillotined in the following weeks, as were Malesherbes and Mme. Elisabeth, while almost all the Auteuil regulars were incarcerated. Chamfort died too soon to benefit from the decree that declared the soul to be immortal. Too soon to learn that the actors of the Comédie-Française, in exile, performed *La jeune indienne* in May 1794 in Charlestown, where the play was set. Too soon to hail Robespierre's death and the end of tyranny that July, following the Thermidorian coup by parliament. Physically, nothing remained of Chamfort—neither corpse nor offspring. The state sold his remaining furniture to pay wages due his housekeeper and Dr. Brasdor as well as the surgeon who finished him off. His manuscripts were stolen just before the apartment was put under seal. The major part of Chamfort's oeuvre thus vanished for good.[12] The bastard child went out the way he came in—empty-handed.

Posterity

Though buried to general indifference, Chamfort was used to settle scores once Thermidor had put an end to the Terror. Journalist Pierre Delacroix denounced Chamfort's role during the Terror, all the while pointing out the value and severity of his sacrifices. "The only difference between me and those who appear to defend his memory, is that they sincerely weep for him after his death whereas I wept for him during his lifetime."[13] But the faithful friends—Ginguené, Roederer, and Sélis—remained wary of those who harbored "the fleur-de-lys in their hearts."[14] Ginguené inherited Chamfort's enemies, while Roederer engaged in an exchange with a writer for *Le Journal de Paris*.

> Roederer: Would you associate him with those who spilled blood?
>
> *Journal:* No, but I wouldn't place him on the side of good souls, either. . . . Wasn't it only when the Terror reached him that he stopped applauding terrorism?
>
> Roederer: It was well before that [and] . . . his conduct never

reflected his own self-interest. Chamfort always showed
himself to be above [his own interest]; further, we could say
that he was the enemy of it.[15]

But an anonymous contributor to the same paper replied that
"[Chamfort] loved only Chamfort. . . . At first he displayed only
gaity, with just a shaft of nastiness, but this shaft . . . became a tree.
It overshadowed his entire life. He wound up by becoming intoxicated on democracy and bad wine; I see a lot of fury in him, but look
hard for humaneness."[16] Baudin des Ardennes, a member of the
convention, then wrote to Roederer, reminding him of the moralist's
outrage at having been called "my dear Chamfort" by the prince de
Condé. "When one is so eager for equality, why not be content to
live among one's equals?"

Ginguené brought the polemics to a temporary halt by publishing Chamfort's *Oeuvres*. These four volumes, which presented the
moralist's aphorisms and anecdotes for the first time, were read all
across Europe. Chateaubriand, having emigrated to London, vainly
sought the anecdotes he had heard from Chamfort's own mouth. He
was one of the first to stress that this "masterpiece of the century"
had been mutilated. Chateaubriand's opinion was shared by the
prince de Ligne, who regretted that Chamfort had never traveled.
From Holstein, meanwhile, the exiled comte d'Angiviller accused
Mme. de Flahaut (his sister-in-law) of having furnished Chamfort
with damning anecdotes about the count.

In 1799, there appeared an account of a prophecy reportedly
made by Cazotte, notorious Illuminati and author of *Le diable
amoureux* [*The Devil in Love*]. The scene took place in 1788, in the salon of a "great lord and man of intellect." In attendance were Condorcet, Malesherbes, the poet Roucher, Bailly (famous for his theory
of a "hyperboreal people"), the duchesse de Gramont (the duc de
Choiseul's "incestuous" sister), and so on. All heard detailed pre-
dictions of their deaths during the Revolution. "You, Monsieur
Chamfort, you will slash your veins with twenty cuts of the razor,
and yet you will not die for several months," announced Cazotte.
"And, as I told you, you will then be governed by reason and philosophy alone. . . . Those who will treat you as such will all be philosophers, who will repeat your maxims." La Harpe, also present at
the meal, then said, "You've predicted numerous miracles, yet I
don't seem to figure among them." Cazotte replied, "You will account for a miracle no less extraordinary—you will become a

Christian." Upon which everyone burst into laughter. "Well, that's reassuring," said Chamfort. "If we are to perish when La Harpe becomes a Christian, we're immortal."

Given the notoriety of Cazotte's prophecies, this account initially sowed confusion. Soon, however, the hand of La Harpe became apparent; he had converted in 1795, becoming as hysterical a Catholic as he had been a Philosopher, then a Jacobin. This was the final settling of scores between the two enemies, La Harpe paying homage to the foresight that he himself lacked, and explaining his "creature's" suicide. The newly conservative La Harpe henceforth provided constant support to Chateaubriand, whom he regularly received at home, all the while continuing to perform his role as sadistic professor in Mme. Recamier's salon.

Purgatory

Following suit, other ex-Philosophers tried to clear their names at Chamfort's expense. Marmontel had the good sense to withdraw to the countryside on August 10, 1792, and to remain there; in his *Mémoires d'un père* [*A father's memoirs*], he denounced Chamfort's responsibility for the 1789 "plot," for the abolition of the Académie, and for the drop in Marmontel's standard of living (the former canon of the Philosopher's clan had owned numerous shares in a butchers' concern). Marmontel's friend and relation, Abbé Morellet, who displayed greater courage by fighting the closure of the Académie right to the end, inveighed in his *Mémoires* against Chamfort's terrorist statements, "similar to all those which, issued from the podium of the Assembly, resulted in nobles and priests from one end of France to the other being hunted down, and having their throats slit." Thus the man whom Voltaire had nicknamed *Mords-les* [Bite 'em] managed to adopt an almost saintly air. The sensitive Suard—a monarchist at heart who took care to say good things about Robespierre before retiring to Fontenay-aux-Roses (and who was accused of closing his door to a Condorcet in search of shelter)—reproached Chamfort, via his wife and her *Mémoires*, of having always been envious. Only Abbé Delille, that happy bastard (who had been set free during the Terror in order to praise Robespierre's cult of the Supreme Being), remained silent.

Chateaubriand had praised Chamfort and preface-writer Ginguené in 1797. "I am fulfilling my role of historian for them," he wrote in *Essai sur les révolutions*, "without being so arrogant as to claim their renown. When I lived among them, I shared only their indulgence." But such opinion found no immediate echo. For the end of Jacobinism and the dawn of romanticism effectly robbed Chamfort of relevance, a relevance increasingly claimed by Chateaubriand. Stendhal was the first to congratulate the moralist for not having repudiated the Revolution,[17] preferring Chamfort's maxims to his contemporaries' musings. "Read Chamfort," Stendhal repeatedly instructed his sister, praising the Attic wit and irony of a style he himself took as a model.[18] In Stendhal's wake, Mérimée found in Chamfort the comment repeated by all those individualists (including the Goncourts) "condemned" to the salons during the restoration and the Second Empire: "M. de Lassay . . . used to say that you should swallow a toad every morning, when going out into high society, so as to encounter nothing more disgusting during the day."[19]

While these heirs to the eighteenth century were seduced by Chamfort and his misanthropic levity, the nineteenth century in general rebuffed the revolutionary zealot. Sainte-Beuve hounded him brilliantly and pitilessly. "He didn't hope for Robespierre's downfall soon enough to merit witnessing it," wrote Sainte-Beuve in his *Les causeries du lundi* [*Monday-Chats*], subsequently accusing Chamfort of wanting to drag all of humanity down in his own fall. These two arch critics (the former having produced only one tragedy, *Mustapha,* and the latter only one novel, *Volupté*) seemed to be made for one another, like La Harpe and Chamfort earlier. It was a specialist on Sainte-Beuve who recognized that "the Chamfort disguised as well-meaning moralist" was obliged to fell the real Chamfort, the one "who truly dared to be himself."[20]

Sainte-Beuve nevertheless had regrets, and probably also regretted revealing his own *poison,* his literary bitterness, his bachelor's frustration.[21] After declaring that Chateaubriand's final portrait of Chamfort was odious, the Monday chatter admitted that his own was perhaps too severe.[22] Chamfort's real rehabilitation came from Germany, however, where his rarely lyrical but often scorching style seduced the early romantics (who also appreciated irony). Right from the early nineteenth century, the romantic theorist Friedrich Schlegel spoke of the moralist's "fragmentary brilliance," winning Schlegel the nickname of *der Chamfortierende.* And it was Pushkin who, in the Russia of 1830, had Eugenie Onegin read Chamfort in despair prior to his final discussion with Tatiana. Schopenhauer felt there was more metaphysics in a single Chamfort anecdote than in all of Hegel's *Phenomenology* and, more concretely, borrowed aspects of Chamfort for his own elitist and pessimistic morality.[23] Nietzsche discovered a literary soul-brother who dared say out loud what Zarathustra confided to the mountains. The Goncourts painted a sprightly portrait of an "executioner with courtly sword," an "immortal champion of the epigram" who succeeded in condensing all the "knowledge of the world" onto little scraps of paper.[24] Fin-de-siècle Paris adopted this half-cynic, half-ascetic, whose contradictions had revolted people a century earlier ("He exceeds all limits," Baudin des Ardennes had claimed). For the "cult-of-self" generation recognized itself in his egotism, and Rémy de Gourmont devoted a now-lost preface to Chamfort. Hence it required several decades for Chamfort to be understood, for time to catch up with his ideas.

Consecration

The twentieth century finally supplied Chamfort with a healthy contingent of misanthropes and ideological dropouts (psychoanalysts remaining strangely silent). Paul Léautaud—"the Rue-de-Condé Chamfort," with his trademark cats and basket—regularly haunted the work, manias, and even the final residence of the moralist. Wartime Collaboration turned Chamfort into a bolshevik, while the Liberation made him out to be a rebel. Céline found Chamfort to be a model of conciseness which "put him to shame." Albert Camus, in his preface to Chamfort's *Maximes*, hailed a willfulness always ready to pay the price for superiority, a hardness toward others and toward oneself, a desperate saintliness that culminated in an exploit "as bloody as the greatest conquests."[25] This became a point of reference for the author of *L'homme révolté* [*The rebel*].

The most recent reader of Chamfort is Emile Cioran, whose balkan expression of French symmetry and skepticism makes him undisputed current heir to Chamfort. In *De l'inconvénient d'être dé* [*The Trouble with Being Born*], which ranges from maxims to long fragments (like Nietzsche), from the criticism of civilization to a godless mysticism, from destructive fury to nihilistic affirmation, Cioran confessed his "bouts of gratitude" for the magnificently ungrateful Chamfort.

Instead of leaving children behind, Chamfort left readers— including some nasty ones. His true descendants are not the revolutionaries of 1789 (those "soul-brothers" attempting to bring forth the "new man" Chamfort invoked), but rather those "solitary minds" (to use Barbey d'Aurevilly's expression) who, through a paradox perfectly consistent with the "skin-deep aristocrat," were generally more or less reactionary (with the notable exception of Camus and Stendhal, although this latter case is debatable). Of all those readers who shared Chamfort's misanthropy, intellectual elitism, pessimism, and misogyny, Nietzsche is obviously the most important and the most accomplished. He reveals the other side of the moralist, not the revolutionary but the lifelong elitist, the individualist who was convinced of the absolute superiority of intelligence over birth and wealth, yet who detested the social trappings of superiority.

Had Chamfort remained just a little more of a philosopher, the Revolution would have missed out on its tragic wit and its sharpest sting; it would be regarded as a much more stupid event and would not seduce so many spirits.

Nietzsche
The Gay Science

Nietzsche read Chamfort sympathetically, in the etymological sense of the term. Though Nietzsche must have known of Chamfort's existence through Schopenhauer, it was sometime between 1879 (when Paul Rée first mentioned Chamfort to him) and the writing of *The Gay Science* in 1881 that Viennese writer Zdekauer gave Nietzsche a copy of Chamfort's *Maximes* with a preface by A. Houssaye.[1] Nietzsche thus discovered a sick man who bared his wounds, a consciousness that placed passion over reason, a fury that was the equal of intelligence. Here was a moralist who challenged all commonly accepted ideas, including his own. Nietzsche recognized himself in this philosopher always ready to assert his *self* against society, and who claimed to study only what appealed to him. Here was a precocious practitioner of *The Gay Science*. Nietzsche appreciated the "aristocrat" who denounced a society in which slaves imposed their law on superior minds, and who gazed on this society with a "sarcastic gaity" and an "indulgent contempt." In Chamfort, Nietzsche discovered the freedom of tone, the nimble intelligence (what he would call "exquisite conciseness" in his *Nachgelassene Fragmente*), and the art of dialoguing with one's self that he had so appreciated in Stendhal and Montaigne. This dialogue had effectively derailed Nietzsche from his youthful goal of establishing a system reconciling all of German philosophy, in order to supersede it. He now understood that contradiction was not merely an inherent aspect of any intellectual autobiography, it could also be a weapon for a thinker who, like Chamfort, tended to "turn around whatever he finds veiled . . . [to see] what these things look like when they are reversed."[2] So, without renouncing his global project, the bludgeoning philosopher considered the piecemeal

263

moralist a sublimated friend, a fellow scholar, a station along an anti-Christ's tortured path.

According to Houssaye, the dying Chamfort supposedly said to Sieyès, "My friend, I'm leaving this world where the heart either breaks or bronzes." This could only delight the hermit hostile to any form of pity and weakness, would please the pagan saint determined to break with country and family. For Nietzsche had decided to forget his mother, and the long line of ministers from which he descended, to follow an increasingly solitary and masculine path, thereby freeing himself—like the illegitimate son—from all forebears and all descendents in order *create himself.*

There is nothing new in comparing the two men. Lou Salomé mentioned Chamfort's influence on Nietzsche, and all of Nietzsche's biographers (Charles Andler in particular), have noted the similarities between these two loners who advocated self-deprivation as the sine qua non for independence. Both of these antisocial beings were ready to do anything—including fiercely attacking the self—to be themselves. But what is perhaps insufficiently acknowledged is the extent to which the elitist and mysogynist philosopher of *Beyond Good and Evil,* that expunger of feminine values in and around himself, represents the culmination of Chamfort. It sometimes seems as though the disciple is held to have preceded the prophet, whereas all the elements of the Nietzchean revolution are already present in the *Maximes:* superior individualism, hatred for petty morality, the cult of energy as sovereign remedy for melancholy, the denunciation of "females" as a factor of decline. Nietzsche was right to praise that "man rich in depths and backgrounds of the soul—gloomy, suffering, ardent,"[3] for Chamfort's struggle against pretense, like his hatred of Pharisees, reveals a bracing and desperate determination to discover that secret knowledge of the entire world (which every philosopher seeks prior to retreating into a special, limited field).

All his life, Chamfort attempted to find a new morality to replace faltering Christianity. This unsuccessful quest led to a tolerant deism following his suicide attempt. But he had already managed to rock religious foundations in his *Products of the Perfected Civilization* by sketching out a morality where good and evil intertwine like a caduceus, where the former unintentionally works for the latter, and where the second unwittingly leads back to the first. It was Nietzsche who best understood this antisystem, in which generosity is sometimes the brash expression of egotism, in which misanthropy can be avoided only through weakness of character and "absence of ideas," in which energetic minds are condemned to "deviations which suppose the absence of all morality" and to a "consuming bitterness" which occasionally renders them "highly odious." In this world, "while you should love thy neighbor as thyself, it is just as fair to love thyself as thy neighbor." Chamfort had envisaged extending this inversion of values to the arts, philosophy, and legislation prior to his conversion to the Revolution; Nietzsche managed to go beyond his iconoclastic predecessor by announcing the end of Christianity.

Both shared the same postulate: the world was not living up to its potential, and civilization diminished the individual. Chamfort identified three culprits—the aristocracy, which suppressed talent; women, who wanted to subject men to their own law; and the "Nazarene sect" which was "the source of human degradation." This sounds like pure Nietzsche. Nietzsche, however, also accused the church of making the powerful feel guilty; sitting on the wooden benches of the University of Basel, he dreamed of a mythic, all-powerful aristocracy. This became his personal ideal, even though he sometimes painted it as that of the French nobility of the sixteenth and seventeenth centuries. Chamfort, however, knew just how far the aristocracy of his day was from this iron-willed model and from the almost dictatorial agenda he had set for himself in 1765. Overlooking the ephemeral greatness of nobility, Chamfort saw only its historic injustice, and so fell back onto a "citizen's" Christianity. Elitist everywhere he triumphed and egalitarian everywhere he was excluded, Chamfort wound up by prescribing a remedy the opposite of Nietzsche's on every point. Nietzsche's revolution was reactionary; he was an anti-Jacobin who preached inequality—or death. There remains an unbridgeable distance between the German's defense of "blond" pagan instincts and the Frenchman's call for the rebirth of natural man. Referring to Chamfort's period of self-sacrifice in 1792 and noting that this avenged nothing, Nietzsche basically reproached Chamfort for only one thing—having opted for a return to bucolic pre-Christian origins rather than the war-like pre-Christianity advocated by Nietzsche, on the grandiose scale of Dionysus and Zarathustra.

It is no coincidence that the trajectory of these two masked minds (which aspired to unmask everything) began with an illness and led to a split in personality. Illness drove the "venereal" moralist and the syphilitic philosopher to begin their sabotage on themselves. Illness was the acid in which they tempered their morality, their defense of an "anti-social" attitude to civilization, their rage for simultaneous rebirth and destruction. "A moralist who would extinguish his passions is like a chemist who would extinguish his flame," observed Chamfort. Nietzsche, also aware that he was dealing with explosive material, asserted in his *Mixed Opinions and Aphorisms*, "During his experiments, a chemist will inevitably poison or burn himself on occasion." Both of these thinkers, determined to strip morality of some of its rust, simultaneously acted as experimenter and experiment, patient and doctor.

Nietzsche's first reading of Chamfort was enthusiastic. He was delighted at the idea of being one of the few Germans still familiar with him, appreciating and understanding Chamfort better than the French themselves. Nietzsche even announced, in the *Nachgelassene Fragmente* of 1881, that the time had come to "rediscover" Chamfort. Nietzsche saw himself as heir to the Enlightenment, a modern *Aufklärer*, and he felt that the "crystalline" style was the best way to translate and give substance to his inversion of values. His discovery of a Frenchman who considered words themselves to be a distortion (a misanthrope was someone who truly loved mankind) was thus every bit as electric as Mirabeau had suggested. Nietzsche claimed again in 1881: "Chamfort's collection of maxims and anecdotes has the advantage over every book in the world of ultimately possessing the power of a torpedo-fish."[4] During the same period he wrote to his friend Peter Gast, "We also have the honor of both holding the *same* opinion on Chamfort. He was a man of Mirabeau's caliber in terms of character, heart, and scope of intellect."[5]

For Mirabeau was crucial to the Nietzsche-Chamfort encounter. In *The Gay Science*, Nietzsche placed Mirabeau "above the foremost statesmen of yesterday and today." This explains the flattering portrait of the French moralist in the same book, as well as a strange posthumous fragment: "Rationality during the French Revolution was Chamfort's and Mirabeau's rationality. Irrationality was Rousseau's irrationality." The German's enthusiasm here got the better of his lucidity, for in the same posthumous fragments he drew up this amazing list: "Zoroaster, Moses, Mohammed, Jesus, Plato, Brutus, Spinoza, Mirabeau, Me. . . ."[6]

Yet, at the same time, Nietzsche recognized the extent to which Chamfort's "rationality" was unconventional, like his own. Chamfort had declared, prior to 1789, that the true philosopher should assume the status of the dead in order to free himself from any involvement with the living, from all error—just as Nietzsche, in another posthumous fragment, wanted "to engender the view-point of the dead . . . to be an invisible spectator."[7] Nietzsche was unable, however, to explain why the wise Chamfort was not content with his superiority, why he wound up rejecting the advantages of his insight, detachment, and misanthropy, to the point of such self-sacrifice and suicide.

For, of course, what amazed Nietzsche about Chamfort was that "a man who understood men and the crowd [so well] . . . neverthe-less joined the crowd and did not stay [on the sidelines] in philo-sophical renunciation and resistance." He was amazed that Chamfort wanted to save men after having fully evaluated the catastrophe, after recognizing that men "become smaller when they flock together." Furthermore, Chamfort deliberately called for revolution, an undertaking that the German always detested. Nietzsche's rationality resided in his hatred of the father and in his desire, defined in almost psychoanalytic terms, to avenge his mother. Nietzsche enjoyed inspired insight into the illegitimate son, just as Sainte-Beuve offered insight on the failed writer and Chateaubriand on the renegade sage. Chamfort's "all too justifiable resentment" sufficed to plunge him into an egalitarian revolution, he who was a priori so inegalitarian. But Chamfort's "hatred and re-venge" also served to "educate a whole generation" which included some of history's "most illustrious human beings." He was, there-fore, an object of envy for the German hermit, who sought disciples all his life. Via Mirabeau, Chamfort even played a significant if secret historical role as prompter, his own convictions having been prompted by "ardent energy" and the circumstances surrounding his birth.

How, then, did Nietzsche get from the flattering 1881 portrait in *The Gay Science* to the scathing depiction of the man of rancor in *The Genealogy of Morals*, six years later? It is possible that Nietzsche, weary of being compared to Chamfort, wanted to conjure away their resemblance and rid himself of his own self-destructive drives. And it is probable that, after having been seduced—to say the least—by the strange osmosis that took place between Mirabeau and Chamfort around 1784, seeing it as an incarnation of his super-human dream (a lion with a cat's mind), the German moralist subsequently wanted to dissect the sick brain of his French forebear, retracing his psychic trajectory from resentment to Jacobinism.

For Nietzsche had meanwhile entered a new, "dionysiac" phase, as illustrated by the preface added to *The Gay Science* in 1886.

Temporarily recovered, he evokes the state of quarantine from which he had just emerged (and which Chamfort had also experienced), "that stretch of desert, exhaustion, disbelief, of icing up the midst of youth, this interlude of old age at the wrong time, this tyranny of pain even excelled by the tyranny of pride . . . this radical retreat into solitude as a self-defense against a contempt for men that had become pathologically clairvoyant—this determined self-limitation to what was bitter, harsh, and hurtful to know."[8] Any belief in a final state or happy outcome, continued Nietzsche, any aspiration for another world placed under the sign of peace, sun, and harmony can only come—like the desire for medication—from a sick philosopher. Chamfort was a philosopher who, unlike Nietzsche, was unable to kill off the human rancor in himself in order to glorify the world *as it is*, unable to do away with the social animal and adopt permanent solitude.[9]

Nietzsche was thus the first to have established, from within, the link between Chamfort's illness, birth, misanthropy, and Jacobinism. He drained the morality from Sainte-Beuve's view of Chamfort—"one of the strangest and clearest [cases] of a mental ulcer," according to the author of *Les causeries du lundi*. This is why Nietzsche deserves the place of honor, far ahead of Schopenhauer, in the pantheon of Chamfort's readers. Nietzsche considered Chamfort a "nobler and more philosophical La Rochefoucauld of the eighteenth century."[10]

"One cannot reasonably expect to arrive at the truth," said Chamfort. "Nothing is true, all is permitted," replied Nietzsche. By stressing the limitations of Enlightenment and rationality, by glorifying vital strength, by deliberately endorsing the Terror and indirectly endorsing the advent of the Nazi "superman," Chamfort and Nietzsche undermined the hypocritical balance of power governing old Europe. The paradox is that these two individualists effectively accelerated the eruption of the masses into history—independently or in collusion with "leaders."[11] By hastening the demise of inequality and religion, they enabled Europe to emerge convalescent and democratic. Thus they are read today less as philosophical theorists than as novelists recounting their own consciousness, as chroniclers of their "ideology," as human case studies revealing constant contradiction in values. This, after all, only does them justice. Both knew that the medicine they prescribed "would kill a horse"—even if they were not yet aware that it would wind up killing them, too.

APPENDIXES

1. THE THEFT OF CHAMFORT'S MANUSCRIPTS

I found [Chamfort] highly entertaining, yet so harsh . . .

Julien Green, in his diary

The missing texts inspire unequal interest. The loss of "the major part"[1] of the *Products of the Perfected Civilization*—over two thousand fragments in all—is irreparable. One is less inclined, however, to be so categorical about the two *Epîtres de Ninon* [*Ninon's epistles*], the poems on the Fronde and Geneva, and the epigrams translated from Greek ("society" tidbits the moralist regularly proffered from 1770 until his death), even though his friends claimed that Chamfort expected such work to significantly contribute to his fame. The date of the theft is unclear. Ginguené was in Saint-Lazare prison when the apartment was sealed, and no one from the group was there when the seals were removed. Ginguené suspected one of Chamfort's acquaintances;[2] "a disloyal act has been committed," he wrote in the Year IX (1800–1801). "But who would dare profit from it?" Who, indeed? Creditors seeking reimbursement? Suppliers to whom Chamfort owed money? The most likely hypothesis remains that of a close acquaintance. For Chamfort had spoken of the existence of his boxes to only a very few people. Mirabeau and Abbé Roman knew, but they were dead. Sélis and Ginguené knew, too, but they were probably the only ones who did.

Unless, of course. . . . Unless his enemies were in the know. There was no lack of them at the time. Some people reproached Chamfort for having betrayed the Republic, others for having served it. Sélis leaned toward the theory of theft by agents of the Terror. While it is true that revolution left little room for introspection, it is striking that there is nothing in the remaining papers on Robespierre, Marat, the Montagne, Mme. Roland, and the Gironde. There are barely ten allusions to the four most dense years of his life during which, by his own admission, he learned the most about human nature.

Ginguené nevertheless thought the theft a private affair. He began an investigation on his release from prison, but it led nowhere. Early in 1795, the magistrate allowed him to examine the two folders that escaped the catastrophe, and Ginguené also found a box containing Mirabeau's letters to Chamfort in a locked room on rue Chabanais. Ginguené thereupon announced his decision to publish Chamfort's *Oeuvres*, with the approval of the Commission de l'Instruction Publique.[3] Ginguené was accused of snatching the bread from Sélis's mouth, but Sélis completely exonerated him. Chalamel, a member of the Montagne, then accused Ginguené of having broken the seals on the two folders without witnesses, practically naming Ginguené himself as the thief. "We're seeing a lot of people put on a good show in society with . . . the wit of others," wrote Chalamel.[4] Once again, Sélis defended Ginguené. Ginguené then hypothesized that the stolen fragments might be coded, as Chamfort once claimed to Abbé Roman. But the argument doesn't hold up. For why would only illegible texts have been stolen? Unless, of course, it was truly a political affair—the Commune or the Comité de Salut Public may have wanted to seize the secrets of an influential "traitor." Or unless, finally, one of the civil servants was a collector—a mighty rare species in 1794.

With a heavy heart, Ginguené decided to publish the "debris" of the masterpiece his friend had bequeathed him. He eliminated more than half of the extant fragments, those he judged weak or repetitive (particularly in the section titled "Characters").[5] He then organized the rest according to an outline left by Chamfort. Ginguené initially published this selection in *La Décade Philosophique*, then again in Year III (1795) in Chamfort's *Oeuvres* (in which the thief was unsuccessfully exhorted to render up the treasure "in the name of friendship, philosophy, and letters"). There the investigation came to an end, even though two of the directors then in power—Barras and Sieyès—had known Chamfort.[6]

Ginguené—who can never be too highly praised for his determination to give Chamfort a second life, that of the moralist we know today—published Mirabeau's *Letters* to Chamfort in 1797, inciting A. Lenoir to have a bust of Chamfort sculpted. Ginguené not only executed Chamfort's literary testament to the letter, he also adopted Chamfort's ideas on education in his role as head of the Comité d'Instruction Publique. In 1798, Ginguené was appointed ambassador to Turin, only to return to France after receiving a humiliating reprimand from Talleyrand (Nancy Ginguené had wanted to replace the "livry of servitude" with short jackets as the official dress for Turin receptions). Whereupon Ginguené retired to the Montmorency area.

But Ginguené had sworn to track down the man who had amputated Chamfort's heritage the way Tobiesen had shortened his life. Ginguené took up his investigation again, sounding out survivors. Finally, he apparently discovered something in 1813. "This is not the place to say what has become of the rest," he wrote in his entry on "Chamfort" for Michaud's *Biographie universelle,* "but someday it will be known. On the very day of his death, all of Chamfort's missing work fell into the very hands from which they passed into those which probably still hold them."[7] But Ginguené took his secret to the grave in 1816. In 1824, the Auguis edition became the most complete by publishing twenty-two tales not included among the papers found on Chamfort's death.[8] Some of those fragments excluded by Ginguené made their way into the three reprints issued during the nineteenth century. But the major part of the collection—which Mirabeau in 1784 had already described as immense—has truly disappeared. In 1857, publisher P. J. Stahl wrote, "It is said that Chamfort's unpublished manuscripts exist and that the person who has them abuses the right of ownership and refuses to give out any information concerning them."[9] They are still at large.

2. PORTRAITS OF CHAMFORT

Chamfort apparently never posed during his lifetime, perhaps because illness had disfigured his face early in his adult life. With the exception of one small engraving, all known portraits of Chamfort are posthumous.

The portrait found on the cover of this book is the handsomest as well as the only psychologically plausible one. The artist and the painting's current whereabouts are unknown; it was photographed early in the twentieth century (cover photo by Roger-Viollet). Although it dates from 1805, it is published here because it inspired the engravings most often reproduced to illustrate the moralist's personality and oeuvre. The first, published by Touquet in 1821, is held by the Carnavalet Museum, and the second, published by Jouaust but undated, can be found in the print collection at the Bibliothèque Nationale. The two engravers took care to show Chamfort in dress more appropriate to the period in which he lived.

The only contemporary engraving was turned up by a print dealer named Mas. It bears an attractive yet anonymous expression which might belong to any young man of the eighteenth century.

In 1797, Ginguené suggested to Alexandre Lenoir that Chamfort be included in Lenoir's Gallery of Great Men in his Museum of French Monuments. Claude Michallon executed a plaster bust late in 1797 or early in 1798,[1] which must have been a faithful likeness, given Ginguené's presence. Late in 1798, Lenoir swapped it (along with others) for stone columns from a church in Chartres. The bust was then placed in the Chartres library, from which it disappeared—probably during bombings in the Second World War. Chamfort's strange fate apparently continues to hound him.

The Mandet de Riom Museum has a portrait of Chamfort in its basement that was painted in 1860 by Nicolas-Auguste Laurens. It was part of an Auvergne gallery made up of portraits—often imaginary—painted during the Second Empire. Presented to the museum by M. Boudet de Bardon, it is supposedly "based on a pastel by Quentin de La Tour." But there is no trace of the original in books devoted to the work of the pastel artist, and the face in this portrait, with its weak chin and empty gaze, is not very convincing. Wildenstein and Besnard do provide a list of unidentified portraits by Quentin de La Tour but without reproducing them. There is, therefore, a small chance of finding the pastel, purportedly used by Laurens, probably in some private collection.

An engraving found in the Bibliothèque Nationale's print collection (Series N 2), occasionally reproduced, bears the legend, "La Tour pinx. Larcher sculpt." This homely, crude engraving, done early in the nineteenth century, only distantly resembles the Riom portrait—unless it is the other way around. The engraving exists in two states.

Another engraved medallion, also "inspired" by La Tour, and signed by Mercier, was published by A. Tradieu in 1878,[2] in a book that hails Chamfort as "one of greatest men of lower Auvergne."

A decent portrait was printed at the front of F. Duloup's version of Chamfort's *Oeuvres principales* published by Pauvert in 1961 (no source information was provided, however, and Duloup is now dead). The subject rests his elbows on four volumes which seem to bear the title *Tableau historique*. Chamfort, of course, authored the *Tableaux historiques de la Révolution française*, illustrated by Prieur.

A drawing by Moine was to be found in the copy of La Fontaine's *Oeuvres*, published by C. A. Walckenaer in 1827, kept in the Bibliothèque nationale's reserve collection. This nineteenth-century drawing was attractive but not very faithful to the eighteenth century. It has, moreover, been stolen.

Finally, there exists a hideous engraving done by Rouargue for the first volume of the 1826 edition of Chamfort's *Oeuvres*—executed, like the others, posthumously.

3. UNANTHOLOGIZED APHORISMS AND ANECDOTES

Translator's note: The third Appendix of the French version of Chamfort contains seventy hitherto uncollected aphorisms and anecdotes that Claude Arnaud compiled from three main sources. The material is of uneven quality and is primarily of interest to French scholars who already have access to Chamfort's complete works. A selection of this material, therefore, is given here; numbers correspond to the French edition.

Mirabeau Papers

These nine fragments are drawn from two volumes of letters and drafts of letters written in England in 1785 by Mirabeau, including several to Chamfort.[1] They were anonymously translated into English and published in London in 1832.[2] The two volumes contain twenty-five "anecdotes" and eighty-two "maxims" attributed to the people's tribune. But all of them were plagiarized either from Chamfort (eighty-seven fragments, of which fifty-five have already been anthologized) or from Rivarol (the twenty remaining fragments).[3] The following nine fragments are taken directly from the 1832 English translation (*Mirabeau's Letters during His Residence in England* [London: Effingham Wilson, 1832], 1:293–311).

3. R., while in company with M. de Créqui and several noblemen, was conversing about the rights of the aristocracy, and exclaimed—"We shall be degraded! We shall be ruined!" M. de Créqui repeated, in an under tone—"We! We!" "Well!" said R., "what is there so extraordinary in that word?" "Only that it is the plural I find so singular!"

6. If the young generally display more courage on a death bed, and greater weakness on the scaffold, than the old, it is because, in the first instance, young men preserve more hope, and in the second, suffer a greater loss.

8. . . . The esteem we have for an author is proportioned to the analogy between his ideas and those of his reader.

9. The least fault a man in distress commits is a sufficient pretence for the rich to refuse him all assistance; they would have the unfortunate entirely perfect.

21. Vices are more frequently habits than they are passions.

24. If poverty makes men sigh, riches make him yawn. When fortune exempts us from labour, nature loads us with the weight of time.

25. R—— used to say of the Duke of Orleans, whose face was covered with pimples, and of a purple hue, [that] debauchery had dispensed [him from] blushing.

26. Little minds triumph over the errors of men of genius, as the owl rejoices at an eclipse of the sun.

32. Man passes his life in [justifying] the past, in complaining of the present, and in trembling for the future.

Anecdotes Never Reprinted

36. A foreigner, finding himself at Mlle. de Lespinasse's residence, along with d'Alembert and many other distinguished people, grew impatient on listening to an inexorable talker. He took d'Alembert aside. "Did you know," he said to Alembert, "that the man who is forcing everyone to be quiet and listen to him is just a poor *bastard* of ——?"

"Sir," replied d'Alembert, "you're addressing the wrong party. I have the misfortune of being in the same situation as that gentleman."

The blundering foreigner then hastened over to Mlle. de Lespinasse, and threw himself on the sofa where she was sitting. "How clumsy and unfortunate I am," he said to her, and recounted the incident.

"I do feel sorry for you, sir," replied Mlle. de Lespinasse, "for I am in the same situation as M. d'Alembert."

Roederer commented that what made this anecdote so singular was that Chamfort, who recounted it to Talleyrand and Roederer, could have said the very same thing to the person who recounted it to *him*. (From *Oeuvres du Comte Roederer*, 4:259 ff. Grosclaude, in fact, included this anecdote in his edition of *Produits de la civilisation perfectionée*)

37. Given his advanced age, Fontenelle had or took nearly every liberty, and one day entered Mme. Helvétius's dressing room to find her almost totally undressed. "Oh, Madam," he said in withdrawing, "if only I were eighty again!" (Fontenelle lived to be almost one hundred.) (See A. Giuillois, *Le salon de Mme. Helvétius*, 2d ed. [Calman-Levy, 1894])

38. Of La Harpe, he used to say, "He's a man who uses his faults to hide his vices." (Grimm's *Correspondance littéraire*, v. XII, p. 248, April 1779)

40. Baculard d'Arnaud was in the habit of borrowing small sums from everyone, which he never paid back. "He owes a million ecus in ten-sou pieces," said Chamfort. (*Biographie des contemporains*, by Rabbe, de Boisjolin, and Sainte-Preuve [Paris, 1834], 1:139)

44. Early in 1789, someone defended the privileges of the nobility. "The comment is obviously that of a gentleman, though not noble," said Chamfort. (*Journal de Paris*, 5 Prairial, Year VI [May 25, 1798])

Russian Papers

Ginguené bequeathed the papers he had found in Chamfort's apartment (only half of which he published) to Alphonse Denis. Denis, respecting Ginguené's selection, steadfastly refused to bring out a new edition. He nevertheless lent the papers to Victor Hugo, with whom he was acquainted; whereupon Abel Hugo, unbeknownst to his brother Victor, then recopied certain fragments rejected by Ginguené. Sixty-one of these were published, complete with inaccuracies, by the publisher Stahl (alias Hetzel), and should, therefore, be added to the one hundred fifty published by Colnet (who offered no explanation of their origin) and the ten hundred seventy-five published by Ginguené. The last French owner of the manuscripts, Feuillet de Conches, allowed Lescure to publish one hundred thirty-three new fragments in 1879. Feuillet de Conches was a renowned collector and expert who, frustrated by history's lapses, wound up forging hundreds of letters by Marie-Antoinette, Louis

XVI, Charlemagne, etc. But he doesn't seem to have "toyed" with Chamfort's manuscripts, which then dropped out of sight. In 1961, J. Sylvestre de Sacy claimed that they were permanently lost.

The whole lot had in fact been sold by the manuscript dealer Charavay to a Russian collector in 1908. In 1958, it was bought by the Lenin library in Moscow from a second Russian owner. Ten years later, the Lenin library published forty-six new fragments in French and in Russian, in a specialized review, *Utshenie Zapiski*, no. 304.[4] Eight of these are given below.

45. When Hamilton finished preparing the comte de Gramont's *Memoires*, he lent the book to his sister, the comtesse de Gramont. She felt that in fact the book presented her husband as nothing more than a witty swindler, and demanded that the *Mémoires* not be published. Hamilton gave his word. Shortly after, the *Mémoires* appeared. The countess reproached her brother, who protested his innocence. On further investigation, it turned out that the comte de Gramont had discovered his wife's copy, and had sold it to a bookseller. The second edition should have mentioned this revealing incident.

46. The Chevalier de Lupé recounted in front of Mme. de Villeroi, who respected women, a trait of some woman or other who was related to Mme. de Villeroi. "I find it extraordinary," she told him, "that you can speak that way of my aunt." "Heavens, Madam," said M. de Lupé, "it's your uncle who speaks thus."

48. Ambition is an avaricious vanity. Love of fame is a vain ambition.

49. It is a profound truth that we only truly love our friends when we love their faults. This doesn't mean flattering them, but simply recognizing that these faults are due to great qualities, which is almost always the case with characters of real substance.

54. A conceited man read a letter from a woman to a group which included the very woman who had written it. The letter happened to be tender and decent, which prompted the woman to say, "Whoever wrote that letter should blush only on account of the address."

61. A woman between two men, [one] of whom says tender things to her, while the other speaks ill of her rivals: She smiles at the former, but listens to the latter.

63. A man hoped to convince a lord to intercede on behalf of an unfortunate friend in prison. He took a serious and moving tone. The lord interrupted him and no more was said. Another, shrewder, man, told a rousing tale in which one of his friends was the hero. The lord laughed and wanted to know the name of the friend. "He's in prison. It's so-and-so."

"That's just the man I wanted to talk to you about," said the first man.

"Then why the devil did you begin with boring talk about a man so appealing?" replied the lord, at the same time handing over the money necessary to clear the unfortunate man.

64. If the Revolution has not yet rid itself of countless small social hypocrisies, those eternal comedies played out in salons and social circles, then the Revolution has failed in its first task.

4. A CHAMFORT SAMPLER

Translator's note: Readers unfamiliar with Chamfort's aphorisms may appreciate this small selection. It is hoped that they will subsequently seek out W. S. Merwin's ambitious translation of all of the maxims and meditations, along with many of the characters and anecdotes (see Products of the Perfected Civilization *[San Francisco: North Point Press, 1984]). The versions here owe much, of course, to Merwin's pioneering work, but greater syntactic liberty has often been taken in order to retain stylistic fidelity to the vigor of Chamfort's prose. In addition, occasional semantic corrections have been made. Yet a number of Merwin's particularly successful translations have been included in this selection, and these are indicated by the initials WSM.*

The numbers of the fragments correspond to the 1982 Gallimard/Folio edition of Maximes et pensées, caractères et anecdotes.

"Maxims and Meditations"

2. Most authors of collections of poetry or epigrams proceed as though they were eating cherries or oysters. They start out by selecting the best, but wind up swallowing everything.

7. In the current state of society, it seems to me that man is corrupted more by reason than by passion. Human passions (by which I mean those found in primitive man) have preserved what little nature still exists in the social order.

36. One prays that a villain will be lazy, a fool silent. (WSM)

53. What is a philosopher? A man who pits nature against the law, reason against custom, conscience against opinion, and his own judgment against injustice.

60. Rank without merit earns deference without respect. (WSM)

65. Men become smaller when they flock together—like Milton's devils, who were forced to become pygmies in order to fit into Pandaemonium.

67. Physical disasters and the calamities of human nature made society necessary. Society's ordeals were then added to those of nature. The drawbacks of society led to the need for government, whereupon the evils of government were added to those of society. Such is the history of human nature.

73. The philosopher who would extinguish his passions is like the chemist who would extinguish his flame.

79. Tragic drama has the great ethical flaw of attaching too much importance to life and death.

87. In getting to know the evils of nature, one comes to scorn death; in getting to know those of society, one comes to scorn life.

94. A man who is poor but independent of others obeys necessity alone. A man who is rich but dependent must obey some other man, or even several others.

95. Ambitious men who fall short of their goals and live in despondency remind me of Ixion who was lashed to the wheel for having courted a cloud.[1]

104. Public opinion claims a jurisdiction which a gentleman should never completely recognize, yet which he should never refuse to acknowledge.

118. The great disaster of passions is not the torment they cause, but the debasing errors and depravity into which they lead men. Without these drawbacks, passion would enjoy many advantages over cold reason, which never produces happiness. Passions enable men to *live*, wisdom merely enables them to *survive*.

120. One needs to be able to unite opposites: love of virtue with indifference to public opinion, a penchant for work for indifference to fame, and concern for one's health with indifference for one's life.

129. An unprincipled man is usually a man without character, for had he been born with character, he would have felt the need to endow himself with principles.

150. Precepts are to conduct what practice is to the arts. (WSM)

152. One is made happy or unhappy by a multitude of things which one cannot see, cannot admit, cannot express.

194. Society is made up of two great classes: those who have more dinners than appetite, and those who have more appetite than dinners. (WSM)

229. On seeing what goes on in society, the most misanthropic of men would wind up amused, and Heraclitus himself would die of laughter.

230. Given equal intelligence and enlightenment, I don't think a rich man can ever know nature, human feelings and society as thoroughly as a poor man. Because any time the former might invest in pleasure, the latter must find comfort in reflection.

239. Experience enlightens private individuals, but corrupts princes and high officials.

240. Today's public is like modern tragedy—absurd, ghastly, and dull.

261. If you wish to be appreciated in high society, you have to let yourself be taught many things you already know by people who don't.

282. Since philosophers claim to take people for what they're worth, it is perfectly clear why such an assessment pleases no one.

284. Rousseau's penchant for solitude is hardly surprising; souls like him tend to find themselves alone, living in isolation like the eagle. But, like the eagle, the scope of their gaze and the height to which they soar lend enchantment to their solitude.

302. Calumny is like a wasp which harasses you. Raise no hand against it unless you're sure of killing it, for otherwise it will return to the charge more furious than ever.

312. Poverty cheapens crime.

336. Whatever I learned, I no longer know. The little that I still know, I've intuited.

354. High society, which diminishes men greatly, reduces women to nothing.

359. Love, such as it exists in high society, is merely an exchange of whims and the contact of skins.

373. A woman of wit once made a comment which may well be the secret of her sex—which is that every woman who takes a lover places more importance in how he is regarded by other women than in how she regards him herself.

376. Ear and mind can recognize pointless repetition, whereas the heart cannot.

425. Most books produced these days seem to have been written in a day, using books read the day before.

434. A little philosophy leads to a contempt for learning; a great deal of philosophy leads to a respect for it. (WSM)

445. Having a great many ideas doesn't betoken a fine mind, just as having a great many soldiers doesn't betoken a fine general.

447. What I admire in the ancient philosophers is the desire to make their conduct conform to their writings. One notices it in Plato, Theophrastes, and a number of others. Practical ethics was so essential to their philosophy that several of them were placed at the heads of schools without having written anything: Xenocrates, for example, Polemon, Heusippus, etc. Socrates, without having offered a single work to the public, and without having studied any science except ethics, was the chief philosopher of his age. (MSW)

457. Economists are surgeons who have an excellent scalpel but a jagged lancet—they operate exquisitely on the dead but torture the living.

468. There's an amusing way to prove that France's Philosophers are the worst citizens on earth. The proof is this: having pub-

lished a great number of important truths concerning politics and economics, and having given practical advice in their books, this advice has been followed by almost all the sovereigns of Europe, with the exception of France. From which it follows that the prosperity of these foreigners will increase their might, while France will remain at the same level, with the same excesses, et cetera, thus winding up in a state of inferiority relative to the other powers. And this is obviously the fault of the Philosophers, as revealed by the duke of Tuscany's well-known reply to a Frenchmen, regarding the felicitous innovations the duke had undertaken in his realm. "You praise me too highly," he said. "All my ideas come from French books."

486. The only history worthy of attention is that of free peoples. The history of peoples subject to despotism is merely a series of anecdotes.

545. A man of wit, finding himself the butt of two malicious wags, said to them, "Sirs, you are mistaken. I am neither a fool nor a dunce, I am between the two." (WSM)

574. Love, said Plutarch, silences all other passions—it is a dictator before whom all other powers swoon.

576. M. de L—— told me that the moment he learned of Mme. de B——'s infidelity, he felt, in the midst of his grief, that he would never love again, that love was vanishing forever—he was a man in a field hearing the sound of a partridge rising and flying away.

592. Conquerors will always be considered first among men, just as the lion will always be called king of the beasts.

"Characters and Anecdotes"

614. M. de Tressan had composed ditties against the duc de Nivernois in 1738, and in 1780 sought election to the Académie. He went to see M. de Nivernois, who received him marvelously, spoke of the success of his latest books, and let him depart full of hope until, seeing him ready to climb into his carriage, the duke said, "Farewell, count, and let me congratulate you on having such a short memory."

641. The young and poor Abbé Raynal agreed to say a mass every day for twenty sous; when he became wealthier, he passed it on to Abbé de La Porte, withholding eight sous. This latter, becoming less beggarly, conceded it to Abbé Dinouart, withholding another four sous. Thus this poor mass, entailed with two stipends, was worth only eight sous to Abbé Dinouart.

643. Lord Marlborough was in the trenches with a friend and a nephew when a cannon shot blew out the brains of his friend, covering the face of the nephew, who recoiled with fright. Marlborough, unmoved, said, "What, sir, stunned?" "Yes," said the young man, wiping his face, "I'm stunned that a man with so much brains exposed himself to such pointless danger."

647. Count Mirabeau had a very ugly face but a fine sense of wit. He was accused of abduction with seductive intent, and pleaded his own defense. "Sirs," he said, "I am accused of seduction; as my only response and my only defense, I ask that my portrait be entered as evidence." The court clerk didn't understand. "Fool," said the judge, "just take a look at the gentleman's face!"

688. Abbé de Molières was a poor and simple man, detached from everything except his own work on Descartes's system. He had no valet, and worked in bed for lack of firewood. He placed his trousers on his head, over his nightcap, with one leg hanging to the left, the other to the right. One morning, he heard someone knocking at the door.
"Who is it?"
"Open up."
The abbé pulled on a rope and the door opened. Not looking up, he said, "What do you want?"
"Give me your money."
"Money?"
"Yes, money."
"Oh, I see, you're a thief."
"Thief or not, I need money."
"Yes, of course, you need money. Have a look there. . . ." The abbé stretched his neck, presenting one of the trouser legs. The thief rummaged.
"There's no money there."
"No, of course not, but there's a key."

"So, this key . . ."

"Take it."

"I've got it."

"Go over to that desk there, and open it."

The thief put the key in a drawer.

"Leave that one alone, don't disturb it, my papers are in there. Zounds, stop that! Those are my papers. You'll find the money in the other drawer."

"Ah, here it is."

"Take it then. And lock the drawer."

The thief fled.

"You, thief, shut that door! Zounds, he's left the door open . . . That devil of a thief—now I have to get up in this freezing cold! Cursed thief!" the abbé lept out of bed, shut the door, and hurried back to his work.

721. Someone said to Donne, the English satirist, "Thunder against the sins, but spare the sinners." "What," he said, "damn the cards and pardon the card-sharps?" (WSM)

774. In his youth, M. Helvétius was as handsome as a Greek god. One evening he was seated peacefully at the hearth, although somewhat near to Mlle. Gaussin. A famous financier whispered in the actress' ear, loud enough for Helvétius to hear, "Mademoiselle, would you care to accept 600 louis in exchange for a few indulgences?" "Sir," she replied (also loud enough to be heard, and indicating Helvétius), "I'll give *you* 200 louis if you show up at my place tomorrow morning with a face like that."

808. King Frederick of Prussia asked d'Alembert if he had ever seen the king of France. "Yes, Sire," replied this latter, "when I presented him with my speech of acceptance to the Académie française."

"And what did he say to you?" inquired the king of Prussia.

"He didn't speak to me, Sire,"

"Then who *does* he speak to?" queried Frederick.

836. Abbé Maury, when poor, taught Latin to an old counselor at high court who wanted to understand Justinian's *Institutes*. Several years later, Abbé Maury ran into this counselor, who was amazed to discover him at a genteel residence. "Well, Abbé," asked the coun-

selor offhandedly, "what stroke of fate ushered you into this house?"

"The same one that brought you here."

"No, it's not quite the same thing. Your business looking up? Have you gotten somewhere in the priestly trade?"

"I'm M. de Lobez' grand vicar."

"The deuce! That *is* something. How much is it worth?"

"A thousand francs."

"Rather paltry," said the counselor, reassuming his light and offhand tone.

"But I also have a priory," continued the abbé, "worth a thousand ecus."

"A thousand ecus!" (*With enhanced esteem:*) "That's a good deal."

"And I made the acquaintance of the master of this house at Cardinal Rohan's place."

"Gracious! You frequent Cardinal Rohan?"

"Yes, he procured an abbey for me."

"An abbey! Well!! That said, Abbé, would you be so kind as to dine at my place?"

853. A wit once told me that the French government was an absolute monarchy moderated by lampoons.

888. Mme. de Maintenon and Mme. de Caylus were walking by the lake at Marly. The water was very clear and the carp could be seen moving slowly, looking sad and thin. Mme. de Caylus pointed them out to Mme. de Maintenon, who answered, "They are like me: they miss their mud." (WSM)

920. M. d'Invau, when he was Controleur-Général, asked the king for permission to get married. The king, when he learned who the young lady was, said, "You are not rich enough." The other mentioned his post, as something which made up for his lack of capital. "Ah," said the king, "posts come and go, but a wife remains." (WSM)

925. A woman of ninety said to M. de Fontenelle, then ninety-five, "Death has overlooked us." "Shh!" replied M. de Fontenelle, putting a finger to his lips.

987. A modest man was told, "Sometimes there can be slits in the bushel under which virtues hide."

990. It was said of a skillful but cowardly fencer—who was also witty and gallant with women, yet impotent—that, "He handily wields both foil and flirt, but shies from duel and delight."

1011. "There are three sorts of friends in high society," M—— used to say. "Friends who are fond of you, friends who don't care about you, and friends who detest you."

1013. D——, a witty misanthrope, used to say, on the subject of human wickedness: "Only the futility of the first flood prevents God from unleashing another."

1017. M—— used to say that the drawback of being inferior to princes was richly compensated by the advantage of being far removed from them.

1046. It was said of a ribald but incorrupt courtier: "He was dirtied by the whirlwind, but remained unstained by the mud."

1069. M. de B—— saw Mme. de L—— every day, and it was rumored that he was going to marry her. At which point he said to one of his friends, "There are few men she would less willingly marry than me, and vice-versa. It would certainly be strange if, in fifteen years of friendship, we hadn't realized how unattractive we are to one another."

1103. Of an idiot over whom no hold could be gotten, M—— used to say: "He's a jughead without a handle."

1132. A girl, at confession, said, "I'm guilty of having held a young man in esteem."
"Esteem! How many times did you hold him in esteem?" asked the priest.

1147. Henri IV used a singular method to demonstrate the different characters of his three ministers—Villeroi, Jeannin, and Sully—to a Spanish ambassador. First he summoned Villeroi. "See that beam? It's about to give way."

"Quite likely," said Villeroi, without looking up. "It will have to be fixed. I'll give orders for it."

Next he called to Jeannin, who said, "I'll have it examined."

Then Sully was sent for, looked at the beam and said, "Surely you jest, Sire. That beam will outlast both of us."

1148. I once heard a pious person say naively, in arguing with people who were discussing articles of faith, "Sirs, a true Christian does not examine what he is instructed to believe. You see, it's like a bitter pill—if you chew it, you'll never be able to swallow it."

1173. The young marquis de Choiseul-la-Baume, nephew of the pious, Jansenist bishop of Châlons, suddenly became despondent. His uncle, the bishop, asked why. The marquis said that he had seen a coffee maker that he would like to have but despaired of obtaining. "Very expensive, then?" "Yes, uncle—twenty-five louis." The uncle gave the young man the money on condition that he would get to see the coffee maker. Several days later, he asked his nephew for news. "Acquired, uncle, as you yourself shall see tomorrow." And, in effect, the bishop saw the coffee maker on leaving mass the next day. It was not a recipient for making coffee but rather a pretty wench who worked in a café, and who has since become known as Mme. de Bussi. It is not hard to imagine the old Jansenist bishop's wrath.

1190. "I don't care for faultless women," M—— used to say, "who are above weakness. It is as though I can see etched over their portals the lines that Dante placed over the gates of hell:

Voi che intrate, lasciate ogni speranza.

Abandon all hope, ye who enter here."

This is the motto of the doomed.

1203. There is an Italian farce in which Harlequin, referring to the shortcomings of each sex, observes that we would all be perfect if we were neither men nor women.

1223. A wife had just lost her husband. Her confessor (in an honorary capacity) came to see her the next day and found her playing cards with a very well-dressed young man. "Sir," she said, "you look surprised; if you'd come a half hour ago, you would have found me bathed in tears. But I staked my sorrows on a card with this gentleman, and I lost." (WSM)

1224. It was said of the former bishop of Autun, who was monstrously fat, that he had been created and placed on this earth to see just how far human skin could be stretched.

1245. An American, on seeing six English soldiers separated from their army, had the unbelievable audacity to rush them, wounding two and disarming the others. He led them to General Washington, who asked how he managed to overcome six men. "As soon as I saw them," replied the American, "I ran up and surrounded them."

1259. A seriously ill man who didn't want to receive the last rites said to his friend, "I'm going to pretend not to die."

1265. An Englishman consulted a lawyer about how to run off with a rich heiress yet remain safe from the law. The lawyer asked if she were consenting. "Yes." "Well, then," replied the lawyer, "take a horse, and have her mount in front, with you on the rump. Then, when passing through the first village, shout, '*Miss X . . . is carrying me off.*'" The affair was executed accordingly . . . and it turned out that the woman thus carried off was the lawyer's daughter.

1326. A man owed some money to a grave digger who had buried his daughter. On coming across the grave digger, he offered to settle. "That's all right," said the grave digger, "we'll make it up some other time. One of your servants is ill, and your wife looks none too healthy."

"Short Philosophical Dialogues"

II

A: You no longer see M——?
B: No, it's no longer possible.
A: Why is that?
B: I could see him as long as he displayed poor morals, but now that he's keeping poor company, it's impossible.

VII

A: You're familiar with all the ministers' scheming!

B: That's because I once lived among them.

A: You made out well, I hope.

B: Not at all. They're gamblers who showed me their cards, who even peeked at the deck in my presence, yet who shared no part of their winnings with me.

XII

A: It's a decent post.

B: You mean lucrative.

A: Decent, lucrative—one and the same thing.

LXVIII

A: According to him, I should remain wary of everyone.

B: And?

C: I do just as he says, starting with him.

NOTES

Abbreviations

The following abbreviations are used throughout:

O.C.   Chamfort, *Oeuvres Complètes de Chamfort*. 5 vols. (Paris: Auguis, 1824–1825).

Ging. Ginguené's preface to Chamfort's *Caractères et anecdotes*, (Paris: Crès, 1924).

Frag. Refers to numbered fragments of Chamfort's aphorisms and anecdotes, according to the system used in the 1982 Gallimard/Folio ed. of *Maximes et pensées, caractères et anecdotes*.

1. A Negative Fairy Tale

1. The question of Chamfort's birth has been discussed in the following publications:

a) P. G. Aigueperse, *Biographie ou dictionnaire des personnages d'Auvergne* (Clermont-Ferrand, 1834).

b) Ambroise Tardieu, *Histoire généalogique de la maison de Bosredon* (Clermont-Ferrand, 1863).

c) A. Tardieu, *Histoire de la ville de Clermont-Ferrand*, 1870–1872

d) *Intermédiaires des Chercheurs et des Curieux* 13 (February 10, 1880).

e) A. Tardieu, *Dictionnaire des anciennes familles d'Auvergne* (Moulins, 1884; Marselle: Laffitte Reprints, 1970.

f) *La Revue Française* (1890): 169.

g) *Bulletin Historique et Scientifique de l'Auvergne*, 1 (1930): 34–35; 2 (1931): 106.

h) *Auvergne Littéraire* 121 (1947): 40–41.

2. A certain Morabin, according to Ginguené's entry on "Chamfort" in Michaud's *Biographie universelle* (1813).

3. See *Intermédiares des chercheurs et des curieux* (February 10, 1880), col. 94.

4. Letter from Chamfort to Thomas, August 1772, in *Revue des Autographes* (January 1899).

5. In 1793, he claimed to have resided in Paris for forty-three years. Archives Nationales, file T. 1458.

6. *La Décade Philosophique* 7, Year IV, 1st quarter.

7. "Epitre d'un père à son fils," *O.C.*, 5:100.

8. Quoted by Jean Dagen in Chamfort's Maximes, *Pensées* . . . (Paris: Gallimard/Folio, 1968), 10.

9. *O.C.*, 5:222.

10. Ging., p. xii.

11. L. S. Mercier, *Nouveaux tableaux de Paris, ou Paris sous la Révolution* (Paris, 1862).

12. "Combien le génie des grands écrivains influe sur l'esprit de leur siè-cle?" *O.C.* (1767), 1:200.

2. Early Struggle against Anonymity

1. Ging., p. xii.

2. Sélis, *La Décade Philosophique*, 7:537 ff.

3. *O.C.*, 5:108.

4. Frag. 1237.

5. Duchesse d'Abrantès, *Histoire des salons de Paris, de Louis XVI à Louis-Philippe* (Paris: Ladvocat, 1836–1838).

6. Letter to Schuwaloff, September 15, 1774, in *Studies on Voltaire and the 18th Century*, 106 (1973): 35–39.

7. La Harpe, *Correspondance littéraire* (Geneva: Slatkine Reprints, 1968), 1:321.

8. "Avis au sujet de la correspondance littéraire de ce journal," *Journal Encyclopédique de Bouillon* (May 1, 1763).

9. Ging., pp. xii–xiii.

10. Letter of March 1764, D. 11781, in the Bestermann ed. of Voltaire's *Correspondance*.

11. Frag. 976.

12. Sainte-Beuve, *Causeries du lundi*, ed. Garnier, 4:342.

13. Letter from Voltaire to Chamfort, May 25, 1764, in Bestermann ed., D. 11890.

14. D'Alembert, *Mélanges de littérature, d'histoire et de philosophie*, (Amsterdam, 1759).

15. Frag. 167.

16. Marquis d'Argenson, quoted by Will Durant, *L'epoque de Voltaire*, (Lausanne: Rencontre, 1966), p. 199.

17. "Combien le génie des grands ecrivains influe sur l'esprit de leur siè-cle?" *O.C.*, 1:201.

18. Ibid., pp. 214–215.

19. Ibid., p. 217.

20. Letter of May 14, 1764, in Bestermann's ed. of Rousseau's correspon-dence, no. 3274.

21. Letter of June 24, 1764, in ibid., no. 3359.

22. "One day Duclos said to Mme. de Rochefort and Mme. de Mirepoix that courtesans were becoming prudish," wrote Chamfort. "He said they were more straitlaced than virtuous women. Whereupon he told a racy story, and then another even racier, and finally a third which began even more boldly when Mme. de Rochefort stopped him and said: 'Careful, Duclos, we're not as virtuous as you seem to think.'" See frag. 909.

23. Aubin, *Chamfortiana*, Paris, Year IX, p. x.

24. Frag. 868.

25. B. and G. Cazes, eds., *La politique naturelle, D'Holbach portatif*, (Paris: Pauvert, 1967), p. 131.

3. The Mask

1. One of Mme. du Deffand's brothers, which would have made Chamfort her nephew, and cousin to Julie de Lespinasse.

2. Frag. 928.

3. Frag. 905.

4. Frag. 773.

5. Frag. 796.

6. Cf. Stendhal's *Le rouge et le noir*.

7. Anon., *Journal de Paris*, 12 Germinal, Year III (April 1, 1795): 716.

8. Quoted by Sainte-Beuve, 4:540, n. 1.

9. Aubin, p. x.

10. Frag. 44.

11. *Le rouge et le noir*.

12. "Epitre d'un père à son fils," *O.C.*, 5:99.

13. *Lettre à M. de XXX, docteur de Sorbonne, sur la pièce qui a remporté le prix de L'Académie française*, by Father Guidi, 1764. (Pamphlet)

14. Letter to Rousseau, August 14, 1764, in Bestermann, no. 3467.

15. Letter to Rousseau, October 6, 1764, in Bestermann, no. 3547.

16. Letter to Rousseau, October 15, 1764, in Bestermann, no. 3575.

4. Herculean Adonis

1. Application for citizen's card, 1793, Archives nationales, T. 1458.

2. Ging., p. xiii.

3. Dumont-Wide, *Le prince de Ligne*, pp. 144–145.

4. Frag. 359.

5. Stendhal, *De l'amour.*

6. See Grimm et al., *Correspondance littéraire, philosophique et critique,* 16 vols. (Paris: Tourneux, 1877–1882). See also letter to Rousseau, in Bestermann, no. 3575.

7. Aubin, p. viii.

8. See Letter to Rousseau, in Bestermann, no. 3467.

9. Ibid., no. 3575.

10. Aubin, p. xiv.

11. *Les amours de Gonesse,* a one-act comedy (Paris, 1765).

12. Grimm, *Correspondance littéraire,* 6:395 ff.

13. "L'heureux temps," *O.C.,* 5:215.

5. Shattered Illusions

1. Letter from Angiviller to Countess Stolberg, published in vol. 7 of L. Bobé's *Papiers de la famille de Rewentlow* (Copenhagen, 1906).

2. See *Maximes,* frag. 1099, in which Chamfort accuses Angiviller of religious and political hypocrisy, as well as being a deceitful courtier. See also frag. 845, where he describes the couple formed by the count and Mme. de Marchais (later Mme. d'Angiviller) as contrived.

3. Grimm, *Correspondance littéraire,* October 1768.

4. *O.C.,* 4:394.

5. Frag. 222.

6. Leprosy and elephantiasis also have been considered. Today granulatosis is mentioned. But the symptoms described are too vague to permit positive diagnosis.

7. G. Gaubras, *Le duc de Lauzun et la cour intime de Louis XV* (Paris: Plon, 1924), p. 20.

8. Mme. de Genlis, *Mémoires* (Paris: Ladvocat, 1824), 9:144.

9. G. Gabor, *Die misanthropie Chamforts* (Berlin, 1928); E. Katz, "Chamfort," *Yale French Studies* 40 (1968). Professor Renwick also deserves special acknowledgment for his insight on this issue.

10. *O.C.* (August 20, 1765), 5:250.

11. Both the date and author of this letter have been the subject of debate, although it was published by Ginguené (*O.C.,* Year III of the Republic, vol. 3, letter 3). A manuscript version is to be found in the Ginguené collection at the Bibliothèque Nationale, N.a.f. no. 9198, fol. 175), but it is not in Chamfort's handwriting.

12. Mme. Necker, *Mélanges,* Year VI of the Republic, 3:26.

13. Laclos, *Dangerous Liaisons*, trans. Lowell Bair (New York: Bantam, 1962), p. 52.

14. Frag. 1043.

15. Frag. 366.

16. Frag. 771.

17. Frag. 125.

18. "Epitre à M____," *O.C.*, 5:112.

19. Chamfort, *L'homme de lettres* (Amsterdam, 1766).

20. See Gaillard, *Encyclopédie méthodique*, vol. 6.

21. Letter to Voltaire, September 26, 1766, in Bestermann, D. 13588.

6. Little Balloon

1. Frag. 1011.

2. Letter of May 24, 1767, Thomas's correspondence published by M. Henriet in *Revue des Autographes* (January 1899), p. 60.

3. Letter of December 11, 1767, in ibid., p. 62.

4. For his "Ode sur la grandeur de l'homme," *O.C.*, 5:123.

5. Thanks to his "Héroide de Servilie à Brutus."

6. For a prize for eloquence.

7. Letter to Audibert, September 5, 1767, in Bestermann, D. 14408.

8. See Thomas's letter of November 13, 1768, *Revue des Autographes*, p. 68.

9. See Lucien Brenel, *Les philosophes et l'Académie française*, p. 179.

10. Diderot, *Oeuvres complètes*, Club français du livre, 7:418.

11. Gaillard, *Mélanges académiques* (Paris, 1806), p. 133.

12. For an "Ode sur la Vérité."

13. Quoted by Peignot, *Recherche sur la vie et les ouvrages de M. de La Harpe*.

14. Bachaumont, *Mémoires Secrets*, August 25, 1769.

15. According to Courchamps, author of the marquise de Créquy's apocryphal *Souvenirs*, compiled from survivors of the Ancien Régime (1834), 7 vols.

16. September 20, 1769, *Correspondance complète* de la marquise du Deffand (Paris: Plon, 1865), 2:1.

17. In Bestermann, D. 15921.

18. *O.C.*, 5:241.

19. Unpublished letter to the marquis de Lezay-Marnesia, September 16, 1769, in catalogue 269 of the Librarie de l'Abbaye, Paris.

20. *Bibliothèque de société*, 4 vols. (1771); and *Grand vocabulaire français*, 30 vols. (1767–1774).

21. Grimm, *Correspondance littéraire*, February 1, 1770.

22. Ibid.

23. "Finally," he continued, "if all the pleasures, feelings and ideas of an entire lifetime could be brought together in the space of twenty-four hours, it would be done. You'd be made to swallow this pill and then be told: Begone!" See frag. 259.

24. "Eloge de Molière," *O.C.*, 1:28 and 31.

25. Letter to Thomas, January 4, 1773, *Revue des Autographes*, p. 148.

26. Mme. Suard, *Essais de mémoires sur M. Suard* (Paris, 1817), p. 151.

27. *Elite des pensée fugitives* (London, 1779), p. 9.

28. Frag. 188.

29. An anonymous writer offered another version of the facts in 1795: "He attempted a career in negotiations; his correspondence was noted only for the outrageous letters against the ambassador he accompanied. He is believed to have returned to Paris and to have said that politics was like Old High German to him."

30. See *Journal de la cour et de la ville* (October 14, 1791).

31. Letter to Schuwaloff, September 15, 1774.

32. Frag. 883.

7. Ironclad in Repelling Evil, a Wax Mold in Accepting Good . . .

1. Frag. 306.

2. Letter of June 10, 1773, to the marquise de Créquy, "Du château de Moutonne par Orgelet," private collection.

3. *O.C.*, 5:144.

4. Letter of August 22, 1773, to the marquise de Créquy, *L'Amateur d'Autographes* 4 (1866): 361.

5. Letter of September 15, 1774, written in Barège, to Mme. de S——, *O.C.*, 5:264.

6. Ging., p. xx.

7. Letter to Guibert, October 25, 1774, *Lettres de Julie de Lespinasse*, ed. E. Asse (Paris, 1876), p. 141.

8. *Epitre à Chamfort sur son eloge de la Fontaine*, 1774.

9. *Correspondance Turque*, published in 1801 by Colnet du Ravel, pp. 31–32.

10. Letter from Voltaire to Chamfort, November 16, 1774, Bestermann, D 19189.

11. Letter to Schuwaloff, November 15, 1774.

12. "Essai d'un commentaire sur Racine," *O.C.*, 5:9.

13. Frag. 428.

14. (Paris: Lacombe, 1776), 3 vols. Ginguené wrote, "Almost all the entries of any importance were by him."

15. Letter to the architect Antoine, Bibliothèque de l'Institut, n.d.

16. Aubin, p. xii.

17. Mme. Suard, p. 151.

18. It wasn't until Joseph II, Marie-Antoinette's brother, came to Paris that Louis XVI unburdened himself and agreed to have his phimosis treated.

19. *O.C.*, 4:284.

20. Weber, *Mémoires*, (Firmin-Didot, 1860), p. 179 n.

21. Metra, *Correspondance littéraire secrète*, vol. 1, October 6, 1776.

22. *Journal Historique*, vol. 3, 1863, p. 245n.

23. Metra, November 11, 1776, 3:417.

24. Frag. 302.

25. Ging., p. xxiv.

26. Ibid.

27. Archives du château de Chantilly, Paris, August 15, 1777.

28. Ibid., undated letter.

8. A Cabal Against Mustapha

1. Open letter to playwrights, dated June 27, 1777, in Brian Morton, ed., *Correspondance de Beaumarchais* (Paris: Nizet, 1969), letter 532.

2. Ibid., letter 546, Chantilly, July 2, 1777.

3. A. Vallentin, *Mirabeau* (Grasset, 1946), 1:296.

4. *Correspondance de Beaumarchais*, letter 538, July 1777.

5. Ibid., letter 537, to La Harpe.

6. A character in a comedy by Piron, Métromane was a playwright who underwent torment during the premiere.

7. Grimm, *Correspondance Littéraire*, December 1777.

8. La Harpe, *Correspondance Littéraire*, 1:378.

9. *Journal des Théâtres* 3–4 (1778): 118.

10. Cousin d'Avallon, ed., *Arnoldiana* (Paris, 1813).

11. Collé, *Journal et Mémoires* (January 1770): 245.

12. La Harpe, *Lycée* (Paris, 1825), 9:440.

13. Metra, January 3, 1778, 5:266.

14. Sélis, *Décade Philosophique* 7, pp. 537 ff.

15. La Harpe, *Correspondance Littéraire*, 2:374.

16. *Mustapha et Zéangir*, chez la veuve Duchesne (Paris, 1778). The binding of a copy held at the Bibliothèque Nationale bears Marie-Antoinette's coat of arms. Chamfort would write later, with a certain lucidity regarding himself: "People who think they love a prince, the moment they have been well treated, remind me of children who want to be priests the day after seeing a fine procession."

17. Bachaumont, *Mémoires secrets*, December 20, 1777.

18. Mme. Necker, *Nouveaux mélanges*, (1801): 1:51.

19. *Journal Encyclopédique* 1 (February 1778), pt. 2.

20. Berlin, *Mustapha et Zéangir* (Paris, 1704).

21. *Journal de Politique et de Littérature* 8 (March 15, 1778): 353 ff.

22. Frag. 333.

23. Frag. 85.

24. Mercier, "La littérature du Faubourg Saint-Germain et celle du Faubourg Saint-Honoré, *Tableaux de Paris*.

25. Rue des Garennes, on the site of what is now 25, rue Boileau in the 16th arrondissement of Paris.

26. Frag. 496. These were the words Saint Theresa of Avila used to describe hell.

9. Auteuil-Passy

1. Frag. 283. The phrase was taken from Horace.

2. Frag. 580.

3. Letter to Mme. d'Epinay, May 18, 1776. Grimm, *Correspondance littéraire*, 11:363.

4. Letter 12, n.d., *O.C.*, 5:302–303.

5. Frag. 470.

6. Abbé Morellet, *Mémoires*, ed. Baudoin (1823), 2:393.

7. Undated letter (probably summer 1781), *Revue des Autographes*, pp. 66–67.

8. Frag. 1020.

9. *O.C.*, 5:224.

10. Chamfort, *Oeuvres choisies*, 3 vols. (Paris: Bibliothèque Nationale, 1866), foreword by M. David, 1:7.

11. Furthermore, one of Chamfort's disciples (probably Grouvelle) had meanwhile published a poem showing his "mentor" on the verge of dying, and refusing the host . . . the doctor having forbidden him "starchy food."

12. Antoine Guillois, *Pendant la terreur, le poète Roucher* (Paris: Calmann-Lévy, 1890), p. 88.

13. *O.C.*, 1:235.

14. Pellisson, *Chamfort*, p. 102.

15. *Registres de l'Académie française (1635–1793)* (Paris: Institut de France/Firmin-Didot, 1906), 3:501.

10. Love, and Only Love

1. Letter to Abbé Roman, March 4, 1784, *O.C.*, 5:275.

2. Notes on Esther, *O.C.*, 5:55.

3. Letter to Mme. ***, *O.C.*, 5:235.

4. Undated letter, erroneously attributed "to Mme. Agasse," *O.C.*, 5:304.

5. Ging, p. xxvii.

6. Frag. 469.

7. Comte de Moré, *Mémoires, 1758–1837* (Paris, 1898), p. 124.

8. Talleyrand, *Mémoires*, ed. Couchoud (Plon, 1957), 1:35.

9. Léonce Pingaud, *Choiseul-Gouffier* (Al. Picart, 1887), p. 34.

10. Talleyrand's manuscripts of Chamfort's aphorisms thus made their way into the auction rooms. One of them sums up their intellectual relationship: "A certain loose woman managed to sell herself, but was unable to give herself away." See Lacour-Gayet, *Talleyrand* (1928), 1:58; and frag. 376. Talleyrand also claimed authorship of Chamfort's reply to Rulhière's statement that "I've only done one nasty thing in my life." "And when will it end?" asked Chamfort. See also *Monsieur de Talleyrand* (1837), 2:17; and frag. 1249.

11. See Casimir Carrère, *Talleyrand amoureux* (Paris: France-Empire, 1975), p. 28; and frag. 453.

12. *Mémoires du comte de Ségur* (Barrière, 1859).

13. The marshal demanded that officers *also* be educated. An amusing thing happened, noted Chamfort: the academic examiner granted certification only to commoners, while the genealogist only granted it to gentlemen. "Out of a hundred candidates, there were only four or five who fulfilled both conditions." See also frag. 1058.

14. Frags. 655 and 911.

11. Long Live Mirabeau! And Long Live the Charmer!

1. *Correspondance Mirabeau-Chamfort*, published by Ginguené, Year V of the Republic, Paris, letter 10, p. 35.

2. Chamfort's replies disappeared after Mirabeau's ashes were withdrawn from the Pantheon.

3. Nietzsche, *The Gay Science*, trans. W. Kaufmann (New York: Vintage, 1974), pp. 148–149.

4. *Correspondance Mirabeau-Chamfort*, p. 34.

5. Frag. 289.

6. The first objectively dated fragment from the *Maximes et anecdotes*—no. 726—is from 1780. But a reference to Abbé Terray's "honesty" indicates that Chamfort had been taking notes as early as 1770.

7. Frag. 522.

8. Letter to Abbé Roman, no. 11 *O.C.*, 5:289.

9. Tilly, *Mémoires* (Paris: Mercure de France, 1986).

10. Besenval, *Mémoires* (Paris: Barrière, 1827), pp. 84ff.

11. Frag. 285.

12. He was from old but undistinguished stock. The Rigaud de Vaudreuil family provided governors of Canada, and his father was governor of the Leeward Islands. Vaudreuil owed his colonial fortune to his mother—"but at every occasion he spoke as a man of high birth," stressed Besenval.

13. Fragment found in *Mirabeau's Letters during his Residence in London* (London, 1832), 2:311.

14. Frag. 1250.

15. *Les Adieux des Evêques aux filles de Paris . . .* (Pamphlet)

16. Letter to Mme. de ——, n.d., *O.C.*, 5:255.

17. Frag. 763.

18. *Correspondance intime du comte de Vaudreuil et du comte d'Artois . . . , 1789–1815* (Paris: Plon, 1889), 1:xxii.

19. Louis de Loménie, *Beaumarchais et son temps* (1856), p. 308.

20. Letter to Abbé Roman, May 4, 1784, *O.C.*, 5:277.

21. Morellet, *Mémoires* (Paris: Baudoin Frères, 1823), 1:393.

22. Vigée-Lebrun, *Souvenirs*, 3 vols. (1835–1837), 1:88.

23. While Chamfort liked to simplify the most complex witticisms—a joke should always make its victim laugh, he would say—he also liked to complicate the simplest details. He once gave his address to a friend with so many detours that his friend never found it.

24. Meister, *Souvenirs de mon dernier voyage à Paris* (Geneva: Usteri & Ritter, 1910), p. 198.

25. P. L. Roederer, *Oeuvres* (Firmin-Didot, 1853), 4:212.

26. *O.C.*, 5:224.

27. Frag. 265 followed, in order, by fragments 672, 785, 937, 1032.

28. "Happiness is like a watch," he wrote. "The less complicated it is, the less likely it is to go wrong." See also frag. 308.

29. Frag. 315.

30. *Correspondance Mirabeau-Chamfort*, p. 2.

31. Ibid., p. 21.

32. Frag. 160.

33. *Correspondance Mirabeau-Chamfort*, p. 44.

12. *Julie*

1. Today named rue de la Victoire.

2. Frag. 186.

3. Frag. 717.

4. Frag. 380.

5. *Correspondance Mirabeau-Chamfort*, p. 23.

6. A famous courtesan who was mistress to Pericles and friend to Socrates.

7. "La Vraie Sagesse," *O.C.*, 5:148.

8. *Correspondance Mirabeau-Chamfort*, p. 42.

9. Unpublished letter, June 1784, in *Catalogue de M. Leroux et Mathias*, Nouveau Drouot, sale of March 15–16, 1983.

10. Frag. 355.

11. Roederer, 5:201.

12. G. Bord and L. Bigard, *La maison du 18 Brumaire* (Paris: Neptune, 1930), p. 85.

13. Frag. 821.

14. To use Georges Poulet's term.

15. Letter to Abbé Roman, May 4, 1784 (incorrectly dated March 4 by Auguis), *O.C.*, 5:276.

16. Letter to Abbé Roman, April 4, 1784, *Maximes, pensées . . .* (Paris: Gallimard/Folio, 1968), p. 379.

17. Letter to Abbé Roman, May 4, 1784, *O.C.*, 5:273–274.

18. Letter 5, *O.C.*, 5:267–268.

19. Frag. 1085.

20. Frag. 417.

13. *From Moralist to Volcano*

1. *Journal de Paris*, 28 Ventose, Year III, pp. 716–718.

2. Frag. 177.

3. "M——" was elsewhere identified as a "true Greek pedant" and "author of a book on Italy," but following Chamfort's death a contemporary confirmed that Chamfort and "M——" were generally one and the same person.

4. Undated letter to Abbé Roman, *O.C.*, 5:292.

5. See Appendix One concerning the theft of Chamfort's manuscripts.

6. Frag. 463.

7. Rousseau's *Confessions* would be published, in their entirety, only in 1788.

8. See his *Tableaux de Paris* [Scenes of Paris], an invaluable account of the prerevolutionary period.

9. For example, "A poet sought Chamfort's opinion on a couplet: 'Excellent,' replied Chamfort, 'except for the boring passages' "—a quip Rivarol repeated in front of Abbé Cournaud. See frag. 1248. Or, "He (ie, Rivarol) said of Rulhière, although the comment has also been attributed to Chamfort, that 'He swallowed poison like a toad and spat it like a viper.' " See Jean Dutourd, *Rivarol* (Paris: Mercure de France, 1963), p. 278. The comments by Lauraguais and baron de Theis are quoted on p. 271 and p. 5.

10. Mirabeau also plagiarized Rivarol, who immodestly claimed, "If there are a few well-turned phrases in his thick books, they must be by Chamfort, Abbé Cerutti, or myself." See Rivarol, *Journal Politique National et Autres Textes*, with an introduction by Willy de Spens, 10–18 Editions (1964), p. 256.

11. Frag. 1049.

12. Poulet, *Etudes sur le temps humain*, 2d ed., vol. 2 (Paris: Editions du Rocher, 1976).

13. Frag. 180.

14. Frag. 212.

15. Frag. 126.

16. Many of his anecdotes are in fact gleaned from contemporary journals, from memoirs by people living under Louis XIV, the Regent, or Louis XV, or from Duclos's writings . . . but these were almost always tightened up and commented on by Chamfort, who added a small "c" at the end of his own thoughts.

17. Frag. 319.

18. Frag. 1257.

19. Frag. 24.

20. Frag. 17.

21. Frag. 472.

22. Frag. 598.

23. Frag. 114.

24. Frag. 387.

25. Frag. 98.

26. Frag. 769.

27. See Hetzel's preface to the Stahl edition of Chamfort's *Oeuvres*, 1857.

28. A text spurned by the Marseille Academy in 1767 and not included in *O.C.*

29. Frag. 455.

30. "Combien le génie des grands écrivains influe sur l'esprit de leur siècle?" 1767, *O.C.*, 1:200.

31. Frag. 899.

32. Frag. 515.

33. Nietzsche, *The Genealogy of Morals*, trans. Francis Golffing (New York, Doubleday, 1956), p. 170.

34. Ibid., p. 173.

35. Ibid., p. 175.

36. Ibid., p. 176 and 164.

37. "As to readers, I will never have any," also claimed the "hero" of *Notes from Underground*, that "irreducible source of negation."

38. Scheler, *L'homme du ressentiment* (Paris: Gallimard, 1970), p. 25.

39. Nietzsche, p. 173.

40. Bernoulli, ed., *Souvenirs de Mme. Overbeck*, 1:236.

41. Freud would take up and fully develop this point to explain the origin of neuroses.

42. Scheler, p. 49.

43. Ibid., p. 53.

44. Note that Mirabeau, the only plausible superman—if such exists—among all those mentioned in these pages, jokingly commented that doctors should have erected a statue of Chamfort in honor of the forgotten illness which he allowed them to rediscover . . . and which Mirabeau considered a nervous condition.

45. Scheler, p. 60.

46. Ibid., p. 22n.

47. Ibid., pp. 140–141n. Scheler once again quoted the German sociologist Sombart (1863–1941) on the subject of the birth of the capitalist spirit and petty-bourgeois behavior.

48. Scheler, p. 23.

49. Quoted by Guy Chaussinand-Nogaret, *Mirabeau* (Paris: Seuil, 1982), p. 150.

14. Half Cockscomb, Half Poppy

1. Marmontel, *Mémoires d'un père* (Paris: Stock, 1943), p. 357.

2. Desmoulins and Collot d'Herbois might also be cited, as well as all those who sunk into oblivion, whom Robert Darnton analyzed in *La Bohème littéraire* [Literary Bohemia] and some of whom participated in the Revolution as a reaction *against* the Philosophers.

3. *Considérations sur l'Ordre de Cincinnatus* (London: Johnson, 1784), pp. 24 and 29.

4. Letter 18, *Mirabeau's Letters during his Residence in London* (London, 1832), 1:82.

5. *Doutes sur la liberté de l'Escaut* (1785). (Pamphlet)

6. Probably the source of the thirty-two unpublished maxims and anecdotes appended to the French version of *Chamfort*. See Appendix Three.

7. *Mirabeau jugé par ses amis et par ses ennemis* (1791), p. 104.

8. Letter dated August 23, 1784, manuscript at the Bibliothèque Publique et Universitaire, Geneva.

9. Frag. 142.

10. Frag. 565.

11. Orieux, *Talleyrand* (Flammarion, 1970), p. 122.

12. Frags. 961 and 499.

13. *Lettre d'un Anglais à Paris*, London, March 18, 1787; and Chamfort's letter of April 15, 1787, 3 p. in 4°, Charavay file.

15. The Palais-Royal Powderkeg

1. Mallet du Pan's unpublished diary, quoted in *Auvergne Littéraire*, 121 (1927): 42.

2. Sélis.

3. Barère, *Mémoires* (Paris, 1842), 1:p. 34.

4. Letter dated December 13, 1788, *O.C.*, 5:293–301. Chamfort would say to Vaudreuil, "I did it out of friendship for you, and for everything you've done for me."

5. Frag. 807.

6. Apparently Mirabeau managed to justify the "theft" of the manuscripts belonging to Condé. Chamfort wrote, "I consider it great good fortune that the friendship was already perfect between M—— and me when I had occasion to render him a service, recently, that I alone could do. If everything that he has done for me had been . . . dictated by self-interest . . . my life would have been empoisoned forever" (frag. 334).

7. Chateaubriand, "Essais sur les Révolutions," *Oeuvres* (Paris: Ladvocat, 1826), 1:160–161.

8. Ibid. The suppers were held at the home of Mme. de Farcy, Chateaubriand's other sister, where Chamfort recounted "the strangest of anecdotes."

9. Letter dated December 13, 1788, *O.C.*, 5:293–301.

10. "I want nothing which creates a role in place of a man," he said. The Revolution was to be a general downing of masks.

11. Chateaubriand, *Mémoires d'outre-dombe* (Paris: Gallimard/Folio, 1982), 1:184.

12. Frag. 519.

13. *La circulaire des districts, ou dénonciation forcée des apôtres du despotisme.* (Pamphlet)

14. *Mémoire et consultation sur la question suivante . . .* (Paris, December 1788).

15. *Liste des Amis du Peuple qui méritent de fixer le choix des électeurs de Paris,* n.d. (Pamphlet)

16. Frag. 511.

17. Lettre de J.-B. Lauraguais à M***, Paris, 1802, pp. 161 ff.

18. *Mémoires pour les académies,* Paris, Year VII of the Republic, p. 26.

19. Marmontel, pp. 357 ff.

20. Réveillon owned a wall-paper factory which was sacked on April 27, 1789, by thousands of rioters, two hundred of whom died. The duc d'Orléans, who was passing by, was accused (as was the court) of having instigated the riot.

21. *Essais sur les Révolutions,* with notes from the confidential copy, ed. M. Regard (Paris: Pléiade/Gallimand 1969), p. 82 ff. And *Chateaubriand politique,* with an intro. by Jean-Paul Clément (Paris: Hachette/Pluriel, 1986), p. 82.

22. Frag. 529.

23. "Tableaux de la Révolution française," *O.C.*, 2:178.

24. Ging, p. xxxvi.

25. "Tableaux . . . ," p. 217.

26. Ibid., pp. 270–271.

27. Ibid., p. 274.

16. The Bastille

1. Etienne Dumont, *Souvenirs sur Mirabeau* (London, 1832), p. 175.

2. Mirabeau's earnest colleagues were known as "Mirabelles," punning on a feminine form of the count's name and on a variety of plum.

3. Bertaut, *Egéries du XVIIIe siècle* (Paris, 1928). Bertaut, however, does not cite his sources.

4. "Tableaux . . . ," *O.C.*, 2:317.

5. Ging., p. xxxvi.

6. "Tableaux . . . ," *O.C.*, 2:340.

7. Letter 14, Wednesday . . . , *O.C.*, 5:305–306.

8. Morellet, *Mémoires*, 1:398.

9. "Tableaux . . . ." *O.C.*, 2:347.

10. Marquis de la Rochefoucauld-Liancourt, *Mémoires de Condorcet* (1862), 2:360.

11. "Tableaux . . . ," *O.C.*, 2:360.

12. Letter of November 30, 1789, *Correspondance du bailli de Virieu*, ed. Grouchy and Guillois (Paris: Flammarion, 1903).

13. Taine, *Les origines de la France contemporaine* (Paris: Hachette, 1922), 3:152. Reprinted by Hachette/Pluriel in 1986.

14. "Tableaux . . . ," pp. 159 and 361.

15. Chaussinand-Nogaret, p. 183.

16. Helena-Maria Williams, ed., *Correspondance de Louis XVI* (1803), 1:187.

17. Frag. 530.

17. Normalcy

1. See A.-V. Arnault, *Souvenirs d'un sexagénaire* (Paris: Librairie Dufey, 1833), 2:208.

2. *Mercure de France*, in *O.C.*, 3:139.

3. Ibid., 3:21.

4. *Le Moniteur Universel*, Wednesday, November 25, 1789. Reprint of 1847, 2:227.

5. "It will be discussed in Chamfort's circle," said Chateaubriand, beside himself with joy on being published.

6. Dumont, p. 196.

7. *L'assemblée nationale aux Français*, Paris, February 11, 1790.

8. *Mercure de France*, January 16, 1790, *O.C.*, 3:132.

9. Ging., p. xxxix.

10. *Actes des Apôtres* 163 (April 1790).

11. Elsewhere, Rivarol would claim, "The people are a monarch who is always hungry; His Majesty is only really at peace when He's digesting."

12. *Le chef des Jacobites aux Français*, Paris, February 11, 1790. See also *Précis de la vie du prélat d'Autun*, and *Letter à M. l'évêque d'Autun et auteurs de l'adresse aux provinces*, 1790. (Brochures)

13. *Mercure de France*, August 14, 1790, *O.C.*, 3:p. 58.

14. Ibid., p. 53.

15. Frag. 1044.

16. *Mercure de France*, *O.C.*, 3:38.

17. *Le Livre rouge, ou liste des pensions secrètes sur le trésor public* . . . , 1790.

18. *Petit dictionnaire des grands hommes de la Révolution* (Paris: Palais-Royal, 1790).

19. *O.C.*, 3:78.

20. Ibid., p. 408.

21. Verses placed under Mirabeau's portrait in *O.C.*, 5:239.

22. Mirabeau, critical of the king's "nillfulness," said, "The king's only man is the queen."

23. *Revue Rétrospective* 7, 2d ser. (Paris, 1836): 312–313.

24. "La jambe de bois et le bas perdu," *O.C.*, 5:135.

25. *Mercure de France*, *O.C.*, 3:120.

18. Shattered Dreams

1. Beaumarchais, letter of July 8, *Théâtre complet* (Paris: Pléiade, 179), p. 691.

2. See Franz Blei, *Talleyrand homme d'état* (Paris: Payot, 1935).

3. Letter to Mme. Panckoucke (incorrectly attributed to her daughter, Mme. Agasse), dated July 16, 1790, *O.C.*, 5:310.

4. Ibid.

5. Ging., p. xxxvii.

6. *Correspondance Vaudreuil-Artois*, ed. Léonce Pingaud (Plon, 1899), 1:32.

7. Note to the court dated October 29, 1790. Guy Chaussinand-Nogaret, *Mirabeau entre le roi et la Révolution* (Paris: Hachette/Pluriel, 1986), pp. 147–148.

8. *Mercure de France*, *O.C.*, 3:143.

9. Ibid., p. 148.

10. "Who are . . . your chosen authors, your favorites?" Mirabeau asked Chamfort. "Can I count on there being Greek and Latin poets among them? And if you had the strength to also include the elite among writers of memoirs and moralists . . ." Letter 20, October 3, 1790, *Correspondance Mirabeau-Chamfort*, pp. 94–95.

11. Letter of November 2, 1790, *Revue Rétrospective*, p. 514.

12. *Intermédiaire des Chercheurs et des Curieux* 27 (March 10, 1893): 611.

13. *Chronique Scandaleuse* 2 (February 1791): 8.

14. Tilly, *Mémoires* (Mercure de France, 1985), pp. 150ff.

15. Ruault, *Gazette d'un Parisien sous la Révolution* (Perrin, 1976), pp. 221–222.

16. Cabanis, *Journal de la Maladie et de la Mort de Mirabeau Aîné* (1791): 26–27.

17. *Esprit de Mirabeau* (1797), 1:xiii. See also Albert Maurin, *La Galerie Historique de la Révolution Française* (n.d.), 1:193.

19. The Académie Dismembered by a Member

1. Chamfort, *Des académies* (Paris: Buisson, May 1791).

2. Abbé Morellet, *De l'Académie française, ou réponse à l'écrit de M. de Chamfort* (Paris, 1791).

3. *O.C.*, 3:443.

4. Ibid., p. 30.

5. "Lettre à mes Concitoyens . . . ," *O.C.*, 5:333–334.

6. Gérard Walter, *Histoire des Jacobins* (Paris: Somogy, 1946), p. 206.

7. Georges Duval, *Souvenirs de la Terreur* (Paris, 1840), 2:319. However, Lauraguais didn't publish his conversation with Chamfort until 1802; and Suard would even dispute the claim that Chamfort was behind Sieyès's title.

8. D'Antraigues and Mlle. Saint-Huberty would be murdered in London during the Empire by their servant, whose defection Napoleon's agents had engineered.

9. Supplement to *Actes des Apôtres* 4 (August 1791).

10. Frag. 518.

11. Frag. 527.

12. Frag. 526.

13. Frag. 520.

14. *L'Ami du peuple*, September 11, 1791.

15. Frag. 526.

20. Doing Away with the Self

1. *O.C.*, 5:342–343.

2. Sainte-Beuve later claimed, "In 1782, everyone wanted a gig for themselves. Not having gotten one, by 1792 they didn't want anyone to

have a gig." Yet many foreigners noted how easy it was to get run over in Paris by speeding carriages.

3. *Chronique Scandaleuse* 28 (late 1791).

4. "Despotism apparently has supporters who feel it encourages the fine arts," wrote Chamfort. "According to these people, the goal of every human society is to have fine tragedies, fine comedies, etc. Such people forgive all the evil done by priests on the grounds that without priests we would be deprived of the comedy of *Tartuffe.*"

5. *Mercure de France, O.C.*, 3:329.

6. Frag. 517.

7. Anon., *Sur l'abus des éloges* (late 1791), which relates to Chamfort's support of Chabanon's position.

8. *Journal-Pie* 12 (March 8, 1792): 4.

9. Letter of January 17, 1792, *O.C.*, 5:313–316.

10. *A deux liards . . .* , no. 25 (March 1792).

11. Letter of January 17, 1792, *O.C.*, 5:313–316.

12. April 21, 1792.

13. Letter from Dumouriez to Robin, quoted by E. Hattin, *Bibliographie historique et critique de la presse périodique française*, p. 9.

14. Unpublished letter dated June 13, 1792, to the chief of staff at the Ministry of Foreign Affairs, 3 p. in 4°, Charavay file.

15. *A deux liards . . .* , no. 25 (May 1792).

16. Williams, *Souvenirs de la Révolution française* (1827), p. 24.

21. The Monarchy's Death Throes

1. Letter of August 12, 1792, *O.C.*, 5:317–320.

2. Ibid.

3. Ibid.

4. Ging., p. lxii.

5. Morellet, *Mémoires*, 1:394.

6. Letter from Daillant de la Touche, December 18, 1809, in the Ginguené papers, Parent de Rosan Collection, Bibliothèque du XVI arrondissement, Paris.

7. Chamfort often dined at their place, along with Racine's daughter-in-law, then aged ninety-two. She still dressed in the style of Louis XIV, about whom she recounted numerous anecdotes.

8. Thiébault, *Mémoires* (Paris: Plon, 1894), 1:312–313.

9. François Albert-Buisson, *Les quarante au temps des lumières* (Paris: Fayard, 1960), p. 170. Albert Buisson provides no date or source for this quotation.

10. Manon Roland, *Mémoires* (Mercure de France, 1966), p. 121.

11. Concerning this entire passage, see John Renwick, "Chamfort patriote en coulisse," *Studies on Voltaire and the 18th Century* 183 (1980), pp. 165 ff. Renwick notably includes a previously unpublished letter from Chamfort to Roland, dated September 17, 1792.

12. Roederer, 4:555.

13. Ginguené hid Chateaubriand's sisters and mother during the massacres. True to form, Chateaubriand would later accuse Ginguené of having "advance knowledge" of them.

14. Roland, p. 120.

15. September 6, 1792, Chamfort file, Archives nationales.

16. Bibliothèque nationale archives, file, 47, pp. 402–404. See also Leprince, *L'histoire de la B.N.*, 2d ed.

17. Letter from Chamfort to Abbé Barthélemy, May 8, 1793, Académie française Archives, Chamfort file.

18. See Louis de Préandau, "Chamfort fonctionnaire," *La Revue Hebdomadaire* (November 1909): 514.

19. Petition by playrights to the National Assembly, *Le Moniteur* (October 14, 1792). Reprinted, 14:1222.

20. Frag. 406.

21. Roland, p. 120.

22. A Bad Dream

1. See Chalamel, *Garat et Ginguené . . . intrigants et dilapidateurs*, (1795), p. 562.

2. Louise Fusil, *Souvenirs d'une actrice* (Paris: Schmid, n.d.), p. 191.

3. It was said that Grouvelle died of remorse (in Varennes!) after a press campaign launched in 1806 on the publication of Grouvelle's edition of the *Oeuvres de Louis XIV* harped on his role as verbal executioner.

4. Roland, p. 121.

5. *O.C.*, 5:346.

6. Frag. 145.

7. *O.C.*, 5:341.

8. Williams, p. 24.

9. *O.C.*, 5:344.

10. Quoted in Pingaud, *Correspondance Vaudreuil-Artois*, p. xxv.

11. Barras, *Mémoires*, p. 87, chap. 11.

12. Application for citizen's card, April 18, 1793, Archives nationales.

13. Hérault de Séchelles, *Théorie de l'ambition*, ed. Guégan (Paris: Ramsay, 1979).

14. Chamfort had already defended freedom of the press, even royalist, during the Constituent Assembly. "Any law against calumny is pointless," he used to say, "because slander sells well."

15. Frag. 143.

16. *Considérations sur l'ordre de Cincinnatus*, p. 6.

17. Report dated 18 Floréal, Year II, May 7, 1794. Quoted in Roederer's *Oeuvres*, 4:513.

18. Letter of August 12, 1792, *O.C.*, 5:319.

19. Ging., p. xliii.

20. *Le Père Duchesne* 256 (June–July 1793).

21. Letter to the Minister of the Interior, July 10, 1793. Bibliothèque Nationale, Van Praet file.

22. Archives Nationales, file on Comité de Sûreté Générale, F₇4638.

23. See J-J. Barthélemy, *Oeuvres diverses* (1823), 1:cvii.

24. Anon., *Citoyen français*, 11 Fructidor, Year X.

25. Letter from Chamfort to Tronson du Coudray, August 8, 1793, B.N. manuscripts.

26. Van Praet file.

27. Delisle de Sales, *Mémoires pour les Académies*, Year VIII of the Republic, Paris, pp. 17 ff.

28. Archives Nationales, file F₇4638.

29. Tobiesen nevertheless asked that the painter Bounieu be rehired— he who, as fate would have it, had painted Mirabeau's portrait.

23. His Own Executioner

1. Quoted in Pellisson, p. 278.

2. Letter to Citizen Laveau, September 8, 1793, *O.C.*, 5:323–324.

3. Report by agent Rousseville, dated September 24, 1793, in Pierre Caron, *Paris pendant la Terreur*, 1:190.

4. Receipt signed Fabre, September 13, 1793, Archives nationales, Chamfort file.

5. Quoted in *Mercure de France*, January 1808, p. 221, article on the second edition of Chamfort's *Oeuvres*.

6. "Lettre à mes concitoyens, 18ᵉ jour du 1ᵉʳ mois de la République française," *O.C.*, 5:325–326.

7. But he cited only the verdict on the king and the departmental guard,

which the Gironde wanted to raise to protect the Assembly from Paris. His initial opposition to the war would have been a more striking argument.

8. Frag. 1184.

9. *O.C.*, 5:340–341.

10. On hearing Chamfort's quip repeated early in Bonaparte's rise to power, Rivarol added, "Every dog winds up finding its master." Lescure, "La vie et la mort de Chamfort," *Le Correspondant*, n.s. no. 81 (October–December 1879): 707.

11. Ging., p. il.

12. Report of police commissioners in the "Le Pelletier" district (formerly "1792" district), 24 Brumaire, Year II, November 14, 1793, Archives nationales, file F₇4638.

13. Ging., pp. li ff.

14. Roland, p. 120.

15. Barras, p. 88, chap. 11.

24. . . . From the Dead

1. Arnault, 2:147.

2. Ging., p. liv. Ginguené explains that this is how Chamfort always referred to the Pantheon once Marat had been interred there, while Mirabeau's remains were scattered in a gutter.

3. Ibid., p. lv.

4. Ibid., p. lvi.

5. The Paris Commune regularly put on free plays for the people.

6. Frag. 598.

7. Ideas being understood in the sense used by Condillac, as phenomena provoked by sensations. Doctor Cabanis would go so far as to "materialize all of man" in his *Traité de morale et de physique* [Treatise on morality and physics].

8. Paris, 29 Nivôse, Year II, Charavay file, 2 p. fol.

9. Ging., p. lviii.

10. Ibid., p. lix.

11. Archives de la Seine.

12. See Appendix One.

13. *Le Spectateur française*, March 12, 1795, p. 694.

14. *"Ginguené au comité d'instruction publique,"* reply to Chalamel, 4 Ventôse, Year III, February 22, 1795.

15. Roederer, 4:259 ff.

16. April 1, 1795.

17. Article in *New Monthly Magazine* (September 1, 1825).

18. See Stendhal's *Journal* (April 24, 1805; January 22 and 26, 1806; etc.).

19. Frag. 863.

20. Roger Fayolle, *Sainte-Beuve et le XVIIIe siècle* (Paris: Armand Colin, 1972), p. 364.

21. Sainte-Beuve explained Chamfort's frustrations with the observation, "They obviously come from a man who never had a family, who knew no tenderness from forebears or descendents."

22. M. Allem, *Chateaubriand et son groupe littéraire* (Paris: Garnier, 1948), p. 98–100. The "Monday chat" devoted to Chamfort can be found in vol. 4 of Sainte-Beuves's *Causeries*, p. 539.

23. See Schopenhauer, *The Wisdom of Life and Other Essays*.

24. See the Goncourts' *La Société française sous la Révolution et le directoire*, as well their *Journal*, vol. 11, October 28, 1886, entry (Paris: Flammarion, 1956).

25. Chamfort, *Maximes . . .* (Paris: Livre de Poche, 1974), p. 15 (Camus' preface was originally published in 1944).

25. Nietzsche-Chamfort

1. Rée had extensively read the French moralists prior to writing *Der Ursprung der moralischen Empfendungen*, published in 1871. Arsène Houssaye published his edition of the *Ouvres de Chamfort* in 1852, with an often inaccurate preface.

2. The 1886 preface to *Human, All too Human*, trans. R. J. Hollingdale (New York: Cambridge University Press, 1986), p. 7.

3. Nietzsche, *The Gay Science*, p. 149.

4. Nietzsche, *Oeuvres philosophiques complètes* (Paris: Gallimard, 1982), 5:625n.

5. Nietzsche, *Lettres à Peter Gast* (Paris: Bourgois, 1981), p. 290.

6. Nietzsche, *Oeuvres . . .* (Autumn 1881), 5:518.

7. Ibid., 5:326.

8. Nietzsche, *The Gay Science*, p. 32.

9. It might be added that, for Nietzsche, this meant overcoming his doubts by exalting his destiny. Cf. this "poem" from *The Gay Science* (trans. Kaufmann, New York, 1974, p. 59), as a response to Chamfort's anxiety about not having been born at the right time to write.

"I come today
Because I feel that way,"
Thinks everyone who comes to stay
Forever. And he gives no weight

To what the world may say:
"You're rather early! You are late!"

10. Nietzsche, *The Will to Power* trans. Hollingdale & Kaufmann (New York: Vintage, 1986), p. 405.

APPENDIXES

1. The Theft of Chamfort's Manuscripts

1. Parent de Rosan Collection, Ginguené papers, f. 154.

2. Ibid., f. 153.

3. Ibid., and note.

4. Chalamel, *Garat et Ginguené . . . intrigants et dilapidateurs*, 1795. See also Chalamel's letter to Garat and Ginguené, dated 27 Pluviôse, Year III, in the Parent de Rosan Collection, f. 235.

5. Several hundred fragments left by the thief therefore remain unpublished.

6. As to Roederer, he became minister and confident to Napoleon. Judging by the emperor's brilliant aphorism, it is not impossible that Roederer encouraged Napoleon to read Chamfort.

7. The Lenin Library (see Appendix Three on unpublished maxims) suggests that Colnet, who published Chamfort's *Oeuvres* in 1808, may have been this second owner. His edition in effect includes 150 unpublished fragments. But why wouldn't Ginguené have spoken up at that point? And why would so few have been published?

8. *O.C.*, 2:viii.

9. Chamfort, *Pensées et maximes, caractères et anecdotes, dialogues* (Brussels: Hetzel, 1857), p. lii.

2. Portraits of Chamfort

1. *Inventaire Général des richesses d'art de la France*, Archives du musée des monuments français, pt. 2 (Paris: Plon, 1866).

2. *Grand Dictionnaire biographique des personnages historiques . . . du Puy-de-Dome* (Moulins, 1878).

3. Unanthologized Aphorisms and Anecdotes

1. These cross-check—taking variations and a collage-like order into account—with those letters published by Ginguené.

2. *Mirabeau's Letters during His Residence in England* (London: Effingham Wilson, 1832).

3. All of these documents come either from the "Cabinet Noir" [postal censorship office], which read and occasionally copied letters exchanged with rival England, or from personal papers seized from those arrested during the Revolution. Certain of these fragments postdate 1785, which tends to prove that Chamfort lent his collection to Mirabeau not only prior to the count's departure for London but also following their reconciliation.

4. They had been previously published in Russian, in the first Russian edition of *Products of the Perfected Civilization,* which met with great success.

4. A Chamfort Sampler

1. Ixion wanted to seduce Hera, who fashioned a false image of herself from a cloud, with which Ixion then made love. But he was caught in the act by Zeus, who lashed him to a fiery wheel which rolled eternally across the sky.

BIBLIOGRAPHY

Manuscripts

Archives of the Bibliothèque Nationale: Van Praet papers, and archive 47, ff. 403, 404, 411.

Archives Nationales: Central index, sec. LXXI^{xx} 109, files T 1458, 0^1 671, 0^1 3887, F^7 4638, F^7 4684, F^7 4759, F^{17} 1001, F^{17} 1035, F^{17} 1206, F^{17} 1350, F^{17} 4339, AF □ 286 and 292.

Bibliothèque Nationale: N.A.F. (Nouvelles Acquisitions Françaises) 22899, ff. 31–32, Rothschild A. XVIII.83. Also Ginguené papers N.A.F. 9192–9220.

Charavay. "Revue des autographes." 1866–1922.

Municipal libraries in Reims, Lille, Paris XIVe arrondissement. Parent de Rosan collection, Ginguené papers, no. 20.

Other archives: Comédie-Française, Puy-de-Dome, Académie française. Archives de la Seine (Estate file DQ^{10} 1436, no. 2328).

Other libraries: Bibliothèque Historique de la Ville de Paris, bibliothèque de l'Institut de France.

Private collection: Dr. Girard, Clermont-Ferrand.

Published Articles and Essays

Barbey d'Aurevilly. *Critiques* (1909): 124–140.

Bord, Gustave. "L'hotel de la rue Chantereine." *Le Carnet* (1903 and 1904).

Citron, Pierre. "Balzac, lecteur de Chamfort." *Année Balzacienne* (1969).

Grouber de Groubental. "Chamfort chez le prince de Condé." *Cabinet Historique* 20 (1874).

Henriot, Emile. *Courrier Litteraire* (18th century) 2 (1962).

Intermédiaire des Chercheurs et des Curieux (March 10, 1893; and July 1952).

Katz, Eve. "Chamfort." *Yale French Studies*, no. 40 (1968).

Lescure. "La vie et la mort de Chamfort." *Le Correspondant* 117, no. 81 (1879).

Menant, Sylvain. "Chamfort, naissance d'un moraliste." *Caheirs AEIF* (May 30, 1978).

Pelisson, M. "Chamfort avant la Révolution française." *Révolution Française* 18 (1890).

———. "L'arrestation et la mort de Chamfort." *Mercure de France* 61 (1906).

Peltier. Obituary on Julie Talma. *L'Ambigu* (May 20, 1805).

Poulet, Georges. "Chamfort et Laclos." *La Distance Intérieure* (1952).

Ridgeway, R. S. "Camus' Favorite Moralist." *Studies on Voltaire and the 18th Century*, no. 199 (1981).

Sylvestre de Sacy, J. "Editor Chamfort." *Mercure de France* (1961).

Sélis. La Décade Philosophique. Year IV of the Republic. A series of articles on the publication of Chamfort's *Oeuvres*, in the following issues: 30 Frimaire (pp. 537 ff.), 10 Nivôse (pp. 29 ff.), 10 Pluviôse (pp. 214 ff.), 30 Ventôse (pp. 540 ff.), 30 Thermidor (pp. 348 ff.).

Todd, Christopher. "Chamfort and the Anecdote." *Modern Language Review*, no. 74 (1979).

Vauthier, G. "La succession de Chamfort." *Annales Révolutionnaires* 13 (1921).

Principal Editions of Chamfort's Works

Caractères et anecdotes de Chamfort. Ed. A. Van Bever and preceded by Ginguené's preface. Paris: Cres, 1924.

Chamfort: Maximes et anecdotes. With intro. by Albert Camus. Monaco: Incidences, 1944.

Chamfort: Maximes et anecdotes. With intro. by Jean Mistler. Monaco: Editions du Rocher, 1944.

Chamfort: Maximes et pensées, anecdotes et caractères. Ed. Louis Ducros and containing a previously unpublished heroic poem. Paris: Larousse, 1928.

Chamfort: Maximes, pensées, caractères et anecdotes. Ed. Jean Dagen. Paris: Gallimard/Folio, 1968.

Chamfort: Pensées, maximes, anecdotes et dialogues. Preceded by P. J. Stahl's account of the Chamfort story. Paris: Michel Lévy, 1860. (An earlier edition was published in Brussels in 1857.)

Chamfort: Produits de la civilisation perfectionnée. Ed. Pierre Grosclaude. 2 vols. Paris: Imprimerie Nationale, 1953.

Dictionnaire dramatique. 3 vols. Geneva: Slatkine Reprints, 1967.

Früchte der volvollendeten Zivilisation: Maximen, Gedanken, Charakterzüge. Ed. Ralph-Raimer Wuthenow. Stuttgart: Reclam, 1977.

La jeune indienne. Ed. Gilbert Chinard. Princeton: Princeton University Press, 1945.

Les plus belles pages de Chamfort (a selection made by Rémy de Gourmont). Paris: Mercure de France, 1905.

Maxim i Mislef: Karaketerov i Anekdotof. 1 vol. with portrait. Moscow and Leningrad: Soviet Academy of Literature, 1966.

Massime e Pensieri: Caratteri et Anedotti. Ed. Giovanni Macchia Milan: Longanesi, 1984.

Maximes, pensées, caractères et anecdotes. Ed. Geneviève Renaux, with Albert

Camus's preface. Paris: Gallimard/Livre de Poche, 1970; reprinted in the Folio series, 1982.

Oeuvres Choisies de N. Chamfort. With preface by M. de Lesclure. 2 vols. Paris: Librarie des Bibliophiles, 1879.

Oeuvres Complètes de Chamfort. 5 vols. Paris: Auguis, 1824–1825.

Oeuvres Complètes de Chamfort. 2 vols. Paris: Colnet, 1808.

Oeuvres de Chamfort. Ed. Ginguené. 4 vols. Paris, 1795.

Oeuvres de Chamfort. Preceded by an essay by Arsène Houssaye, 1852.

Oeuvres principales de Chamfort. Ed. F. Duloup. Paris: Pauvert, 1960.

Products of the Perfected Civilization. Trans. and with an intro. by W. S. Merwin. San Francisco: North Point Press, 1984.

General Source Material

Abrantès, Duchesse d'. *Histoires des salons de Paris, de Louis XVI à Louis-Philippe.* Paris: Ladvocat, 1836–1838.

Amiable, Louis. *La loge des noeuf soeurs.* Paris, 1897.

Andler, Charles. *Nietzsche, sa vie, sa pensée.* Paris: Gallimard, 1958.

Augustin-Thierry, A. *Le tragédien de Napoléon, F. J. Talma.* Paris: Albin Michel, 1942.

Aulard. *La Société des Jacobins.* Paris: Jouaust, 1892.

Baillio, Joseph. *Elisabeth Louise Vigée Le brun.* 1983.

Balayé, Simon. *La Bibliothèque Nationale des origines à 1800.* Geneva: Droz, in press.

Bardoux, A. *Etudes d'un autre temps.* Paris: Calmann-Lévy, 1889.

Bayet, Jean. *La Société de Auteurs et Compositeurs Dramatiques.* Paris, 1908.

Bénétruy, J. *L'atelier de Mirabeau.* Geneva, 1962.

Bénichou, Paul. *Le sacre de l'ecrivain, 1750–1830.* Corti, 1973.

Bertaud, J. *La vie littéraire en France au XVIIIᵉ siècle.* Paris, 1954.

Boiteux, L.-A. *Au temps des coeurs sensibles.* Paris: Plon, 1948.

Boncampain, Jacques. *Auteurs et comédiens au XVIIIᵉ siècle.* Paris: Perrin, 1976.

Bord, Gustave. *La maison du 18 Brumaire.* Paris: Neptune, 1930.

Broglie, Gabriel de. *Ségur sans cérémonie* Paris: Perrin, 1977.

Buchez, P. J. B. *Histoire Parlémentaire de la Révolution française.* Paris, 1845.

Castries, Duc de. *Figaro, ou la vie de Beaumarchais.* Paris, 1985.

Castries, Duc de, *Mirabeau.* Paris: Fayard, 1960.

"Chamfort." *Encyclopédie universalis.*

Chassin. *Les elections et les cahiers de Paris.* 4 vols. Paris, 1883–1889.

Chevalier, Pierre. *Historie de la Franc-Maçonnerie française*. Paris: Fayard, 1974.

Darnton, Robert. *Bohème littéraire et Révolution*. Paris: Le Seuil, 1983.

Dauban, C. A. *Les prisons de Paris sous la Révolution*. Paris, 1870.

Dutourd, Jean. *Les plus belles pages de Rivarol*. Paris: Mercure de France, 1963.

Duval, Georges. *Souvenirs de la Terreur*. Paris, 1841.

Ehrard, J., Charlier, G., and Mortier, R., eds. *Marmontel: Le Journal Encyclopédique (1756–1793)*. Paris: Nizet, 1952.

Fayolle, Roger. *Sainte-Beuve et le XVIIIᵉ siècle*. Paris: Colin, 1972.

Flammermont. *La journée du 14 Juillet 1789*.

Furet, François. *Penser la Révolution française*. Paris: Gallimard, 1979.

Furet and Richet. *La Révolution française*. Paris: Hachette/Pluriel, 1970. Translated by Stephen Hardman, under the title *The French Revolution*. New York: Macmillan, 1970.

Goncourt, E. and J. *Histoire de la Société Française pendant la Révolution*.

Goncourt, E. and J. *Journal*. 3 vols., Paris: Laffont, 1989. Translated under the title *The Journal of the de Goncourts: Pages from a Great Diary*. Ed. Julius West. London and New York: T. Nelson, n.d.

Goncourt, E. and J. *La femme au XVIIIᵉ siècle*. Paris: Flammarion, 1982.

———. *La Guimard*.

Guillois, Antoine. *Pendant la Terreur, le poète Roucher*. Paris: Calmann-Lévy, 1890.

Héron de Villefosse, R. *L'anti-Versailles, ou le Palais-Royal de Philippe-Egalité*. Paris: Dullis, 1974.

"Homage à Chamfort." *Revue Doloriste*. 1951.

Hunter, A. C. J. *B. A. Suard*. Paris: Champion, 1927.

L., E. M. du. *Mme. Elisabeth*. Paris: Perrin, 1932.

Lancaster, H. C. *French Tragedy in the Reign of Louis XIV (1774–1792)*. Baltimore, 1953.

Le Bourgo, Léo. *Duclos*. Bordeaux, 1902.

Le Breton, André. *Rivarol*. Paris, 1895.

Madelin, Louis. *La Révolution*. Paris: Hachette, 1938. Translated under the title *French Revolution*. New York: Ams Press (reprint of 1938 ed.).

Manceron, Claude. *Les hommes de la liberté*. Paris: Laffont, 1972–1979. Translated by Patricia Wolf, under the title *The Age of the French Revolution*. New York: Simon and Schuster, 1989–.

Meunier, Dauphin. *Chamfort and Mirabeau*. Paris: La Jeune Parque, 1928.

———. *Autour de Mirabeau*. Paris: Payot, 1926.

Michelet, Jules. *La Révolution française*. Paris: Laffont, 1979. Translated by

Charles Cocks, under the title *History of the French Revolution*. Chicago: University of Chicago Press, 1967.

Moreau, Pierre. *La conversion de Chateaubriand*. Aléan, 1933.

Painter, George Duncan. *Chateaubriand: A Biography*. London: Chatto and Windus, 1977–. Original is in English; translated to French under the title *Chateaubriand: Une biographie*. Paris: Gallimard, 1979.

Pellisson, Maurice. *Les hommes de lettres au XVIIIe siècle*. Paris: Colin, 1911.

Priouret, Roger. *La Franc-Maçonnerie sous les lys*. Paris: Editions 10–18, 1976.

Regaldo, Marc. *Un milieu intellectuel: la décade philosophique (1794–1807)*. Champion, 1976.

Registres de l'Académie de France. Institut de France/Firmin-Didot, 1906.

Richard, P. J. *Aspects de Chamfort*. Paris, 1959.

Sainte-Beuve. *Chateaubriand et son groupe littéraire*. Ed. Maurice Allem. Paris: Garnier, 1948.

Soboul, A. *La Révolution française*. Paris: Editions Sociales, 1973. Translated by Geoffrey Symcox, under the title *A Short History of the French Revolution*, Berkeley: University of California Press, 1977. Also translated by Gwynne Lewis, under the title *The French Revolution, 1789–1799*. Westport, Conn.: Greenwood, 1964.

Todd, Christopher. *Voltaire's disciple: J.-F. de La Harpe*. London: King's College, 1972.

Tourneux, Maurice. *Bibliographie de l'histoire de Paris pendant la Révolution française*. Paris, 1890–1913.

Tucoo-Chala, S. *Charles-Joseph Panckoucke (1736–1798)*. Pau: Marrem-Povey, 1979.

Contemporary Publications

Allonville, Comte d'. *Mémoires secrets de 1770 à 1830*. Paris, 1868.

Angiviller, Comte d'. *Notes sur les mémoires de Marmontel*, with intro. by L. Bobé. Copenhagen, 1933.

Anon. *Mirabeau jugé par ses amis et ses ennemis*. Paris, 1791.

Barère de Vieuzac. *Mémoires*. Paris: Lafitte, 1824.

Barruel, Abbé Augustin. *Mémoires pour servir à l'histoire du jacobinisme*. Reprint; Paris: Diffusion de la Pensée Française, 1933.

Bensenval. *Mémoires*. Paris: Mercure de France, 1987.

Boigne, Mme. de. *Mémoires*. Paris: Mercure de France, 1986.

Bombelles. Marquis de. *Journal*. Geneva: Droz, 1978–1982.

Brissot. *Mémoires*. 1832.

Chabaud, A., and Perroud, C., eds. *Correspondance et mémoires de Barbaroux.* Paris, 1923.

Collet, Charles. *Journal et mémoires du règne de Louis XV (1748–1772).* Ed. Henri Bonhomme. 1868.

Colnet du Ravel. *Correspondance Turque.* Paris, 1801.

Condorcet. *Mémoires.* Ed. marquis de La Rochefoucauld-Liancourt. Paris, 1862.

Constant de Rebeque, Baronne de, ed. *Lettres de Julie Talma à B. Constant.* Paris: Plon, 1933.

Cousin d'Avallon. *Arnoldiana.* Paris, 1813.

Cushing, M.-G. *P. Letourneur.* New York, 1908.

Dumouriez. *Mémoires.* Firmin-Didot, 1848.

Dussault, *Annales littéraires.* Paris, 1838.

Fleury. *Mémoires de Fleury, de la Comédie-Française.* Paris, 1835.

Frénilly, Baron de. *Souvenirs.* Reprint; Paris: Mercure de France, 1987.

Fusil, Louise. *Souvenirs d'une actrice.* Paris: Schmid, n.d.

Garat. *De la conspiration d'Orléans.* Paris, 1797.

Garat. *Mémoires sur M. Suard.* Paris, 1829.

Hardy, J.-P. *Le triomphe de la vérité sur Mirabeau.* Maestricht, 1785.

Hérault de Séchelles. *Théorie de l'ambition.* Ed. G. Guégan. Paris: Ramsay, 1979.

La Harpe. *Lycée.* 13 vols. Year VIII of the Republic.

———. *Cours de Littérature.*

Laborde, J.-B. de. *Pensées et maximes.* Paris, 1802.

Ligne, Prince de. *Oeuvres.* Vol. 27. 1804.

Lucas-Montigny. *Mémoires de Mirabeau.* Paris, 1834.

Mercier, L.-S. *Tableaux de Paris.* Paris: Reprint Maspero, 1979.

Meunier, Dauphin. *Lettres de Mirabeau à Yet-Lie.* 1929.

Nougaret, J.-B. *Anecdotes du règne de Louis XVI.* Paris, 1791.

Oberkirch, Baronne d'. *Mémoires.* Paris: Mercure de France, 1970.

Rivarol. *Journal Politique National.* With intro. by Willy de Spens. Paris: Editions 10–18, 1964.

———. *Petit dictionnaire des grands hommes de la Révolution.* Paris, 1790.

———. *Mémoires.* Ed. M. Berville. Paris: Galic, 1962.

Romilly. *Memoirs of the Life of Sir Romilly, Written by Himself.* London, 1840.

Ségur, Comte de. *Mémoires.* Ed. A. Barrière. Paris, 1859.

Thierry, M. *Guide des voyageurs à Paris.* 1787.

Tilly, *Oeuvres melées.* Berlin, 1803.

Van Doren, C. *Autobiographical Writings.* New York: Viking Press, 1945.

Contemporary Periodicals

Les Actes des Apôtres

L'Ami du Peuple

L' Année Littéraire

L'Arétin Français

La Chronique de Paris

Courrier de l'Europe

Le Courrier de Provence

L'Espion Anglais

La Feuille Villageoise

Journal des Débats de la Société des Amis de la Constitution

Journal Encyclopédique

Journal Général de la Cour et de la Ville

Journal de la Montagne

Journal-Pie

Journal de Politique et de Littérature

Journal de Trévoux

Magasin Encyclopédique

L' Orateur du Peuple

Le Père Duchêne

Les Sabbats Jacobites

Le Spectateur Français

Biographies of Chamfort

Dousset, Emile. *Chamfort et son temps.* Paris: Fasquelle, 1944; republished, Clermont-Ferrand: Volcans, 1974.

Pellisson, Maurice. *Chamfort, étude sur sa vie, son caractère, ses écrits.* Paris, 1895; Geneva: Slatkine Reprints, 1970.

Sleek, D. *Chamfort.* Gand, 1886.

Teppe, Julien. *Chamfort, sa vie, son oeuvre, sa pensée.* With a preface by Jean Rostand. Paris: Clairac, 1950.

INDEX